BIG BILLION STARTUP

Mihir Dalal is a writer based in Bangalore. He studied at the business school and the South Asia Studies department at Columbia University in New York, where he was a Knight-Bagehot Fellow. He was previously Bangalore Bureau Chief at *Mint*. *Big Billion Startup* is his first book.

BIG BILLION STARTUP

The Untold FLIPKART Story

MIHIR DALAL

PAN

First published 2019 by Macmillan
First published in paperback 2023 by Pan
an imprint of Pan Macmillan Publishing India Private Limited
707 Kailash Building
26 K. G. Marg, New Delhi 110001
www.panmacmillan.co.in

Pan Macmillan, The Smithson, 6 Briset St., Farringdon, London EC1M 5NR
Associated companies throughout the world

www.panmacmillan.com
ISBN 978-93-89109-15-3

Typeset in Minion Pro by R. Ajith Kumar, New Delhi
Printed and bound in India by Manipal Technologies Limited, Manipal

MIX
Paper | Supporting responsible forestry
FSC www.fsc.org
FSC® C043100

For my grandparents

CONTENTS

1	Breeding Ground	1
2	The Bansals Go to IIT	22
3	Exodus from Amazon	41
4	The Desertion	53
5	Up, Down, Hello, Goodbye	59
6	The Kart Gets Rolling	80
7	The Eye of the Tiger	92
8	'*Binny Ke Batch Se Ho?*'	106
9	Boom	125
10	The King of Shaktipeeth	141
11	Setback	154
12	No Respite	166
13	The Tiger Cub	180
14	Hello, Moto	193
15	Another Bansal Joins the Family	203
16	A Billion Dreams	207
17	The Comeback	216
18	Reinventing the Kart	234
19	Chaos and Confusion	254
20	After Bansal, Bansal	273
21	The Tiger Cub Returns	294

22 Kalyan Raj 311
23 The Son 329
24 A Journey to Bentonville 338

Epilogue 363
Afterword 368
Author's Note and Acknowledgements 376
Notes 379
Index 412

1

BREEDING GROUND

One morning in August 2004, a few days ahead of his twenty-first birthday, Ajay Bhutani was woken up by a persistent knock on the door. It was 7 a.m. and Ajay was lying exhausted in his small hostel room at the Indian Institute of Technology in Delhi.

Ajay had dropped into bed only two hours ago, after a gruelling night at the computer laboratory on campus. He was in the penultimate semester of his four-year programme in computer science. Campus recruitment – the reason IIT students had put carefree college life on hold – was just days away. Ajay, a Punjabi boy from Faridabad, had been preparing for recruitment season for the last three years. He needed to sleep to be awake for it.

But the knocking wouldn't stop. Outside, one of his hostelmates called out, '*Abey, uth ja, ek company aayi hai.*' Hey, wake up, a company's here.

Ajay rubbed his eyes. '*Kaun si*?' Which one?

'Amazon.'
'Amazon?'
'*Kitaabe bechti hai online.*' They sell books online.
'*Usse kya hota hai*?' What's the use of that?
'*Paise bahut de rahi hai.*' They're offering high salaries.
'*Achha? Chalo.*' Really? I'm coming.

AMAZON, THE AMERICAN online retail pioneer, had opened its India offices in the southern city of Bangalore the previous month. In the early 2000s, dozens of dotcoms – as internet companies were then known – had gone bankrupt. Amazon, which had been one of the prominent faces of the technology boom and bust, had managed to emerge from this gloom, albeit with a diminished reputation and stock price.

In August 2004, the young search engine Google listed its shares, fetching a valuation that was far higher than that of Amazon.[1] EBay, an online marketplace and auctions site and Amazon's rival, earned higher profits and was considered a better-run company.

This may not have bothered Amazon's founder Jeff Bezos, who coincidentally was an early investor in Google. Bezos was known to mainly be obsessed with keeping Amazon's customers happy rather than worry about rivals or stock-market valuations. But there was one other goal that kept him occupied – he wanted to transform Amazon, a hawker of books, toys and electronics, into an all-purpose technology company. Yet, all Amazon seemed to be doing was selling books, toys and electronics. It was time the company started experimenting and venturing onto new avenues. One of these initial experiments happened to be a search engine called A9. Introduced in September 2004, A9 set out to be a more advanced version of Google.

Bezos put Udi Manber, an accomplished Israeli technologist he had lured away from Yahoo, in charge of A9. In turn, Udi persuaded Bharat Vijay, one of Yahoo's early employees and a brilliant engineer, to join the A9 team in 2004. After working at Yahoo's headquarters in San Francisco for nearly five years, Bharat had moved back to his country in 2000 to set up Yahoo's India office in his home city of Bangalore. Four years on, Bharat's mandate now was to launch Amazon's India office. He had to assemble and lead a team that could make image searches on the internet easier, an area in which Google wasn't exactly breaking new ground.

Bangalore seemed like a good place to hire engineers for A9. Some of the smartest employees at technology companies in the US were Indians, many of whom were graduates of the Indian Institutes of Technology, a chain of government-subsidized engineering colleges that Jawaharlal Nehru had established in the 1950s. Amazon had arrived armed with the knowledge that IIT-educated engineers could become real assets to a company. After all, it was a group of IIT engineers who had started Junglee – a website that allowed people to compare product prices across shopping sites – which Amazon had acquired in the late 1990s. Determined to recruit the exceptionally talented, Amazon was keen to open its doors to more such inventive engineers.

The company had another reason to set up shop in India: it was an unrealized market. Since the early nineties, when India opened its economy to foreign investment, brands and retailers had swarmed the country from overseas, buying into the notion that hundreds of millions of Indians had money to spend and were raring to devour all kinds of consumer goods after decades of forced socialist deprivation. Consultant firms and research agencies happily fed the naivete of foreign companies with wild estimates of the potential of India's retail market. The local media even labelled Kishore Biyani – the founder of Pantaloons and Big Bazaar – India's Sam Walton.[2] In 2004, Amazon's arch-rival eBay would buy Bazee, an Indian clone of eBay, for $50 million.[3] Gradually, after the dawn of liberalization, the forbidding, socialist India of the last forty years had transformed into a virgin consumerist paradise for American and European brands.

Indians, of course, had their own view about this representation of their reality. In 2004, the Indian people ousted a coalition led by the Hindu nationalist Bhartiya Janata Party. The BJP had campaigned on the premise that until the party's most recent tenure in the central government, Indians had never had it so good, an idea encapsulated in its election slogan 'India Shining'.[4] Shockingly, in a country where nearly forty per cent of the population was poor and most of the rest just got by, Indians didn't think their hunger to consume was a cause for celebration. It wasn't that life under the BJP hadn't improved for many; the improvement had just been incremental rather than the miracle claimed by the party. Politicians, like astrologers, are usually better off promising a happier tomorrow rather than glorifying a barely tolerable present.

But in fact, just as Amazon opened its office in the IT city of Bangalore in July 2004, India entered a period of unprecedented economic expansion, building on the foundation laid by the reforms of 1991 and then further solidified by the BJP. Thirteen years after he had helped implement the liberalization policies as Finance Minister, Manmohan Singh, now Prime Minister of the Congress-led coalition government, began a five-year term during which India came as close to 'shining' as it ever has.

In this period, from 2004 to 2009, many Indians bought basic commodities like soaps and biscuits for the first time. They bought mobile phones and television sets, installed telecom connections. From country liquor, they switched to whisky, even if it was a local variety. In fewer numbers, Indians acquired scooters and cars. A few million lavished cash on computers and internet connections. For a time, it seemed not impossible that Kishore-ji could actually become a 'poor man's' Sam Walton, as not only consumer goods makers, but many kinds of businesses blossomed in this period. IT services lost their glamour – the call centre myth, like the actual experience of working at one, was unsuited for longevity – but sales and profits at IT companies soared to record levels. From just two billionaires in the mid-nineties, India boasted as many as forty-nine billionaires by 2010, as was pointed out in *Forbes* magazine.[5] Capitalism replaced socialism as India's guiding economic philosophy, as consumerism went mainstream, enthusiastically taken up as a way of life by a growing middle class.

They weren't aware at the time, but this was the new India that Ajay and his IIT-mates – among whom were Sachin Bansal and Binny Bansal – would witness in the first phase of their careers. And in their impressionable years, Ajay, Sachin and Binny, along with a hundred other unformed engineers, were indoctrinated in the practice of perpetuating consumerism by Amazon, a company that existed solely to convert every living person to this faith and keep them entranced through its unending cycle of product accumulation and delivery.

TECHNOLOGY ENTREPRENEURSHIP HAD taken off accidentally in the US and China. In the 1950s, the US government funded research in California aimed at improving America's defence and aviation technology. These research projects, and the lure of prestigious institutes such as Stanford University, drew some of the smartest minds in science and technology to California. As these innovators – the most prominent of whom was William Shockley, winner of the Nobel Prize in 1956 for his role as one of the inventors of the transistor – collaborated, they birthed inventions that would eventually lead to the introduction of personal computers and pave the way for mass adoption of the internet. In the 1960s, the counterculture movement supplied the ethos that induced people to believe that personal computing would transform the world for the better even as they enriched themselves beyond belief. In a nutshell, an unlikely combination of government-funded research, the madness of flawed geniuses like Shockley,[6] a small number of adventurous financiers, along with the hippie movement, created and nurtured entrepreneurship in Silicon Valley. Companies like Fairchild Semiconductor, Intel, Apple, Netscape and Paypal were born, which in turn spawned hundreds of entrepreneurs.

The evolution of India's internet ecosystem was slightly more straightforward. Its epicentre was Bangalore, which was once described by Nehru as 'the city of the future'.[7] Modern Bangalore traces its origin to 1537 when Kempe Gowda, a ruler of the Vijayanagara Empire, built a fort and established a settlement in the region. In 1799, the British won the state of Mysore. A decade later, a cantonment area was established for British officers in Bangalore, in close proximity to Kempe Gowda's old town.

After India's independence in 1947, Bangalore became the country's tech centre. The city was home to the Indian Institute of Science, many engineering colleges and government-owned companies such as Hindustan Aeronautics which were engaged in technology work. Many of these institutions had been established before independence through the efforts of the great technocrat M. Visvesvaraya with help from industrialists such as Walchand Hirachand and Jamsetji Tata and the progressive ruler of Mysore state, Krishna Raja Wadiyar IV.[8]

In 1985, Texas Instruments, an American hardware firm, opened an office in Bangalore and rapidly attracted some of the country's best engineers. Around the same time, Infosys, an unknown startup in those days, moved offices to Bangalore from Pune. The success Infosys achieved soon after proved something important: it was possible for entrepreneurs from India's middle class to establish hugely successful businesses by dint of sheer innovation and hard work, without having to curry favour with bureaucrats and ministers to get ahead. Infosys' success also firmly anchored Bangalore as the tech hub of India for the private sector. The city's pleasant weather, cheap rents and cosmopolitan ethos made it all the more attractive to prospective migrants. In the mid-2000s, the term 'Bangalored' entered the political and economic lexicon.[9]

Soon, India's booming economy caught the attention of American venture capitalists hunting for promising new markets in software, internet and consumer businesses. The venture capital scene that had lapsed into a moribund state after the American tech bust was quickly rebuilt around 2006. Indian-American tech executives, such as Ashish Gupta (one of Junglee's founders), Vani Kola and Vinod Dham, moved to India to set up venture funds. Entrepreneurs like Avnish Bajaj, Suvir Sujan and Alok Mittal entered the venture capital arena after making a few millions selling off their internet businesses in India. Other early venture capitalists like Sudhir Sethi, and the Subrata Mitra–Prashanth Prakash duo – whose fund Accel Partners would become the first institutional investor in Flipkart – had spent their careers in India's IT sector but now wanted to be at the frontier of the country's next technology boom.

While all these factors created a hospitable environment, a crucial formative influence on internet entrepreneurship in India was that of Amazon.

By helping establish Bangalore as India's tech city, IT companies led by Infosys and Wipro had provided a foundation for new internet startups. But in the aesthetic sense, Infosys and Wipro weren't purely technology companies. Students at top engineering colleges such as the IITs had little regard for IT companies – they didn't fancy work associated with terms such as 'body shopping', 'BPO', 'call centre' and 'labour arbitrage'. And the narrative of these companies' founders who had built staid, stable businesses through many years of toil held little appeal in an India that was thirsting for instant success and wealth. This immediacy was still linked to getting a job at an international organization. A different and fresher corporate environment was needed to change this mindset, to attract the youth to participate in entrepreneurship in the new India.

The first generation of internet companies in India had collapsed in the early 2000s and never recovered. There were exceptions: Infoedge, a conglomerate of digital businesses, and the online travel company MakeMyTrip. But the glamorous aspect of the startup myth – rookie engineers creating extraordinary products or websites from their garages and becoming rich and famous overnight – that inspires entrepreneurs, was perhaps missing from these companies. Their respective founders, Sanjeev Bikhchandani and Deep Kalra, were outstanding businessmen, but their old-fashioned outlooks and staid personalities were in the Infosys mould. They were also based in Delhi. In the internet business, location is paramount in an ecosystem's early days – the desire to start one's own company is a physical sensation that spreads like a fever from people who take the plunge to their colleagues, friends, acquaintances. Unlike Bangalore, Delhi did not yet have a large enough network of skilled engineers itching to quit their jobs to code up their own websites. (A few years later, however, Gurgaon would emerge in its own fashion as a rival startup centre to Bangalore.)

So it was that the American internet companies, despite the big bust of year 2000, brought fresh inspiration to India's would-be entrepreneurs. Synonymous with instant wealth, fame and the glamour of innovation, these companies wielded irresistible powers of seduction. They were at the frontiers of economic and social transformation, the new messiahs in the age of globalization. And they seemed to be saying that the rewards they had enjoyed were within one's grasp; all one had to do was take the leap into entrepreneurship. Out of these companies, it was Amazon that became the breeding ground for the first consequential batch of internet voyagers, providing them not with the skills and knowledge necessary for entrepreneurship, but with something more fundamental and important: confidence, the belief that you could do it. Most of those who took the plunge from Amazon and ventured into entrepreneurship didn't succeed in creating big companies. Instead, what mattered was that they went on to *start* something when few in India believed in such a thing as an internet business.

In 2005, Infosys co-founder Nandan Nilekani found global fame after the *New York Times* writer Thomas Friedman published his bestselling book *The World Is Flat*. Friedman had derived the phrase from a similar statement – '... the playing field is being levelled' – that Nilekani had expressed to him in an interview.[10] By this time, however, Infosys had almost completely lost its appeal in the elite tech colleges – few engineers wished to join their ranks, the work seemed boring, the pay meagre. As if to prove Nilekani's theory about the world supposedly flattened by globalization, it was Amazon, not Infosys, that came to inspire the next generation of tech and internet entrepreneurs in his home town of Bangalore. A reverse outsourcing, as it were.

AMAZON GOT OFF to a slow start in India. Bharat Vijay, tasked with setting up Amazon's India office, started at the company in July 2004. He asked a family friend, Anand Rao, to join him. Anand, an upcoming sales manager used to dealing with uber-formal corporates, turned up for his interview in a suit, only to bemuse his interviewer, who had spent the past eight years in the outlandishly casual setting of Yahoo, dressed in shorts, T-shirt and flip-flops. That day, Anand gave up formal attire for the rest of his life.

Soon began the groundwork for the launch of Amazon's retail business in India. Following its trajectory in the US, Amazon planned to launch itself here, too, as a retailer of books. Anand studied the market, met books suppliers, distributors, logistics companies and drew up a strategy to launch operations. A part of his mandate was to look for potential acquisitions – Amazon had just entered another Asian market, China, by buying the online retail company Joyo for $75 million.[11]

But it was A9, Bharat's search engine project, that formed the centrepiece of the India office. A team of Amazon leaders from the company's headquarters in Seattle visited India towards the end of July to supervise the launch. They were in town also to institute Amazon's singular corporate culture, particularly its recruitment process. That Amazon was serious about its India operations became evident from Rick Dalzell being part of the delegation – he was a deputy of Jeff Bezos and one of the most well-respected officials at the company.

Amazon's first office in Bangalore was located in Divyashree Chambers, a three-storied building in an area known as Langford Town, which forms part of Bangalore's colonial district. Apart from hosting Amazon, the building, packed with engineers, also housed an IT services firm called e4e Labs.

Amazon had found its India office; now it needed people. Bharat, Anand and a few of their colleagues spent July and August visiting engineering colleges and research institutes while also soliciting candidates from other technology companies.

Each candidate was put through many rounds of interviews. Aspirants were judged on their academic and professional record, intellect, skills and temperament. Amazon only hired people it considered truly elite engineers who would also unquestioningly adapt to the company's distinct ethos. Its recruitment process was especially rigorous in the US and it would be no different in India. Even though India was known to have hordes of cheap engineers, Amazon's primary purpose was to gather the smartest ones available. This limited its options as there were few Indian firms doing high-level technical work. The IT services champions, Infosys and Wipro, weren't known for their technical proficiency. The reservoirs of India's best engineers were to be found at two companies – Trilogy Software and Yahoo India, Bharat's former employer. But Bharat, who knew the Yahoo founders Jerry Yang and David Filo personally, was reluctant to raid their troops. Besides, it was possible that Yahoo, already upset by Bharat's defection, would go on to sue Amazon. So, in the months of July and August, it was Trilogy's employees who received job offers from Amazon. Very few engineers were found to be suitably equipped, and those who were thought fit would need a month or two to move jobs. Amazon's high recruitment standards had come at a price: delay. Bharat was eager to get started with A9 but there wasn't enough of a workforce to build the search engine.

A solution was sought and found. From its Seattle headquarters, Amazon sent back a few of its many Indian-origin employees to Bangalore. These were highly skilled engineers, already schooled in the Amazon worldview. Chief amongst them were Vijay Subramanian, a tall, imposing Tamilian who, many would observe, had adopted the manner of a stereotypical south Indian film star; Vikas Gupta, who was considered a tech genius within the company; and Amit Agarwal, who had joined Amazon in 1999 after studying computer science at IIT Kanpur and then at Stanford University, the mecca of technology learning. Amit was considered part of a species that Amazon insiders called Jeff Bot. The term referred to employees who had so wholly internalized the ways of the company and its founder that they may as well have been robots programmed in the Bezos school of thought.

Sujayath Ali, who was hired by Amazon from the Indian School of Business in 2005 and worked for nearly seven years at the company, recalls how Amit was 'a true Amazonian'. In fact, he isn't sure if Amit was any different even outside the office. There were quite a few people like Amit who measured everything in life by 'Amazon values'. After leaving Amazon, Sujayath founded an online shopping site called Voonik in 2013.

Amit, Vijay and Vikas were joined by more than a dozen others from Seattle in the second half of 2004. By now, there was an additional project that needed attention. Apart from A9, Amazon had decided that it would work on another initiative in Bangalore, a micro-payments product called Flexible Payments Service that would let any small merchant receive money online immediately after a sale. One could sell something for even a cent or a rupee and receive payment for it. This service would have to be so sturdy, so fast, so secure as to be able to handle tens of millions of transactions on any given day. If it worked, it could transform commerce – all kinds of everyday buying and selling may then be done over the internet using Amazon's payments service. The goal was to make this payment mechanism an integral part of Amazon Web Services (AWS), a new division of Amazon that would later settle the question of whether the company was simply a retailer or the most elitist of tech companies.

Vikas, the tech genius, and Amit 'Jeff Bot' Agarwal, took charge of the payments unit while Bharat oversaw the search engine. Vikas reported to Amit even though he was widely seen as the brains behind the payments unit.

Slowly, over the next nine months, after interviewing more than 1,000 people, Amazon painstakingly accumulated a team of about sixty by the middle of 2005. One fourth of this workforce had come from the company's Seattle headquarters, others came from software companies like Trilogy and Tavant Technologies, and the rest straight from colleges, business schools and research institutes. Even a small number from Infosys passed through Amazon's fine sieve. Most of the recruits were in their mid-to-late twenties, a couple in their early forties, and almost all were men, in conformity with the unwritten mores of the early twenty-first-century tech era.

Amazon's recruiters believed that every single engineer from that initial team of sixty had the ability to start their own business; they had chosen to join Amazon only because they relished working with other young, driven, overachievers like themselves.

In fact, it so happened that more than three dozen people out of Amazon's early hires, along with the Bansals who joined later, would go on to become entrepreneurs, influential tech leaders and investors in India's startup world. Apart from Flipkart, many of the founding members of notable early startups including Infibeam, TutorVista and Chakpak, came from this batch. It was in part Amazon's insistence on hiring only the most superior engineers that inadvertently fostered the entrepreneurship spirit in this group.

Gaurav Singh Kushwaha was one of the earliest members of the payments team at Amazon. In March 2006, eighteen months after he joined the company, Gaurav would become one of the first to leave in order to start his own business. His firm, a movie information site called Chakpak, would later be acquired by Flipkart. Gaurav's co-founder at Chakpak, Nitin Rajput, was another early employee at Amazon India.

To attract these talented engineers, Amazon had adopted an unfamiliar approach. In the US, the company was known for its extreme frugality. It used old doors to make desks. Junior and senior employees alike flew economy and stayed in cheap hotels. Amazon was an outlier in the US tech world, where companies were known to spoil their engineers with inflated compensation and perks. In India, however, Amazon broke its own rules and splurged in order to draw the smartest engineers. It offered outsized compensation packages to all employees; the salaries of mid-level and senior managers were sweetened by allotments of Amazon stock. The company created extravagant office spaces which shocked visiting executives from Seattle. Perks were offered in abundance: free cab travel, subsidized food from expensive caterers, the latest computers, fast internet. No other company could hope to match such lavishness.

Within a few months of opening its first India office in July 2004, Amazon moved to the top floor of a three-storied building overlooking the Bangalore Race Course. Standing on the terrace of the third floor, employees could bet on horse races. That office was the most luxurious space the company's new engineers had ever worked in. Everyone had large desks, comfortable chairs, powerful computers, lounge sofas and shower rooms. There were video games and a ping-pong table. But the clincher was the bar, always well stocked and frequently used. In the early years there were many parties, too, often thrown by Anand Rao, Amazon India's second-ever employee and facilitator-in-chief of various vices. At one such party in 2005, nearly all employees who attended were pushed into the pool on the premises of O2, a rooftop bar on the uptown Residency Road. Even Bharat Vijay wasn't spared (although Amit, ever the proper Amazonian, didn't attend). Phones were damaged, wallets lost, clothes were discarded. Some people walked home in their underwear. Later, Amazon was forced to pay tens of thousands of rupees as recompense to O2.

But more than anything else, employees remembered their time at Amazon for the absorbing assignments and the distinct work culture. Finding the best engineers was just the start; Yahoo India and Trilogy had hired the best engineering minds, too, in their day. What set Amazon India apart was the unusual way in which they made their employees work with each other. It was this corporate culture that almost permanently moulded the mindset of the many people who worked for the company in its early years.

Amazon in India essentially operated like a startup filled with aggressively smart people who were given abundant cash to create innovative technological products. Their employees weren't engaged in lowly back-office work; they didn't have to kowtow (yet) to faceless superiors in the US. Instead, two newly put together teams, working independently of each other, had been charged with creating two exciting and complex products:

a search engine and a payments system. These teams were further divided into smaller groups of five to six people. In Amazon parlance, the smaller groups were called 'two pizza' teams. A meal of two pizzas had to be sufficient for a team to be labelled thus. The Amazon engineers worked within the framework of the company's processes, but apart from these fundamental strictures, they were unfettered and could function with little concern for organizational hierarchy, work hours, dress code or personal hygiene. The youngest engineers, college graduates like Ajay Bhutani, who had reacted with puzzlement on being told of a company that sells books online, were encouraged to challenge Jeff Bots and Tech Geniuses. There were even awards to be won for being unconventional. 'The Emperor Has No Clothes' award, for instance, would be conferred on individuals for pointing out fundamental flaws in products.

Amazon thus created an environment that pushed its meticulously chosen employees to battle each other over ideas, so that the ones which emerged out of the process would have been comprehensively thought through and fought for passionately.

Work at Amazon was informally organized according to a set of what it called 'leadership principles'. These weren't fluffy ideals; rather every employee was required to memorize and abide by these prescriptive directives. These principles urged one to 'think big', show 'bias for action', and demanded other such peculiar compliances. It was no surprise that the A9 project was deemed The Google Killer by some employees. They were not joking – having a sense of humour wasn't one of Amazon's leadership principles.

But the supreme directive was the dogma of customer obsession. At the centre of everything at Amazon, acting like a centrifugal force governing ideas, processes and decisions was this principle: 'Leaders start with the customer and work backwards. They work vigorously to earn and keep customer trust. Although leaders pay attention to competitors, they obsess over customers.'[12]

Customer happiness achieved, business expanded prodigiously, this principle then acted as a centripetal force, self-validating and completing the cycle which was repeated every day, every hour within Amazon's premises.

At the India office, too, Amazon fashioned its Brave New World, making sure the customer obsession principle became a part of its employees' consciousness. Abhishek Goyal, an early employee, recalls that if someone was late for an internal meeting, they would say, 'Sorry, my customer obsession is a bit down today.' Every meeting hosted an empty chair – for the customer. Every single employee had to talk about 'customers, customers, customers.' Abhishek later joined Accel Partners, where he would convince his bosses to become the first investors for Flipkart.

It wasn't surprising that the customer obsession principle was applied with such rigour in India – Jeff Bezos took a personal interest in the two Indian projects and would sometimes even conduct reviews. If one didn't obsess over customers, it wouldn't be easy to answer any of Bezos' questions. The intensity with which this principle was applied deeply affected everyone who worked there, including the few who weren't greenhorns. N. S. Amarnath (known to his colleagues as Amar), a senior engineer in the payments team, was by far the oldest employee at Amazon India. In his mid-forties, he was nearly fifteen years older than his managers and about two decades older than most of his colleagues. 'That level of customer obsession ... it was very novel, very profound for us,' says Amar. 'At that time, IT services companies were the only other benchmark in India and that kind of customer obsession wasn't there. They just weren't used to thinking of it.'

Indeed, this maniacal focus on pleasing customers and other characteristics of Amazon's corporate culture – thinking big, hiring young people and letting them loose, creating a combative work environment, treating engineers like gods – would be later adopted at Flipkart by the Bansals. Sachin, in particular, was radicalized by Amazon's dogma of customer obsession.

OF THE BANSALS, Sachin joined Amazon first, in January 2006. A few months later, the company moved its office to Ali Asker Road. Named after the Persian horse trader who settled in Bangalore a few years after it was set up by the British,[13] Ali Asker Road is a wide, tree-lined stretch of concrete. In the heart of colonial Bangalore where streets display their British lineage with names like Cunningham Road, Brigade Road and Richmond Road, Ali Asker Road stands out primarily for tracing a different ancestry.

By the time Amazon hired Sachin, its employees had completely absorbed the company's ethos. Sachin, then twenty-four, was placed in the payments team. After graduating from IIT Delhi, he had spent a few months at a Bangalore IT firm called Techspan.[14] He came to Amazon as a young, intelligent, but somewhat naive man, eager to prove himself, but without much knowledge about how the world worked. He was also confident – getting into the IITs can take care of that – but had no idea of his worth. Amazon loved hiring people like Sachin; they were easily lured onto the company's internal battlefield with temptations of wealth, power and glory, shown to be always within reach, but only attainable if one complied with Amazon's methods and mandates.

Sachin entered a team of overachieving men with supreme technical skills and attendant egos. Some of these men were engineering managers such as Amar Nath and Ashish Agrawal. Sujayath Ali and Raghu Lakkapragada, who had been hired straight from the Indian School of Business, worked as product managers. There was Ajay Bhutani, Sachin's junior from IIT. The seniors – by experience – included Gaurav Kushwaha, Mohan Varadarajan and Aditya Lal, who would all soon start their own firms. Among the engineers Sachin worked closely with were Vijay Subramanian, the self-styled Tamilian film star, Sachin Dalal and Alok Chandra – all of whom would later help build Infibeam, an online retailer that played a small but nearly climactic role in Flipkart's first year. And at the top of this pyramid were Amit the Jeff Bot, and Vikas the Tech Genius.

In Amazon's elite engineering crowd, Sachin had come to be regarded as a middling programmer, competent but not outstanding. There were several others like him, but many more were considered better. A former teammate of Sachin remembers him as a 'regular' guy, neither too quiet nor too shy and not very social either.

Sujayath Ali, who was briefly Sachin's colleague at Amazon, recalls that Sachin was as inclined towards understanding how a product would be used as he was towards writing code. The tech world broadly categorizes these two areas respectively as 'product' and 'engineering'. A product-oriented worker prioritizes the ease of use, while an engineer cares more strongly about the strength of the code they write. Product and engineering work together but are often in conflict over what needs to be prioritized. 'Coding-wise, Sachin was average but he had a sharp business sense ... if you gave a feature to him, he would develop it in a very consumer-friendly way,' says Sujayath.

Soon, these qualities would come together to propel the rise of a singular Indian startup.

2

THE BANSALS GO TO IIT

The first few years of an engineer's professional life can be like an extension of college. It is often the case that Indian college students – many of whom come from middle-class households – with certain proclivities gravitate towards classmates with similar interests. Once a student has moved to a new city with a new job, it isn't uncommon for them to share their accommodation with friends from their college hostel who might have moved to the same city. A group of friends will often stay in the same flat, sometimes two or three people to each bedroom. The living arrangements aren't necessarily salutary. Cheap furniture, bean bags and mattresses are common fixtures, arranged so weed and alcohol can be consumed and video games played with minimal expenditure of effort. It isn't too unreasonable to say that in many cases, this extended adolescence is brought to a close only by marriage, often arranged by the engineer's family. It can even be argued that some engineers never truly grow out of their adolescence.

Sachin Bansal's post-IIT life was no different. When he moved to Bangalore in 2005 after graduating with a B.Tech., he called upon one of his closest hostel friends, Ankit Agarwal. Ankit and two of his IIT friends, Kapil Makhija and Prayank Swaroop, shared a three-bedroom apartment at the National Games Village complex and worked at different tech companies. Soon after relocating, Sachin moved in with them. Located in the upcoming Bangalore suburb of Koramangala, the NGV was built in the 1990s to host the athletes participating in the 1996 National Games in Bangalore. It was a large apartment complex with dozens of buildings, many of them named after rivers. The flats were compact, but the complex boasted gardens, badminton courts, a swimming pool and walking lanes. In the nineties, the NGV had played an important role in the gentrification of Koramangala.

Koramangala is situated a few miles away from Bangalore's former cantonment area. Year 2008 onwards, this suburb developed into a thriving startup centre. Just two decades ago, however, its landscape had been dominated by an artificial lake. (Such lakes have been the major source of water in the city since it was established in the sixteenth century.) Koramangala's gentrification began in earnest after Infosys launched operations in the suburb in the late 1980s. Over the next decade, as the IT industry burgeoned, many companies, including Infosys, moved their offices to the nearby Electronic City. Koramangala benefited from its proximity to this new IT hub. Wealthy IT businessmen like Nandan Nilekani and Ashok Soota took up residence in Koramangala. The construction of the NGV complex and the launch of the grand Forum Mall helped transform the area in the 2000s into an exemplar of

Indian suburbia.[1] Now in the new millennium, Koramangala had become an attractive residential area for migrant engineers like Sachin. It had cheap, plentiful housing like the NGV complex, and many restaurants and bars had come up to meet the demands of the area's new demographic. It also offered easy access to the city's main business and entertainment sectors.

At the NGV complex, there was another group of four IIT graduates who shared a separate three-bedroom apartment and were friendly with Ankit and his flatmates. One of these young men was Binny Bansal.

IN A WAY, it was fitting that both Sachin and Binny, who would become India's most famous internet entrepreneurs, hailed from Chandigarh.

As with the IITs from where both Bansals had graduated, Chandigarh, too, had been established as a manifestation of Nehru's faith in modernity and technology. After India ceded much of the Punjab province in the Partition of 1947, Nehru wished to build a city within the Indian state of Punjab that would symbolize modern Indian ideals. Chandigarh was to be 'unfettered by traditions of the past ... an expression of the nation's faith in the future.'[2] It wasn't dissimilar to what Nehru had said of Bangalore. In 1951, Nehru hired the pioneering Swiss architect Le Corbusier to create the layout for Chandigarh city. Corbusier died before work on Chandigarh could be finished but it was his design, with a few tweaks, that was implemented when the city was finally set up. Chandigarh was divided into approximately thirty roughly equal rectangular blocks of concrete connected by wide tree-lined roads. A large public square was created, which was surrounded by three imposing government and legislative buildings.

Chandigarh, located at the foothills of the Himalayas, is about 270 kilometres from Delhi. The city's landscape which used to be barren owing to the largely semi-arid climate of north India, was replaced by concrete buildings and attendant greenery, a forced order symbolic of the rise of science and technology.

By the time the Bansals were born in the early 1980s, Chandigarh had long been designated as a union territory that served as the capital of both Punjab and its neighbouring state of Haryana. It had grown in size, too. There were now nearly fifty sectors, new parks and gardens, a proliferation of restaurants. It had become a wealthy little city. Much like Bangalore, well-to-do government and military pensioners found it hospitable. Chandigarh had also produced one of India's most famous cricketers, Kapil Dev. But the city wouldn't exactly turn out to be the new urban paragon imagined by Nehru and Corbusier. As the role of the government in India's economy weakened after liberalization, the private sector's importance grew sharply. But Chandigarh couldn't attract many companies, leaving few employment avenues for its young residents. Many of them, especially bright, ambitious young men like the Bansals, were eager to set off for more exciting terrain.

APART FROM THEIR surname, Sachin Bansal and Binny Bansal had few things in common.

Sachin was born on 5 August 1981 to a business family. His father ran a grain-trading business while his mother has been a homemaker. Sachin is the older of two brothers. Binny was born the following year, on 3 December 1982. His father worked at a public-sector bank and his mother is a retired central government employee. Born to middle-class families, both had comfortable childhoods.

Sachin studied at the D. A. V. School in Panchkula, a town close to Chandigarh. He was known to be a quiet, well-mannered boy with few friends and his academic record was superior throughout. Uma Nijhawan, Sachin's English teacher, remembers him as rather bright but equally shy and introverted, so much so that she was taken by surprise once when Sachin pulled off a small literature event with distinction. 'He wouldn't take the initiative but was very responsible and competent if you gave him something to do. He would come into his own then,' Nijhawan recalls.

Binny went to St Anne's Convent School in Chandigarh, and unlike Sachin, developed a passion for sports. He was captain of the basketball team and played football as well. He had also become familar with computers at a young age. In 2013, Binny told a journalist, 'One major point of inflection [in school] was that I was introduced to computers at class four. It was love at first sight … I was probably the only one at school who could program.'[3] In the early 1990s, this level of familiarity with computers was rare. Most Indians had never seen a computer, much less used one.

Like other children of their age in Chandigarh, Sachin and Binny were relatively privileged, their teenage years mostly unaffected by a preceding period of disturbance in Punjab. In the 1980s, the state was a violent, volatile place. Sikh terrorism, orchestrated by the militant leader Bhindranwale, was at its peak in the first half of the decade. Punjab was haunted by the rise of Bhindranwale, who was eventually killed by the Indian Army in 1984 at the Golden Temple complex. The subsequent assassination of Indira Gandhi by her Sikh bodyguards in the same year unleashed another cycle of violence in Punjab that extended even to Delhi. By the time the Bansals entered their teenage years in the mid-nineties, the state had become relatively peaceful again.

After clearing their tenth-standard exams, both Sachin and Binny enrolled for their final school years at the D. A. V. College, where they were two years apart. College was a mere formality. Classes were sparsely attended, as parents put their children through private coaching in the hope that it would help them secure a seat at any one of India's reputed engineering colleges, the most sought-after of which were the IITs. An IIT degree was the surest way of landing a secure, well-paid job at an IT firm or a multinational company. And getting such a job was considered no small achievement in the early years of the new millennium. Middle-class parents, who had grown up with the fear that such rewarding, stable employment would be out of their reach, hammered their insecurities and aspirations into their children with uncompromising zeal. If they didn't study relentlessly, what awaited them was a dire life on the streets, they were assured.

Sachin made his first attempt to clear the IIT-Joint Entrance Exam in 1999 but failed to secure admission. He joined a lesser institute, the Punjab Engineering College, but took the IIT-JEE test again while still enrolled there.

A local tutor by the name of Ashok Chitkara had achieved fame in Chandigarh as someone who could identify the brightest kids and help them secure admission into the best colleges. Sachin signed up for Chitkara's classes. Chitkara had a peculiar teaching style. He would sometimes explain complex mathematical concepts in Hindi, using *muhavares*, or draw on well-known historical events to make his point. He was also eminently methodical. He assigned class slots and devised seating arrangements based on his estimation of his students' abilities. Students had to regularly take mock exams. Sachin's scores were often in the top tier even though he was never to be seen at the 'front benches'. After a year of Chitkara's coaching classes, Sachin got his break. He pulled off an impressive national rank of 49 in the IIT-JEE test in 2000, surprising Chitkara himself.

That was a record year for both Chitkara and his city with respect to the IITs.[4] Every one of Chitkara's front-benchers – his most obviously sincere students – made it into the IITs. Many of the 'back-benchers', which included members of Zomato and Grofers' founding teams, also got in. Chitkara's fame grew, and so did his ambition. He launched his own university a few years later. Unfortunately, by then Chandigarh was producing IIT-worthy students in far fewer numbers.

In 2000, Sachin and most of Chandigarh's other star pupils, hoping to become engineers, chose to go to IIT Delhi. This would be the first fortuitous step in Sachin's drift towards entrepreneurship. Later, taking a job at Amazon India would be another.

At IIT Delhi, Sachin would meet the people who would later become crucial early employees at Flipkart. He would build his first technology product at this institute, learn how to overcome the humiliation of failure, how to give up addiction. He would cultivate deep friendships here and, for the first time, be able to venture out of his sheltered life in Chandigarh. He would get his first taste of life in a metropolis, and of the West. In fact, IIT Delhi's graduating classes of the early 2000s turned out to be the most significant suppliers of the country's initial entrepreneurs. The founders of some of India's most influential startups, such as Snapdeal, Zomato and Delhivery, were students at IIT Delhi at the turn of the century.

Hostel life greatly characterized one's time at IIT Delhi. There were several social networks apart from classes – study groups, sports groups, cultural activities – that brought people together. But the hostel ranked the highest in importance. Loyalty to one's hostel was paramount; some of the competitive-minded senior students enforced this unwritten law and passed on their zeal for their respective hostels to the juniors. Rivalries grew intense during inter-hostel competitions and campus elections. It was common for students to lose their voice after screaming abuses against rival hostels. This subsequent inability to speak was considered a badge of honour. By usual Indian campus life standards, what went on at IIT Delhi in those years wasn't exactly outrageous.

Among the programmes, computer science was easily the most in demand, owing to the IT boom and the general hype around computers and the internet. This was followed by electrical engineering. The rest of the programmes were perceived as inferior. It was believed that the academic abilities of the computer science students were far greater than those enrolled in civil engineering, for instance. Sachin's exceptional rank in the IIT entrance exam ensured that he was one of a select group of about sixty admitted into the computer science programme in 2000. Many engineers who became entrepreneurs later boasted degrees in computer science from the IITs or other engineering colleges.

The computer science programmes at the various IITs aren't identical. At the Delhi campus, the focus is on the fundamental principles of programming rather than a specific manner of writing code, which is an ever-evolving process. Many IIT Delhi graduates benefited from this approach as working professionals.

The professors, mostly middle-aged or elderly men, were unsparing. One professor would spend his class hours writing complex equations on the blackboard in tiny handwriting, without stopping to check if his students were able to keep up. On finishing, he would simply wipe the board clean and no explanations would be proferred. Instead, he would inform his clueless students that assignments were going to be based on his blackboard notes. Harsh Dhand, one of Sachin's batchmates, compares the computer science programme to being 'thrown into a deep well'. If one emerged victorious, this victory could be replicated in their career. But there are always a few who can't handle the pressure.

Each semester lasted about four and a half months, during which time students had to take a variety of tests; there were also class assignments, cultural events, sports competitions and the call of hostel life.

Ajay Bhutani, who knew both Sachin and Binny at IIT Delhi, says that the programme ensured students learnt how to cope in a high-pressure environment. 'The number of things you have to do ... you don't necessarily [have time to] get organized – you just figure out how to do things. You learn to solve problems faster, more efficiently.'

SACHIN'S FIRST FEW days at IIT were not pleasant. He was an '*ek thappa*' – cricket slang adapted into IIT Delhi lingo to refer to those who had passed the entrance exam after one failed attempt. Those who secured admission on the first try were called 'full toss' and the ones who needed three attempts were crowned 'dead ball'. All first-year students had to endure being 'ragged' by the seniors from their respective hostels. These ragging sessions were called 'interactions' or 'interviews', which often lasted a few weeks. The severity of the ragging depended on the personalities of the victim and the interviewer. First-years were meted out tasks that could range from having to scream slurs against other hostels or wear full-sleeved shirts in the choking Delhi summer; only in the rarest cases were the freshers physically abused. Mostly, these sessions ended with juniors and seniors finding a degree of bonhomie amongst one another. Very few juniors rebelled. Sachin was one of them. He took an instant dislike to these interactions. He didn't do his tasks properly, his displeasure evident, and on a few occasions, he refused his seniors outright. Nevertheless, in the years after Flipkart's founding, one of his 'interviewers', Sujeet Kumar, would become one of the most influential employees at the company.

Sachin was assigned to the Jwalamukhi hostel, Jwala for short. Some hostels such as Kumaon and Aravalli were known for producing skilled sportsmen and hosting impressive cultural activities. Jwala, which means flame in Hindi, was the most infamous. True to its name, it was considered to be the most aggressive hostel when it came to student body elections. The hostel's frequent success in these elections made it all the more unpopular. It also boasted an excellent canteen which served a weekly chicken biryani of great repute. But Jwala's notoriety was primarily due to its high population of Instant Chutiyas or ICs. IC is IIT slang for an abrasive, irritating fellow, instantly recognizable by their off-putting personality. According to Pranay Gupta, a student at IIT Delhi in the early 2000s, the ICs were essentially oddballs. 'You would come across them and think, "*Faltu mein apne aap ko hero samajh raha hai.*" He thinks too much of himself for no reason.' ICs were misfits, and not in an interesting way. They were considered uncooperative and duplicitous, not willing to help their classmates with homework even if they had completed it with ease.

Sachin wasn't considered an IC, but he was made an involuntary member of the Chandigarh Chutiya Association, or the CCA. All IITians hailing from Chandigarh were clubbed together in this imaginary group. Students from Chandigarh tended to stick together and there were many of them at IIT Delhi. Several of them exuded confidence, were generally liked and, most importantly, were popular with the very few girls on campus, hence condemned by their less-fortunate mates into the infamous CCA.

Sachin assimilated at IIT Delhi after the first-year ragging sessions. His hostelmates and classmates alike remember Sachin as a regular guy, who was just one of the boys. Short and dark, with glasses perched loosely on a square, smooth face, Sachin was of medium build. He mostly stuck to his small group of friends and did well in his first-year exams.

Varun Gupta was Sachin's roommate in their first two years at IIT Delhi. The Jwala hostel rooms were small at just twelve feet by twelve feet. A half-wall of concrete separated two rooms. In this cramped space, Varun found Sachin to be a quiet, serious fellow, a pleasant roommate who even had a sense of humour. Varun was the highest scorer in Sachin's batch and later found success as an academic in the US. Many people in class would borrow Varun's notes, but not Sachin, who preferred to read the textbooks. 'Sometimes he would lose interest in a topic and ignore it. But if the topic interested Sachin, he would be really good at it,' Varun recalls.

Sachin was also rather blunt. Harsh Dhand, a fellow CCA member, believes that with Sachin, one always knew where one stood. 'If he didn't like something about you ... he would tell you that without caring much for the consequences.'

In Sachin's second year, the college installed internet connections in the hostels. This prompted some of the more well-off students to install computers in their rooms. Previously, students could use computers only in a communal laboratory. Now, this new infrastructure changed the way students lived. It is probable that Sachin had some exposure to computers before coming to IIT. Binny, by his own admission, was familiar with the machines to a great extent before starting college. As for many of their classmates, especially those from smaller cities and towns, it was at IIT where they were introduced to computers for the first time. Some of these people, who had not seen or used computers, much less the internet, until just a few years prior, would soon find success as internet entrepreneurs or senior executives in the technology world.

As soon as some students installed computers in their hostel rooms, they began to spend large parts of their days cooped up; Sachin confined himself in his room more than others. While he was neither popular nor notorious at IIT, occasionally his independent and rebellious traits came to the fore.

During his intermediate years at IIT, Sachin created a new file-sharing software. It was his first foray into creating technology products, which would later become a full-time occupation. This software allowed users to share photos and videos with each other. The product had a sleek, well-designed interface that made files on one computer accessible to all computers within the same network. Theirs being a network of adolescent male engineering students, Sachin's software was mainly used to share pornography.

A few weeks after Sachin designed the file-sharing system, it caught the attention of the forbidding IIT administrators, who made sure that it quickly fell out of use. The students quietly moved on to a more covert alternative. Sachin was crestfallen. He had hoped the software would become a fixture and bring him lasting recognition and popularity.

Despite this setback, Sachin soon displayed his tech skills again. An electronic game of anagrams had become popular on campus. Those who decoded anagrams fastest would be awarded the highest scores. Naturally, the players most proficient in English did better than the rest. Sachin, whose English was only passable, grew very irritated with the game. So, he wrote up software, that could help him solve the word puzzles – he had not beaten hundreds of thousands of fellow nerds in the entrance exams only to be shown up by the English language. Other players started using software, too, and soon several students deleted the game in disgust because it was impossible to tell man from machine. This was exemplary engineering retribution by Sachin, and a classic example of Instant-Chutiya-like behaviour.

By the end of 2002, in the third year of his programme, Sachin had become addicted to computer games. While many students would spend hours on these games daily, Sachin's addiction was more serious. He was also *very* good at gaming, which was why the anagram game had rankled. Students regularly played two games in particular – *Age of Empires* and *Quake*. *Quake* required expert hand-eye coordination while *Age of Empires* was a strategy game, testing the player's ability to plan their moves in a shrewd, tactical manner and allocate resources efficiently. Sachin was among the few who excelled at both games. He was almost unbeatable at *Quake*. His hostelmates frequently heard his shouts at the end of a session – 'Killed it!' – late in the night as he celebrated his latest victory.

Ram Singla, one of Sachin's hostelmates at Jwala and a fellow involuntary member of the CCA, would lose to Sachin every time, often within seconds. Ram would ask Sachin, 'What's the point, man? Why are you even playing with me?'

'*Koi aur hai nahi. Tu hi khel le*,' Sachin would say. (There's no one else around. So, I have to make do with you.)

In 2003, Sachin and three of his hostelmates, Harsh Dhand, Ankit Agarwal and Pankaj Garg, were selected for a two-and-a-half-month research internship at the University of Essen in Germany. The city of Essen lies on Germany's border with Belgium and the Netherlands. For the four young men, the internship turned into a pleasure trip. On a university-allocated budget of €1,500 each, they embarked on a Europe trip, visiting more than a dozen countries including France, Italy and Spain. In the early 2000s, very few young Indians had the means or the opportunity to travel to the West. It wouldn't be surprising if this trip had stirred and broadened Sachin's imagination to some extent.

Although, on returning in the summer of 2003 for his fourth and final year at IIT Delhi, Sachin quickly resumed his manic gaming. He was possessed by video games. His friends speculated that he sometimes left exams early just so he could return to his games. He had lost interest in the programme, and a few months into his final year, it became clear that he wasn't going to pass – a calamitous outcome. Getting into an IIT is considered a momentous, life-changing event. But this is based on the assumption that one will obtain the degree that fetches the big jobs. It was a reasonable assumption – most students attained passing grades without great difficulty.

Sachin, however, was so consumed by video games that he considered quitting IIT altogether to take up gaming professionally. It was an absurd plan. IITians are known to rave about the excellence of their education, but it is often only later in life. It isn't necessarily for the quality of the institute's education or for intellectual enrichment that multitudes of aspiring young Indians seek admission into the IITs. The higher goal, for both the aspirants and their parents, is for the former to obtain the best-paying jobs and ward off a proverbial life on the streets. In the early years of the new millennium, dropping out just wasn't considered acceptable.

But Sachin didn't care. He informed his friends of his latest accomplishment – he had apparently clinched one of the highest ranks in a national gaming competition. The aim was to win the next time. Only at the end of his fourth year at IIT, as he watched his classmates land jobs at marquee companies like McKinsey and Microsoft or move abroad for post-graduate studies, did Sachin change track and vow to get his degree. Like a chain smoker quitting determinedly, he withdrew himself from gaming.

Over the next year, Sachin experienced the humiliation of staying behind for an additional year. He worked diligently, spending hours at the computer lab rather than thinking of ways to improve his gaming scores. He finished his final-year research project, completed the mandatory courses and finally secured his degree. In July 2005, he joined the small Indian software firm Techspan in Bangalore. It was hardly a dream job, but at least he wasn't killing it or getting killed by video game characters. And he wasn't out on the streets either.

Outside IIT campuses, Sachin may have come across as an extreme character, unusually passionate, an eccentric who would consider giving up an IIT degree for gaming. But not at the IITs, where students like Sachin were hardly uncommon. As Ram Singla succinctly puts it, 'There's another guy [bestselling paperback writer Chetan Bhagat] from IIT who wrote a book called *Five Point Someone*.[5] He could've been describing Sachin.'

THERE WAS NOTHING eccentric about Binny Bansal. He truly was a regular campus guy.

Binny joined the computer science programme in 2001, one year after Sachin. He was a 'full toss', securing admission in the first attempt. His classmates included Rohit Bansal, who would go on to launch Snapdeal, Flipkart's arch-rival for many years. Binny and Rohit were 'best buddies'[6] in their first year at IIT but they drifted apart after that. Their class came to be notorious for low attendance and relatively poor grades. Their seniors would scoff at them. '*Tum log yahaan kahaan se aa gaye?*' How did you guys end up here?

The four years Binny spent at IIT Delhi passed satisfactorily.

He was overall a bright student, even though his grades slipped in later years. He played sports – basketball and squash were his favourites. Despite being introverted and a tad socially awkward, like the stereotypical Indian software engineer, Binny had a mild, pleasant personality. His peers found him likeable. One of his classmates recalls, 'Binny was not impulsive; he was analytical, logical. And he generally came across as a nice guy. He was one of the few who had a normal life at IIT.' Like Sachin, he had a small group of friends, and he, too, was made a member of the CCA.

Binny's reputation, however, rested on something else entirely: he had a girlfriend. He was dating Aparna, one of his three female classmates in the computer science department, and considered attractive. The men in his class numbered more than fifty. Being in a relationship was 'the rarest of the rare thing' at IIT. Binny was of average height and had what is considered quintessential Punjabi good looks – clear green eyes, fair skin and a sportsman's lean physique. He often invited jealousy but such ill feeling would never escalate thanks to his agreeable personality.

Engineering students are often known to lack rounded personalities, as they spend their late teens confined in the bleak rooms of Taylorist[7] coaching institutes in the single-minded pursuit of securing admission into a reputed college. Very few of these aspirants make it to the college of their choice, or in many cases, of their parents' choice. Many of those who do, spend their college years in a vacuum of sorts. Their conditioning is such that education is seen strictly as a utilitarian means towards the end goal – a respectable job. Humanities programmes – there is one at IIT – are dismissed as superfluous. Social development in this environment is thus stunted, and gender sensitivity is nearly absent. Many male engineering students struggle to hold a basic conversation, much less form friendships, with women.

In this abnormal environment, it was hardly surprising that Binny was one of the few men who led a 'normal' life.

Binny lived in the Shivalik hostel. In other hostels, first-years had to share their rooms with a roommate. Shivalik was the only hostel where every student had a room to themselves from the beginning. It was the least distinguished of the ten IIT Delhi hostels. It had been opened up to students in the four-year programmes only a couple of years before Binny came to the campus (IIT Delhi also offers a five-year programme). Anil Kumar, Binny's hostelmate, describes Shivalik as a 'very laid-back kind of place, a sleepy hostel, almost like for retired people'.

Anil and Binny worked together on the student publications board which published the campus magazine. The magazine contained student profiles, information about events, study groups and other on-campus activities. Anil, who came from Agra, was in the civil engineering programme. He and Binny had joined IIT in the same semester. Unlike Binny, whose involvement in the publication board's activities seemed perfunctory, Anil was an energetic member of the group. He organized events, put together a literature festival that boasted Keki N. Daruwalla as one of the speakers, and won praise across hostels for his efforts. Binny, on the other hand, 'was a bit in his hostel's image,' says Anil. 'He was not too enterprising and he didn't really show any signs of leadership then.'

One of Binny's teachers at IIT Delhi was Professor M. Balakrishnan, who had graded his main research project in the programme's final year. Professor Balakrishnan has no recollection of either Binny or Sachin being his student. He only realized years later that he had taught Binny, as he watched an interview of the Bansals with journalist Shekhar Gupta on NDTV's show *Walk the Talk*, where Binny mentioned his project.[8] According to Professor Balakrishnan, it is largely the mediocre, anonymous students such as the Bansals who excel at entrepreneurship.

It hasn't escaped Anil Kumar's attention either that the highest scorers in his batch may have done well in their careers but they weren't the standouts. The people who truly excelled were the average students, nearly anonymous in college.

3

EXODUS FROM AMAZON

This is the story of how Sachin Bansal and Binny Bansal met, an extraordinary tale as befits all matters of grave importance such as politics, caste, religion and war.

There are often varying accounts of the same historical event. This isn't unreasonable – memory is fickle, events lend themselves to different interpretations, old opinions get coloured by newer perceptions that are bound to evolve with time. But what Sachin has said publicly about how he met Binny differs so much from the accounts of people who knew them during Flipkart's early days, that one must delve into the concept of the 'creation myth' to understand Sachin's claims.

In Flipkart's later years, Sachin came to idolize Steve Jobs. He treated the Jobs biography, *Steve Jobs* by Walter Isaacson,[1] like the gospel. Closely associated with Jobs and Apple Inc, the company he co-founded in California, is the idea of the creation myth, a practice entrepreneurs often follow, whereby the story behind their company's creation is embellished by at least some imaginary element.[2] The purpose is to pad up the romance, glamour and providence already associated with the company and its founders. The fact that Job and his friend Steve Wozniak built the Apple computer in a garage all by themselves is only a half-truth. Such accounts presented as the real and romantic version of how a company was founded become a source of inspiration to aspiring entrepreneurs who look up to these successful entrepreneurs as business icons and role models. Most founders perpetuate the creation myth to some degree, even if they add minor imaginary touches. It is but expected that an innovative entrepreneur who has founded a business worth billions of dollars, will be able to creatively present their founding story to the public. Jack Dorsey, co-founder of Twitter, who, like Sachin, also idolized Jobs, has been known to fabricate his own creation myth around Twitter. It has been alleged that Dorsey gave the impression that he was the sole person responsible for the founding of the online social networking company, thus erasing the role of his partners.[3] In telling the story of how he met Binny, Sachin certainly has no such intention. His purpose is simply to tell a good story. It's the inventive details in his account that make it intriguing.

In 2015, during the *Walk the Talk* interview, Shekhar Gupta asked Sachin and Binny how they had met. Sachin's version went thus:

'[It was during] one of the summers in IIT Delhi. In [the] IITs, what happens is that when your project is unfinished during a semester, your professor asks you to stay over for a summer project to finish that project. And I had an unfinished project during one of my semesters. And Binny also accidentally had an unfinished project. Our professors asked us to stay back. We were alone. I actually did not expect anyone to be in the college at that time and I was surprised to see Binny in the lab. I think for the first few days we just maybe thought the other person would go away and they're just there for a few days. But then we started talking and we actually realized that we're from the same city.'[4]

Sachin's 'unfinished project' was a euphemism for the classes he had failed at IIT Delhi. After most of his classmates graduated in 2004, Sachin had to stay back and retake some of the mandatory courses so he could achieve a minimum score of 190 points. He also needed to submit a mandatory research project. This is what would lead to Sachin finally getting his degree in 2005, nearly one year after most of his classmates had graduated.[5] Despite idolizing Jobs, Sachin was clearly embarrassed by his failure at college. Not only Jobs, many famous entrepreneurs, Bill Gates and Mark Zuckerberg included, have spoken openly about dropping out to become entrepreneurs. Indeed, this was one of the essential ingredients that went into the making of their very own creation myths. But the IITs have such strong significance for the Indian middle class that even the country's most radical internet entrepreneur who otherwise embraced Silicon Valley values wholesale, couldn't find it in himself to admit to relative failure at the hallowed institution.

The other loophole in Sachin's account had revealed itself previously, in 2010, at a startup event called UnPluggd, in Bangalore. While delivering a talk about Flipkart, he had said, 'We were batchmates from IIT Delhi – 2005 batch ...' Faltering noticeably, he continued, 'Uh ... right, so this is how we started.'[6] Sachin's unease with public speaking is sympathetically evident.

It is clear he is not comfortable in the limelight, speaks without affectation, and is ultimately a passionate champion of his company. One feels willing to excuse him for saying that his co-founder was also his classmate.

It is a known fact that Sachin came to IIT Delhi in 2000, and Binny in 2001. By all accounts, the Bansals didn't know each other in Chandigarh. So, where did they actually meet?

It is clear that even if they had met in the IIT Delhi computer lab in 2005, this meeting had no bearing on their later friendship and partnership, both of which developed only in Bangalore.

THE BANSALS TRULY got to know each other at the NGV complex in late 2005 after Sachin moved to Bangalore to work at Techspan. They cultivated an easy friendship without becoming particularly close, as is often the case in a large group. Sachin and Binny had become part of a group of eight IIT graduates of similar age. The friends would meet often, go out for movies, dinner and drinks. Some of them, including Sachin, owned cars, which they would take on long drives around or away from Bangalore. A favourite destination was Hampi, an ancient town in Karnataka known for its temple ruins and hippie scene. The sports enthusiasts of the group, which included Binny, played squash and football together. Geeks like Sachin took up hobbies such as coding challenges and puzzle-solving which one commonly faced at job interviews. Sachin also resumed gaming, although not with the obsessiveness of his IIT days.

After graduating from IIT, Binny had taken a job as a programmer at Sarnoff Corporation, an American technology hardware-maker. His stint there lasted eighteen months.

Towards the end of 2006, he applied for a job at Google – which had just set up shop in India – and a few other tech companies. Google rejected Binny.[7] Around the same time, Sachin referred him to Amazon. If Binny made the cut, Sachin would earn a small referral bonus.

Binny was almost rejected by Amazon, too. Another Sachin, a Sachin Dalal, was one of the several Amazon employees who had interviewed Binny. Binny was so nervous that he trembled while writing the code that had been asked of him. Sachin Dalal had to leave the room so Binny could feel at ease. He describes Binny's candidature as 'borderline'. A few positives, such as Binny's IIT degree, ultimately worked in his favour. In late 2006, Amazon gave Binny a job offer.

Right from the start, Binny came across as shy to his colleagues, addressing his superiors as 'sir' even though they were barely older than him. There was no doubt, however, that his technical proficiency was impressive. Sachin Dalal could see that Binny was a highly skilled engineer, better than even Sachin Bansal.

By the time Binny started at Amazon in January 2007, the Indian outpost had evolved vastly from a year ago when Sachin had joined the ranks. Work on the search engine A9, and the payments product Flexible Payment Service, had crept along. Amazon leaders in Seattle had initially found that the India team had done a stellar job with FPS. But there were procedural gaps as certain technical processes were impermissible given that payments was a tightly regulated space. The FPS team was asked to plug these gaps and make a few other changes. FPS was finally launched to a few merchants in the US in 2007 but Amazon didn't promote it enthusiastically. The search engine project was a mess. It had suddenly been thrown into turmoil in February 2006 – soon after Sachin had started at Amazon – when the A9 CEO, Udi Manber, left Amazon to join Google.[8]

Just days later in India, Bharat Vijay, who had been hired by Manber, also quit Amazon. Over the next month, some of the most consequential leaders at Amazon India followed suit. Vikas Gupta, the head of FPS, returned to the US to launch a startup called Jambool, which built payments software for online games. (Jambool would be acquired by Google in 2010 for $70 million.)[9] Vikas was frustrated with the pace of work at the office and didn't get along with his boss Amit Agarwal either. He was independent-minded and no longer cared for a long career at Amazon or any other corporation. He became the first engineer to leave Amazon India to be an entrepreneur. At the same time, Krishna Motukuri, another important Amazon executive, also left to start a comparison-shopping website called uGenie. This company, too, would be acquired by Lulu.com a few years later.[10]

The departures of these leaders marked the beginning of the end for Amazon's experiments building innovative products at the India base. Technical skills aside, Bharat, Vikas and Krishna were also popular, charismatic leaders. Amazon had turned out to be a rewarding workplace for many employees, but the peculiarity of its work culture was grating and could lead to burnout. Bharat and Vikas' easygoing personalities as well as Amazon's initial extravagance had made working here seem gainful to its employees. As these two well-liked leaders made their exits, the environment of bonhomie at the office began to disintegrate.

By this time, Amazon had also decided against launching

its operations in India. Its China venture was faltering, so the company chose to sort out those issues rather than rush into another difficult market. Amazon had evaluated the benefits of buying Indian online retailers such as Indiaplaza. But it passed up the opportunity to buy these firms, realizing they were too small and shoddily run. Amazon had also initially considered starting its own operations; they would've just had to find ways to circumvent the prohibitive foreign investment laws. But the risk of being trapped in a regulatory minefield overshadowed this temptation. Amazon's decision to abandon its India plan was a pivotal factor in the launch of startups like Flipkart and Infibeam. It is doubtful if the Bansals and the Infibeam founders would have launched e-commerce ventures with Amazon as a rival.

By the start of 2007, when Binny joined Amazon, the India base had morphed into a typical back office engaged in specialized routine work. Amazon had come to India with the goal of creating world-beating products. Less than three years later, the dream had died. No one was calling A9 the Google Killer any more. Employees were disenchanted; Amazon had lost its hold over them. When a member of the A9 team was on his way out, he was instructed, by the same company that had lured employees with its office bar and commuter benefits, to return his laptop bag. In a bold act of white-collar solidarity, nearly every employee on the floor threw down their own bags.

Earlier, the Amazon India office operated almost like two different startups, each team working towards building its respective product – A9 and FPS. But after Amazon moved to the Ali Asker Road office in 2006, it introduced many new processes that employees found constraining. Amazon teams in Seattle had also started hiring engineers in Bangalore to handle routine tasks for the headquarters after realizing that they could adhere to high professional standards, and would cost much less than their American counterparts. For many employees in India, it was their first experience of 'seeing a startup become a corporation'.

As Amazon's appeal waned, entrepreneurship became a more enticing prospect, and the entrepreneurial urge that had seized some senior executives at the company in early 2006 gradually turned into a broader movement over the next two years, drawing dozens of engineers from Amazon and other companies, and even some colleges.

Inspired by the likes of Vikas Gupta and Krishna Motukuri, a few mid-level Amazon employees left the company in 2006 to launch their own ventures or enter the startup scene in some capacity – as investors or senior employees. Among the first of such deserters was Gaurav Singh Kushwaha. After graduating from IIT Delhi, Gaurav had worked independently as a freelance software engineer for a German company. Ever since, he had felt inclined to start his own company.

At Amazon, Gaurav had seen how the power of the internet could change lifestyle choices. This got him thinking about what kind of internet services could work specifically in India. It was an optimistic period for the country. The economy was booming. Indian companies were buying foreign ones, including companies based in the land of their former colonial masters. Mobile phones were selling faster than manufacturers could make them. Telecom connections were hitting record numbers every month. Everyone assumed that the masses would be introduced to the internet soon. Bursting with confidence, Gaurav felt his time had come.

This was the spirit with which many people like Gaurav left their jobs to pursue entrepreneurship. India's flourishing economy and their stint at Amazon led these would-be entrepreneurs to ask themselves why they were working for someone else. Why couldn't an internet company be built in India, for Indians, by Indians?

The Silicon Valley entrepreneurs were driven partly by the belief, however misplaced, that they were changing the world for the better. In Bangalore, in those days, it was the urge to prove that an Indian engineer had the wits and the audacity to be an innovator, to create something indigenous, reject the middle-class championing of professional 'service', combined with a lust for excitement, wealth and fame that propelled many to take up entrepreneurship. Over the next few years, many of these startup founders would fail to realize their dreams. Even for the Bansals, who became entrepreneurial icons admired for their energy, skill and inventiveness, this idealism would culminate in a transformational but complex achievement.

AFTER QUITTING AMAZON in early 2006, Gaurav wanted to launch a mobile ads company. But he dropped the plan after realizing that the field was crowded and began searching for other startup ideas. A few months later, his roommate and longtime friend, Nitin Rajput, who was also employed at Amazon, joined forces with him. Soon, they noticed that there were no Indian websites that offered film content the way IMDB did internationally. This was a surprising omission in a country of over a billion people known for their love of movies – and potentially a big business opportunity. In early 2007, Gaurav and Nitin launched Chakpak, conceived as a social network for all content related to Bollywood.

To expand, they needed capital. Gaurav approached Subrata Mitra, his former boss at Tavant Technologies, who had started a fund, Erasmic Venture, to invest in young startups. Erasmic and Canaan Partners invested $2 million in Chakpak. It was one of the biggest cheques written for a nascent internet company, a rare instance of a classic venture investment in India. Gaurav and Nitin had little idea of the market's size. They lacked a long-term vision, couldn't tell a balance sheet from a profit-and-loss statement. But they did relish the everyday excitement of running their own startup and offering for the first time in India quality film content in an online space where users could interact with one another.

To attract customers Chakpak 'gamed Google'. Chakpak would feature at the top of Google search results to do with Bollywood films and film stars. Ensuring such a result and attaining virality on Orkut and Facebook wasn't just a proud achivement, it was Chakpak's business model. The site drew as many as 150,000 users a day – an impressive number for its time.

Gaurav and Nitin worked out of the Erasmic Venture office on Bangalore's Cunningham Road, less than half a mile away from Amazon's Ali Asker Road office. A few months after Chakpak's launch, Sachin and Binny sought out Gaurav and Nitin for advice.

AT AMAZON, SACHIN and Binny were bored. Work had become uninspiring. The payments product they were working on hadn't taken off and the office had lost the energy of the early years. They did enough to escape censure but preferred to spend work hours playing video games and in various other pursuits. Sachin Dalal recalls that the Bansals played truant for several months in 2007. They would be 'out all day and work late when they could order pizzas and take it easy' after the bosses had already returned home to their families.

In reality, when Sachin Dalal thought the Bansals were just evading work, they were actually out conceiving a plan to start their own company.

In early 2007, Sachin had started talking to his friends about launching a startup. By mid-year, he felt more confident about his plan as well as teaming up with Binny. Sachin had said to a colleague at Amazon, 'This doesn't work … working for someone doesn't work for us.'

By now, Sachin and Binny had known each other well for nearly two years. They were still not close friends, but out of their NGV group, they were the only ones inclined towards entrepreneurship. This formed the basis of their bond, which would grow into a strong partnership that would take their friends by surprise. Sachin would admit to his mates that while he and Binny weren't best friends, they got along well and thought on similar lines.

Years later, in a 2013 interview, Binny spoke about his early interactions with Sachin. 'The journey [with Sachin] started seven years back, I think, when I joined Amazon. And we started interacting more ...'[11]

Sachin and Binny resigned from their posts at Amazon in the second half of 2007. This caused some consternation at the office. The company was losing people in hordes but two employees resigning in the same week was especially worrying. The bosses had reason to be surprised, too. Owing to his fine performance in 2006, Sachin had been promoted only a few months ago while Binny had barely completed six months at Amazon. Why would they leave now? A manager of theirs wondered if a rival company was methodically stripping Amazon of its prized talents. But there was no such nefarious plot. Amazon India had lost its way and its ambitious employees were simply moving on to pastures new.

On one of Sachin's final days at Amazon, he had a brief exchange with his namesake, Sachin Dalal. Dalal had said, 'I heard you are leaving and starting your own company. *Haan*, why not try it? You've anyway got a promotion and can always come back.' Sachin had laughed in response.

The only downer for the Bansals was that Sachin had to return the referral bonus he had earned for recommending Binny to Amazon.[12]

4

THE DESERTION

Sachin and Binny knew Nitin Rajput, Gaurav's co-founder at Chakpak, from Amazon. Gaurav had interviewed Sachin at Amazon in early 2006. And all four of them lived in Koramangala.

Initially Sachin and Binny considered starting a website that would offer product reviews. It would collate information on products on various e-commerce sites and guide customers to the most reliable ones. The modus operandi would be the same as Chakpak's: 'game Google'.

This trick – better known as search engine optimization (SEO) – was to use all kinds of mechanisms to have one's site at the top of Google search results. At that time, internet awareness was still low; most users were not familiar with more than a handful of websites, and Google had become their gateway to the internet. Naturally, it became critical for websites to find a prominent place on these search results. Gaurav had gamed Google to make sure Chakpak would get noticed whenever anyone in India browsed the internet for movies. Similarly, Sachin and Binny wished to make their website popular for shopping-related searches. But why wouldn't they just sell the products themselves? Sachin later explained that the Bansals 'didn't want to do the dirty work of packing and shipping of books, handling of operations and all that'. They were software engineers who knew only 'how to write software'.[1]

Soon, the Bansals realized that a price comparison website would contain the most fundamental of flaws: when all suppliers are substandard, there's no value in comparing them. The e-commerce landscape was laughably tiny with only a few well-known sites, among them Indiaplaza, Rediff and Indiatimes. These sites claimed to sell a wide variety of products including books, laptops and CDs. But altogether, the annual sales of products over the internet amounted to less than $40 million.[2] In 2007, Amazon's sales in North America alone exceeded $8 billion.[3] The Indian market, on the other hand, had failed to pick up primarily because the shopping sites were notoriously poor in usability, product quality, delivery – nearly every aspect of e-commerce. Directing users to these sites would be akin to a search engine that inevitably throws up inaccurate, inadequate information.

About a month later, sometime in September 2007, the Bansals decided they would get their hands dirty. Sachin explained this move later while giving a talk at a 2010 startup conference, 'We basically asked ourselves the question, "Can two people, working from home … compete with bigger e-commerce players?" … [We] did market research, talked to a few vendors, looked at revenues of current e-commerce players ... We basically found that the answer is yes. Because the problems that the bigger players were facing were really basic ... around technology, around service, which we thought were very simple problems. Technology was something we were good with. And the service was the only part where we thought that if we can make a difference ... we can probably compete with them.'[4]

The Bansals' previous jobs had paid well and, aided by their frugal lifestyles – video games, puzzles and sports don't require all that much upkeep – they had saved well. In all, Sachin and Binny put up ₹400,000 together to launch their startup.[5] It wasn't an insubstantial sum, even for young, well-paid engineers.

The news shocked their flatmates. What had seemed a passing fancy had turned into a purposeful, irreversible act. They had strongly discouraged the Bansals from taking up entrepreneurship. Moreover, online retail seemed like an especially foolish business idea. Their reaction was similar to Ajay Bhutani's during campus recruitment season at IIT Delhi, when he learnt what kind of business Amazon did: *who sells books online for a living!* It was considered mad to start an internet company, especially when one's career was advancing nicely. But the Bansals were determined to at least 'try something'. They reasoned that even if their startup failed, they would get better jobs afterwards because they had 'tried something different'.

After launching the company, Sachin and Binny continued to live in separate apartments at the NGV complex. In the short period between relinquishing the price-comparison idea and choosing to start an e-commerce firm, two momentous events transpired.

Sachin and Binny finalized the name of their website. Not having enough money to buy a domain of their preference, they settled for a name that cost them just ₹500. Sachin set the parameters – the name was to have no more than eight characters or it would be too much to type, it had to sound 'cool', make the brand stand out. A few brainstorming sessions later, 'Flipkart' was found to be suitable. They ran with it, hoping that 'kart' with its recall of shopping carts, would resonate with customers.[6]

The second event nearly caused the startup to fold up before it had even been launched: Sachin and Binny lost their third co-founder. When the Bansals had started working on their startup idea, they had enlisted a third entrepreneur in the team.

The story of how the Bansals ended up as Flipkart's only two co-founders is rather comical. While the founding of Facebook and Twitter saw ideas being 'borrowed', people ruthlessly discarded, one-upmanship adopted by all sides as the norm – typical American stories of capitalist greed – the story of Flipkart's founding is in the Indian middle-class idiom.

The third entrepreneur who was part of Flipkart's founding team was Varun Sharma*, a friend of Binny. Unlike many of his NGV friends, Binny was a part of other social networks, too. It was not that he was especially social; he was just less socially awkward than the others. Binny had expressed his wish to start his own business to some of his friends outside the NGV circle, and Varun was one of the few who saw merit in the idea. He didn't need much convincing.

It was decided that Sachin, Binny and Varun would be equal partners in the startup. Varun worked with them for a few weeks and their partnership got off to a promising start.

---

* Name changed

He seemed to offer a way of thinking that was different from Sachin and Binny's, something both Bansals valued. The trouble was that Varun had not revealed his entrepreneurial ambition to his parents.

Varun visited his parents sometime after he had started working with the Bansals. When he told his parents that he was going to quit his job to launch a startup, they were appalled. 'Have you gone crazy?' they said. 'Forget about it and move on with your life.'

In the decades after India's independence, when Varun's parents were growing up, job security was paramount and getting a job was often a hard-won victory. To give one up, especially a job at a multinational corporation, and gamble on internet entrepreneurship instead, would have seemed ridiculous to them. Thus thwarted, Varun told the Bansals he was backing out.

Varun's desertion deflated Sachin and Binny. They debated whether they should move forward at all. They were giving up stable, rewarding jobs, staking their savings on a venture which their friends had called foolish. Now, to have a co-founder leave even before the venture had begun, shook their confidence. It hit Sachin particularly hard. He had told his friends earlier that with him and Binny almost always being 'on the same page', a third person was needed to challenge them. After Sharma's departure, he vented to his friends and sought commiseration. It so happened that some of them, despite their misgivings, encouraged Sachin to keep going.

The Bansals soon overcame their setback and started work on the e-commerce website in September 2007. Their resolve and the increasing strength of their relationship took the people around them by surprise. For the most part, Sachin and Binny didn't even discuss Flipkart with their friends, who took this as a sign of maturity, and suggestive of the trust that had developed between the duo. At least at an interpersonal level, Flipkart was starting to work out.

5

UP, DOWN, HELLO, GOODBYE

As Sachin and Binny recovered from the shock of Varun's desertion, the Flipkart website took shape. Coding up a site was no problem for the two IIT computer science graduates. But the Bansals also wanted it to be seamlessly easy to use. Ever since he had created the file-sharing system at IIT, Sachin had nursed an interest in product design. Now, both he and Binny were determined to produce a neat, uncluttered website that would stand out from the messy interfaces of existing e-commerce portals such as Indiaplaza and Indiatimes.

The website was ready in October 2007. The Bansals tinkered with it some more after showing it to their friends and gathering feedback. Finally, they felt confident enough to unveil it to the public. Flipkart.com highlighted all of Flipkart's promises in clear, simple terms: a large selection of books, low prices, free delivery and secure transactions. The letters 'f', 'l' and 'p' were treated in an orange font, the 'i' was inverted to make it look like an exclamation mark, and the last four letters that formed 'kart' were a sapphire blue. The search bar was prominently displayed.[1] The website's design wouldn't have won awards but the Bansals had produced a clean, functional interface. They asked their friends and family members to try it out. Ankit Agarwal, Sachin's flatmate at NGV and former IIT-mate, was among the first to successfully place an order on Flipkart. The Bansals were elated.

That is how it is in the early days of entrepreneurship. One day the entrepreneur is flailing, filled with self-doubt, anxiety, frustration. The next day, a task done well, they feel superhuman, chest out, adrenaline pumping, ready to take on the world. Likewise, with the website launched and the first orders placed on Flipkart, the Bansals felt on top of the world.

They had decided to start with books. The cue had been taken from the Amazon playbook. It made sense to do so, especially in India. Books are cheap, standardized, easy-to-deliver items that many customers might not feel compelled to physically hold before buying. The hope was that if a website sold original, first-hand books at a discount and ensured that the books reached customers in a few days, they wouldn't mind buying from the website.

In online retail at the time, the books category was primarily a means of establishing that essential factor in the success of commerce anywhere: trust. In 2007, no Indian e-commerce firm allowed customers to pay with cash. Transactions had to be completed online using credit or debit cards. And only the most well-to-do Indians, a demographic that included people who spoke English and spent money on books, had credit cards. But this upper class did not trust online retailers yet. Many customers had had bad experiences in the early days of online shopping. Payments failed often, products turned up after months when one could no longer remember why they had placed the order, sometimes the wrong product would be delivered, or it would turn out to be defective, the delivery worker would have difficulty finding the recipient's house – it seemed every time someone bought something online, e-commerce firms would discover a new way of botching up the centuries-old practice of selling things. In this scenario, the Bansals realized that they would first have to win their customers' confidence, and history had shown that books were the easiest means to accomplish it.

A few months after Flipkart was launched, Sachin told a friend over dinner: '*Yaar*, we'll make an Amazon in India. Why should we work for them when we can run our own business? If they can do it, so can we.'

ONE IMPORTANT ASPECT that internet entrepreneurs in India tend to skip in their creation myth-making is the matter of caste.

Both Bansals hail from families that identify as being from the larger Bania caste which has for long been India's single-most powerful business community. The Ambanis, the Birlas, the Ruias, even Dilip Shanghvi, are all Banias. Within the Bania caste, the Agarwals are a prominent community. Businessmen such as the Jindals, Airtel's Sunil Bharti Mittal, and Anil Agarwal, founder of Vedanta, belong to this community.[2] This predominance of Banias in the business world extended into the internet space through the Agarwals, and in particular through the Bansal community. The Bansals are one of the eighteen *gotras*, or clans, within the Agarwal community.

Apart from Sachin and Binny, other well-known internet entrepreneurs from the Agarwal community include Myntra co-founder Mukesh Bansal, Snapdeal's Rohit Bansal and Ola's Bhavish Aggarwal. These entrepreneurs are not usually found referring to the dynamic mercantile history of their communities – the creation myth has to be unique after all. In any case, to say that one is endowed with business acumen at birth is far-fetched. And of course, it's not as if all Banias are inclined towards entrepreneurship and neither are all people of a different caste inclined towards one specific occupation. But one can argue that caste-based practices and traditions in dominant mercantile communities such as the Agarwals can cultivate in the younger members of a family an inclination towards entrepreneurship. If one happens to be born to a business family, one is likely to be inclined to follow suit.

When Sachin moved to Bangalore in 2006, he drove one of his father's used cars instead of buying himself a new one. Ajay Bhutani – who worked with Sachin at Amazon India after graduating from IIT Delhi – wasn't surprised by Sachin's decision. 'Conditioning does play a role,' he says. 'The basics of running a *dhanda* don't come to just about anyone. Those who've seen how it's done do seem to have an advantage over others.'

Even at the IITs, observes Professor Balakrishnan, career choices of students were often shaped by caste and class. The large demographic of students from business communities at IIT Delhi and IIT Kanpur commonly show a strong inclination towards entrepreneurship. He contrasts the success of many of these ventures with his former startup, Kritikal Solutions. The first-ever on-campus technology startup at IIT Delhi,

Kritikal Solutions was set up in 2002 by Balakrishnan and four other professors, along with seven students. It was launched with the intention of producing cutting-edge technical work for corporate clients in the field of digital imaging. But the firm went nowhere. 'We were all from salaried, middle-class backgrounds. Not one of us had any business sense – complete absence of risk-taking ability.' Besides, he adds, five professors can hardly agree on anything.

For the Bansals, and particularly for Sachin who came from a business family, the support of their folks was crucial in the first few months. While Varun's parents forbade him from taking up entrepreneurship, Sachin's father encouraged him and even offered significant practical help, the lack of which could have killed his ambition.

Setting up a functional e-commerce startup meant working with other businesses, including a payment gateway firm that would allow Flipkart to receive customer payments online. In 2007, it wasn't easy for two anonymous entrepreneurs in their mid-twenties to get access to a payment gateway. For weeks Sachin and Binny ran around meeting banks and payment firms. But the payment processing fees were either too high or the Bansals were sent packing as soon as the banks realized they were novices. In despair, Sachin finally turned to his family. With little effort, Sachin's father was able to procure the elusive services of a payment gateway on account of his long-standing trading business. This important milestone achieved, on Sachin's father's advice, the Bansals went on to register the startup as a proprietorship, rather than a limited liability company, as was the norm for new businesses. This reduced their administrative burden, freeing them to direct their energies towards running

Flipkart. These were some of the small but important tweaks that a Bania family background supplied.

Sachin's newfound identity as a proprietor even helped him get married in 2008. In a rare nod to his family background, Sachin admitted in 2010, 'In our community, a person with a salaried job is less valued than someone who runs their own business. As it happened, I was married within a few months of starting out on my own.'[3]

IN THE FIRST few days after the Bansals launched Flipkart, their family members and friends placed orders on the website. At the end of the third week of October 2007, the Bansals noticed an order from an unknown person named V. V. K. Chandra. The order had been placed from Mahabubnagar, a small town in Andhra Pradesh (now in Telangana). Chandra had purchased a book titled *Leaving Microsoft to Change the World* by John Wood.

Still working out of their NGV apartments, Sachin and Binny had planned to source books from nearby bookstores after a sale had been booked. Thrilled to have received their first legitimate order on Flipkart, they went hunting for John Wood. But their excitement soon turned into embarrassment as they couldn't locate the book in any store. Binny personally wrote an email to Chandra informing him that the book was in scarce supply, but the search was still on. A copy of the book was finally found at the Sapna bookstore on the edge of Bangalore's upscale Indiranagar suburb, a few miles west of Koramangala. But the copy Binny had traced was old and he now felt unsure if Chandra, already seemingly disappointed by the delay, would accept it. So, he emailed Chandra again asking if he would accept an old copy or prefer to wait for a week so that Flipkart could look for a fresher one. Additionally, Binny also offered Chandra a ten per cent discount to compensate for his troubles. Chandra, a software engineer who ran a consultancy business, was so eager to read the book that he asked Binny to send the old copy. On 31 October, the Bansals shipped the book. Two days later, it reached Chandra. He was rather impressed. He held in his hands a book he had desperately wanted but not found in any bookstore in all of Hyderabad. An unknown website not only procured it for him but displayed unheard-of solicitousness in the process. The delayed delivery of an old copy of a book wasn't the ideal start the Bansals had imagined for their company, but Flipkart's customer service had already entranced the company's first real customer.

Chandra left a comment on Flipkart's website, which was proudly displayed for several months:

'The best Indian online book store I have ever seen. Fast and free shipping, discounts and a large number of titles. I could not have expected more. You guys really rock. Good luck.'[4]

Over the next few months, Sachin and Binny applied this rigour and sincerity to win over many more customers. Their business model was crude. After receiving an order, either Sachin or Binny (Binny more often than Sachin) would make a bookstore run – Sapna, Gangaram's and Blossoms were the most frequented – wrap the book in attractive paper and ship it to customers through a courier service. They also tried sourcing books directly from book distributors but were turned away by many. After much persuasion, a couple of distributors finally agreed to give the Bansals access to their inventory. Now a few times every week, by turns, Sachin or Binny would pay a visit on Binny's motorbike to the distributors' warehouses located across Bangalore and pick up books so they could fulfil new orders.[5] The Bansals employed part-time workers who helped with the packaging, but they were otherwise on their own.

Around this time, the Bansals uploaded one of their personal mobile phone numbers as the Flipkart helpline. They worked on improving the website and attracting more users. Sachin quickly became adept at manipulating Google. Having initially received advice on the matter from the Chakpak founders, Sachin now learnt new tricks on his own. Soon, Flipkart was featuring at the top of Google searches, not just for books but for all sorts of products. Sachin's newfound expertise didn't just bring more customers to Flipkart; it accidentally started a chain of events that would transform the company two years later, at the end of 2009.

Through trial and error, Sachin and Binny gradually discovered what strengths each possessed. In the company's early days, their roles weren't clearly defined. Both tried their hand at everything. But it quickly became evident that Sachin excelled at marketing, website design and other tasks directly linked to attracting customers, while Binny showed proficiency in organizing the supply operations. In Binny's own words, 'In four to five months, it just happened. Sachin would think ahead, how to grow the business, how to get customers. And I would think about how will all this work at scale.'[6] This was the template they followed over the next few years. Sachin formulated the vision for the company – how much they should expand, what direction it should take – as Binny set up the infrastructure to realize that vision.

Despite a few milestones, Flipkart's first year was a period of struggle for the Bansals. They found great success in pleasing a few thousand customers who bought books through the website, but in almost every other aspect, they faced one setback after another. One of the biggest jolts came from their failure to convince any of their friends to join them. In the first few months after launching Flipkart, Sachin and Binny had asked more than a dozen friends and acquaintances to join the company. Among the persons solicited were Sachin's former hostelmates, nearly all of Sachin and Binny's NGV flatmates, and a few other people known to Binny. But not one of them was willing. These engineers were sceptical about entrepreneurship, the potential of e-commerce, selling books online (*Who reads books anyway?* they said). They were especially unsure about Sachin and Binny. In college, Sachin and Binny had been mediocre students, as unimpressive outside the classroom as they were within it. No one had thought they could be leaders. In those years, when entrepreneurship was almost a middle-class taboo, the Bansals' venture had struck their friends as a whim, an amusing but eccentric pursuit. They were to be indulged, like children, but joining them was considered preposterous. They were so alone that when Sachin got married to Priya in April 2008, Binny could not attend the wedding. He had to stay back in Bangalore and keep the website running as he was still one of the only two employees at Flipkart.

Anil Kumar, Binny's batchmate from IIT, also lived in Koramangala, just a few minutes away from the Bansals. After graduating, Anil had found work as a management consultant. He too lived with old IIT classmates in an apartment. Anil had found Binny to be an unimpressive guy in college, lacking ambition, energy and purpose, much like his hostel, Shivalik. Despite being on the board of IIT Delhi's student publications, Binny had achieved little other than an influential position. When Binny and Anil ran into each other in Koramangala in late 2008, Anil asked him, 'What are you up to?'

'Startup ...' said Binny.

'What kind of startup?

'We sell books.'

'*Abbe,* who sells books? Where is your salary coming from?'

'How will we get a salary? We're looking for funding.'

'*Funding kaun dega be*?' Who will give you funding, man?

Anil had thought that Binny was talking gibberish; why would anyone offer capital to two novices, especially when one of them was his neverdowell classmate? 'I thought he had gone mad,' says Anil today. 'I left the conversation at that ... And now I keep talking with my other IIT friends that if I had just managed to even put together one lakh – begged, borrowed, stole – and given it to them ...'

A few months later, in 2009, Anil launched a consultancy startup, RedSeer Management. He would meet Binny a few more times that year and exchange notes about real-estate prices in Koramangala, where both their startups were located. He didn't see Binny for nearly two years after that. During this time, Anil and his friends forgot about Flipkart, their scepticism entrenched.

This is why, the next time Anil heard about Flipkart, he would have an identity crisis.

BY MARCH 2008, six months after launching the website, the Bansals' commitment to their customers materialized into a tangible benefit: Flipkart had broken even. The startup was generating sufficient revenues and achieving profit margins high enough to be self-sustaining. It was pulling in a few dozen orders every day. Customers were happy and kept coming back to buy more. Encouraged, Sachin and Binny moved to their first office, a small two-bedroom flat in an area called Wilson Garden, a few kilometres away from their apartments in NGV.[7]

Soon after, Flipkart hired its first official employee. Until now, Sachin and Binny had employed part-time workers to help them with sourcing and handling packages. But the increase in orders prompted them to look for a full-time employee to oversee the procuring and packaging of books. A delivery worker at First Flight Couriers, one of Flipkart's courier partners, pointed the Bansals to a former colleague of his named Ambur Iyyappa. After working at First Flight for four years, Iyyappa had taken a break to complete a diploma course. First Flight had warned him that he may lose his job. By the time he returned to Bangalore a few months later, the company had already replaced him. Out of a job, Iyyappa, who came from a poor Tamilian family, was desperate. Flipkart took him on at a monthly salary of eight thousand rupees.

Iyyappa turned out to be an excellent hire. At this time, Flipkart had a simple operations process. After customers placed their orders, Sachin and Binny entered the book titles and quantities on an Excel sheet, handed out printouts of the sheet to their packaging workers, who then bought the books from various bookstores. Iyyappa had an extraordinary memory, and he knew how courier services worked. He was skilled at organizing the procurement process and managed the packaging and courier workers well. Iyyappa and Binny worked closely over the next two years. They developed a patois of English, Hindi and Tamil that only the two of them could understand.

Soon, Iyyappa took charge of most of the physical operations work. This allowed Binny to direct his energies on expanding product assortment and automating the processing of orders. The Bansals were so pleased with Iyyappa's performance that, within a month, they gave a referral bonus of ₹5,000 to his acquaintance at First Flight Couriers.

Iyyappa was Flipkart's 'human ERP*'[8] until it reached a thousand orders a day. He had a sensational career at the company. In a year's time, his salary soared from eight to nearly eighty thousand rupees a month. Over the next decade, he would become a *crorepati* by selling Flipkart shares and secure a BBA degree.

THE OFFICE ESTABLISHED, their first employee hired, the company financially stable, the website running smoothly, and customer numbers increasing every week, it was now time for Flipkart to raise venture capital. The Bansals knew how their friends at Chakpak had attracted funding, so, when asked, the Chakpak founders Gaurav and Nitin advised the Bansals to approach venture funds. The Bansals were looking for an initial $1 million so they could fulfil their expansion plans.

In early 2008, around the time they had hired Iyyappa, the Bansals had gone to a networking event for entrepreneurs called Open Coffee Club. This is where they met Abhishek Goyal.

---

* enterprise resource planning

Abhishek, who had previously worked at Amazon India, had been hired by Erasmic Venture a few months ago. After leaving Amazon in 2006, he had moved to a software firm called 3i. But Abhishek was a perennially restless employee. He had started an HR firm before joining Amazon but it had failed. He was bored at 3i and considered launching a mobile payments company with his friend, Mekin Maheshwari. But they gave up on the idea after another payments startup announced a large funding round. Still, Abhishek wanted to be part of the startup world in some way. Gaurav, the Chakpak co-founder who knew Abhishek from their Amazon days, introduced him to Subrata Mitra of Erasmic Venture. Subrata soon agreed to hire Abhishek as an associate. Abhishek's task was to find promising startups and bring them to the notice of Subrata and his partners, Prashanth Prakash, Mahendran Balachandran and Gagan Kumar.

Abhishek had heard of Flipkart from friends and acquaintances, some of whom had tried and appreciated Flipkart's service. A college senior of Abhishek used to joke that Flipkart was like an ATM for books – just as an ATM dispenses notes one after the other, Flipkart delivered book after book in quick succession. Abhishek had asked a mutual friend to introduce him to the Bansals but as fate would have it, they unexpectedly ran into one another at Open Coffee Club. It was organized by Amarinder Singh, an engineer with an MBA who worked as a sales executive and wanted to encourage entrepreneurship in India.

Abhishek hit it off with Sachin and Binny instantly. The three of them had similar personalities. In his mid-twenties, Abhishek was a shy computer science graduate from IIT Kanpur. He had a nervous laugh which gave away his social awkwardness. He was very serious about work and desperate to find his calling. In the Bansals, Abhishek saw two young software engineers who were living his dream of being an entrepreneur. He found them to be 'very geekish' and straightforward, like typical computer science students. The Bansals didn't try to hardsell Flipkart, there was no posturing, no real pitching. It was a trait that even Abhishek's superiors at Erasmic appreciated. 'Sachin and Binny came across as a couple of tech guys who wanted to write code rather than run around doing operations. That was not surprising – most tech entrepreneurs were like that,' says Abhishek.

After the first meeting itself, Abhishek decided to urge his bosses at Erasmic Venture to invest in Flipkart.

Over the next few months, Abhishek, who also lived in Koramangala, spent many weekends with the Bansals. He became a friend and mentor to Sachin and Binny. When gauging entrepreneurs, Abhishek would look for small clues that pointed to their problem-solving abilities. Every time he met the Bansals, they would talk of a new trick learnt, a discovery made or a problem solved. It was clear that Flipkart was unceasingly moving forward. Even its website was well made and unusually fast for the time.

During one meeting, the Bansals described their customer support email address to Abhishek. It was cs@flipkart.com, kept intentionally short. Many e-commerce sites featured long, complex email addresses, perhaps because they didn't want to be assailed by customer complaints. Sachin didn't see the point to this. His rationale was simple. He explained to Abhishek, 'If you don't want customers to write to you then don't publish your email. If you want to actually help customers then make it easier for them to write to you.' It was a continuous trickle of such cues over many months that strengthened Abhishek's belief that these were uncommon, dedicated entrepreneurs, on to something big.

Abhishek noticed that the Bansals would take a problem and break it down into 'manageable pieces'. Other e-commerce firms would typically wait to source all the books that a customer had ordered and deliver them together to save costs. Almost always this caused long delays in deliveries because some books would inevitably be out of stock. But the Bansals split up orders, delivering instantly the books their suppliers had in stock, and shipping the rest when they became available. They would also promptly process refunds or order replacements. Abhishek recalls how 'it was magical for that time. The benchmark was so low that when you saw a company do reasonably well at execution it compounded the impression that those guys are very capable. And they weren't even losing money.'

Sachin and Binny had realized that they would have to decide who between them should take on the role of CEO. It mattered to investors who was at a company's helm. Too many startups had been broken up because their founders fought over who was more important. It had become clear that Sachin was the one with the vision – the big thinker. Binny's contribution, however, was no less important. Managing operations was critical to Flipkart's success, but it was inherently secondary to Sachin's role. So, the Bansals agreed that Sachin would be Chief Executive Officer and Binny the Chief Operating Officer. When they met the higher-ups at Accel Partners, it was clear that Sachin was CEO and Binny the COO. This was reassuring.

Abhishek tried to nudge them on the subject, but the Bansals didn't seem to have any differences. They were very thick, very close. They would almost always meet Abhishek together. Abhishek noticed that Sachin and Binny could predict each other's thoughts and opinions on any subject. Their chemistry was evident – they took trips together, ate out together – it almost seemed like they were brothers.

Abhishek was also struck by the Bansals' perseverance. They regularly worked more than twelve hours a day. Even on weekends, Sachin and Binny would be in the office until 8 p.m. Sachin liked going on long drives to unwind and eating dosa chicken and other Indian dishes at local restaurants. Both Bansals, along with Abhishek, would also go to the far-off Windsor Pub for beers. But the Bansals were particular about spending only so much time outside of work. After Abhishek had convinced Sachin to go out and take it easy one Sunday afternoon, the Flipkart CEO had relented, only to come back to Abhishek later half-jokingly, '*Yaar, chaar ghante barbaad ho gaye. Main tere saath nahin aaonga phir se!*' Man, you wasted four hours of my time. I'm not going out with you again!

As impressed as Abhishek was with the Bansals, he couldn't convince his fund to back Flipkart. The Erasmic Venture partners weren't even alone in their scepticism towards the company. The Bansals had approached every venture fund in India for capital. They met partners and associates at all the marquee funds, from Sequoia Capital, NEA-Indo US, Matrix Partners, IDG Ventures to Nexus Venture Partners. Not one of them showed serious interest. Some fund managers scoffed at them. Others didn't like the name 'Flipkart'. *Why was it spelt kart, not cart?* The Bansals considered renaming Flipkart to

WSpot but finally decided against it. One investor even asked the Bansals if their operations had Six Sigma certification. Six Sigma is a complex mechanism of business processes made famous by General Electric, a giant manufacturing company. Operating out of an apartment office in Koramangala, Flipkart managed its supply chain using Excel sheets, printouts and the human ERP, Iyyappa. The Bansals had, of course, not even heard of Six Sigma. To add to their woes, there were venture capitalists who even offered unsolicited career advice, 'You guys are educated – why are you trying to do this?'[9]

These reactions were in keeping with the times. Venture capitalists were considered lords, and their sense of self-importance matched this stature. Entrepreneurs were expected to be in their thrall, grateful that they were given a few minutes to pitch their unconvincing ideas to the masters whose *gyan*, wisdom and aura were to be absorbed and admired. This equation would change over the next decade; VCs now compete to prove who is the most humble servant to star founders. In 2008, however, it was the venture lords whose egos had to be massaged by startup founders, who had to be courted and coaxed diligently into writing cheques, never mind that these lords were paid crores in management fees to do so. When it came to e-commerce, the verdict of the pantheon was unanimous: it wasn't going to work in India, and even if it did, two software engineers would be the least likely to make it happen.

In those days, no e-commerce website worked smoothly. This was primarily because of the founders' ineptitude in running operations. 'E-commerce is all about warehouses, factories, moving goods – the website is the easiest part,' says

Abhishek. 'If you're doing millions of transactions, how would you maintain quality? ... How would two software engineers succeed in such an operations-heavy business?'

Books also allowed very low margins, which made profitability in an e-commerce set-up dubious. It didn't matter that the Bansals eventually wanted to sell all kinds of products. The VCs remained unmoved. To them, the numbers still didn't add up. Even if a business such as Flipkart were to grow very fast, it would still not amount to much. If somehow the startup defied the odds and achieved significant scale, it would require at least $20 to $25 million in capital. And no one was willing to risk that kind of cash.

IN 2007, APART from Flipkart, two other e-commerce startups had emerged from the detritus of Amazon India. One was Anand Rao's Pustak, which focused solely on selling international books unavailable in the country to domestic customers. The other was Infibeam, founded by Vishal Mehta, who came from a wealthy Gujarati business family that owned a large Toyota dealership. After working in Amazon's acquisitions team in Seattle for five years, Vishal had moved back to India in 2007. He sensed that there was an attractive opportunity to build an e-commerce firm as Amazon had cancelled its plan to launch in the country. He gathered a stellar founding team to start Infibeam, persuading Ajay Chandra and Vijay Subramanian, two among Amazon India's brightest engineers, to join forces with him. A month before Flipkart started, Vishal launched Infibeam in September 2007, selling cars online with help from his family business. Like Flipkart, Infibeam wanted to become the Amazon of India. Unlike the Bansals, however, Vishal had no shortage of startup capital. After its launch, Infibeam quickly expanded into other categories such as books, mobile phones and laptops.

Sometime in the middle of 2008, Vishal approached the Bansals. Flipkart was doing well with books, but it was still very small. He had heard of the Bansals from Ajay Chandra and Vijay Subramanian, who had been their colleagues at Amazon. Vishal invited Sachin and Binny to Ahmedabad for a meeting.

In Ahmedabad, Vishal made his proposal: he wanted the Bansals to sell their website to Infibeam. Flipkart would complement Infibeam's book selection, and Vishal would, in turn, acquire the services of two young, talented engineers who had limited but intimate experience of running an e-commerce business. It would be a great deal for Infibeam. Vishal convinced the Bansals that e-commerce was a complex business that required years of arduous work and massive quantities of capital, that all this was beyond the Bansals – they would surely get crushed. The Bansals could join Infibeam instead and they could all create something big together.

Vishal's pedigree and his family's standing lent him an imposing aura. Before Amazon, Vishal had studied at Cornell University and the Massachusetts Institute of Technology. He was well spoken and the Bansals found him impressive. They had been rejected and ridiculed by the venture lords. They had failed to convince their friends and IIT-mates to join Flipkart. Their former flatmates had advised them against entrepreneurship. On the other hand, here was Infibeam. The Bansals were not just convinced by Vishal's stature and wealth, they also knew how good Ajay Chandra and Vijay Subramanian were. On their own, the Bansals didn't stand much chance against such excellent engineers and Vishal's personal financial strength. Flipkart was yet to be incorporated as a company. Sachin had recently got married – it was perhaps time to cut his losses. Selling out didn't seem like a bad idea.

Thinking they were out of options, the Bansals agreed to sell Flipkart. The paperwork for the buyout was prepared. Vishal was offering the Bansals less than five per cent of Infibeam in exchange for all of Flipkart. The compensation would be paid entirely in Infibeam shares, and they were to move to Ahmedabad.

Vishal sent them the paperwork for the sale. When he saw the employment letter, Sachin was shocked: Infibeam was offering him and Binny less than ₹15,000 each as monthly salary. It was a humiliating proposal. Sachin asked Vishal for a higher amount over the phone, only to be told haughtily that it was a fair offer. Now, Sachin was truly offended. He told Vishal that they would get back to him in a few days, and hung up.

That conversation helped the Bansals recover their senses. Vishal's spell was broken. They realized that Flipkart's progress may not seem impressive to an outsider but it was, in fact, substantial. They were growing rapidly, learning new things, improvising and improving every week. And they had done it all by themselves, with help from a human ERP. The VCs hadn't been kind to them, but they were hardly the only ones to receive such treatment. In those days, not many startup deals materialized. And they were certainly not going to sell out in such a demeaning fashion. All things considered, they would continue to persevere with Flipkart. Though Vishal kept following up for weeks, eager to wrap up the deal, he was carefully fended off every time.

By now, Flipkart had met most of the VCs in India, including one Shailendra Singh of Sequoia Capital. Shailendra had acquired a reputation among some entrepreneurs as someone 'who dated but never committed'. During a meeting with him, the Bansals discussed the hypothetical prospect of selling Flipkart, without mentioning that they had a standing offer from Infibeam. Shailendra instantly dismissed the idea, 'You've only been working at it for a few months. Are you mad to be thinking of selling right now? Give it a few months more at least.'

They had already decided to refuse Infibeam by now; the validation by a venture lord, even one whom they didn't particularly like or respect, gave them comfort. Once again, the Bansals uncovered reserves of steel and confidence that would have surprised people who knew them. The setbacks they had faced – deserted by a co-founder, rejected and ridiculed by friends and investors – would have drained the confidence and drive of many a strong-willed, experienced entrepreneur. Selling out to a bigger, pedigreed company would have allowed them an honourable exit and mitigated their financial risk. But they dug deep, holding firm, with a venture lord as an unwitting prop.

A few weeks later, Sachin told a friend over beer, '*Yaar, bach gaye*. Vishal had completely brainwashed us. What a crazy thing we were going to do!'

6

THE KART GETS ROLLING

In the second half of 2008, a few months after the Infibeam episode, Sachin and Binny received an email from a stranger. It was addressed to 'Bansal and Bansal (not in a particular order).' The sender, Tapas Rudrapatna, was familiar with Flipkart. He liked to read and had ordered books on the website. His family had recently moved back from Bombay to their home in Mysore. Tapas had come to Bangalore to look for a job and had found temporary accommodation at a friend's place in the same Wilson Garden neighbourhood where the Bansals worked. He had noticed a Flipkart signboard and, on a whim, written to the Bansals asking if they were hiring. Sachin and Binny responded; a meeting was set up.

The Bansals were startled by Tapas. He was an unlikely startup employee, and would probably have made an unlikely employee anywhere. He was around the same age as Sachin and Binny, but seemed to have lived many lives. After studying commerce at Sydenham college in Bombay, Tapas had worked in advertising, helped run a shack in Goa, and played a clown – an actual clown – in a circus act. He was a talented musician, having played bass guitar in a metal band in Bombay; he could even handle a rhythm guitar and drums. He had tattoos all over his body, wore his hair long over a thin, bearded face. He loved his *chai-and-sutta*. The Bansals were fascinated by him, but they weren't sure what Tapas could do for them. He wasn't a coder or an operations man, and they couldn't imagine how couriers and distributors would react to his unusual personality. What sealed the decision was Tapas' prized possession: a laptop. Tapas also admitted that he needed only enough money to cover his rent and chai–sutta needs. This came to less than what the Bansals were paying Iyyappa. They hired Tapas and asked him to work in customer service and do a variety of odd jobs.

Unexpectedly, Tapas became an integral part of Flipkart for the next four years. He performed the widest range of duties out of all its employees. He helped set up new offices, wrote Flipkart's blog, oversaw social media marketing and became the most important member of the customer support team. Most of all, along with Sachin, he was the strongest advocate of the customer at Flipkart, ensuring that the company never veered from its motto of keeping shoppers happy. Whenever there was a prickly user issue or a call from an angry shopper, Tapas would handle it, pacifying them with apologies, jokes, conversation. He spoke to Flipkart users in an informal, friendly, almost-irreverent manner and wrote blogs and Twitter posts that charmed them. He handed out free books and offered additional discounts. While within Flipkart, employees in charge of any mishandled order would be treated with swear words, scorn and contempt. In these moments, the funny, friendly Tapas would transform into a raging bully. Without an official role, Tapas was simply seen as Flipkart's conscience-keeper in the early years, ready to help wherever there was a crisis.

Tapas' presence diminished quickly after 2011 as Flipkart exploded into a mid-sized firm and then into a huge company. During the company's first three years, however, Tapas played a crucial role in building Flipkart's cult-like brand. He also became a confidant to the Bansals, who found it easy to trust Tapas as he was singularly uninterested in acquiring power. In Flipkart's final years of independence, he was perhaps the only employee, out of all former or existing Flipkart employees, who was close to both Sachin and Binny.

BY THE TIME Tapas joined Flipkart, the company had completed a year. It was handling a few dozen orders every day and word about the website was spreading. Flipkart needed more employees; there was a lot of work to be done. The website itself had to be upgraded. Until then, Flipkart's use of technology had been rudimentary. Now, it needed engineers who could build sophisticated tech systems. But more importantly, it needed someone to do the dirty work of dealing with suppliers and courier partners whose cooperation was vital for the company's survival. Binny had a knack for designing supply chain processes, not so much for the daily grind of negotiations with stubborn partners.

Despite the multiple rejections from his friends, Sachin had kept in touch with some of his former IIT-mates. One of these people was Sujeet Kumar, Sachin's senior at the Jwala hostel whose 'interviews' Sachin had resented when he had first started at IIT. After some initial awkwardness, Sujeet and Sachin had become friends. Like Sachin, Sujeet had also not secured passing grades in the first attempt and had to stay back on campus to obtain his degree. During those six additional months in 2003, the two of them spent a considerable amount of time with each other over *teen patti* and chai–sutta.

The youngest of three children, Sujeet was born into a land-owning family in Bhabua, a small city in Bihar. His father and grandfather were lawyers. In college, Sujeet had been a mediocre civil engineering student, but his boisterous personality had made him one of the best-known people on campus. Sujeet was dark, of average height, his hair was always dishevelled, and he wielded an earthy, raucous sense of humour. He immersed himself in college life, participating in cultural events and joining several clubs. At once, he was on the committee to prevent ragging as well as the organizer-in-chief of the ragging at Jwala. Sujeet was the big bully of the hostel but also its most popular resident. He also organized hostel activities and was an energetic participant in hostel politics. He lost an election for the post of the college's cultural secretary but played a key canvassing role in the victory of a Jwala candidate.

Ankit Agarwal, Sujeet's junior and a resident of Jwala, confirms that Sujeet was 'really good at managing people', but both he and his hostel were notorious as every year Jwala would 'ditch other hostels and try and win all the elections for itself'.

After graduating from IIT, Sujeet wanted to join the Indian Administrative Service. But two failed attempts later, he gave up and started working for an offshoring firm in Delhi in 2006. In 2008, the company went out of business owing to the global financial crisis following the bankruptcy of Lehman Brothers in the US.

Sujeet had kept in touch with Sachin after college. In the period when the offshoring business was unravelling, Sujeet noticed that Sachin's status message on an internet messaging service indicated that he was hiring engineers at Flipkart. Sujeet wasn't interested in a tech job, nor was he equipped for it, but he offered to help Sachin find coders. A few weeks later, Sachin told Sujeet that Flipkart wanted someone to run operations, inviting him to join them. This piqued Sujeet, as in this role he could put to use his hyper-energetic personality and intuitive ability to read people and get work done. 'I'll come to Bangalore and talk to you,' he said to Sachin.

In November 2008, Sujeet visited the Bansals in Bangalore. He wanted to see for himself how Flipkart worked and size up the co-founders. He didn't know Binny, and it was important to get a sense of the COO's personality if they were to work together. They went out for drinks, reminisced about their IIT years, discussed their common friends. He found Binny to be a pleasant fellow, with whom it would be easy to get along.

Sachin, on the other hand, had changed a little from the guy Sujeet had known in college. He didn't even seem to exactly be the man he had spoken to at the beginning of the year. The new Sachin sounded very enthusiastic about Flipkart. It was clear that he thought Flipkart could become big. His confidence was striking, a significant transformation from Sachin the IIT student. He also seemed careful about what and how much information was to be shared with someone else.

Encouraged by his observations, Sujeet decided to give the job a try. He decided to spend the next few months working with the Bansals. If it worked out, he would stay on at Flipkart.

When he agreed to join them, Sachin and Binny brought up the matter of compensation. Sujeet told them, '*Comp-womp chhod yaar*. Let's see if I'm comfortable working with you and if you are comfortable working with me. We'll talk after six months.' Sujeet had enough money. What he wanted was to 'build something', to prove himself. His salary was finalized only in June 2009. After that, they never again spoke about it.

As soon as he started at Flipkart, Sujeet began focusing on establishing relationships with book suppliers. Until then, Flipkart had built partnerships with a few book distributors but had no relationships with publishers. It still sourced at least some of its orders from bookstores. This mode of operations had been necessary in the beginning, but it wasn't sustainable. Flipkart's raison d'être, as is that of most internet businesses, was to replace the offline stores rather than depend on them. Even though the Bansals worked with a few middlemen, Flipkart now needed to move up the chain and establish direct connections with the businesses that controlled the supply of books.

SUJEET WAS A mirror image of Sachin and Binny. Sujeet's inability to write code was complemented by the Bansals' lack of interpersonal skills which had made it difficult for them to break into the closed world of publishing. Sachin and Binny were introverted coders; Sujeet was an extroverted, all-action hustler. It was an ideal combination, one that worked in a symbiotic manner to catapult Flipkart into an explosive startup. From the day he went to work there, Sujeet was given complete independence to run his function. His role at Flipkart grew as fast as the company's business. Sujeet became the engine of the company. Outside the technology and marketing functions, it was his word that became the writ in the key functions of sales and supply chain. Sujeet would quickly become the most powerful man at the company, after the Bansals. During his first four years, the Bansals rarely questioned any of his decisions, even though they didn't always approve of his unconventional methods and aggressive tactics.

This became Flipkart's guiding philosophy with respect to its employees: hire smart people and don't tell them what to do. It was applied to Sujeet, and to most of the senior employees the Bansals brought into Flipkart.

In the early years, the Bansals also openly admitted to their weaknesses. After Sujeet joined them, he asked the Bansals for the contact details of Indian publishers. But they didn't know any. They had struggled to establish contact with publishers, who showed little interest in engaging with two anonymous software engineers. The Bansals were happy to leave it to Sujeet to build relationships with publishing firms. 'It [was] a great thing. Many others would have wasted time lying,' says Sujeet.

Meanwhile, at Infibeam, Vishal Mehta still hadn't given up hope of convincing the Bansals to sell Flipkart. In early 2009, Vishal flew to Bangalore. At a Café Coffee Day outlet in the eastern part of the city, he met Sachin, who had brought Sujeet along for the meeting. It was here that they politely but firmly told Vishal that Flipkart, with its five employees and a-few-dozen-orders-a-day business, wasn't up for sale.

By April 2009, the few dozen orders shot up to more than 200 as the company began working directly with more book distributors in Bangalore. But Bangalore represented a minuscule part of the publishing world, the centre of which was Delhi. To become a force in the books business, Flipkart would have to cultivate relationships with the publishing houses and distributors in the capital. In the summer of 2009, Sujeet and Tapas travelled north to set up Flipkart's first office outside Bangalore. This office properly complemented the company's headquarters located inside a two-bedroom apartment. Situated in Daryaganj, the Delhi office was a single room of twenty square footage on the first floor of a dingy building. A few minutes' walk from Jama Masjid in Old Delhi, Daryaganj is home to many large and small book distributors and hosts regular *kitab bazaars* that attract thousands of thrifty book buyers.

In the summer heat, the poorly ventilated room which lacked air-conditioning and had just one small window, felt suffocating. But it was here, amidst the blaze of the madly cramped lane, that Flipkart established itself as a major force in the books world. Sujeet used all his sociability and cunning to jostle, charm and manipulate distributors, who agreed, one after another, like fish taking bait. He immersed himself in every aspect of the books business. After it became evident to Sujeet that he would have to be stationed in Delhi for a while, he installed an old used air-conditioner in his tiny office.

Within three months, Flipkart's assortment of books widened considerably as it signed up dozens of small distributors in Delhi. 'You had to figure out how the local networks worked. Distributors needed permission from publishing houses, which controlled the pricing of books,' Sujeet says. He built relationships with the decision-makers at the distribution firms, activated their fear of missing out on an unknown yet promising new source of business and played one against another.

AS 2009 DAWNED, the world found itself drowning in a post-Lehman Brothers era. The financial markets had collapsed, banks had stopped lending and businesses of all kinds were cutting jobs and curtailing investments. India would recover quickly from the recession, but at that time the economic environment looked dire.

Inside Flipkart, however, things were better than ever. Yet, funding remained elusive. The financial crisis rendered e-commerce ventures even less appealing to the venture capitalists. In that bleak climate, only the safest of investments were entertained.

Previously a proprietorship, Flipkart incorporated itself as a limited liability company in October 2008. This newly registered entity was called Flipkart Online Services Private Limited.[1] By the end of 2008, Erasmic Venture, the funding company Abhishek Goyal worked for, was showing serious interest in Flipkart. Erasmic had recently been bought by Accel Partners, an elite venture capital firm headquartered in the Silicon Valley. Erasmic would be renamed Accel Partners India but allowed to retain its team.

Accel was unlike most other venture capital firms in India. To begin with, the fund invested in very young startups. Other funds at that time had adopted the models of their prototypes in the US. The ones in India had raised large amounts of capital, anywhere between $150 million to $200 million, and they looked for relatively mature startups that could absorb a cheque of $5 million to $10 million. But the paradox was that such companies were extremely rare. Most startups were young and needed capital to take off, but most funds were unwilling to invest in these ventures. The venture lords would take several years to realize that the US model wouldn't work in India, ironic for a community that criticized many local startups for being copycats of American companies. Accel was one of the few funds that backed very young companies. The partners at Accel were also generally more friendly and considerate towards entrepreneurs. What also set Accel apart was the kind of startups it invested in; its portfolio largely comprised internet and software companies, whereas most other funds preferred traditional businesses, making room for only a handful of internet firms. One well-known VC even declared that the 'internet is dead in India'. Accel, whose partners had previously worked at software firms, had funded companies like Chakpak, the software firm Mu Sigma, the travel portal HolidayIQ, and Myntra, a gift-selling website.

But when it came to e-commerce, even the partners at Accel had serious doubts. For nearly a year, Abhishek had tried to persuade his colleagues Subrata Mitra and Prashanth Prakash to invest in Flipkart. They had felt impressed by the Bansals, but their conviction about the futility of e-commerce could not be shaken. It was, in turn, strengthened as they considered the example of eBay. The American online marketplace, which was regarded as one of the more wisely run internet companies, had bought the Indian e-commerce startup Bazee in 2004. Five years since, eBay had failed to make its mark in India.

The partners at Accel had long debates regarding India's ability to sustain large internet businesses. Many firms were trying but not one offered hope. Of all niches, e-commerce seemed to have the bleakest prospects. It required huge quantities of cash, but who would supply so much capital in India? Then there was the immense problem of operations.

Even eBay was struggling in that respect. These were all sensible arguments against investing in an e-commerce startup. But there were still many more. Accel had even begun to have doubts about its own strategy of betting on internet startups. Many of the internet companies in Accel's portfolio, including HolidayIQ and Myntra, were growing slowly. Chakpak was popular with users but its revenues were meagre. Most funds were investing sparingly in internet startups. Only a few search engines, travel sites and social networks received funding. Accel already had significant internet holdings; it seemed too risky to add an e-commerce venture.

But Abhishek kept prodding his superiors. His thesis was simple: if people are funding the Googles and Facebooks of India, why not fund the Amazon of India? Obviously, that didn't convince his bosses at Accel.

Yet again, the Bansals' resilience in the face of such resistance was remarkable. Despite being turned down by every fund they had approached, the Bansals took the rejections in their stride. After so many months of discussions, they were understandably desperate, but they did not let it derail their objective of building a high-quality e-commerce site.

It wasn't just Abhishek who wanted Accel to invest in Flipkart. Gaurav Kushwaha of Chakpak had also pushed Flipkart's case with Subrata and Prashanth, the two leading partners at Accel. Even Mukesh Bansal, co-founder of Myntra, had spoken highly of Flipkart. At one point, Abhishek and Gaurav separately considered financing Flipkart with their personal cash. In spring 2009, Abhishek told his superiors that he wished to invest in Flipkart out of pocket. At this, Subrata and Prashanth finally gave in. 'We'd rather put [in] a bit more and do it from the fund.'

Thus, in the end, all logic was defeated. This is how many deals are struck, as feelings, intuition, persistence and luck come together to influence a decision. 'Exact math doesn't work. If you did a lot of math you wouldn't end up doing any investment because almost always there's nothing at the start,' reasons Abhishek.

In the summer of 2009, Accel agreed to invest $1 million in tranches into Flipkart. Accel was to have a twenty-five per cent stake in the company. It was a raw deal for the Bansals. But in that moment, after being rejected for more than a year, all they felt was relief.

7

THE EYE OF THE TIGER

Flipkart received the first instalment of about $250,000 from Accel Partners in the first half of 2009. By now, the company had moved into a new office in a charming part of Koramangala. The new premises, on the first floor of a large, sunlit bungalow surrounded by trees, was an upgrade from the drab space that had so far housed the Bansals and their first few employees. Subrata Mitra from Accel joined Flipkart's board as part of the funding round. But there had been a problem with wiring the money. For some reason, Accel was unable to send the entire amount to Flipkart. So, Subrata reached out to his friend Ashish Gupta, head of the venture capital firm Helion Venture Partners. This was the same Ashish who, along with his friends, had sold his price comparison site Junglee to Amazon in the late nineties. He later founded the IT services firm Tavant Technologies. In 2006, Ashish set up Helion to invest in Indian startups. Helion had looked into Flipkart but concluded an investment in the company was too risky. But Ashish didn't mind investing in his personal capacity. In 2009, he wrote a cheque of about ten lakh rupees to Flipkart which was sent along with one of the Accel tranches. Less than nine years later, that bet would turn into one of the most lucrative startup investments in India, yielding Ashish more than a hundred crore rupees.[1]

With Accel's funding, Flipkart finally had the cash to hire engineers and supply chain staff. By now, they desperately needed more support. Sales were beginning to soar as Sujeet signed up distributors in Delhi, expanding Flipkart's assortment by thousands of books every month. In the mornings and afternoons, Sujeet would pitch Flipkart to both small and large distributors. In the evenings, he would meet with courier services and oversee the packaging and shipping of books. In all of this, Tapas played a key supporting role. Apart from accompanying Sujeet on some of the visits to distributors' offices, he trained the packaging workers and courier personnel. Binny, too, spent a few months at the Delhi office, working closely with Sujeet as he designed Flipkart's supply processes. It was areas such as this where Binny was gifted – he enjoyed setting up structures and systems. How does one upload the pricing and volume data of books onto the Flipkart system? How would the Bangalore and Delhi offices sync up? How could packaging workers make use of the systems? Binny had all the answers.

As business grew, Flipkart rushed to hire more people in Delhi. Sujeet got in touch with a few people from his IIT gang. He usually moved around with his troops. He had brought along some of his IIT friends even to his previous outsourcing startup. At Flipkart, Sujeet persuaded Maneesh Mittal and Anuj Chowdhary, his mates from IIT Delhi, to join him. It was a measure of Sujeet's interpersonal abilities: Anuj had declined to join Flipkart in 2008 when he was approached by Sachin. Of course, the funding from Accel helped this time around. But it was Sujeet's association with the company that had ultimately been reassuring. Maneesh joined in early September 2009, Anuj a few days later. They quickly settled into their new roles.

Maneesh and Sujeet had been batchmates at Delhi while Anuj had been in Sachin's class. All four of them had stayed at the Jwala hostel, a detail that was presented as a toxic nexus in a controversial magazine story some years later.[2] That story scarred Flipkart for years, but in the beginning, Maneesh and Anuj did turn out to be productive recruits in the operations function. Sujeet had the force of personality to bring together a driven, talented team and cultivate a spirit of kinship. But it was Maneesh and Anuj who had a head for details, for thinking up and implementing the day-to-day processes that allowed Flipkart to thrive. Maneesh oversaw warehousing activities while Anuj took up the responsibility for signing up publishers and distributors. Both men reported to Sujeet. Just as the Bansals had given Sujeet free rein, Sujeet, in turn, chose not to interfere in Maneesh and Anuj's work.

Even though the orders for books were increasing by multitudes, Flipkart maintained its diligence in pleasing customers. Each order would be handled with the same rigour – every customer's tweet would be taken seriously, customer complaints would be investigated with the seriousness of a murder inquiry, lessons learnt would be applied and processes improved. The company instilled this 'customer obsession' in all employees. Maneesh, who loved reading, would urge employees to treat books like *heeras*. It was even common for many of the company's senior members to deliver books personally if orders piled up.

Sachin and Binny were also continuously refining the packaging and delivery processes. When they had started out, the two of them would gather books on the office floor, then organize them as per customer orders. As the orders increased, this process became untenable, so they moved to a shelf-based system. Books would be loaded onto shelves rather than stacked on the floor. Both these systems were designed for speed and efficiency; books had to be packed and shipped almost as soon as they would come in. But by October 2009, Flipkart was fulfilling a few hundred orders every day, up from just a few dozen a year ago. The shelf-based process had to be shelved. Sachin and Binny designed a new system which they called the 'pigeonhole'. This system was based on orders rather than individual books. If a customer ordered three books and Flipkart had at least two or all of them in stock, it made little financial sense to ship them separately as orders increased manifold. The pigeonhole method thus allowed Flipkart to upgrade from a book-by-book delivery system to an order-based system.

A MAJORITY OF Flipkart's sales came from Bangalore and Delhi simply because the company could deliver quickest to these cities. The financial capital Bombay was an obvious gap on both the demand and supply sides. The city had many book buyers as well as a number of book distributors that stocked important works of fiction and non-fiction. With the Delhi office up and running, Sujeet now set his sights on Bombay. In

October 2009, he rented a small room in the western suburb of Andheri. It was one of the few places he could afford. There he once again settled into the routine he had devised in Delhi. Every morning, in the rush-hour madness, he would take a local train to Churchgate, the southern tip of the city. He would interview potential employees and have his lunch before paying visits to distributors' offices.

A few weeks after Sujeet moved to Bombay, a recruiter reached out to Indranil Dutta, a young sales executive at Berger Paints. The recruiter told Indranil that an exciting new e-commerce startup was looking to hire a head for its newly launched Bombay office. When Indranil heard the name of the startup, his immediate reaction was, 'Flip-what?' Soon, he interviewed with Sujeet and Binny who promised to give him complete control over the western operations. Indranil was excited – after all, how many twenty-five-year-olds, just eighteen months into the corporate world, would even be considered for such positions? Indranil had wanted to launch a startup of his own, but the Flipkart offer was compelling. And Binny and Sujeet had seemed sincere. They were also offering a sizeable increase in salary. All options weighed, Indranil decided to join Flipkart as the head of its Bombay operations, which included Pune, Ahmedabad and a few other western cities.

After hiring Indranil, Sujeet moved east to set up Flipkart's operations in Calcutta in early 2010. Yet again he repeated his bait-and-switch trick with book distributors as he launched Flipkart's office and hired people. The company had now established its presence in all the four major regions of India.

MEANWHILE IN BANGALORE, the Bansals had hired a few coders. In July 2009, they also recruited Flipkart's first head of product, Shivakumar Ganesan. They were now on the lookout for an engineering chief. Accel's investment in Flipkart had strengthened the bond between Abhishek Goyal and the Bansals. Abhishek was the lone man in the venture capital world who had believed in them. He had even been willing to put his personal money into Flipkart. Abhishek empathized with the Bansals and saw the world as much as an entrepreneur as he did as a venture capitalist. He had become a valuable advisor to Sachin and Binny. When the Bansals told him they were looking for an engineering head, he introduced them to Mekin Maheshwari. Abhishek and Mekin had worked at Yahoo and had considered starting a company together. When that didn't pan out, Mekin joined Ugenie, the startup that had been launched by former Amazon India employee Krishna Motukuri. After a two-year stint, Mekin quit Ugenie. Now in his late twenties, he wanted to be an entrepreneur. Neverthless, Abhishek urged him to meet Sachin and Binny.

Their meeting lasted more than three hours, after which Sachin offered Mekin a job as Flipkart's chief of engineers. But Mekin wasn't sure and asked for a week to consider his options. In that week, he placed an order from Flipkart – he had never used the website before. He sought advice from his friends and conducted a quick investigation of Flipkart online. Of the dozen or so people he asked for advice, most warned him against joining an unknown startup. They were also convinced that e-commerce wouldn't work in India. Still, Mekin felt drawn to Flipkart – customers were raving about it on social media: 'Finally found the book on Flipkart!'

'Got the book in two days flat!'

Mekin could tell that customers loved Flipkart's service.

A week later, he had another long conversation with the Bansals. He also visited Flipkart's small headquarters to observe how the company handled its operations and figure out if Sachin and Binny's spiel about customer obsession had been genuine. It didn't take him long to notice that the entire company was designed to deliver books fast. A packaging worker coming back after picking up books from suppliers would first put aside current orders even though the more efficient move would have been to record all the books in the system together. He was also taken by the manner of the Bansals; they weren't very talkative, neither did they try to hardsell Flipkart to him. Instead, they came across as two serious engineers who were absorbed by the challenge they had taken up. Mekin decided his startup could wait.

Along with Sujeet, Mekin became one of the two seniormost executives at Flipkart for the next three years.

By September 2009, when the Bansals hired Mekin, Flipkart was in pursuit of serious expansion. It adopted the famous Amazon motto: Get Big Fast. Before the Accel round was finalized in the summer, Flipkart had been marked by a series of setbacks and near-blunders, the Infibeam episode being just one of them. It got off to a painfully slow start due to shortages of capital and employees. The travails had strengthened the Bansals, turned them into shrewd business-boys. Now with dedicated, energetic employees on their side, their ambition was soaring. Even the venture lords had started to relent. The astonishing jump in Flipkart's revenue had turned the heads of a few in the pantheon, who were finally ready to move past their scepticism about Flipkart and e-commerce in general. Around this time, firms such as Nexus Venture Partners entered into investment discussions with the Bansals.

Sachin, in particular, was charged up. From this period until the start of 2012, he would take centre stage at Flipkart. The dynamic between the Bansals that had developed in the early years would consolidate. It was already becoming apparent that Sachin defined Flipkart's vision and ambition while Binny designed the blueprint to realize it all. To their colleagues Sujeet, Mekin and several others, the partnership seemed ideal. 'Taking courageous calls and thinking bigger – that was always Sachin. Binny wouldn't take the lead, but he used to go along with Sachin's calls one hundred per cent. Sachin was super aggressive, and Binny would say, "*Haan, dekh lenge kaise karna hai* – we'll figure it out." It worked wonderfully,' recalls Sujeet.

SINCE FLIPKART'S LAUNCH in October 2007, Sachin had become an expert at manipulating Google. The thousands of hours Sachin had spent on *Quake* and *Age of Empires* were finally coming in handy. Fixing a search engine, of course, wasn't strictly like gaming. But their mechanisms weren't entirely dissimilar. Deploying dozens of tricks, such as displaying the Indian flag on the website, Sachin made Flipkart into a prominent shopping destination without spending on marketing. In fact, Sachin's excellence in coming up with these fixes in Flipkart's early years not only made the website popular, it even ensured the company's survival. By attracting large numbers of users to the site, Sachin helped bring in significant advertising revenues which provided the cash Flipkart needed to spend freely on pleasing customers.

From the second half of 2008, Flipkart was pulling in lakhs of rupees every month as the website appeared prominently on Google searches. If someone searched for a mobile phone they were likely to see Flipkart at the top of their search results, even though the company didn't sell phones. As people converged on the website, it became an attractive advertisement platform. The Bansals even made money from their old employer. At the time, a small number of wealthy Indians were ordering products from Amazon.com. Amazon had a scheme which rewarded other internet firms that directed users to its site, and one of the participants in this scheme was Flipkart.

The Bansals had started out in October 2007 with a capital investment of four lakh rupees. That meagre sum couldn't have sustained the company for the twenty months that it survived before its first successful financing round. The money from the sales of books wasn't sufficient either. It was the advertising revenue that turned out to be crucial for the company's sustenance. In essence, Google and Amazon bankrolled Flipkart's early years. These three ingredients – Sachin's search engine mastery, and internet giants Amazon and Google – would soon come together to serve up many other benefits to Flipkart.

IN NEW YORK, Lee Fixel, a Jewish-American fund manager, was looking to make investments in emerging international markets. Born in 1980, Lee was the eldest of three children. His father was a lawyer and his mother a fashion designer. After becoming a chartered financial analyst (CFA) and obtaining a management degree, Lee had joined an investment firm, Alkeon

Capital, where he examined internet companies as an analyst. In 2006, he was lured to Tiger Global, which wanted to increase its investments in internet firms, especially in emerging markets such as India, China and Eastern Europe. Lee was peripatetic. He had investments in many countries, and he spent much of his time in aeroplanes.

Lee had travelled to India a few times and, in 2007, had invested in the online travel company MakeMyTrip. He was eager to add to his portfolio. India's economy was booming, lifting middle-class incomes. Its retail sector was one of the largest in the world, and one of the least modern. This created a lot of room for new retail companies. The poor infrastructure, India's infamous traffic in urban areas, especially in Bangalore, along with the fact that real-estate costs there were unusually high, had convinced Lee that offline retail would have limited reach in the country. The corollary was that the same forces would make for a hospitable environment for e-commerce. In 2009, Lee hired the consultancy firm McKinsey to conduct market research on the internet space in India.

The firms mentioned in McKinsey's report did not impress Lee. He considered online retailers such as Infibeam and Indiaplaza but passed up on them. One day, restless in his New York office, he ventured online to conduct some armchair research of his own. On Amazon.com, he started looking up popular books that he thought an Indian might want to read. From there he transposed the book titles onto Google to see which Indian websites were selling them. Every search threw up Flipkart in the top results. Lee was surprised; the McKinsey report hadn't mentioned Flipkart. Yet it seemed to be a popular search destination with a large assortment of books. On an impulse, Lee emailed Flipkart's customer service team asking to speak with the company's founders. But no one responded. He then called the customer service number mentioned on the Flipkart website. He introduced himself and asked to be put through to the Bansals. An employee told him that they weren't available and hung up after assuring Lee that they would call back.

When Sachin and Binny were informed about Lee's call, they were incredulous. In those days, venture lords didn't call on fledgling entrepreneurs; entrepreneurs went to them. And even if they wanted to speak with a promising startup founder, no venture lord would demean himself by calling up customer care. And why would someone call Flipkart from New York anyway? All the US venture firms had Indian arms. The Bansals' suspicions deepened after they looked up Lee and Tiger Global online and found little. In the US, Tiger Global was a famous name in the investment world. It traced its origins to Julian Robertson, one of the most successful investors on Wall Street in the eighties and nineties. The outstanding performance of Robertson's firm, Tiger Management, had once earned him the nickname 'The Wizard of Wall Street'.[3] Even though Tiger Management shut shop in 2000, many of Robertson's acolytes started investment firms of their own. One of these was Tiger Global. It was such a secretive and elite firm that it didn't need a website. Of course the Bansals weren't aware of this. To them, the name Lee Fixel didn't even sound very American. Amused, they concluded it was a prank call and moved on.

A few days later, Lee emailed Flipkart's customer service team again. Feeling intrigued, the Bansals decided to call this persistent man to ascertain once and for all if he was indeed a prankster. But they couldn't even make the call because their phone connection lacked an international calling feature. His pursuit still fruitless, Lee now asked Deep Kalra, founder and CEO of MakeMyTrip, to speak with the Bansals on his behalf. Deep was a well-known and respected entrepreneur and the Bansals saw him as a mentor of sorts. Only after Deep spoke to them did they start taking Lee seriously. In early September, they spoke to Lee for the first time. After a few more phone conversations, Lee flew to Bangalore to meet the Bansals. Immediately he was impressed. Sachin and Binny were young but Lee could see that they were very sharp and thoughtful about payments, logistics, and various other matters that needed to be sorted out in order for e-commerce to expand in India. The Bansals' obsession with pleasing customers pleased Lee, too; he had seen Amazon apply that principle to great effect in the US. His conversation with the Bansals turned out to be very different from the ones he had had with other Indian e-commerce startups. Not only were the Bansals far more ambitious, they also seemed to know how their vision could be accomplished.

In later years, the speed at which Lee made investment decisions would become legendary. He displayed the first instance of this speed when he decided to invest in Flipkart. Less than six weeks after his first call with the Bansals, Lee made his offer. The amount was astronomical: $9 million. Flipkart's first round of funding from Accel had come after more than a year of talks, and after the company had been passed up by every other venture capitalist. Now, just a few months after Accel finally agreed to put up a grand sum of $1 million, and that too in tranches, Flipkart was on the cusp of securing a funding that was ten times as large and negotiated in less than forty days.

The talks with Tiger Global moved so fast that Flipkart had by then not even received all the Accel tranches. Accel would now have to renegotiate its investment terms. In October 2009, Flipkart signed a term sheet, also known as a preliminary investment agreement, with Tiger Global. In early 2010, after completing all financial diligence, the deal was signed. The total investment came up to $10 million, of which $9 million was contributed by Tiger Global and $1 million by Accel. Flipkart's valuation soared to nearly $40 million.[4]

Tiger Global's investment was just the vindication for which Sachin and Binny had been so desperate. Finally they had found an investor who understood their vision and was willing to fund it. While they were relieved when Accel had invested in Flipkart, the Bansals had been unhappy with the terms. Flipkart had been valued at less than $5 million and the Bansals had felt shortchanged. But in this new round of investments, they would call the shots and Accel would have to acquiesce to their terms. Sachin pushed especially hard, seeking a valuation of $50 million. He seemed to be a man transformed. The previous year, he had felt overawed by Infibeam's Vishal Mehta, grateful that someone was offering to put him and Binny out of their misery. Now he had the brazenness to ask for a valuation of $50 million, and the skill it took to be granted as much as $40 million. There was no science behind this – it was a matter of demand and supply, a confluence of similar sensibilities.

When Lee had made the decision to invest in Flipkart, he hadn't spoken to the other venture lords in India, most of whom were sceptical about the company's prospects. His decision had been simple. It wasn't as if he could foresee the Bansals' success in running a large e-commerce operation. It was futile to make that kind of judgment at this early stage. Instead, what he could see were two serious entrepreneurs who had studied the retail market deeply and had bright ideas about unlocking it using technology. And he was getting a chance to pick up a large stake in a promising venture for a relatively small sum. This was all the evidence he needed.

It was one of the biggest startup deals of the time, but for Flipkart employees such as Mekin and Sujeet, the only surprise was the speed at which it happened. Even before Lee's endorsement, they had little doubt that Flipkart was going to become something special. Business was doubling and tripling in size every quarter. They were assembling a stellar team. For anyone who had seen Flipkart from the inside, one thing was clear: you did not want to miss this journey.

Those were happy days for the Bansals. In November 2009, as the deal with Tiger Global was being finalized, Sachin became a father. His wife, Priya, had given birth to a boy. A few months later, in February 2010, Binny married his girlfriend Trisha, a graduate of the Indian Institute of Foreign Trade. The two had serendipitously met nearly five years ago just before Binny graduated from IIT Delhi. While Sachin's decision to become a businessman had enhanced his marriageability, Binny had to work hard to bring around Trisha's family who were initially unsure about the groom's choice of career. But they had eventually relented. Binny's wedding only added to the general feeling of positivity that had been permeating through Flipkart's halls.

8

'BINNY KE BATCH SE HO?'

Lee Fixel stressed the 'Fast' in Get Big Fast. By the time he had invested in Flipkart in early 2010, the company was already expanding at a frenetic pace. It generated revenues of ₹11.6 crore in the financial year 2009–2010.[1] Lee's entry redoubled Flipkart's ambition and confidence and turbocharged its expansion efforts. The fresh capital allowed the company to spend more freely on launching new product categories, hiring employees and pursuing audacious experiments.

Sachin and Binny began to make preparations for a Flipkart that would be many, many times its current size. They had already established a foothold in books. Now the company hungrily entered new categories. In the second half of 2010, Flipkart started selling mobile phones, music and film CDs, DVDs, and cameras. To launch these categories and to move to the next stage in its evolution, the company needed a capable management team. When a startup receives venture capital, investors insist that the company hire experienced leaders.

Its new executives are expected to have previously worked at larger companies so they are able to bring to the startup their subject matter expertise or general management abilities. They are seen as necessary for propelling the startup to the next level or two. The startup is thereby able to attract larger amounts of capital which is supposed to help it grow even bigger, which then necessitates the management to be replaced by a newer set of leaders. At Flipkart, this cycle began in 2010 and would continue for the next eight years, as the company would see ceaseless growth, churn, volatility and drama.

The Bansals had formed a 'Core Team' that consisted of themselves, Mekin, Sujeet and Tapas. The five of them would meet for dinner every Wednesday to discuss the week's events and make plans for bigger strategic moves. In 2010, the core team spent much of their time interviewing prospective candidates for a variety of new positions at the company. Within a few months Flipkart had added more than two dozen senior and middle managers. Finance, marketing and human resources departments were set up and the existing sales, operations, customer support and technology functions were expanded. This concept of the Core Team was one more peculiarity the Bansals had adopted from Amazon, apart from the principles of customer obsession, thinking big, and bias for action.[2]

Just like Amazon, even at that early stage, Flipkart instituted a high standard when it came to recruitment. All candidates who applied for jobs in the technology department were made to take tests and quizzes. They were asked to apply their technical skills to solve real problems that Flipkart was facing. But the company didn't hire only from the IITs; engineers from Delhi College of Engineering, Punjab Engineering College, colleges in Tamil Nadu and other states were all welcomed. Mekin, who had devised the hiring process, was open to recruiting anyone who cleared the interviews, regardless of the candidates' pedigree. The candidates would be posed technical questions, but these were mostly designed to test the engineers' problem-solving abilities.

For the other departments, the company hired experienced professionals, entry-level workers, generalists, specialists – anyone and everyone who suited their needs and met its standards. Flipkart was an unknown internet company operating in an environment where startups were seen as career graveyards. But the Bansals knew they would need to attract highly capable people in order to succeed. More importantly, the people they hired would need to adopt Flipkart's cause completely, become warriors for the company. Flipkart was creating a new industry from nearly nothing. Its employees would have to put the company at the centre of their lives – long hours, working weekends, fulfilling different roles at different times, relocation, and constant volatility would be the features of their lives. In return, Flipkart wasn't even willing to offer exorbitant salaries. Understandably, many of the people Flipkart hired at that time were men and women who hadn't experienced much professional success, felt a keen sense of insecurity, were desperate to prove themselves and discover their self-worth, not too different from Sachin's situation when he joined Amazon, or Sujeet's when he agreed to work for his former IIT juniors. At Flipkart, the prototype of the ideal hire was Ankit Nagori.

Ankit was born in Bokaro, a small town in Jharkhand, where his father ran a steel trading business. He had moved to Delhi with his family when he was five years old. A graduate of IIT Guwahati, Ankit had wound up his startup Youthpad, a social media platform, in early 2010. He was lost. A keen reader, Ankit visited a New Delhi book fair in March 2010, and found a stall with a sign that read Flipkart. Curious, Ankit looked up the company and realized that it was an emerging internet firm. Although his venture had failed, Ankit was keen to continue working at a startup. He emailed Binny, asking for a job. Some days later, Ankit interviewed with Sujeet and Anuj Chowdhary, Flipkart's sales head. They were impressed by Ankit's energy and the eagerness his fresh, clean-shaven face seemed to exude, and agreed to hire him. Ankit was to steer the launch of CDs and DVDs, what Flipkart referred to as 'media', another adoption from the Amazon playbook. At twenty-four years, Ankit was young even by Flipkart standards. He was a category head for all practical purposes but his formal position was at the lowest level of the hierarchy. It didn't matter; as soon as he joined, Ankit completely bought into Flipkart's mission. Flipkart hired many other executives in the coming weeks and months. They included Anuj Rathi, who headed product and worked closely with Sachin; Marcus Terry, who oversaw customer support; Vaibhav Pandey, who oversaw electronics; and Vipul Bathwal, who launched the mobile phones category.

Hiring people was relatively easy, but it was impossible to know whether one had made the right choice. As early as 2010, a pattern emerged at Flipkart that would haunt the company for a long time. Many executives would quit soon after they were hired. Some left of their own accord, many were forced out. Flipkart had already lost its first product chief, Shivakumar Ganesan. The day Ankit joined, Anuj Chowdhary, one of his two interviewers, put in his papers. Anuj had been doing well as the head of sales. But he was torn between staying at Flipkart and taking up entrepreneurship. Finally, he left in April 2010 to start his own venture. A few months later, Anuj's replacement, Satyarth Priyedarshi, also left.

As much as Flipkart encouraged its employees to operate independently, it seemed the company had little patience for those who didn't fit in or perform well immediately. These people were either fired or sidelined ruthlessly, treated like pariahs. One can argue this is a more or less well-established characteristic of internet companies. Obsessed with frenetic growth, anyone or anything that proves to be an impediment to the company must be removed immediately. The 'Move Fast and Break Things'[3] creed made famous by Facebook captures how internet companies are often run. The merciless approach towards employees is an essential aspect of this culture, where workers are the means to an end. At Flipkart, corporate ruthlessness reared its head mostly at the senior level. In the company's early years, its junior employees, who comprised a majority of Flipkart's workforce, felt secure in their jobs, revelled in the company's freewheeling culture, embracing the thrill of taking on important tasks they wouldn't be allowed to come near at most other companies.

A BIG ADVANTAGE Flipkart had over its rivals was its clever application of technology. It had divided its engineering teams loosely into two groups: demand and supply. In 2010, with a sizeable team of coders in place, Flipkart implemented its first set of major technological changes on both sides with the intention that this would complement the work of its sales and operations teams towards increasing revenue.

The website especially saw major improvements. In April 2010, Flipkart's technology chief, Mekin Maheshwari, had hired a senior engineer named Amod Malviya, who took over the engineering function of the website. Amod was a skinny, strong-headed twenty-nine-year-old, an IIT Kharagpur graduate who had spent most of his young career working at startups. He was both technically proficient and a skilful manager of people. He believed that technology was the Supreme Function, a view Sachin shared with him. But in his first week at Flipkart, Amod clashed with Sachin. The Flipkart CEO enjoyed working closely with engineers and would often issue instructions to them without consulting with their managers. To this, Amod objected: '*Yaar, ya tum bolo ya hamey bol ne do* – either you take over or let me do my job.' Sachin sulked, but he also stood down, and over the next five years, forged a close relationship with Amod that was often volatile but rewarding for Flipkart. In his first year alone, Amod oversaw many of the developments on the website.

The company's plain, functional website had pleased users from the start. But the site, like all other e-commerce platforms in India, was dogged by transaction failures. For a customer, buying online was almost like playing the lottery – as much as forty per cent of all transactions fell through. This would happen due to technological glitches on the sites or on the part of their payment providers, or even because of inconsistent internet connectivity. No matter the reason, some customers who were victims of failed transactions would inevitably not return again. Amod had set up a 'two pizza' payments team under a subordinate, Santosh Dwivedi, that found a solution by experimenting with several payment gateways. By fusing the gateways with its systems, Flipkart could switch amongst them based on the success rates of the various gateways at any given point. By early 2011, the transaction success rate jumped to more than eighty-five per cent from less than sixty per cent. Many other e-commerce firms did not have the technological abilties or the imagination to pull off such a deep integration with several payment gateways; consequently their failure rates remained high even as Flipkart's dropped.

Flipkart further simplified the checkout process for customers. At that time, many e-commerce companies would ask users to share unnecessary personal information, leading to long checkout times. Sachin was insistent that Flipkart should have the smoothest possible checkout process that required minimal information about customers.

In 2010, Flipkart also developed many basic functions on the website that allowed it to showcase newer categories. The company introduced technology tools that made it possible for them to process refunds and returns within a few hours, a significant improvment from the previous days-long process. The search feature was also refined. On other sites, the search function was so poor that customers would often fail to locate products even though the company actually had them in stock. But even Flipkart's superior search function would falter in the coming years as its product assortment multiplied at a brisk pace.

IN E-COMMERCE, PRODUCTS require specialized treatment, and success in one category is no guarantee of prosperity through others, as Flipkart discovered when it expanded beyond books.

Mobile phones turned out to be a particularly tricky category. Flipkart's first investor, Accel Partners, had warned the company about the problems it would face. The Accel VCs had told the Bansals, 'Losing a phone isn't like losing a book – you can lose a lot of money.' But Sachin decided, 'Screw it, we'll do it.' Flipkart's mobile phones category went live in early 2010. The first order came in shortly: a customer had purchased a Samsung phone. At that time, Flipkart still followed its 'just-in-time' system. After a customer ordered a product, Flipkart would source it from a distributor or an offline retailer. The company did not hold its own stock yet, which was illegal as per Indian laws. And just as it had been with Flipkart's first-ever order in October 2007, the Samsung phone could not be located anywhere. Finally, after three days of hunting, a single unit was found at a small retailer in Bangalore.

While no one knew it at the time, this inauspicious start was a sign of things to come in the mobile phones business. Phone brands scoffed at Flipkart's approach. Their message was the same as Accel's warning: selling phones isn't like selling books. 'You can't just stick a picture of a phone on your site and expect people to buy it,' brands complained to Flipkart executives. Phone dealers set onerous conditions: no credit, upfront payment, low margins. For weeks, Flipkart executives pleaded for better terms but the dealers wouldn't budge. Finally Sachin told his executives, 'Just get it done. They will come around. I've seen the same thing happen with books.' So, they gave in to the dealers who remained sceptical despite Flipkart's acceptance of their steep terms. A large dealer of HTC phones proved to be especially frustrating. He had refused to return calls from Flipkart executives for weeks. When he finally met with them, he was contemptuous: '*Chalo, ek phone bech kar bata do* – let's see if you sell even one phone.' A month later, Flipkart sold about fifteen HTC phones. The next month it sold a few dozen, and soon a hundred. The dealer who had initially proven rather difficult was now begging Flipkart to buy more phones.

This became the pattern with Flipkart and its suppliers. Just as Sachin had said to his employees, the suppliers would ultimately come around. When Flipkart had first started to woo them, publishers, distributors and brand custodians alike had treated Flipkart with ridicule. In 2010, this was the case even in the books category, the company's mainstay at the time.

INDRANIL DUTTA'S ANDHERI office was a set of two rooms, twelve feet by twelve feet in size. In one room, books were packaged, while in the other, a few white-collar employees worked at their computer desks. Indranil had hired a dozen people mostly to fulfil operations and sales roles. Every day he and his team went to meet distributors at their offices. There, the Flipkart executives would be kept waiting, sometimes for as long as an hour. It was done deliberately, to make them feel small.

Distributors even struggled to get the company's name right. They would say, 'Flip-what?'

'Flipkart.'

'Flip-card?'

'Flip-KART.'

'Flip-kart? What's a kart?'

'Have you seen a shopping cart? Perhaps at Big Bazaar?'

Conversations about the company's name would often go like this. Indranil could hardly complain; his reaction had been no different. What exasperated him instead was the steadfast refusal of the books industry to see the benefits of e-commerce. Managers at publishing and distribution houses would seem set in their ways, refusing point-blank to even consider how e-commerce could transform their business. 'Who are you and who is Flipkart?' they would say with condescension.

Indranil and his colleagues tackled this problem the old-fashioned way – by going to the top. They would reach out to a manager, then to their boss, and so on, until they could talk to the CEO. 'Once the CEO is aligned … everyone gets aligned,' was Indranil's belief. By early 2010, many large book distributors had signed up with Flipkart, and the remaining few would soon follow suit. But the company had still had no breakthroughs with publishers, local or international.

Readers in India frequently wanted books from abroad. Either these books were not available here or would only be published after a delay. Binny had identified a handful of international publishers that controlled the supply of books that readers here might like. Binny cold-called – Flipkart had got international calling installed after being unable to call Tiger Global – and emailed executives at these publishing houses. He had arranged to meet some of them at BookExpo America, the biggest annual book fair in the US, in 2010. But he couldn't get his visa in time and sent Mekin instead. At the book fair, one major publisher agreed to supply books to Flipkart. Over the next year, several other international publishers came on board. Every time Flipkart signed up with a new publisher, the orders shot up. More customers were able to find books they were looking for, which led to higher sales, benefiting the publisher in question, and leading to more publishers wanting to work with Flipkart.

After this achievement, Flipkart began to make headway with domestic publishers, too. Just four months after he joined the company, Ankit Nagori was asked to lead the books category along with media. He had done well with launching CDs and DVDs. To his surprise, music labels were willing to work with Flipkart. It was the final phase of the era of analogue music. People were increasingly downloading pirated music and movies, but there were still enough people buying CDs and DVDs for Flipkart to feel interested in the category. Many customers bought their CDs from a handful of retailers such as Landmark, Crossword and Odyssey. Before launching the category, Ankit conducted market research – which were the most popular labels, who were the bestselling artists, and so on – by literally visiting these stores. When Flipkart launched the category, it simply offered the bestselling CDs at a lower price. That's all it took for customers to switch their loyalties to Flipkart. Music products were similar to books: relatively inexpensive, standardized and easy to ship. A few years later, Flipkart's rise would permanently damage Landmark, Crossword and Odyssey's business.

As head of the books category, one of Ankit's immediate tasks was to build partnerships with domestic publishers. It was important to work with publishers in order to obtain pre-orders, develop relationships with authors and generally acquire influence in the books world. Together with Sujeet, who had become his mentor, Ankit set to work. Even though Flipkart had begun to make contact with publishers in early 2010, it would take the company more than eighteen months to convince the major publishing houses. Most were wary – their dealings with e-commerce companies hadn't gone well. Publishing executives told Sujeet and Ankit that other companies like Flipkart had made similar promises but had ultimately just looted them and left. Their other concern was that Flipkart would recklessly resort to heavy discounting, which would hurt the publishers' long-standing offline partners. But Sujeet and Ankit allayed their concerns, promising lucrative sales. 'Sujeet had built amazing relationships in the books industry. He would know the CEOs, the sales heads. He made sure that we had a seat at the table with publishers. Once the relationships were built, I would keep following up and finalize the deals,' says Ankit. In 2011, the company finally began working with the country's major publishing houses, including Penguin India and HarperCollins India. Popular authors such as Chetan Bhagat soon began to patronize Flipkart, appearing at book events organized by the company, participating in social media chats it hosted, and promoting Flipkart in various other ways.

As Flipkart's books business expanded, local bookstores in Delhi would sometimes send email warnings to Ankit and Sujeet about Flipkart's discounting practices. One retailer even sent a threat over email. This didn't deter the company, which continued to cut prices. By 2011, Flipkart had also grown large enough to demand better credit terms from distributors. This helped them cut working capital, the cash needed to run the business.

Apart from strengthening its supplier relationships, in 2010, Flipkart focused on further improving its delivery speed. Working with courier companies had proved to be a constant struggle. Flipkart executives would try a variety of approaches to coax better service out of them. They would plead, charm, harangue, and as a last resort, refuse to do business with repeat offenders. After increasing its order volumes and consolidating them with one courier company, Flipkart would suddenly move on to others. At the Bombay office, for instance, Indranil Dutta would stop using a courier service for a few days if it refused to fix persistent issues. Starved of orders, executives at the courier company would come running to him in 'full panic' mode.

'*Sir, kya ho gaya? Do din se order nahin aa rahe hai.*' Sir, what happened? You haven't sent us orders for two days now.

'*Haan sir, karte hai. Sir, aap aaiye, mere boss se milwana hai.*' Sure sir, it'll be done. My boss would like to meet you.

Indranil and his colleagues in Bangalore and Delhi would keep repeating this exercise until they got their way.

While such dealings by themselves may not seem too significant, these hair-splitting negotiations with the couriers and suppliers, along with Flipkart's technological improvements and enhancements in marketing and customer support, together constituted a gestalt. A process of continuous, relentless improvement was in motion at the company every day, propelling its business from one milestone to another. The ecosystem at the time was so resistant, the infrastructure so rudimentary, that e-commerce could have only been willed into existence through such painstaking persistence.

In the words of Vaibhav Pandey, a former Amazon executive who joined Flipkart in 2010 as one of its senior sales executives, 'Flipkart was building the road and walking on it at the same time.'

SMALL IMPROVEMENTS ASIDE, Flipkart introduced in 2010 what would turn into the biggest expansive force for its business and for e-commerce: cash on delivery.

E-commerce transactions until that point were predominantly fulfilled using credit cards. This was for a variety of reasons, the chief among them being a fundamental mistrust between the websites and their shoppers. Websites were wary of being defrauded, while shoppers mistrusted websites that seemed incompetent when it came to fulfilling their basic obligation to deliver products they had already sold. Banks, too, were sceptical about e-commerce which meant that the technology for internet banking and debit card payments was underdeveloped. Credit cards had become the default payment option online, but less than ten million people owned one. India's economy worked on cash.

Keenly aware of this fact, Sachin wondered, as he hankered for faster growth at his company, whether more people would buy products if they could pay in cash. Cash payments would mitigate the worry of receiving wrong or defective products; customers could simply refuse to pay. On an impulse, Sachin instructed the Flipkart operations team to launch a cash-on-delivery payment option. In preparation for this launch, Binny and Sujeet asked Flipkart's courier service providers if they had the infrastructure to handle it. One of these courier partners, a company called Aramex, agreed to try it out. In April 2010, Flipkart introduced cash payments. A few weeks later, other courier providers began offering the service as well. The orders instantly jumped. But Flipkart wasn't the first shopping site to think of cash payments. Indiaplaza and Rediff had introduced the option earlier. Flipkart would soon find out why cash payments had never picked up.

As Flipkart's orders increased, all kinds of operational issues began assailing them: cash would be stuck with courier partners for weeks, products wouldn't reach on time, customers would complain of the rude behaviour of delivery workers. The system was a mess. Every unpleasant incident would leave a stain on Flipkart's image.

Flipkart executives were initially confounded by the problem. It was clear that they would have to offer cash payments. But there would be a backlash from customers if the courier companies kept messing up. Cash-flow issues also had to be considered. A few months into the launch of cash on delivery, the problems showed no signs of abating. The Flipkart brand had been painstakingly built. It was the only asset the company had, in essence. It had to be shielded. For days, Binny, Sujeet and other senior executives studied the issue, and soon the solution became obvious: Flipkart would have to launch its own logistics service.

It was going to be risky. A logistics service involved setting up complex processes to ensure that sales, warehousing, delivery and customer support divisions would seamlessly work together. Thousands of delivery workers would need to be hired and trained. Handling cash orders was fraught with hazards, too: fraud, theft, loss, delays. For months, Flipkart remained indecisive about entering logistics. The company's executives had been studying the Chinese market closely. Tiger Global's Lee Fixel had made investments in e-commerce companies in China and encouraged the Bansals to speak with Chinese entrepreneurs and senior executives. They soon learnt that even in China, transportation was a major problem for e-commerce companies which had taken to developing their own logistics services. In late 2010, Binny and Sujeet decided that Flipkart would also have to take the plunge.

They assigned the logistics launch to Vinoth Poovalingam. Twenty-four-year-old Vinoth had joined the company in April after graduating from the Indian Institute of Management in Bangalore. Flipkart, much like the American internet companies that had influenced it, wilfully handed important responsibilities to inexperienced employees like Vinoth, Ankit Nagori and many others like them. Vinoth had worked on the launch of cash payments and was familiar with the logistics processes of courier companies. He was thrilled when Binny asked him to launch logistics in the latter part of 2010, and eagerly waited for a team and budget to be assigned. But a few days later Binny asked him, 'Why haven't you started it yet?' With five delivery workers armed with just Excel sheets and barcode scanners, Vinoth launched the service in Koramangala, which had the largest concentration of Flipkart customers in the city of Bangalore. Soon, Vinoth, with help from Binny, Sujeet and a few others, devised a process to make logistics work at scale.

Having its own logistics service allowed Flipkart to exercise complete control over order deliveries. It could now gain exact knowledge about the movement of each order. When customers called to inquire about their orders, Flipkart was ready with answers. Earlier, customers would feel vexed when Flipkart would fail to explain why their orders had got delayed. 'That was the biggest problem before, when we had no control over the delivery process,' explains Vinoth. 'If there was a sudden spike in volume, the delivery speed would suffer and we were helpless. We were at the mercy of couriers.'

Within a few months of its launch, the logistics service was capable of handling more than one hundred deliveries each day. It was then expanded to serve other areas within Bangalore. The most telling result was a big hike in customer satisfaction scores. Customers started receiving their books in one or two days, sometimes within hours after the purchase. They were thrilled. The in-house service had been initiated as a hopeful project but it was clear that running a logistics fleet could bring huge benefits. The company began to think about how to implement it in other cities.

To expand the logistics service, Flipkart would first need technological systems. It would be impossible for people using Excel sheets to track the movement of thousands of orders – the use of technology was essential. Six months after the service was introduced, the tech systems were ready. In 2011, the company decided to expand the service to Delhi. It also decided that a supervisor was needed to oversee the entire logistics operation. Vinoth had got the service off to a promising start. But there was one problem: he wasn't fluent in Hindi. Sujeet and a few others believed this would be a handicap, especially in the high-demand cities of Bombay and Delhi where Hindi was the lingua franca of blue-collar workers. By this time, Sujeet had convinced Anuj Chowdhary to return to Flipkart. Anuj's startup wasn't going anywhere and he didn't mind coming back to the familiar environs of a company which had grown considerably in the short time he had been away.

THE INTRODUCTION OF cash on delivery and the subsequent creation of the logistics service was another instance of how Sachin and Binny complemented each other. Sachin had pushed Flipkart to launch cash payments, but to make it a success,

Flipkart had to enter a new, complex area of logistics, where Binny excelled.

By the end of 2010, Flipkart was flying. The addition of new categories, the expansion in books, the website improvements, combined with the introduction of cash payments and other advances, had kept pushing up sales. At the end of the year, monthly gross sales had increased to more than ₹10 crore from less than ₹1 crore at the start of the year. It was like seeing a skyscraper being built in record time.

What was equally remarkable was that Flipkart had become a cult brand without spending on advertising. In 2011, as it strived to become a bigger retailer, the company would invest large amounts of cash on marketing, but its initial success was almost entirely based on the customers' word of mouth. Flipkart users would rave about its service, encouraging others to sign up. Those who did weren't disappointed, and they, in turn, enlisted their friends. This meant a rapid rise in orders, which helped the company win the trust of its suppliers and courier partners. Flipkart was benefiting from what is known as 'the network effect'.[4] The primary force behind this self-fulfilling vortex was Flipkart's relentlessness in pleasing customers – just like it was at Amazon.

With Flipkart's rise, Sachin and Binny were quickly gaining fame in the startup world. Their ascendance startled their IIT friends and acquaintances. Some of their former flatmates at the NGV apartment complex, and former IIT acquaintances who had declined the Bansals' offer to work with them, were jealous, filled with regret. Others who knew them were simply confounded.

One such acquaintance was Anil Kumar, Binny's batchmate

from IIT Delhi. When Anil had met Binny in 2008, he had laughed off Binny's efforts to raise capital, thinking that Binny had lost touch with reality. More than two years later, Anil's startup RedSeer was doing well. It worked on contract with larger consulting firms such as Bain, earning fat commissions. When he started RedSeer, Anil had no doubts that he had a better chance of success than Binny. Now the truth was out, irrefutable. For Anil, and many others like him, their IIT Delhi pedigree was a badge of honour. It instantly made one more respectable. Many graduates of the institute are known to proudly reveal their alma mater at every opportunity. When Anil introduced himself as an IIT Delhi graduate in Bangalore's tech circles, he would draw what became a familiar response.

'You're from IIT Delhi, are you?'

'Yes, batch of 2005.'

'*Achha, toh Binny ke batch se ho*?' Oh, so you would be from Binny's batch?

Anil did double takes the first few times he heard this. He couldn't believe that his identity had become linked to Binny's. It became clear to him that his nondescript, laid-back classmate from IIT Delhi's unremarkable Shivalik hostel was on to something big.

9

BOOM

By early 2011, about a year after Tiger Global had invested in Flipkart, the e-commerce market was in a frenzy.

Tiger Global's investment in Flipkart had changed the rules of the venture capital world. Over the next two years, Lee Fixel financed more than half a dozen e-commerce companies. Later, many founders would come to look at Lee warily because of his outsized influence in the startup world and his openly ruthless approach to portfolio companies. But his aggressive investments in his early years as a venture capitalist paradoxically moved the needle towards founders in the power equation with investors. It also shaped the startup ecosystem into a high-risk, winners-take-all business.

Venture capitalists in India had been deeply pessimistic about internet startups, writing cheques to these companies sparingly. It was the Flipkart deal that forced them to loosen up. It is a well-known fact that investors display herd behaviour, especially during the extreme cycles of boom and bust. In 2010 and 2011, following the lead of Tiger Global and Flipkart, investors and entrepreneurs moved like hyenas into e-commerce. This pattern would repeat again during subsequent boom-and-bust periods, and always with Tiger Global–Flipkart as the trendsetters.

The same venture capital pantheon that had pronounced e-commerce dead on arrival now flipped, and investments into internet startups began to soar.[1] Most of this money went to online retail companies, which sprang up by the dozen in Bangalore, Delhi and Bombay. A majority of these firms raised very little cash. But there was no doubt that e-commerce had become a seasonal favourite. EBay, which had been quietly present in India since 2004, arose from its slumber and began spending freely. Kishore Biyani, CEO of Future Group, bought Chaupaati Bazaar, a phone and online commerce company. The founders of FabMart, an online retailer that was born of the first internet boom in the late nineties, made a comeback with a new e-commerce startup called BigBasket. Many others like Myntra, Letsbuy, Snapdeal, Homeshop18, Naaptol and Shopclues were either founded or received significant funding in this period. Even Indiaplaza, that e-commerce dinosaur which had wobbled along since 2000, received $5 million in 2011. The hysterical activity in e-commerce drew comparisons with the great dotcom bubble.[2]

There was some logic behind this frenzy. By September 2010, there were still only ten million broadband connections in India.[3] It was the dizzying growth in mobile phone usage that caught one's attention instead. The popularity of the iPhone, introduced in 2007, prompted predictions that internet browsing would increasingly shift to smartphones. As other phone manufacturers produced a spate of iPhone rivals, internet use on mobiles increased rapidly. Some eighteen million new mobile connections were being purchased every month. This vast base of mobile phone users would soon have access to 3G services, which could lead to widespread mobile internet consumption. The Boston Consulting Group estimated that India would have 237 million internet users by 2015, an astounding increase from 2009's eighty-one million. For e-commerce firms, this prediction came like a beacon. In 2010, most people used the internet for email, messaging and casual browsing; it was estimated that less than ten per cent of internet users bought products online.[4] This gap was bound to close with faster internet connections – all one had to do was offer a reliable e-commerce service and the market would multiply.

AT THE AMAZON headquarters in Seattle, Jeff Bezos was excited by the burst of e-commerce activity in India. Amazon had set ambitious targets for its international business. But there weren't many countries that could satiate its appetite for growth. In China, Amazon was floundering. Now India looked like an obvious new avenue. For the last several years, its strengthening economy had been drawing global attention. Indians were eagerly taking to the internet, and Amazon wasn't unfamiliar with the country's booming tech scene. Although the company had discarded its plan to launch its India operations in 2006, it had continued to expand its office here as a support centre for its US headquarters. The time had now come to revisit the retail space. Just as it had done in 2004–05, Amazon first considered the acquisition of a local company. In early 2011,

Amazon officials approached Flipkart, which had become the most prominent e-commerce brand in India's rapidly developing market.

The Amazon officials who were in charge of international expansion for the company, were led by Amit Agarwal. Amit had previously headed the company's India office. In late 2007, around the time the Bansals had started Flipkart, Amit had moved back to Seattle to take up the role of technical advisor to Jeff Bezos. This was a coveted position as it gave the chosen employee access to the Amazon founder and his singular mind. Amit impressed Bezos enough to be rewarded with a promotion in 2009 – the IIT Kanpur graduate would soon lead Amazon's international expansion.

When Amazon approached Flipkart in early 2011, the latter's business was on a tear. The Bansals were convinced that Flipkart would become a huge company over the next few years. They were discovering their entrepreneurial prowess, like gifted sportsmen discovering their talent. They were in no mood to sell. Lee Fixel, the company's most influential investor, didn't think they should either. Flipkart's growth had taken him by surprise. It had become his most promising bet, a potentially career-defining investment – an investor's dream. It made little sense to cash in so early.

Sachin and Binny decided that they would ask for an outlandish valuation to which they knew Amazon would never agree. They would not be cowed down the way they had been with Infibeam. This time, they would direct the discussions.

The teams met at the plush ITC Maurya hotel in central Delhi. Sachin made his terms clear to Amit, his former boss: Flipkart would agree to a deal only if the company would be valued at $1 billion. This was truly an outrageous demand. Here was a company that had been valued at less than $40 million only a year ago, that was generating about a few crore rupees in gross sales, operating in an e-commerce market which was smaller than most US cities. It was yet to make any profits; there was not even any likelihood of it earning profits for many years.

Predictably, the Amazon executives scoffed at the Bansals' demand. Amit Agarwal said to them, 'What is [it] that you've built? We can do all this in a month.' But the Bansals stood firm, and the discussions had to end.

While Amazon did not buy Flipkart, it was clear that the American online retailer would enter India one way or another. Sachin and Binny used the occasion to send a clear signal to the company: Flipkart was ready for it.

After the talks with Amazon, Sachin returned to his offices in high spirits. He said to his men, '*Maine unko bol diya*: "You can't afford my team."'

A few months later, around June 2011, Tiger Global invested $20 million in Flipkart.[5] This was the single-biggest round of funding secured by an e-commerce startup in India. Flipkart's valuation soared to more than $200 million, making it by far one of the most valuable internet startups in the country.

After this fund raise, Flipkart made a startling statement of intent. The company set a target of generating $1 billion in gross sales within four years. It was a wildly ambitious goal. In the financial year 2010–11, it had pulled in sales worth ₹44 crore.[6] While this was an impressive jump from sales of ₹11 crore in the previous year, it would take consistently stellar performance to get there. No one took the target seriously.

By now, Flipkart regularly featured in newspaper stories

and news channels. It was held up as the most promising e-commerce company in the country. Some newer startups had even adopted 'kart' as part of their names, Healthkart and Lenskart being just two such instances. It was an echo of what had happened during the US dotcom boom of the nineties as Amazon, called Amazon.com at the time, saw scores of new online retailers add '.com' to their names.[7]

The Bansals had become the faces of the new era of internet entrepreneurship in India. Sachin was invited to speak at several events and panels on entrepreneurship. One such panel was attended by Pranay Gupta, whom Sachin knew from IIT Delhi. In an attempt to avoid awkward conversation about their IIT years, Pranay fibbed that Sachin had always been 'super-smart', an outstanding student at IIT, the implication being that Sachin was destined to become a successful entrepreneur. But he was surprised when Sachin responded, '*Nahi, yaar*. I must confess – if you had asked anyone in my batch if I would be an entrepreneur, no one would have said that. I was normal, nothing special.' At IIT, Sachin had indeed been a regular guy, another face in the crowd.

Pranay did notice that Sachin was now a changed man. 'There was a distinct difference ... He had a presence about him ... a certain confidence.'

FLIPKART HAD STARTED off by sourcing products from distributors and brand companies as and when it received orders. But in late 2010, in its push to cut delivery times, the company had started stocking books, phones and other products before customers even ordered them. Flipkart also started developing mechanisms to predict demand. In most product categories, a majority of sales came from a small selection of the products. So, Flipkart began buying many of these products in advance. This was, in fact, illegal. Indian law prohibited e-commerce companies that had raised foreign capital from stocking goods, allowing instead a marketplace model whereby an e-commerce platform could connect shoppers with third-party sellers. There was no reasonable rationale behind the law. It was in place mostly because the government exercised tight control over the retail business. Powerful lobby groups with political influence had ensured that foreign retailers were barred from operating directly in India on the grounds of protecting domestic trade. The checks on e-commerce stemmed from these regulations.

Nevertheless, Flipkart had realized that in order to maintain its high service standards, it would have to hold inventory. There was no ecosystem of sellers capable of delivering the excellence in service that Flipkart wanted to give its customers. The company began to consult with law firms about ways to circumvent the law. A new plan was drawn up. On paper, Flipkart would present itself simply as a marketplace that operated the website Flipkart.com. An entity called WS Retail Services was created that would act as an external seller to the company.[8] WS Retail was a nod to the name 'WSpot' they had once considered as an alternative to Flipkart. In practice, however, the entity was controlled by Flipkart.[9] Sachin and Binny, along with a relative of Sachin, were the owners and directors of WS Retail.[10] Through this questionable structure, versions of which were later adopted by other e-commerce firms, Flipkart managed to skirt India's rigid investment laws.

AS ORDERS INCREASED through 2010, the company's tiny offices in Bangalore, Delhi and Bombay that had doubled up as warehouses, ran out of space. The growth in sales had convinced Flipkart executives that the company would need far bigger warehouses. By the end of the year, the company opened two huge warehouses in Bangalore and Bombay. A few months later, in 2011, it rented an even larger one in Delhi.

Flipkart had now turned into a proper operations company, doing real-world things, getting its hands dirty. It was no longer just engineers running a website, tapping away at their keyboards, writing clever software. Technology was an essential aspect of Flipkart's business, but its scope and application were limited. At the centre of the company was the operations machine. (This was, however, not how Sachin saw it.)

There were essentially two Flipkarts. One was the Flipkart of the Bansals, located in Bangalore. This was the brain of the company, the direction-setter, the part that kept customers happy through smart use of technology and marketing. The other Flipkart comprised the sales and operations machinery. This was the brawn of the company, the part that made it tick every day, that negotiated with suppliers, wrangled with courier companies, packed books, laptops and phones in big warehouses, hit the road every hour, every day, to deliver orders to the homes and offices of customers.

The two sides of Flipkart coexisted awkwardly. While Sachin recognized from the early days the importance of a powerful operations machinery, he was insistent that the technology function would be ascendant at Flipkart. Sachin was like a father favouring the child who had taken up his profession. A sales executive says that Flipkart functioned like two different companies. According to him, 'the product–tech people used to have their offsite in Goa. We would have to make do with some random resort near Bangalore. We had to work six days a week. They had weekends off. They had Nintendo, company food, Red Bull. We had roadside *chhole kulche* every day in Delhi. The product–tech guys also had loose accountability. Even if there was a delay in shipments and it was proven that it was because of a tech glitch, we had to manage the customers' wrath.'

The two sides clashed often. To please brands, sales executives would frequently ask engineers to make changes on the website. But engineers were given free rein to resist these requests if they believed that the website's look and feel would suffer. It was a privilege they exercised frequently. Still, the bonhomie amongst the senior leaders meant that both teams ultimately worked towards the benefit of the company and rivalries were kept in check.

Sachin and Binny had divided responsibilities so that Sachin loosely oversaw the 'demand' side (technology, marketing, customer support), and Binny the 'supply' side. But the man who exercised tremendous control over the operations function – the most important aspect of the supply side – as well as much of the sales function, was Sujeet Kumar. When he had joined, Flipkart was little more than a books-selling website struggling to make headway with distributors and courier partners. In less than three years, the equation had reversed: book distributors and courier partners were now at Flipkart's mercy. The company had developed the confidence to start its own logistics fleet. Much of the credit for this belonged to Sujeet and his team. Sujeet was also a popular figure at the company. He had hired hundreds of people, mentored many young sales and operations employees, promoted them to leadership positions. His closest associate, Ankit Nagori, recalls that Sujeet was a 'big factor' in building camaraderie at Flipkart. 'Sachin and Binny are a bit introverted, but Sujeet is the biggest extrovert. He would organize team dinners, lunches and outings. He was always on his toes to ensure everyone was united.'

But Sujeet came across as abrasive to some employees. His personality hadn't changed from his college days and people who didn't know him well found his manner coarse, improper for a corporate environment. He had no qualms about calling out what he thought was substandard performance. As the seniormost Flipkart executive after the Bansals, he had the authority to do so, and he asserted it freely. When Sachin or Binny wanted to remove someone but were feeling awkward about having the difficult conversation, they would sometimes leave it to Sujeet, a task he would take up without reluctance. He deployed very aggressive tactics to undercut Flipkart's rivals – while this helped the firm, it discomfited the Bansals at times. Sujeet ran the supply chain function in a freewheeling manner. In the rare case, he hired employees to dole out a personal favour rather than purely based on their competence. He would also sometimes remove employees without due process. On the whole, however, the Flipkart co-founders had great trust in him, and both sales and supply chain functions thrived ceaselessly. This was primarily why, in spite of themselves, the Bansals didn't rein him in. Instead, they generously awarded him large quantities of Flipkart stock in recognition of his contribution.

In 2011, Flipkart formalized its hierarchy. Sujeet and Mekin, who were already part of the Core Team along with Sachin and Binny, were both given the title of President. There were other promotions, too. Ankit Nagori, Anuj Chowdhary, Amod Malviya, Maneesh Mittal and Vaibhav Pandey were all made Vice Presidents. The move further strengthened Sujeet's hold over the sales and operations functions. Ankit, Anuj and Maneesh were close to Sujeet and reported to him. Through them, Sujeet had complete control over operations and significant influence on the sales and business development teams.

Ankit's rise at Flipkart had been spectacular. After joining the company in April 2010 at age twenty-four at the lowest level in Flipkart's hierarchy, he had become one of the highest-ranking employees at the company. His role was now expanded to include digital products such as e-books and music.

The first person Sujeet had hired after coming to Flipkart was Maneesh. For the first few months, the Bansals used to refer to Maneesh – who was about the same age as them – as 'sir', a persistent habit from their IIT days. Maneesh had a knack for identifying small fixes in the supply chain that led to huge improvements. He was the brains behind the warehousing systems and processes. The process of collecting thousands of books in a day, sorting, packaging, labelling them, ensuring that no label and book were mismatched, had been designed by Maneesh. He had ensured that the process worked efficiently and at scale. Maneesh had set up a smart, diverse team that included MBA graduates, software engineers and operations experts.

Another key associate of Sujeet was Anuj Chowdhary, who had returned to Flipkart to head logistics. In 2011, the logistics service, which would later be named Ekart, was expanded to many cities. The company hired and trained hundreds of delivery workers, whose navy blue T-shirts with the Flipkart logo would become a familiar sight on the streets. By the end of 2011, Flipkart shifted a large volume of its deliveries from external courier companies to Ekart. In its biggest markets of Delhi, Bangalore and Bombay, the expansion of Ekart enabled the company to maintain its lightning-speed deliveries even as thousands of new customers came to shop at Flipkart every month.

Sujeet, Maneesh, Ankit and Anuj were all based in Delhi until the middle of 2011. The Delhi office operated independently from the Bangalore headquarters. The Flipkart founders were, in fact, rarely seen in the Delhi office. The operations team in Delhi jokingly referred to the Bangalore headquarters as Shaktipeeth, the seat of power. In Hindu mythology, 'shaktipeeth' refers to places of pilgrimage and worship linked to the god Shiva. The inspiration for the name had come from Jwalamukhi, the IIT Delhi hostel where some of Flipkart's senior executives had lived. Jwalamukhi is a shaktipeeth in Himachal Pradesh.

In 2011, on a rare occasion, Sachin visited the company's warehouse in Delhi. The security guard there had been instructed to allow only those employees to enter who could show their Flipkart identity cards. That day Sachin had forgotten to carry his. Not knowing who Sachin was, the guard wouldn't allow Flipkart's co-founder into the warehouse. Despite Sachin's requests and orders, he refused to yield. Soon after, a seething Sachin had to be coaxed out of firing the unsuspecting guard!

In its early years, Flipkart tolerated irreverence from its employees. In 2011, in an attempt to rile the marketing head Ravi Vora, an engineer had wondered out loud in the former's presence, 'Who made this Flipkart campaign? It's so full of shit!'

Ravi, who had come to Flipkart from more formal workplaces such as Unilever and Heinz, had maintained a stiff upper lip in response. The same engineer had also caused a furore by making Salman Rushdie's *The Satanic Verses* – banned in India in 1988 after Rushdie was issued a fatwa by the religious leader of Iran – available on Flipkart. In reality, Flipkart didn't stock the book. But the engineer wanted to read it and believed that Flipkart should source any book that a customer asked for. Soon, word spread on social media that Flipkart was selling *The Satanic Verses.* Many orders were placed. Eventually the company had to cancel them and apologize to the buyers. When the infuriated Flipkart executives asked this engineer to explain himself, he responded, 'I don't know … I just wanted to read it.'

FLIPKART STRUGGLED INTERNALLY with the problem that blights every fast-growing internet startup: chaos. By late 2011, the company's staff numbered a few thousand employees, up from less than 100 employees two years ago. It had several offices in Bangalore and one each in Delhi, Bombay and Calcutta. It was no longer a startup; Flipkart had become a medium-sized company.

The Bansals and their team were locked in a constant struggle to control and direct the ever-growing beast. Every day new problems arose: goods would get stuck at state borders, the warehousing software would break down for hours, there would be a severe shortage of packaging workers during a spike in demand. Dealing with cash was an intractable issue; on occasion, Flipkart delivery workers carrying cash given to them by customers, were attacked by robbers. The company even had to deal with criminal offences by its own delivery workers, a few of whom would abscond with large amounts of cash. Some of the areas where Flipkart had set up warehouses were notorious for poor law and order – this was especially true for northern India. In 2012, a guard working at a warehouse in Gurgaon was murdered by a group of men. Executives in the logistics team filed a police complaint. Thereafter, more cameras were installed across the company's various warehouses and collection centres, security staff were increased, stricter processes implemented.

There were several less serious problems which also sprang up on a daily basis. In 2010, the company shipped a mobile phone that exploded in the customer's hands, an event that naturally drew negative publicity. Sachin and the head of the phone brand jumped onto a conference call with the aggrieved customer and begged for forgiveness.

The Bansals believed in hiring bright young people and giving them free rein. But they were unable to build a strong human resources function. Hierarchy was loosely imposed, systematic routines were largely absent. Flipkart rewarded people who 'took ownership.' 'It's better to ask for forgiveness rather than permission' was the company's mantra, which permeated its corporate culture. Young hires just a few years out of college were given enormous responsibility. Those who did well were instantly handed out promotions and pay hikes in an unstructured manner. Many employees received generous stock options, or employee stock ownership plans (ESOPs). This was one of the most beneficial aspects of Flipkart's legacy in the startup ecosystem. After the company awarded and honoured ESOPs, other startups were forced to follow suit so they could attract talented employees. Until Flipkart instituted a proper

ESOP policy, stock options had largely been worthless assets for employees. Flipkart's rise changed that; employees elsewhere now grew more vociferous in their demand for ESOPs, and startups had to set aside anywhere between five and fifteen per cent of the company's stock for employees.

While Flipkart's freewheeling approach in managing employees paid off, it had significant drawbacks as well. The company became an intense political battlefield at the senior levels. Hierarchical restructuring took place every few months. Senior executives would often be found locked in shouting matches. Roles were changed depending on the need of the hour. Most employees came to believe that they had played a pivotal role in the company's success, that they were indispensable to Flipkart. But suddenly, without notice, they would lose favour. Those who were put on a pedestal would be rudely pulled down, without warning. Many senior employees felt they had done the best work of their careers at Flipkart. But this is where they also experienced their most bitter parting, finding themselves burnt out by the end. For junior employees, the shocks were not as brutal, but the pattern held. Flipkart was like a slaloming rocket: it was great to ride it, but if you fell off, you would meet a devastating end. The growth was so enthralling and all-consuming that no one seemed to care if there was collateral damage.

By early 2012, many of the better-performing employees had left the company. The ones who stayed behind weren't too concerned, and neither were the company's founders.

Flipkart's was also a corporate culture cultivated and designed by men, for men. Until 2012, the company had no woman employee at the senior level. It wasn't simply because there were very few women in the tech world at that time; the company's male executives were also more comfortable working with other men. It seemed that the culture of India's engineering colleges had been replicated at Flipkart.

10

THE KING OF SHAKTIPEETH

Sachin may have been an unfamiliar figure at the company's warehouses, but at Shaktipeeth he ran the show. In the words of one of his colleagues, 'Whatever Flipkart was until 2013, it was what Sachin had imagined.' In interviews with reporters, Sachin came across as energetic, geeky, and he was always quick to smile. At Flipkart's offices he was an impulsive, ruthless capitalist, given to temper tantrums and serial impatience. Sachin was perennially unhappy with the state of affairs at Flipkart, constantly finding fault, always demanding more, and stingy with compliments. His inherent shyness notwithstanding, he had long transformed into a daring businessman, relishing the high-risk game that was internet entrepreneurship. In many ways, Flipkart's internal environment was a reflection of his personality – volatile, chaotic, excited, constantly churning in the rush to grow by leaps and bounds. Thinking small was discouraged and executives who delivered moderate performance failed to survive for long.

In 2011, Sachin moved into a new apartment near the Flipkart headquarters in Koramangala so he could walk to work every day. He was at the peak of his abilities and immersed himself in all functions at the company. From the start, Sachin had taken charge of the product department, unrelenting in his efforts to offer the cleanest, smoothest interface to users. He directly oversaw many of the improvements on the website. Along with Binny and Sujeet, he backed Flipkart's push into logistics. While he hadn't taken much interest in the supply side and had little knowledge of the field, that year he led a project called Flo to design a new supply chain system. Flipkart's previous software, Open Taps, used to constantly collapse under the ever-increasing volume of orders.

Working with a small team of engineers, Sachin now hunkered down in the company's second-ever office, the bungalow in Koramangala. He believed in providence – this was where Flipkart's rise had begun in earnest. The team emerged only weeks later, when the new software was almost ready. Initially, the new supply chain system caused severe disruption with vendors and at warehouses but over time, after several fixes, it resolved many of the problems with the old system. Some Flipkart employees still complained that the software fell quite short of being sufficiently reliable.

On the demand side, Sachin left no such room for criticism. He led the company's email and other digital marketing efforts. He personally crafted the first set of marketing emails that Flipkart sent to customers. He set absurdly high targets and pushed his team hard towards them. In 2016, when Sachin, who had now become an investor in startups in a personal capacity, was asked about what he looks for in an entrepreneur before investing, he said, 'Is the entrepreneur going after really big problems? To the extent that it should almost feel scary. Is it really possible what this guy is thinking?'[1] He consistently urged his colleagues and investors to think along similar lines. The greatest instance of this was when he set a sales target of $1 billion – to achieve this, the business would have to grow by one hundred times in four years.

The number one billion held special significance for Sachin – he was in its thrall, and would be for many years to come. An in-house brand would be coined Billion; Flipkart's annual shopping event would be named Big Billion Day. To Sachin, this was a fitting nomenclature in a country of more than a billion people. It was an expression of Flipkart's mission to take e-commerce to the masses, and also, perhaps, an expression of Sachin's own desire to become a visionary billionaire entrepreneur.

In Binny, Sachin had the ideal foil. Where Sachin was given to grandiosity, Binny was grounded. Sachin took the bold decisions, while Binny was more thoughtful about how to implement them. It wasn't as if Binny was less ambitious; he completely backed his business partner's larger-than-life vision, and was just as demanding. But he was the calmer of the two. Where Sachin glared and shouted, Binny was more willing to hear out employees who had done disappointing work. He had an eye for details and numbers. He would deliver post-mortems of failures or underperformance in a cold, even tone, often using sarcasm, that would make the recipient feel diminished.

When Flipkart was still new, Sachin ensured that the company stayed true to its promise of pleasing customers. He would insist that new employees spend their first few days fielding calls from customers and would obsessively track what customers said about Flipkart on social media.

A key associate of Sachin in this enterprise of pleasing customers was Tapas Rudrapatna. Tapas didn't have an official title. On his LinkedIn page, he described his role as Flipkart's 'Sex Appeal Bringer'. With his long hair, exceedingly thin frame and many tattoos, Tapas resembled the hippies at the US technology startups of the seventies. His two-bedroom bungalow, full of books and guitars, was located near a popular Koramangala bar called Sathya's which Tapas visited every evening. He ate little, often getting by on just one meal a day, and kept odd hours. His house served as the unofficial guest house for Flipkart employees. In the US, hippies like Stewart Brand, editor of a popular counterculture magazine in the sixties, and John Perry Barlow, a member of the band Grateful Dead, had later turned into the cheerleaders of the internet, subsumed by the cause of capitalism. In the India of the new millennium, Tapas was no different. He was as relentless a 'customer advocate' as Sachin. But while Sachin's mania was informed by his experience at Amazon, Tapas' stemmed from his idealism, his belief that the internet was a force for the good and that Flipkart was driven by high-minded principles, unlike a typical corporation that only cares about sales and profits.

Tapas was friends with many of his Flipkart colleagues. But this wouldn't stop him from screaming at them if a customer lodged a complaint. 'Why the fuck has this customer not received his book?' he would yell. 'You guys are useless.' And yet, he was well-liked around the Bangalore office. When out drinking with his colleagues, Tapas would unfailingly foot the bill. His only condition was that each person present had to contribute one hundred rupees in tips for the waiters – Tapas was the most popular patron at many Bangalore bars.

In the early years, it was Tapas who kept Flipkart true to its more idealistic impulses. Rohan Jahagirdar, a friend of Tapas who worked in Flipkart's marketing team, recalls that there would often be a debate around who the company should value more: the customers who spent more money or the ones who ordered more often. 'But Tapas always insisted that you can't bucket customers like that. You have to treat all customers equally. Since he always came from the point of view of the customer, it was very tough for anyone to argue against him because Flipkart was built around customer obsession.'

Tapas would spend three hours every day, from midnight until 3 a.m., reading customer emails. The volume of these emails increased exponentially over the years; he would still read them all. By 2011, Flipkart had set up a large call centre team under Marcus Terry, an experienced customer service leader. Marcus' team would handle hundreds of customer calls, social media messages and emails daily. Sachin had allowed his team leeway to resolve customer issues directly. But the really truculent customers would be left to Tapas. To placate the particularly difficult customers and win their trust, and sometimes just to delight them, Tapas would simply send them free books. During Flipkart's first few years, Tapas gifted his customers thousands of books. He would make conversation with his customers, speaking with them in a friendly manner and winning them over with his charm. Many people who would call to rage about their orders would end up as fans of Flipkart.

Before Flipkart had a large marketing team, Tapas oversaw all its social media promotions and wrote the company's blogs. These blog posts sported a witty, irreverent style similar to that of Hugh MacLeod, an American cartoonist whom Tapas idolized. MacLeod is known for his cartoons about business and marketing and is the author of *Ignore Everybody: and 39 Other Keys to Creativity*,[2] among other books. One of Tapas' blogs intended to encourage people to apply to Flipkart read: 'Come, join us. As a perk, we give free samosas.' Another blog recounted how Flipkart employees, including the CEO, would come in on Sundays to sweep the floors themselves. His blogs and social media posts gave the impression that Flipkart nurtured a bohemian culture. In reality, however, Flipkart was a fast-growing startup engaged in the age-old business of selling products to people. It was true that Flipkart's corporate culture was refreshingly democratic, merit-based and far less uptight compared with the '*lala*'[3] culture with which Indian businesses are typically associated. Most of Flipkart's employees enjoyed working there, relishing the independence and power they were given at a young age. But it was ultimately a Darwinian workplace run by capitalists, whose lead investor was a financier in New York, the mecca of capitalism. The company's purpose was to expand its business as fast as it could and get higher valuations. So, bohemian it wasn't. Yet, working at an internet startup, a continuum of the real world and the virtual, especially one at the frontiers of a new industry, allows for such romantic ideas.

Tapas' idealism was an encapsulation of how Flipkart saw itself in its preliminary years – it helped the company believe that it was an underdog pursuing a noble mission, that it was unique in its endeavours and ambitions.

Sachin and Tapas would compete to come up with the most popular Flipkart post on Facebook. Tapas won one of these rounds by posting a plain white image, which was so odd that many customers found it arresting. In the next round, Sachin countered it by posting a plain black image. They were also responsible for commissioning and approving Flipkart's first television advertising campaign which was set in an old English village. Unsurprisingly, the campaign bombed. When Flipkart finally hired a specialist marketing head in early 2011, their colleagues were understandably relieved.

Tapas was Sachin's most trusted associate; he was also quite selfless. A few months after Flipkart restructured itself and created WS Retail, it was Tapas who was projected as one of the owners and directors of this new company.[4] It was a very risky undertaking – if Flipkart was ever investigated by regulators, Tapas would be in the firing line.

Tapas was also one of the few Flipkart executives who could stand up to Sachin, oppose him, even ridicule him on occasion. When Flipkart began, Sachin and Binny were not in favour of luring customers with heavy discounts. In the first few years, the company, in fact, sold books at higher prices than some rivals. The Bansals believed that if they delivered consistently excellent service, customers wouldn't mind paying a small price for it. But after raising venture capital, the company's solitary objective was to grow fast. Discounting increased 2010 onwards. Tapas would constantly taunt Sachin about how Flipkart had turned into a discount brand. In 2011, when Flipkart had come up with a set of corporate values, 'excellence' being one of them, Tapas emailed Sachin a Hugh MacLeod cartoon that ridiculed how companies abused the word, rendering it banal, meaningless. 'Excellence in excellence,' Tapas wrote.

This was a common phenomenon in the early years: the only

people Sachin truly respected were the ones who stood up to him. Not only did he wield power because of his position as Flipkart's co-founder and CEO, he also had unusually strong views about most things. He was a formidable geek–bully. It took courage and intelligence to spar with him, and he showed regard for those who did so and could prove themselves right.

ONE OF THE biggest drivers of Flipkart's growth in 2011 was forced on the company by Sachin against the advice of many colleagues. Even though Flipkart was expanding at an extraordinary rate, Sachin hankered for more. He was particularly unsatisfied with the mobile phones business. A year after launching the category, Flipkart was selling up to a couple of hundred phones every day. Vipul Bathwal, who had overseen the mobiles category, had left the company to join a rival. In early 2011, he was replaced by Flipkart's Bombay office head, Indranil Dutta, who had moved to Bangalore to take up the new role.

Sachin had gone to the US for a visit that same year. There, he observed that Amazon and other e-commerce companies offered shoppers the choice of returning or exchanging products that didn't satisfy them. In India, however, it wasn't easy for customers to return products as most sites struggled to get products to customers in the first place! No Indian e-commerce company had built the infrastructure to handle returns; the logistical cost was thought to be prohibitive. This prevented them from allowing shoppers to return unsatisfactory products, who, in turn, would be displeased on being stuck with products that didn't match up to their expectations. Since

Flipkart's founding in 2007, Sachin and Binny had known that Indians lacked trust in online retailers, preferring to go to malls or independent stores to buy books, electronics and clothing. There was too much uncertainty online, too many annoyances. This only compounded the customer's inherent resistance to buying things they hadn't seen or felt. Although Flipkart's unrelenting pursuit of pleasing customers had won over a few hundred thousand sceptics, e-commerce was still just a niche business.

Sachin came to realize that Flipkart would have to constantly coax and lure customers with special incentives to encourage them to overcome their mistrust of e-commerce. He also understood that offering product returns wasn't even a special incentive; it was an essential feature of commerce anywhere. In a low-trust society like India, how could a retailer not offer this facility? It would have to be done. In the middle of 2011, he proposed the introduction of an ultra-flexible thirty-day returns policy.

Flipkart executives were shocked. The company had just begun expanding its nascent in-house logistics service; it wasn't equipped to handle returns. Besides, Flipkart's overhead costs would shoot up. Even Binny protested, pointing out that their spending might go up by two per cent. To this, Sachin had a ready counter: 'But our business will grow as well.' Another senior Flipkart executive insisted that a returns policy would lead to fraud, that it would be misused. Sachin shot back angrily, 'For that one per cent, why would you penalize the ninety nine per cent? We'll just blacklist them.'

In the second quarter of 2011, Flipkart introduced its returns policy. Customers could return any product within thirty days without having to provide an explanation. It turned out to be an inspired move. Customers took to the policy immediately and orders increased further.

But introducing the returns policy wasn't enough in itself. It had improved Flipkart's popularity with its existing customers, but it didn't attract large numbers of new users. The problem was that while the company had surpassed its predecessors and peers and greatly improved the online shopping experience, most Indians, even in the cities, were yet to hear about Flipkart. And most of its present users still saw Flipkart primarily as a books retailer that happened to sell other goods. They were tremendously loyal, but their numbers were insignificant within the overall retail market; Flipkart was still just a cult brand. To take e-commerce to the masses, at least in the urban areas to begin with, the company would have to turn to mass advertising.

Around the time it launched the thirty-day returns policy, Flipkart had started considering marketing seriously. This was hard to believe if one was familiar with the company's first advertising campaign of April 2011. Set in an old English village, the ad featured an English grandmother who ordered books online through her pet mouse. Ordering books online was presented as an act of magic. After ninety seconds, the fantasy abruptly ended with the punchline: 'You don't need magic. Just log on to Flipkart.'[5] Few bothered to. In 2016, Sachin spoke about how he had unsuccessfully described the concept of Flipkart to his own grandmother, 'I have tried [to describe Flipkart to my grandmother]. But I don't think my grandmom really liked it. I told her, "This is a phone. You press a button on it and the product arrives at your doorstep." She told me,

"Why would somebody do that? Why wouldn't you just go to the shop and buy?'"[6]

By early 2011, Ravi Vora had joined Flipkart as the head of marketing. A short, dour-looking man, Ravi had spent nearly a decade with the consumer goods makers, Hindustan Unilever and Heinz, known for their expertise in marketing and sales. He was unimpressed by the previous advertisement that had been overseen by Sachin and Tapas. Immediately he set to work on a new campaign.

It had two primary goals – to attract new users, people who had never shopped online before, and to position Flipkart as an all-purpose retailer that sold a range of products from phones and laptops to cameras, and not just books. The overarching feeling that the ads would need to cultivate among viewers was that of trust. It was decided that this would be best achieved by promoting Flipkart's cash-on-delivery and flexible returns policies, its low prices and expansive product assortment. After some hesitation, Ravi retained Happy Creative, the agency that had helped create Flipkart's first ad.

Work on the new campaign went on for more than three months. A few weeks before Diwali, it was ready. The ads featured two children conversing in would-be adult voices about shopping on Flipkart. One child was sceptical about online shopping, their scepticism playfully dismissed as ignorance by the other, who pointed out the various benefits of shopping on Flipkart. The tagline 'No Kidding No Worries' suggested that one could shop on Flipkart without anxiety, and it was so easy that even children could do it.[7] The ads were memorable and created a general feeling of warmth and familiarity about Flipkart. In the weeks and months after the ads were released,

Flipkart's brand was transformed. The company saw a huge increase in traffic and sales. It continued to run the campaign for two years. Internally, Flipkart executives cleverly transposed the message of the ad campaign. Flipkart had once been dismissed as a kids' enterprise by cynical suppliers, investors and rivals alike. The company had now proved that the kids could hold their own.

The Kids campaign, as it came to be known, was launched towards the end of a spectacular year for Flipkart. The gross sales of ₹10 crore in December 2010 had more than quadrupled a year later. The company was hurtling from one milestone to another, month after month, demolishing barriers, becoming stronger and greedier for more.

Flipkart's rise had helped spawn an entire startup ecosystem in the country. Naturally, it also attracted critics. Future Group CEO Kishore Biyani continuously predicted that the end was near for Flipkart and other internet startups that burned through investor cash with no concern for profitability. The larger corporate world was similarly dismissive. But in its early years, the most vociferous Flipkart critics were from within the startup ecosystem. Prominent among them was Mahesh Murthy, the chief of Seedfund, a venture capital firm. There were many others. They had valid and irrefutable reservations about the poor economics of e-commerce, as evidenced by the fact that Flipkart's soaring sales were offset by its losses. It was commonly believed that this trend would continue for many years. Sceptics also thought it was futile to invest in a business that would some day have to compete with Amazon. While these reservations were legitimate, Flipkart was mocked for being a 'copycat' of Amazon, one of the most innovative companies in the world. This analogy would come to be well established. It also happened to be nonsensical.

Selling goods to people was not an idea for which Amazon deserved credit. It wasn't even the first company to think of selling products online. What made Amazon inventive was that it discovered, through trial and error, a series of business innovations that made buying online a habit for a majority of Americans, and Amazon the country's most compelling shopping destination which remained indispensable to its customers through constant improvements to its service. In effect, Amazon had invented the rules of e-commerce. Even if a new competitor entered the field, that company would have to operate within the paradigm Amazon had created. Flipkart had done the same thing in India. There was no doubt that it had taken inspiration from Amazon. But e-commerce in India had few similarities with the retail space in the US. The innovation of cash on delivery, the creation of unique warehousing and logistics processes, the introduction and implementation of the product returns policy, the unique methods of managing everyday dealings with customers, and dozens of other smaller inventions particular to the Indian ecosystem, are what comprised the paradigm of e-commerce in this country. Here, Flipkart had set the rules of the game. Amazon's entry later and its adoption of these ways and means would validate just how innovative Flipkart had been as a company.

Sachin had come up with a pithy counter to the 'copycat' argument. A venture capitalist who had remained sceptical about the company had once told him, 'So what's the big deal about Flipkart – you're just copying Amazon.'

Sachin had replied, '*Haan, theek hai. Tu kar ke bata de.*' Yeah, sure. You show us how it's done.

11

SETBACK

In 2011, every experiment at Flipkart seemed to yield gold. Every successful initiative made the Bansals more confident, prompting them to think bigger and grander. A few months after raising $20 million from Tiger Global, they decided to seek as much as $150 million from new investors. Sachin had already set his sights on a valuation of $1 billion. For a company that was barely four years old, it would be an extraordinary achievement. Future Group, the largest retail chain in the country, had taken nearly two decades to get there.[1] Even other prominent entrepreneurs like Dhirubhai Ambani, Sunil Bharti Mittal, Narayana Murthy and Azim Premji had built their corporate empires over decades.

The company also began to look at acquisitions seriously. Until then, it had bought just one startup, a book discovery tool called WeRead. In late 2011, Flipkart finalized the acquisition of Mime360, a Bombay-based startup that provided music-streaming software to record labels. The deal was part of Flipkart's plan to sell digital services such as music and e-books. Flipkart executives were also eager to work with the Mime360 team which was led by two product-engineering experts, Sameer Nigam and Rahul Chari. Ankit Nagori, who was in charge of Flipkart's digital business, had met Sameer and Rahul through common contacts at the record labels. Ankit was in negotiations with them to source content for the launch of Flipkart's digital products category. Used to meeting executives at publishing houses and record labels that were proudly Luddite, he was floored by Sameer and Rahul. 'Sameer was a mix of media and technology, and a great salesman. Rahul was pure tech. I called up Binny immediately and told him that here are two guys whose company we absolutely need to acquire,' says Ankit.

A few weeks after buying Mime360, Flipkart took over Chakpak, the film content website founded by Gaurav Singh Kushwaha and Nitin Rajput, the Bansals' colleagues at Amazon India. Chakpak had started off in 2007 on a promising note but the rise of Facebook had crippled its ability to attract advertising revenues. Realizing that the company had no future, its founders arranged a sale to Flipkart. It was just a way for them to avoid firing their employees, who were hired by Flipkart; there were no cash or stock payments. Nitin and a dozen other Chakpak employees joined Flipkart while Gaurav went his own way, to conceive his next startup idea.

Later on, as part of Flipkart, the Mime360 team launched Flyte, an online music platform. Users praised it for its attractive interface and easy delivery of music. But Flyte had to be shut down in 2013 – Indians didn't want to pay for music when it was available for free on the internet. Sameer and Rahul remained with Flipkart and went on to become senior leaders at the company. Nitin Rajput also took up an important role in Flipkart's product team.

By the time these acquisitions took place, Flipkart was engaged in fundraising discussions with General Atlantic, a private equity firm based in New York. Other investment companies had shown interest in Flipkart but baulked at its asking price of $1 billion. General Atlantic was one of the few willing to meet this demand. It wasn't a typical investment company; General Atlantic was a highly regarded private equity firm globally. It had been a picky but intelligent investor in internet startups, boasting holdings such as Facebook and Alibaba. An investment by General Atlantic would put an elite stamp on Flipkart. Lee Fixel was friendly with a partner at the firm, and had introduced him to the Bansals. Sachin had led the talks, visiting the General Atlantic headquarters in New York several times along with Binny. Sachin believed that the deal would mark the moment when Flipkart – and he, its CEO – had arrived. It would catapult Flipkart to the global stage and validate the Bansals' status as visionary entrepreneurs.

After several months of discussions, in late 2011, General Atlantic finally signed a term sheet to invest in Flipkart. While a term sheet is not binding, it typically converts into transactions. General Atlantic then began their due diligence process, auditing Flipkart's books and financial records.

The auditing took another few months. At Flipkart, the founders and investors were growing increasingly anxious. After signing the term sheet with General Atlantic, they had ended discussions with other investment firms. Now they were worried about cash flow. Flipkart's business, ever expanding, was sucking up increasing amounts of cash. They had expected the General Atlantic deal to close by now but the firm had raised questions about the state of Flipkart's accounts. It was also concerned that Flipkart might not be compliant with India's foreign investment rules that prohibited inventory-based e-commerce firms from receiving foreign capital.

It was true that in the rush to expand, Flipkart had neglected setting up proper accounting systems. The company had hired a finance chief in 2010 but he had turned out to be a misfit – as were many others who were confounded by the speed at which Flipkart was moving and had urged the Bansals to slow down in order to put proper processes in place. But the Bansals explained to the fund managers at General Atlantic that Flipkart's frenetic growth had overwhelmed its accounting systems. They assured the financiers that Flipkart was close to hiring an established chief financial officer who would soon help fix its systems. They also explained that the company's legal structure was sufficiently clean – most e-commerce firms had similar structures. General Atlantic seemed pacified – they knew that weak accounting systems were a common feature at high-growth startups across the world. Yet they kept postponing the signing of the deal. At the same time, they assured Flipkart that their extensive diligence process was a norm and that the issues it had discovered were minor.

Finally, at the end of 2011, General Atlantic informed Flipkart that its investment committee had approved the deal. The firm had agreed to the $1 billion valuation. The Bansals were elated – months of painstaking discussions had finally concluded. Flipkart's investors, Tiger Global and Accel Partners, were relieved after having watched the slow progress of the discussions with increasing concern.

A day before General Atlantic had indicated it would sign the deal and send the investment amount, Lee Fixel got a call from his friend at the investment firm. The conversation was brief, tense. In an apologetic tone, he told Lee, 'Sorry, we're pulling out.'

Lee, usually unflappable, was furious. Flipkart had carried on in the belief that the General Atlantic deal would come through. Now the company was on the verge of running out of cash – it was utterly helpless. To save Flipkart, Lee would have to persuade his partners at Tiger Global to put up $50 million in emergency funds. It wasn't a conversation he was looking forward to having. It was a humbling moment for the young fund manager, one of the most frightening points of his promising career, something that could have caused serious damage to it.

A few days after General Atlantic backed out, Tiger Global injected $50 million into Flipkart. Accel Partners India, which was a far smaller fund than Tiger Global, had to ask its US parent to wire funds to Flipkart whose capital needs were beyond its capacity.

The episode was a watershed moment for Flipkart. It marked the point at which Lee Fixel became heavily involved in the company's affairs, when his career became inextricably linked with Flipkart. Until then, Lee's role had been confined to that of an investor, board member and advisor to the Bansals. After this event, Lee's involvement went far deeper; he frequently weighed in on the company's strategy, sometimes even on new executive appointments. And he took charge of fundraising. According to another Flipkart shareholder, Lee became 'the company's lead investor and investment banker'.

Sachin, on the contrary, receded from the daily administration at Flipkart. As much as the General Atlantic pullout had shocked Flipkart's investors, Sachin took it the hardest. It was his first big failure, a blunder that could have brought about the end of Flipkart. While he could blame General Atlantic, the responsibility for the fiasco would still have to be borne by the CEO. There was no escaping the reality that Flipkart had been on the brink. It was now painfully clear to Sachin that despite his company's substantial achievements, it was ultimately at the mercy of investors – outsiders to Flipkart. His dream of fetching the $1 billion seemed to have been crushed. His confidence was shot, his stature diminished. He continued to be the face of the company and to lead the fundraising discussions. But it wasn't until the end of 2014 that he would recover his former influence over Flipkart's everyday affairs. It was evident to those who worked closely with Sachin that he had taken the blunder personally. 'He was crushed,' recalls a former Flipkart employee. 'Who had seen that kind of success so quickly before? And then suddenly to come so close to seeing it all collapse … he couldn't deal with it.'

In 2016, Sachin referred to the chastening experience at a panel on entrepreneurship at IIT Bombay: 'One [piece of] advice I would give to [entrepreneurs] is that you should raise funds when you can rather than when you have to. Which means that you don't get into a situation where your business needs funds and you have to really look for investors. Don't push the company to that point. Raise funds when you can.'[2]

At General Atlantic, history would repeat itself. In the mid-nineties, the firm had lost out on investing in Amazon before the American online retailer listed its shares. Amazon had chosen an upcoming venture capital firm in Silicon Valley over General Atlantic.[3] It turned out to be a costly miss for the fund: Amazon's shares vaulted after the company went public a few months later. This time, with Flipkart, it was General Atlantic that had chosen to stay out, and the miss wouldn't look any better for it.

AFTER SUPPLYING THE emergency funds to Flipkart, Tiger Global and Accel Partners began to reduce their risk elsewhere. By now, these two firms had invested in many e-commerce startups. One of these was Letsbuy, a website that sold electronics goods. Letsbuy had rapidly established a large business mostly by luring customers with heavy discounts. Occasionally, the company was even generating higher monthly sales than Flipkart's electronics category. *BusinessWorld* magazine had decided to profile the company for its cover story.

Since Letsbuy had burned a lot of cash, its founders Amanpreet Bajaj and Hitesh Dhingra needed the next round of capital to carry on. Lee Fixel had told them he would back the company. After talks with Lee, the Letsbuy founders pulled out of discussions with other investors. But suddenly in January, Lee told them that he had changed his mind.

While Letsbuy was showing impressive growth, it had major flaws. Its logistics and warehousing systems were a mess. Its technology platforms were substandard. Some employees had even complained to its board of directors that the company was badly run. Lee and the other Letsbuy shareholders suggested to the founders that they sell the company to Flipkart. With little cash left and no new investors on hand, they had no real choice.

Flipkart bought Letsbuy in a distress sale in February 2012.[4] *Business World* had to pull its cover on deadline day. Within a few months, Flipkart promptly shut down the Letsbuy business.[5]

By early 2012, e-commerce in India had become a crowded space. There was eBay, and even though it was flailing, continually changing its strategy and leadership team to little effect, it was still a big name. Over the past eighteen months, a large number of domestic e-commerce startups had entered the fray. But most of these startups lacked the sincerity, ability and resources to last. None had built the kind of sturdy infrastructure of warehousing, logistics and technology that Flipkart had developed. They kept only one weapon in their arsenal: discounts. Every month a new website, fresh from receiving a dose of capital, sprouted up, bearing goods at massive discounts, only to collapse as soon as the money ran out. One could argue that this was like a self-fulfilling prophecy. But during a funding boom, when investors move in a herd, logic is swept aside by the momentum of the crowd; whatever investors and startups decide in the moment is right – until it's not. It was Flipkart's takeover of Letsbuy and its ensuing shutdown that suddenly made investing in e-commerce startups a questionable gamble. Over the next two years, dozens more e-commerce startups would fold up.[6]

Few survived the capital famine. Among the ones that came through were Infibeam, Snapdeal, Shopclues, BigBasket, Myntra and the Rocket Internet group.

Infibeam, whose founder Vishal Mehta had come so close to convincing the Bansals to give up their dreams for a pittance, were now far behind in the game. The Ahmedabad-based firm was only a fraction of Flipkart's size.

It was Snapdeal that was emerging as a serious rival to Flipkart. Snapdeal was founded by Kunal Bahl, its CEO, and Rohit Bansal, the COO. Of the two, Kunal was the face of the company. Born into a business family, Kunal had studied at the Delhi Public School. He had met Rohit when they were teenagers. Kunal, who exuded the easy confidence born of a privileged upbringing, came across as a charismatic man. Rohit, a small-town boy, was awed by him. Soon, Kunal converted the vegetarian Rohit into a meat-eater. Kunal had wanted to study at the IITs, but unlike Rohit, had failed to make it despite trying for two and a half years. Dejected, he moved to the US and got his engineering degree from the University of Pennsylvania, and later studied business and marketing. After college, Kunal got a job at Microsoft but was forced to return to India as he couldn't get a work visa extension. On his return, he immediately called on Rohit and the two started working on a business idea.

In 2007, they began by distributing coupons. Soon, they turned this into a daily deals website. Finally in 2011, they moved into e-commerce. Such dramatic shifts in the business may have seemed implausible and suspect, but Kunal had little trouble in convincing investors to back him. He was a slick talker, a master of PR. In meetings with journalists, Kunal would make it a point to talk about two elements of his life: his schooling at Delhi Public School – the R. K. Puram branch – 'the only DPS that matters', and how he had bravely overcome the denial of a visa extension in the US. Kunal's mannerisms and personality made a mark; he often broke out in guffaws, not unlike Jeff Bezos. He relished the spotlight that came along with Snapdeal's rise; his Twitter handle read: 'Entrepreneur. Maybe Politics.'[7]

Kunal stood out in an e-commerce ecosystem populated by introverted software engineers such as the Bansals – Sachin, Binny, and even Rohit. In fact, Snapdeal's shift to e-commerce had made Rohit feel a bit awkward. It put him in direct opposition to Binny, who had been his classmate at IIT Delhi. In their first year of college, they had even been close friends. When Snapdeal entered e-commerce in late 2011, it chose the marketplace model – the goods listed on its site were owned by third-party merchants; the company didn't have inventory of its own the way Flipkart did. Over the next five years, Snapdeal would be a constant irritant for Flipkart and Kunal would become a bitter opponent to Sachin. Every time it seemed certain that Snapdeal would run out of cash, Kunal would miraculously pull off a fund raise. Snapdeal came to be known as The Cat With Nine Lives.

There was also Myntra, which had been funded by Tiger Global and Accel Partners as well. Myntra had started life in 2007 as a seller of personalized gifts. In 2011, Myntra changed its business to become a fashion-selling website. Its co-founder and CEO Mukesh Bansal was familiar with Sachin and Binny. They had known each other since 2007. Mukesh's startup had, in fact, received funding from Accel Partners more than a year before Flipkart did. Despite having less capital in the years to come, Myntra would stay ahead of Flipkart's fashion business for nearly three years.

As Indian e-commerce startups struggled in 2011 because of the funding slowdown, Amazon made its first concrete move to enter the market. In early 2012, Amazon launched Junglee, a price comparison website (of the kind Sachin and Binny had initially wanted to launch in 2007).[8] The purpose of launching

Junglee was to supply Amazon with important information about the shopping habits of Indians. Amazon would use this knowledge later to plan its own e-commerce business in the country. The launch of Junglee further unnerved investors in local startups.

AROUND THE TIME of the Letsbuy acquisition, Flipkart tweaked its hierarchy again. It hired a new chief financial officer, Karandeep Singh. Karan, a soft-spoken Sikh chartered accountant, was an accomplished finance leader; he had worked in senior finance positions at large companies including Yum Brands and Dell. In his early forties, he came to Flipkart as one of its oldest employees.

The company also asked Ankit Nagori, who was heading its books and digital business, to take over all product categories. He would continue to report to Sujeet Kumar. It was yet another significant promotion for Ankit. Along with his inexhaustible stamina, Ankit had also displayed impressive business acumen as well as the cunning to get ahead of other shrewd, ambitious men, most of whom were older than him.

Ankit's promotion further strengthened Sujeet's hold over the company. He now wielded complete control over Flipkart's operations and sales through his lieutenants. Sujeet, too, had joined Flipkart as an unaccomplished young man. It had been an exhilarating ride for him. After Sachin and Binny, and apart from the institutional investors, he was the biggest shareholder in the company. The financial reward was huge. But Flipkart was special to Sujeet for another reason: he had made something of himself there, as had Ankit and hundreds of others.

In January 2012, Sujeet got married. As was his wont, he invited 'half of Flipkart'. The *baraat* lasted for hours; the dancing wouldn't stop. Sachin, Binny and many Flipkart employees came together to participate in the revelries. This was a rare moment of camaraderie in a year that would eventually see its demise.

12

NO RESPITE

Flipkart had received significant media coverage by 2012, and almost all of it had been favourable. Business dailies, magazines and TV channels had named the company one of India's most promising startups. But beyond the obvious facts, internet businesses like Flipkart and the accompanying venture capital space weren't well understood. One reporter took it upon himself to change this in spectacular fashion.

Earlier that year, Flipkart was approached by *Forbes* for a cover story on the company. The *Forbes* reporter, Rohin Dharmakumar, was on friendly terms with Flipkart's newly appointed communications head, Karthik Srinivasan. Rohin had made an unusual entry into journalism. An engineer with a business degree from IIM Calcutta, he had worked as a business analyst at a consultancy and made partner at the public relations firm Genesis Burson-Marsteller.[1] In 2008, he joined *Forbes*, which was entering India through a partnership with the local media group Network18, to write on technology, media and telecoms. In India, *Forbes* had acquired a reputation for publishing well-researched, hard-hitting stories. Rohin persuaded Karthik to give him access to Flipkart, promising an extensive profile of the company.

Karthik, a genial, energetic PR executive, was excited by the prospect of the *Forbes* story. He thought it would be a nice way for him to begin his stint at Flipkart – a splash on the cover of a respected magazine. He convinced Sachin and Binny to grant full access to Rohin. Initially, the interviews went well. Over a few weeks, Rohin met Flipkart leaders including Mekin Maheshwari, Ravi Vora and the company's CFO, Karandeep Singh. They declined to disclose exact details about Flipkart's valuation, revenues and losses, as private companies do, but the interviews still covered a wide range of topics. When Rohin met Sachin, the line of questioning took a different turn altogether. Rohin challenged the Flipkart CEO about the company's accounting practices, its exclusionary corporate culture, and the disproportionate influence of Sachin's IIT Delhi mates. His interrogation would make it seem as if a litany of problems assailed Flipkart and the way it was run. Another meeting was arranged, this time between Rohin and Binny, who was accompanied by Karandeep Singh. That didn't go well either. At the end of the interview, Karan told a colleague, 'This guy has an agenda. He wasn't interested in hearing out what [Binny] had to say.'

'Can Flipkart Deliver?' hit the stands in June 2012.[2] The story turned out to be so outrageous that it shocked the Flipkart executives even though they had anticipated by now that it wouldn't be an enitrely flattering piece. The article presented Flipkart as a sinister, unethical workplace run by a coterie of scheming IIT Delhi graduates. It painted the Bansals as megalomaniacal entrepreneurs for believing they could build a large e-commerce business in India in record time. Their 'hubris and foolhardiness' might drive the company to ruin, the article prophesied. It declared that Tiger Global's investment practices were unscrupulous, its strategy dubious. It even implied that Flipkart was cooking its books. The photograph accompanying the piece showed four Flipkart executives sitting in a delivery van wearing grim, almost angry expressions. *Forbes* had taken several photographs; its final choice was revealing. Sachin was enraged. '*Yeh kya bakwas hai!* What the hell is this!' he said to Karthik.

The story spread quickly on social media. Like a good conspiracy theory, it showed enough 'research' and 'evidence' to sound compelling. It was the talk of India's startup world for months. Ironically, for a piece that later turned out to be laughably unrealistic, it was one of the last stories by a business magazine in India that would leave a profound impact on the subject it had covered.

At Flipkart, the entire senior management team got together to figure out how to respond. Ravi Vora, who was on vacation in Singapore, had to get on a conference call with his colleagues in Bangalore. Mostly, they vented their anger at the hatchet job. But the immediate danger facing Flipkart was that the story would put off the dozens of senior and middle managers that the company was in the process of hiring. Later, in an unusual move, Karthik convinced Sachin to fire off a long email to the *Forbes* editor protesting that Flipkart had been misrepresented. The email alleged that *Forbes* had published the piece because Homeshop18, a rival of Flipkart, was owned by *Forbes*' parent firm. Sachin had requested that his email be published on the *Forbes* website, which the magazine did, followed by a rejoinder by the *Forbes* editor.[3] The candidates Flipkart wanted to hire came to their interviews with the *Forbes* issue in hand, demanding to know why they should join a company with a tarnished name. Flipkart executives pointed to Sachin's email on the *Forbes* website and the messages of support on social media from customers who continued to believe in the company. Despite their misgivings, many of these candidates agreed to join.

The company had averted immediate disaster, but the story would leave a deep scar. Flipkart, having only received positive coverage until that point, was in a state of shock for weeks. Flipkart leaders were forced to conduct all-employee meetings to restore calm. They pointed to the glowing customer reviews that were posted apparently in response to the company's negative portrayal. It was a non-sequitur – problems related to corporate culture, business models and accounting have no direct link with customer satisfaction – but Flipkart needed its workforce to regain composure. For nearly eighteen months, its leaders had to field questions about its work culture from the candidates they interviewed. Several talented executives abided by *Forbes*' portrait of Flipkart and refrained from joining the company.

BY THE MIDDLE of 2012, Flipkart decided to raise its next round of funds. Despite the General Atlantic setback, Flipkart's sales had continued to rise rapidly. The company had launched many new categories such as fashion, large electronics and beauty products. But the emergency funds from Tiger Global and Accel Partners now needed to be supplemented. The next round of capital would have to be supplied by new investors – Tiger and Accel had invested far more than they had anticipated. Besides, Flipkart would need more cash injections in the future. It was essential to gather a consortium of investors.

Lee Fixel had introduced Sachin to Naspers, a South African media and internet conglomerate. Naspers had invested in internet companies in Africa, Asia, Europe and Latin America. Its best-known holding was Tencent, a large Chinese messaging and gaming startup. Lee was familiar with Naspers' executives; the company had bought into a few Tiger Global-held companies such as Allegro, a Polish e-commerce business, and Mail.ru, a Russian internet conglomerate. Naspers also had some presence in India already. It owned an online travel company called Ibibo and another e-retail company, Tradus. It was eager to fund more startups in the country. (In 2008, when Flipkart was just a few months old, Ashish Kashyap, a Naspers representative, had met the Bansals in order to explore an investment. But after just one meeting, Naspers had decided against pursuing a deal at that time.)

Lee also introduced Sachin to Masayoshi Son, the founder and CEO of the Japanese multinational conglomerate SoftBank Group. Son, a Japanese citizen of Korean descent, was well known in Asia's technology sector; he was once hailed Japan's 'answer to Bill Gates'.[4] When Sachin wrote to him asking for a meeting, he told the Flipkart co-founder that he was leaving for a holiday but would be keen to meet on his return. While this meeting didn't take place, in less than a month, after just a few discussions, Naspers was ready to invest in Flipkart. Within a few years, Flipkart had established itself as the preeminent internet startup in India. Its business was doubling every six months or so. The Bansals and their leadership team seemed exceptionally bright. To Naspers, investing in Flipkart was almost a no-brainer.

Naspers funded Flipkart in August 2012, after an audit that lasted a few weeks. Iconiq Capital, another firm that Lee had introduced to the Bansals, participated in the funding round. In all, the two investors put $150 million into Flipkart, enhancing its value to nearly $900 million.[5] Not long after its survival had been called into question by a cash crunch, and just a few weeks after a damaging article had dented the company's morale, Flipkart had secured the firepower to pursue its objective of taking e-commerce to the masses.

But Sachin continued to feel unsatisfied – Flipkart's valuation had fallen short of his magic number: $1 billion. Still, he was now a wealthy man, and so was Binny, each boasting a net worth higher than $100 million.

Earlier that year, Tiger Global and Accel Partners, whose holdings had multiplied in value, had rewarded the Bansals and some senior employees for their stellar performance. More than a dozen such employees, including Sujeet Kumar and Mekin Maheswari, received crores of rupees in bonuses, as part of the company's stock option scheme.

It was unprecedented in Indian business for such a young company to share wealth with its employees. It was also one of the first instances of ESOPs turning out to have real value. Infosys was considered a benchmark in the aspect of awarding generous amounts of shares to its staff. The employees would, however, have to wait nearly two decades before they could encash these benefits. Flipkart's first cash payout for employees, on the other hand, happened less than five years after the company had been founded. As more Indian startups prospered in the coming years, Flipkart's example became a norm.

It was through such gestures that Flipkart reinforced belief in the idea of internet entrepreneurship. By 2012, Flipkart had not only become the biggest internet startup in India, it was also the 'too big to fail'[6] firm. One by one, Flipkart continued to defy the sceptics, who had overwhelmingly outnumbered the believers. As it came closer and closer to fulfilling its vision, the company uplifted the entire startup ecosystem. The belief – among other entrepreneurs, investors, startup employees, as well as those who had chosen to stay out – that India could sustain a thriving startup scene grew stronger.

The Flipkart executives weren't shy about displaying their wealth. Sachin, who had been driving a Chevrolet, bought a Mercedes, while Binny's Hyundai i20 was replaced by a BMW. Both Sachin and Binny also bought new homes in Koramangala. In 2012, even Sujeet bought a Mercedes.

AFTER THE CAPITAL infusion from Naspers, Flipkart's investors demanded that the company fix its finances and accounting systems. It would also have to adopt a new legal structure to ensure it didn't violate India's investment rules. Its current arrangement was too risky. While the entity that owned the Flipkart website and WS Retail were separate on paper, the Bansals were owners and directors of both. Even a casual observer would have spotted the sham. *BusinessWorld* had informed the company that it was working on a story about the questionable legal structures of e-commerce firms including Flipkart. It was time to devise a new legal ploy to skirt the country's investment rules. And all of this had to be done while the company grew rapidly. In the internet business, current valuations are determined primarily on the basis of estimated future sales growth – one of the costs of accepting venture capital. Flipkart's valuation had swung from less than $5 million to $900 million in just three years based on the hope that its business would continue to fly. If its growth slowed, the company would be in serious trouble, its ability to attract more capital would diminish.

After consulting lawyers, Flipkart finalized a new legal structure. In 2011, it had moved its holding company from India to Singapore.[7] Apart from avoiding regulatory trouble, Flipkart also wanted to prepare for a public listing abroad. Indian stock markets did not allow loss-making companies to list their shares. And neither did India have a specialized ecosystem of analysts and investors that understood how internet companies were valued.

As part of the new structure, Flipkart created several new entities under its Singapore holding company. Separate units were created for the marketplace platform that owned the Flipkart website, the logistics operation and a new payments business. The biggest change was at WS Retail, the entity that was purportedly a third-party seller for Flipkart. Sachin and Binny along with Sachin's relative, B. K. Bansal, who were directors of WS Retail, would need to end their association with the entity.[8] Tapas Rudrapatna, who was already an employee and director of WS Retail, would be joined by a Flipkart colleague. It was decided that WS Retail would have to be padded up; it would be given ownership of Flipkart's logistics unit to pretend that it wasn't a shell company.

For a Flipkart employee to move to WS Retail would be dangerous – if regulators ever looked into Flipkart's relationship with WS Retail, executives at the latter would certainly be investigated. The risk wasn't restricted to financial penalties; it possibly involved jail time. Sujeet Kumar, the most powerful leader at the company after the Bansals, volunteered to move to WS Retail. In the second half of 2012, Sujeet's transfer and the simultaneous exit of the Bansals from WS Retail were finalized.[9] At least at that time, Sujeet's brave move would not affect his position at Flipkart.

The changes in Flipkart's legal structure came just in time. In September 2012, India's commerce ministry made it explicitly clear that foreign investment was prohibited in direct online retail or inventory businesses; only marketplaces were permitted to receive foreign capital. Again, there was no defensible rationale for such a distinction. What mattered was that retail was a politically charged space in India; both right-wing and left-wing parties had opposed the infusion of foreign capital in Indian retail.

A few days later, in October, *BusinessWorld* published its article on how e-commerce firms were violating Indian laws. 'FDI Escapades' detailed the dodgy legal ruses adopted by online retailers to bypass foreign investment laws.[10] It proved that most e-commerce companies, including Flipkart, Myntra and Rocket Internet, were in fact running inventory businesses rather than marketplace platforms. Holding stock was essential to ensure that customers received original, first-hand products in a speedy manner. Without the inventory model, there would be no consistency in service, which would translate to low sales growth and insignificant valuations. Since the inventory model was prohibited, e-commerce firms pretended to be marketplace platforms, claimed the *BusinessWorld* piece. It was an indictment of the regulatory failure in the e-commerce space. This would soon change.

Towards the end of 2012, Flipkart and many other e-commerce companies were hit by a shocker. The Enforcement Directorate, the feared regulator in charge of enforcing foreign investment laws and investigating related violations, had sent them notices.[11]

The ED was inquiring about their legal structures. The regulator was out to prove that the online retailers were operating under the inventory model. While many e-commerce companies received notices, it was clear that the primary target of the ED's inquiry was Flipkart. This was hardly a surprise: Flipkart had raised more capital than all other internet companies combined.

THE ED INQUIRY came at a troubled time for Flipkart. Three worrying trends had endured at the company since the middle of 2012. It was losing more money with every passing month. While this was expected, what made it a cause for concern was the second trend: Flipkart's sales growth had nearly stalled for the first time since its inception in 2007. In June 2012, it was generating about ₹100 crore in monthly gross sales. By December 2012, this number had inched up by less than ten per cent.[12] Even worse, customer complaints about its service had multiplied. Altogether, these trends established beyond doubt that Flipkart was suddenly in a proper crisis. It was an unusual experience for the company where most employees had only known good times.

The crisis at Flipkart was of its own making. The company had grown overconfident. It had launched many new product categories all at once, believing that it could force its way through any barriers. But categories such as large electrical appliances required logistical expertise that could only be accumulated after several months of trial and error. Others necessitated specialized sourcing and logistics mechanisms. Stretched in too many areas, the company's sales function was in disorder. Ankit Nagori, who was now at its helm, could not exert his authority the way he had when leading the books and media categories.

There were other problems as well. The company's new supply chain software, Flo, was found to have flaws that resulted in increased expenditure and troubles with vendors. A new accounting process was introduced with haste, and this caused further disruptions with vendors. Flipkart had also lost many talented senior employees who had suddenly fallen out of favour; executives who had replaced them needed time to acclimatize. Within a year, the company had nearly tripled in size to about 5,000 employees. Older employees were wary of newer colleagues; camaraderie had been replaced with self-interest. Flipkart struggled to impose a uniform corporate culture. In the second half of 2012, the company failed to measure up.

What Flipkart missed the most at this time was the decisive leadership of Sachin Bansal. After the General Atlantic talks fell through, Sachin had loosened his grip on the company.

He seemed distant to his colleagues. The *Forbes* story had also made him less trustful of people. The Core Team had not been meeting frequently. Flipkart's business and staff had grown at a pace that had made centralization impractical, futile even. But the Core Team meetings were still important. These had been a weekly fixture, a ritual that had helped the management exercise some control over what was becoming an increasingly chaotic environment. At that time, when the company desperately needed direction, the diminished influence of its management team and Sachin's withdrawal only worsened the situation.

Sachin and Binny finally took action in December. In a sweeping restructuring exercise, they announced a new hierarchy. Mekin Maheshwari was given a new role in Flipkart's digital products and services unit; Amod Malviya replaced him as the head of engineering. Ankit Nagori was told that his role had been cancelled. He was to now head the company's fashion category, a far smaller responsibility compared with his earlier position as the leader of all categories. It was a hard fall for him, especially painful as it happened soon after he returned to work from a two-week-long break to get married.

Apart from implementing these measures, Sachin decided to step back completely for some time. He told colleagues that he would take time out to work on new ideas for the business and return to a full-fledged role shortly. He was also supposed to represent Flipkart in the ED inquiry, which would be time-consuming. Until Sachin was ready to return, Binny would run the company. He was to directly oversee sales and operations, and the heads of all other functions would report to him. The reorganization jolted the company. Until now, it had been run in a collaborative, concerted manner by a close-knit group of senior employees. The restructuring suggested to Flipkart employees that suddenly Sachin and Binny had laid down the law, that they were unquestionably the bosses.

There would also be a new finance chief at Flipkart: Kalyan Krishnamurthy. Karandeep Singh, who had joined as CFO less than a year ago, was leaving after a disappointing stint. Flipkart had decided to appoint Kalyan, a Tiger Global executive, as interim CFO. It was, in a way, a rebuke to the Bansals – when investor representatives enter their portfolio companies, it is usually because the founders and their management team have stumbled.

Another startling outcome of the restructuring was the near-complete diminishment of Sujeet Kumar's role. While he had ostensibly moved to WS Retail a few months ago, it was assumed that Sujeet would continue in his role at Flipkart. But now that Binny had taken over sales and operations – Sujeet's dominion ever since he joined the company in 2008 – the erstwhile president was like a king without a kingdom.

Not surprisingly, in the months before the restructuring, Sachin and Binny had grown more and more uneasy about the influence Sujeet exerted at Flipkart. For some time, they had had concerns that Sujeet's crude manner could hurt Flipkart's image of a pioneering technology company. Their anxieties may even have been amplified by the *Forbes* story that had painted Sujeet as an insecure, power-hungry executive, an ultra-constitutional authority to whom even Sachin and Binny deferred because he was their senior from IIT Delhi. It was an implausible theory. The Bansals were the founders of the company; it is hard to imagine that seniority in college can solely determine the stature of an employee when billions of dollars are at stake. Rather, they had let him have a free hand mostly because he excelled in areas that neither of them had a knack for. Still, *Forbes*' presentation of the Bansals as weak and Sujeet as all-powerful was disconcerting.

It was a tricky situation for Sachin and Binny. On the one hand, Sujeet was a popular leader who had contributed more than anyone else towards establishing Flipkart's command in sales and operations. The functions he ran had been tremendously successful, apart from the last six months. The extroverted Sujeet had also been instrumental in cultivating a sense of fellowship at the company. On the other hand were the Bansals' fears about Sujeet's untamed manner and their insecurities about the outsized authority of any employee. Soon, in a decisive act, they would send a clear message to all employees that no one at Flipkart was indispensable.

13

THE TIGER CUB

In 2011, Lee Fixel had brought Kalyan Krishnamurthy over to Tiger Global from eBay. Kalyan had begun his career at Procter & Gamble, before moving to eBay where he worked in the company's finance operations for seven years.[1] Lee had initially interviewed Kalyan for the CFO position at Souq.com, a Dubai-based online retailer in which Tiger Global had invested. But Kalyan was hesitant about moving to Dubai, so Lee had asked him to join Tiger Global instead. Within a few months, Lee developed great confidence in Kalyan. He had sent Kalyan to Souq on assignment. The startup needed help in expanding its business. Kalyan had taken charge and turned Souq into a thriving, fast-growing firm, impressing Lee with his dynamism and acumen in sales and finance.

Now, Lee asked him to repeat his performance at Flipkart. The forty-one-year-old Kalyan was expected to bring his expertise to bear on matters such as sales management and setting profit margins. Sachin and Binny initially welcomed

Kalyan's appointment as they knew that the company was weak in these areas. But not wanting to lose control, they would watch his moves carefully.

Kalyan was familiar with Flipkart. He had been on its board of directors as the second representative from Tiger Global. Along with a junior Tiger Global colleague, he had also spent time with Flipkart's marketing team in the second part of 2012. Kalyan had tried to get Flipkart to cut its spending on brand advertising and focus on performance marketing instead. This would increase sales immediately – performance marketing was like an ad informing viewers about a discount sale. Brand advertising, on the other hand, mainly enhances a company's image; it may or may not deliver an immediate improvement in sales but is considered an important tool in enhancing a product or company's appeal. Kalyan believed that brand advertising was a largely wasteful exercise. On this matter, he would often clash with Flipkart's marketing head, Ravi Vora. What was the point of spending heavily on ads that didn't achieve much? Citing the example of the Kids campaign of 2011 that had transformed Flipkart's brand, Ravi would protest that the exact benefits of brand advertising could not always be quantified. 'But it's a well-established method of building a brand and customer loyalty,' he would say to Kalyan.

Kalyan had also pressed the Flipkart team to cut their budget for books and increase spending on promoting fashion products. Flipkart had started selling clothing and other fashion items in 2011 but the category hadn't taken off. This frustrated Lee Fixel, who had been urging the Bansals to develop the category. Of all products, it had the highest margins. By increasing fashion sales, Lee believed Flipkart could move towards generating profits without sacrificing sales growth. Books, on the other hand, were a drain on finances. Flipkart lost money on every book order and it was unlikely that the category would ever yield profits. In 2012, Kalyan urged the Flipkart marketing team, 'Forget books. Get people to buy T-shirts and shoes.' Flipkart did increase spending on fashion products, but it also continued to promote books.

When Kalyan formally moved to Flipkart in early 2013, it was hard to question his authority. In fact, many executives at the company feared for their jobs on learning that Kalyan would come on board in a full-fledged role. He was introduced to senior Flipkart leaders in January that year. Kalyan had appeared peremptory, belligerent. Right after the customary introductions, he had asked some of them, 'So why did the business go down when you guys were in charge?' It was evident he had come to crack the whip.

In his first few weeks at Flipkart, Kalyan was shocked to find out that the company was running its business without paying heed to contribution margins, a key metric for e-commerce companies. Starting with the implementation of a margin structure, Kalyan set about putting the finance function in order. Contracts with suppliers were renegotiated, better credit terms secured. A key project was devised to improve working capital. Within six months, the money Flipkart generated from operations was enough to fund its existing business. It was a major achievement – capital that was earlier being used to sustain the ongoing business was freed up for expansion. Consumed by its expansionary ambition, the company had been spending wantonly. Little effort had gone into making operations efficient. This was hurting Flipkart as it grew bigger.

As an e-commerce company expands, its cost per unit is expected to reduce. In theory, as this cost reduces, the increase in sales is supposed to ensure that the company becomes profitable at a certain scale. At Flipkart, profitability was out of reach and would be for many years, but Kalyan ensured that at least its unit costs were kept under control.

He assembled a small group, comprised of relatively junior managers. Kalyan gave these managers complete freedom to accomplish the tasks assigned to them. They fit a uniform description: around thirty, hungry to prove their worth, enthusiastic about taking on extra work, spending day and night at their desks. And they were completely prepared to swear their loyalty to Kalyan.

Kalyan's approach was straightforward, formulaic. He would tell his handpicked executives, '*Mujhe itna growth chahiye* – I want this much growth. Tell me what you need to get this done.'

One of Kalyan's trusted understudies was Nitin Kochhar, who had overseen the working capital project. Nitin had moved to Flipkart from ITC in 2012. He noticed that Kalyan had an uncanny ability to spot mid-level managers who could 'take the company to the next level', and let them loose. Kalyan preferred not to interfere, spending only an hour or two a month checking in with his team. According to Nitin, 'all he cared about was that targets were met'.

SACHIN HAD ALWAYS been the main man at Flipkart, with Binny close behind. But in 2013, as Sachin stepped back, it was Binny who took centre stage. When General Atlantic had pulled out of investing in Flipkart, Binny, too, had been rattled. But unlike Sachin, he recovered quickly.

Binny's approach and priorities differed from Sachin's. Sachin was instinctively drawn to the demand side of things. When he was in charge, Sachin had enjoyed being among the company's engineers, tinkering with the website to give it a pleasing, smooth interface which was continuously improved by new features. When Binny ran Flipkart in 2013, it was the supply side of the company that prospered more, especially in the technology function. Binny directed his energies towards strengthening the company's plumbing – the foundational structures that kept it all together. Taking Binny's cue, the company's leaders now adjusted their priorities. Amod Malviya, who had been made engineering head, had earlier worked mostly on the demand side. After his promotion, he became absorbed with building better technology for the supply chain function. Inventory planning, warehousing, pricing systems – these aspects improved significantly.

After the volatility of the previous year, Binny's leadership brought stability and acted as a unifying, central force. According to Ankit Nagori, who worked closely with both Binny and Kalyan in 2013, Binny did a 'great job' in keeping the company together. 'Binny would coordinate between the demand and supply teams and ensure everyone was on the same page.' He directly oversaw the warehousing and logistics function in this period, taking decisions on the number and size of new warehouses, hiring blue-collar workers and improving the efficiency of the company's warehousing processes.

In the second half of 2012, sales and customer service had suffered partly because the company had been overwhelmed by its headlong expansion into various businesses. At the end of the year, Binny reorganized the sales team, splitting it into three parts: books and general merchandise, electronics, and fashion. He shut down some categories like large electrical appliances, after acknowledging that the company had dived into them before being ready. The division of the sales team was one of the smartest moves Flipkart had made in months, as it brought back the focus and discipline that had vanished for the past half-year. It paid off almost instantly.

Under Ankit Nagori, the sales of fashion products began to briskly go up. Ankit had to prove himself all over again after the debacle of the previous year. By June 2013, the fashion category quadrupled – it had only taken six months. Flipkart promoted itself as an alternative to rivals like Myntra and Jabong by listing a vast merchandise of accessories such as belts, watches and sunglasses. It offered these products at deep discounts and used its excellent logistics network to deliver them quickly to customers. Ad campaigns promoting the fashion collection also served to accelerate the expansion in sales.

Nipun Mehra, a former Amazon executive and management consultant, was now given charge of the books and general merchandise section. In the early 2000s, he had ordered a T-shirt from a shopping website in India as a birthday gift for his brother. But the website delivered a beer mug instead. His mother was outraged – Nipun's brother was yet to turn twenty. In 2011, Nipun had been working in the US with the Boston Consulting Group, a management consultancy. On a visit to India, Nipun heard about Flipkart from a colleague who was praising its service. So, when the company's recruiters reached out to him for a job, he was intrigued. Having worked at Amazon's Seattle headquarters for four years, he had wondered why a large e-commerce business hadn't come up in India.

After interviews with a dozen Flipkart executives, he joined the company in July 2012. He had instantly hit it off with Binny. As he began working with Binny, Nipun found that the Flipkart co-founder was 'someone who was able to balance the everyday details and the big picture very well'.

As the head of the books division, Nipun extracted higher margins from publishers and distributors, rationalized discounts and expanded the selection of books. In May 2013, Flipkart launched a sale through which it sold a record number of books in a month. By the end of 2013, its dominance in books was such that offline chains like Crossword and Landmark, which were already struggling, were forced to shrink further.

But it was the electronics category at Flipkart that was on fire. This department was run by Amitesh Jha, an IIT Delhi graduate and a senior of Binny from the Shivalik hostel. After trying for years, Flipkart had finally started establishing direct relationships with Micromax, Samsung, HTC and other manufacturers of mobile phones and laptops. This helped the company gain access to some of their popular models. As with books and fashion, it offered these products at discounted prices. It introduced Equated Monthly Instalment (EMI) schemes and periodically held big sale events, becoming one of the fastest-growing retailers of electronic products in the country.

AS THE MONTHS went by in 2013, Kalyan's influence at Flipkart grew. Until his entry, the Bansals had had the last word on important matters. Now, suddenly, it wasn't really clear who was boss. On the surface, Sachin and Binny still had the final word. But as the representative of Flipkart's largest investor, Kalyan's authority was unquestionable. While his position – interim CFO – suggested that his involvement would be restricted to the finance function, Kalyan's influence began to spread rapidly.

Along with Binny, Kalyan would be present at the key sales meetings. In fact, the two worked well together. As the year progressed, Kalyan and Binny came to a tacit understanding that Binny would oversee operations while Kalyan would take charge of finance and sales. Kalyan had developed close relationships with many of the key sales leaders. He didn't have much to do with Flipkart's engineering team, which he believed was too slow in fixing errors and developing essential features. He didn't much care for the technological experiments that excited engineers, believing that the objective of the technology team should be to support the sales function. He made it clear that the sales department should be at the centre of Flipkart. The sales executives were elated – finally, here was a leader who had answered their prayers. Executives such as Ankit Nagori and Amitesh Jha enjoyed having Kalyan as their boss.

Although he was nominally an investor representative, Kalyan dispensed with hierarchy and formalism. Casually dressing down, he was always accessible. He spoke in Hindi and engaged directly with his colleagues. While he, too, had a ruthless streak, he was less volatile, and more predictable than the Bansals. Nearly a decade older than Flipkart's founders, Kalyan seemed more mature. His energetic, brisk manner of speaking was infectious, and his deep knowledge of e-commerce validated his authority. Every time one of his trusted associates asked him for something, Kalyan would say, '*Kar le tu* – go for it.' He ran the business as a finance expert would: with a sharp focus on sales, margins and cash flow.

By the end of 2013, Kalyan had fixed the company's finance function. But it wasn't that he had cut spending; he had rationalized and rationed it, created a sound financial framework. The main objective of this framework was to allow Flipkart to pour *a lot more* money into the pursuit of sales growth. Under Kalyan, the company's spending on discounts increased significantly. In 2013, rival websites such as Homeshop18, eBay and Snapdeal had started a price war. Kalyan instructed his team, 'Whatever their price is, we'll be five per cent lower.' He pointed out that the retail market was huge, and e-commerce a minuscule, insignificant part of it. Investors weren't interested in a retailer growing moderately and losing (or earning) a small amount of money. What drew them was whirlwind growth – this is what fetched a company high valuations. Both Kalyan and his boss, Lee, were experts at working out what investors wanted in a company, and at constructing business strategies that made for compelling investment stories.

What helped Kalyan extend his influence at Flipkart was his relationship with Lee. Only an investor representative could give quick, unequivocal instructions on perilous matters such as spending huge amounts of cash on discounts. A former Flipkart employee recalls, 'Earlier we were always nervous about burning too much. But when Kalyan came and told us to increase discounting, there was no fear because we knew that whatever he was doing, it was with Lee's blessings. We were able to move fast and not worry whether it was the right thing to do or not.'

RUMOURS ABOUT AMAZON's launch had been circulating in e-commerce circles for almost two years. In May 2013, Flipkart got wind that Amazon was indeed launching operations in India the following month. The company prepared for war, its executives wary, but excited. They believed that Flipkart's hold over the market was so strong that even a giant like Amazon would struggle to break it.

To prepare for Amazon's launch, the company had been developing software to manoeuvre product prices on the website. Until 2013, prices had been set manually on Excel sheets. This was no longer viable. The company's assortment of products was ever-expanding, running into millions; it would be foolish to delay the use of technology in price-setting. Without software, the company would lack the means to respond quickly to pricing changes on rival sites. In early 2013, it began building the new technology, which would collect product prices from across its competitors and adjust its own accordingly. Flipkart was determined to match Amazon's prices, whenever it launched.

It was common knowledge that Amazon would kickstart with books. Flipkart executives came to know that Amazon had planned a big surprise to announce its arrival in style. The company had persuaded a few well-known authors to deliver books to customers in person. Nipun Mehra, Flipkart's books head, was worried. If Amazon marked its entry with a big bang, it would spell trouble for Flipkart – and for Nipun. He called up his contacts at publishing houses and told them, 'I can't tell you to not do something for someone else. But if you're doing it for them, then you have to do it for me as well.' Reluctantly, they agreed. Flipkart even managed to get some authors to do book deliveries before Amazon's plans got underway.

Amazon launched its India website in the first week of June. On 4 June 2013, the pricing team at Flipkart worked through the night. It was worth the effort. Amazon launched at midnight, and by 4 a.m. Flipkart was matching its prices. The next day, Flipkart executives noted with satisfaction the tweets from users pointing to the pricing parity between the two sites.

Flipkart had ensured Amazon's launch was rather subdued. But this was just the start. Amazon was here to stay. It was going to be a long war.

IN 2013, INDIA'S economy was struggling. After overseeing the country's most prosperous period in its first five-year term beginning in 2004, the Congress-led government under Manmohan Singh was mired in corruption scandals. In the final phase of its second term, it had run out of ideas; its end couldn't come fast enough. The rupee had slumped, inflation was high and economic growth had slowed down. The expansion of the economy in the previous decade seemed like a fleeting surge out of a morass, only for it to be dragged back in when its limited energy was exhausted. The government's combative taxation moves had put off businesses, which had also been complaining about a 'policy paralysis' for years.[2] Investments by companies, many of which were also plagued with internal problems, dropped. Big business was recovering from the excesses of the 2000s. IT and telecom companies, the standout performers of the previous decade, showed lacklustre performance. Narayana Murthy had returned to Infosys, but he couldn't seem to halt the company's slide into mediocrity.[3]

E-commerce was no different. Out of the fifty-three e-commerce firms that had received venture capital since 2010, less than a dozen managed to raise more money.[4] Soon, many would vanish, either forced shut or sold at fire-sale prices.

Out of this gloom, a new corporate star was emerging: Flipkart. By the middle of 2013, its sales had nearly doubled in just six months. Its finances were improving rapidly. Its service had recovered its earlier excellence. Customers seemed to love the brand again; lakhs of new users were signing up every month. Flipkart was now an established retail brand. It was no longer just a seller of books that happened to peddle other goods. In fact, books now contributed to less than a fifth of the company's sales by value. The diversity in the business greatly enhanced the company's standing with investors, as did its improving finances.

In July 2013, Flipkart raised a new round of capital, pulling in as much as $200 million. Its existing investors Tiger Global, Naspers, Accel Partners and Iconiq Capital, all chipped in. There was a party at Shaktipeeth. Senior leaders, including Kalyan, danced. In an emphatic statement, Sachin declared, 'It's a big validation of Flipkart and Indian e-commerce. There have recently been a lot of sceptics in the media and in business circles who have questioned – rightly so – whether e-commerce is healthy and whether Flipkart is running the way it should be, whether it has the right strategy. This event should put those questions to rest.'[5]

Three months later, the number of sceptics would reduce further. In October, Flipkart announced another injection of cash – this time it had raised $160 million from four new investors, Dragoneer Investment, Morgan Stanley Investment

Management, Sofina and Vulcan Capital Management.[6] By the close of financial year 2012–13, Flipkart's losses had soared to ₹644.37 crore. But investors were taken by the growth in revenues, which now stood at ₹1,163.1 crore.[7]

Finally, Flipkart's valuation jumped to more than $1 billion. It was a monster in India's tiny startup ecosystem. Earlier that year, Redbus, a startup that sold bus tickets, had been bought by Naspers. Redbus was one of the biggest and most successful startups in India. Its sale price was $135 million, only about a tenth of Flipkart's valuation.[8] Flipkart was in a league of its own. Its two recent funding rounds had been orchestrated by Lee Fixel – purveyor of legendary investment stories – and Sachin. Although, by this point, the Flipkart story was writing itself.

14

HELLO, MOTO

When temporarily stepping back from his role, Sachin Bansal had imagined he would return to the driver's seat in the near future. But that wasn't to be. He ended up spending much of 2013 outside Flipkart. The Enforcement Directorate's inquiry proved to be demanding. It required him, as Flipkart's representative, and Tapas Rudrapatna, as WS Retail's delegate, to make several visits to Delhi. There, government officials grilled the two about the relationship between Flipkart and WS Retail. But by the end of the year, the inquiry was losing its intensity. Sachin gradually became convinced that the company would be let off. The structure Flipkart had created for itself and for WS Retail was a classic example of abiding by the 'letter of the law rather than the spirit'.[1]

Apart from the ED's inquiry, Sachin had also been preoccupied with the fundraising exercise that not only secured Flipkart's immediate future but had also elevated it to the status of India's most outstanding young company. The fund raise had also resulted in a tremendous increase in Sachin and Binny's wealth. Back in Chandigarh, Sachin built a large house for his family and bought another Mercedes. The house was a statement of his prosperity, an indisputable mark of high status and power in his family circles.

Sachin was also crowned Entrepreneur of the Year at the 2013 ET Awards, an event organized by the *Economic Times*.[2] He accepted the award in the presence of India's biggest business tycoons. It announced his arrival as a promising new player in the corporate world. The award was proffered to him by none other than P. Chidambaram, India's finance minister at the time. The irony was impossible to miss – the award came at the end of a year in which Sachin had been interrogated by the financial police of the government.

Sachin had, in fact, begun to grow restless within his company. Dealing with the regulatory inquiry and fronting the fundraising discussions were essential tasks, but they were removed from the company's business operations. On the periphery of daily affairs at Flipkart, he had to watch the company thrive from a distance. It was unsettling. Sachin had loved being in charge, directing the company, taking it onto new, unexplored avenues. He enjoyed the power, the successes – the thrill of entrepreneurship was beckoning him back.

But in what way could Sachin go back? What would he do now at Flipkart? The company's growth in 2013 owed much to its strong foundation created largely through Sachin's vision and key insights about cash payments and a flexible returns policy. But it was now one year since Sachin had stepped back; the dynamism of the internet space is such that even a short spell on the sidelines can lead to a loss of understanding, and disorientation.

Still, Sachin was determined to find a way back. When he was in charge, the engineers had been the masters of the company, at least in his view. Every month he would ask his team, 'What new features have we built for our customers?'

Now, under Binny and Kalyan, the sales team had become ascendant, and the technology team only played a supporting role. This was unacceptable to Sachin. Towards the end of 2013, he began to complain to colleagues that Flipkart had stopped 'innovating' and was being run in a 'blindly tactical' manner. According to a former Flipkart executive, Sachin was especially peeved with the company's product function. He wasn't happy that Flipkart had failed to produce exciting new features on its website. Sachin noticed that engineers had become subservient to their sales counterparts, and weren't 'creating new experiences for customers'. While this was true, according to the executive, it had its benefits. 'It wasn't like the sales team was asking the engineers to make random features.'

Sachin had watched Kalyan's growing stature with alarm. Their relationship wasn't great. Kalyan was a straight-up *dhanda* guy. He had little time for technological tinkering that didn't provide a direct, immediate boost to sales. He thought of Flipkart as a retail business whose sole purpose was to grow its sales as fast as it could, through the most economic means, and thereby increase its valuation. Sachin, on the other hand, thought of himself as a technologist and inventor, and of Flipkart as a company that was using the power of software to offer a high-quality commerce service. Their personalities, too, were mismatched. Kalyan sometimes travelled with Sachin for meetings with investors, recounting later to his friends that these were awkward trips, filled with long silences and conversations that ended as abruptly as they would begin. Kalyan was an extroverted leader who liked shooting the breeze with his trusted colleagues; Sachin was an inward-looking engineer, inherently awkward around people, whom he found less interesting than his video games.

Nevertheless, it was clear to Sachin and Binny that many people at Flipkart, especially executives in the sales and finance functions, enjoyed working with Kalyan. Sachin may not have been happy about it, but there was no denying that Kalyan with his single-mindedness had helped transform Flipkart from a promising startup into a highly efficient machine ruthlessly achieving its goals every week, every month, every quarter. Lee Fixel was insistent that the interim CFO prolong his stay at the company. Besides, even Binny held Kalyan in high esteem.

In December 2013, despite Sachin's reservations, Kalyan was rewarded with the role of Head of Categories – Retail. The move legitimized Kalyan's growing influence at the company. He had initially moved to Flipkart for a few quarters to help fix its finance function; it was now clear he would be here much longer.

Despite promoting Kalyan, Sachin continued to express disapproval at the way Flipkart was being run. One of his more persistent complaints had to do with the slow progress of the company's mobile business. He pointed out that customers were increasingly using their phones to browse and shop. Soon, the launch of 4G connections and the introduction of cheaper smartphones would trigger a huge shift in browsing from desktops to the mobile. Yet, Flipkart remained stuck in the 'desktop era'. Its mobile app and mobile site were substandard, Sachin moaned. And they weren't improving fast enough. He would often raise hell with the engineers working on the mobile technology team. In turn, they would vent to their bosses, '*Humare haath dho ke peechhe padha hai Sachin.* He is being relentlessly demanding. Can't you tell him to go easy on us?'

IN EARLY 2013, a recruiter had reached out to Michael Adnani on behalf of Flipkart. The fifty-something Michael was a veteran of the American retail and technology sectors. He was employed at the Chicago offices of Sears, the retail pioneer that was struggling to survive, partly because of Amazon's rise. The recruiter told Michael that an upcoming Indian e-commerce firm called Flipkart was looking for a senior sales executive. Michael was intrigued. Not only was he unaware of Flipkart, he had never even visited India. After a few conversations with the Bansals, Michael realized that they had reached out to him because his last name, Adnani, sounded Indian. Michael was, in reality, an Iranian-American who had lived in the US most of his life. But the conversations had gone well, so they continued to stay in touch.

Flipkart had reached out to him because the Bansals were keen to prepare a long-term strategy to keep Amazon at bay. While Amazon's launch had been a meek affair, they knew that the American company would soon turn into a serious rival. Amazon was struggling in China, which meant India was the last big retail market that remained unconquered. It was obvious that Amazon would throw its might behind succeeding here. Its country manager in India, Amit Agarwal, was a highly regarded leader. Amit had also led Amazon India when the Bansals worked there as junior engineers. His appointment was proof that Amazon wanted to avoid the mistakes that had crippled its China venture, where its management team had felt unfamiliar, unable to grasp the nuances of its retail market. (Amit was the same Amazon leader who had laughed off Sachin's asking price of $1 billion for Flipkart in 2011.) Michael, on the other hand, had worked at companies that had been through the trying experience of an Amazon onslaught. The Bansals believed that his experience would be useful in the coming years.

It wasn't just Amazon; Flipkart had another rival to consider: Snapdeal. The company's shift to e-commerce was going well. Its CEO Kunal Bahl had made a bold announcement that Snapdeal would register gross sales of ₹2,000 crore in the financial year 2013–14. Taking a dig at Flipkart, he said that its inventory model was 'dead', and touted the superiority of Snapdeal's bazaar.[3] Actually, despite its fast growth, Snapdeal was a distant second to Flipkart. But Kunal was an articulate, persuasive young man, a consummate salesman. In early 2013, he persuaded eBay – the inspiration for Snapdeal's new avatar – to invest in the company.[4] The investment, which was announced just a day before Amazon's entry into India, included a commercial partnership between Snapdeal and eBay.[5] Snapdeal had snagged a highly credible name in the e-commerce world. It was unsettling for the Bansals to see a local rival being strengthened thus, even as a renowned international giant was entering the fray.

After many months of talks, Michael joined Flipkart in late 2013 as the head of its electronics business. Sales of electronics products were increasing rapidly, but the heavier spending on discounts was also pushing up losses. Michael pointed out to his colleagues that their method wouldn't endure. He explained that one could cut prices to boost sales, but ultimately, the P&L would suggest that it had all been in vain. This would be self-destructive, the surest way of losing to Amazon, which was brutally competitive. He warned, 'There will be no Flipkart in 2015.'

Along with his teammates, Amitesh Jha and Sandeep Karwa, Michael devised a new plan: exclusivity. They would convince certain phone brands to sell their products only on Flipkart. It was a wildly ambitious idea. While e-commerce was expanding, an overwhelming majority of Indians still did all of their shopping in physical stores. And even though brands had grown more accepting of e-commerce, they hadn't embraced it. They used online retailers primarily to clear out stocks of old phones. Some brands had reluctantly agreed to allow pre-orders on Flipkart – it was free of risk. But restricting the sale of their latest products to a shopping website was inconceivable to them. Even Flipkart executives were incredulous. When Michael presented the exclusivity idea, Sachin responded, 'Are you kidding me?'

Michael met with the leaders of some of the biggest phone-makers – Samsung, Apple and Micromax. As Sachin had warned, Michael's idea met with laughter and ridicule. One executive scoffed, 'Flipkart is just another website. You sell a few thousand phones. We don't even think this e-commerce is going to last.'

But Michael persisted, with a tweak to his plan: he would find brands that needed Flipkart as much as it needed them. One of the phone companies that Flipkart had been in talks with even before Michael came on board was Motorola. Once the world's leading mobile phone brand, Motorola had lost its way. It was now trying to recapture its glory days. Sandeep Karwa, the team leader for Flipkart's mobiles business, had been tipped off by a collegemate about Motorola's India plans. Flipkart also reached out to Xiaomi, a Chinese startup that was winning praise for its cheap, high-quality smartphones. But Xiaomi was undecided about entering India. Motorola, on the other hand, had been working on its India launch for months. Flipkart's talks with Motorola had gone well. In January 2014, Michael, Amitesh and Sandeep flew to Delhi to meet their team one last time. Before leaving, Michael – whose desk was next to the Flipkart founders' – mentioned to Sachin where he was going, only to be dismissively laughed off.

All the key leaders of Motorola were present at the meeting. They said they were willing to work with Flipkart, but not exclusively. Moto G, the phone with which it would launch in India, had been well received in other markets. The obvious strategy in India would be to sell it in stores nationwide, and Motorola was inclined to do just that. But the Flipkart executives deployed a mix of flattery, persuasion and admonition to convince the company to discard that plan. They warned the Motorola team that the phone was overpriced, that the overheads of sales demos, advertising, and so on, would add up. Very soon, Micromax and Samsung would undercut Motorola, weakening them yet again. They'd exited the market once before and were now just repeating old mistakes.

Instead, Michael and his colleagues implored Motorola to sell only through Flipkart, which would bear all logistics and marketing costs. Motorola could take the opportunity to lower the phone's price and make it more enticing for customers. To be able to cut prices without losing margins was tempting for the company. What clinched the deal was Flipkart assuming obligation of selling 125,000 Moto G phones in six months. By now, Kalyan, the newly appointed sales head, had also grown confident about the proposed deal. He backed his team's efforts to woo Motorola. The financial risk was now Flipkart's. In the bargain, Motorola had reduced the price of the phone by more than fifteen per cent, a substantial swing in an ultra-competitive business.

In early February 2014, at a flashy event in Delhi, the companies jointly announced the launch of the Moto G phone. Flipkart had also prepared a national advertising campaign, which included featuring the phone on the front pages of newspapers. At midnight, several hours before readers would discover the ads, Flipkart launched the Moto G sale. Within five minutes, the company had sold 10,000 units, the quantity it had expected to sell in a month. The deluge of customers was so strong that, within twenty minutes of the sale opening, the site crashed. Another 15,000 units had been sold. At the Flipkart office, Sandeep Karwa was alarmed. He immediately called his boss Amitesh and said, 'There's been an attack on the site. Something's wrong.'[6]

The huge demand had a flip side: it seemed that Flipkart would soon run out of stock. People were going to wake up in the morning to Motorola's ad campaign. Going to Flipkart's website would be like walking into an empty store – a disaster for the company. Acting on instinct, Sandeep's team created a banner on the site, 'Thank you for the overwhelming response. We are out of stock.' The sale would resume later in the day. Sandeep was breaking all kinds of rules within Flipkart – a banner like that had to be approved by many bosses. But this was important. And there was no time to check with anyone. If he didn't act instantly, Flipkart's brand would suffer serious damage, which would probably put his job on the line.

The rationing turned out to be a smart move. It saved Flipkart from public embarrassment. Many customers were able to place orders in the morning. By the end of the day, Flipkart had sold more than 100,000 Moto G phones. Its six-month target would be achieved in one week.[7]

The launch of the iPhone in 2007 had transformed Apple's business. It was the 2009 launch of the 'Like' feature for Facebook. For Flipkart, which had seen so many highs already, it would be this Moto G sale.

In February 2014, Flipkart raked in gross sales of $1 billion on an annualized basis.[8] The company had achieved its goal with a year to spare. When Sachin had announced the outrageous target in early 2011, Flipkart's gross sales were barely around $10 million. In less than three years, the company had grown by a multiple of one hundred.

15

ANOTHER BANSAL JOINS THE FAMILY

By 2014, only a few e-commerce companies had displayed the ability and stamina to stay the course. One of these was Myntra, whose CEO, Mukesh Bansal, had remained on friendly terms with Sachin and Binny. They had started their companies around the same time. Even though Flipkart was now the bigger company by a great measure, Myntra was successful in its own right.

It was the largest online seller of fashion in the country. Its website, with a pleasing interface, was considered superior to other shopping sites and enjoyed a loyal following. Its order delivery was speedy and reliable. Myntra was growing fast, generating healthy margins and continuously improving its service. But in 2013, when Myntra hit the market to raise fresh capital, it found few takers. Investors were generally pessimistic about the Indian economy. They told Mukesh that they would wait until the results of the national elections next year before investing further in the country. They were also wary of financing a startup that was competing with Flipkart, which seemed to have an inexhaustible supply of capital. It was deeply frustrating for Mukesh. In his own words, 'The feedback from most of the investors was: "We are interested and we like what you are doing, but not now." But we needed money then so "not now" was not very helpful.'[1] By the end of the year, the company had just a few more months' worth of cash left. Finally, in early 2014, it persuaded Premji Invest, the family office of Wipro founder Azim Premji, to invest in the company. Myntra was saved from disaster, but for Mukesh the experience had been disconcerting.

By this time, Sachin Bansal had already reached out to Mukesh. Their common investors, Tiger Global and Accel Partners, had been encouraging Flipkart to buy Myntra. They reasoned that Flipkart's war with Amazon, which had just begun, would be long and draining. It made little sense for the Flipkart investors to continue backing two companies doing similar things. But initially, Sachin wasn't convinced. He said to the investors, 'We will win in fashion regardless. Flipkart is a technology company. We don't need acquisitions to grow our business.'

A few months later, Sachin came around to his investors' proposal. By early 2014, a couple of Flipkart executives were championing it as well. Vaibhav Gupta, an IIT Delhi graduate who had become the seniormost finance leader under Kalyan Krishnamurthy, and Ankit Nagori, who had redeemed himself by developing Flipkart's fashion business, separately made the case for the Myntra buyout. Flipkart's fashion sales had multiplied in the last year. Still, Myntra had held its own and maintained its leadership position in the category. An alliance between the two would be formidable – perhaps essential – as fashion was a category that Flipkart simply had to win. Not only did fashion allow for the highest margins, many business analysts had predicted that it would become the largest category in e-commerce within a few years. And this was where Amazon was vulnerable – in the US and other international markets, fashion retailers had continued to thrive despite Amazon's overall dominance.

The discussions between the two companies lasted nearly six months. Finally, in May 2014, the merger was finalized. At a press event in Bangalore, Mukesh went on stage to say that he had an 'exciting' announcement to make. After a pause, he added, 'Let me introduce two colleagues of mine.' Out walked Sachin and Binny.[2] 'Flipkart and Myntra are getting together to create one of the largest e-commerce stories and together we will dominate the market,' Sachin declared.[3]

Flipkart had agreed to buy Myntra for about $330 million, mostly with company stock. Myntra would continue to operate as an independent entity. For Sachin and Binny, one of the attractions of buying Myntra had been to enlist the services of Mukesh, whom they regarded as an exceptional entrepreneur. Mukesh was given charge of Flipkart's fashion business and he also retained responsibility of running Myntra.

The deal made Mukesh and his Myntra co-founder, Ashutosh Lawania, very rich men. Mukesh would eventually become one of the largest individual shareholders in Flipkart while Ashutosh would be worth more than ₹150 crore. Myntra's senior employees, too, received large payouts. It was a big day not just for the two companies but for the entire startup ecosystem. The deal was by far the biggest ever in India's internet sector. Until now, investors had poured money into startups for many years with almost no returns to show for it. This deal finally offered evidence that, in the end, startup investing could be very rewarding indeed.

In May 2014, a few days after the Myntra buyout, Flipkart made another spectacular announcement: the company had received $210 million in a funding round led by DST Global, a Russian investment firm.[4] Headed by billionaire venture capitalist Yuri Milner, DST had made its name by spotting the early promise of startups such as Facebook, Twitter and Alibaba. It was a mark of prestige for Flipkart to bag DST as an investor. As with Naspers and many of its other investors, DST had been introduced to Flipkart by Lee Fixel, who had been investing together with the Russian firm for many years.

Such was the momentum in Flipkart's business that in less than a year its valuation had more than doubled – to $2.5 billion.

16

A BILLION DREAMS

All technology companies crave the glorious moment in which they can let the world know that they have arrived. It could be with the launch of an exciting new product, a big acquisition, a public listing of shares, or even the hiring of a renowned chieftain.

In 2014, Flipkart experienced not one, but many such moments. By June, the company had already witnessed its most successful product launch with the Moto G phone, become the first Indian e-commerce firm to record $1 billion in gross sales, and completed the buyout of Myntra, a sector-changing deal.

But its biggest moment, one that immediately turned India into a global internet battleground, was yet to come. Less than two months after agreeing the funding round with DST Global, the Bansals ushered in a new era for themselves, for Flipkart, and for Indian startups. In the last week of July 2014, Flipkart announced that it had raised as much as $1 billion.[1] This funding round, too, had been orchestrated by Lee Fixel, along with the

Bansals. Lee's firm, Tiger Global, contributed about a quarter of the capital. Other large contributions came from existing investors such as Naspers and Accel Partners and new investors including GIC, Singapore's sovereign wealth fund. For an Indian company to raise this kind of equity capital in private markets was unprecedented. Not just in India, globally, too, there were just a few other companies that had received such a large capital infusion all at once. For the Flipkart investors, it seemed foolish to pass up the chance to load up a company that was growing so fast. Flipkart, for its part, knew that it needed to arm itself for the long war ahead with Amazon.

Flipkart's worth now increased to $7 billion, more than twice of what it had fetched only two months ago. It had become one of the most prized internet startups in the world, one of the most valuable private companies in India. Its valuation exceeded that of all other Indian internet startups put together. Until that point, Flipkart had seen itself as a rebellious startup, an underdog with its back to the wall, striving to prove that it was a serious business with seriously big ambitions. It had never been properly accepted as a significant player by corporate India. The big global technology investors, too, had viewed the company, and the Indian market, with something approaching boredom. All of this changed in one moment. The billion-dollar funding round transformed the company's place in the world. As Sachin summed it up, 'We were a little kid waiting to grow up. Now we have grown up.'[2]

That year, a great deal of optimism about India spread both inside and outside the country. After adopting capitalism on its own terms in the early eighties, China had realized a transformative economic boom. Some of the biggest beneficiaries of this boom, and of the Chinese model of state-controlled, nationalistic capitalism, were its internet companies such as Alibaba, JD.com, Tencent and Baidu. In the mid-noughties, more than a decade after liberalization, India, too, looked like it could achieve an economic miracle of its own. But after a promising first term, the Congress government, led by Manmohan Singh, had faltered badly. In the 2014 general elections, Hindu nationalist politician Narendra Modi irrepressibly rose to power as the head of the BJP government. Many voters overlooked his troubling past, when, as Chief Minister of Gujarat, he was criticized for not actively thwarting the 2002 state riots that had led to the massacre of hundreds of people, mostly Muslims. In 2014, Modi, with his slogan '*Sabka Saath, Sabka Vikas*', was seen as a business-friendly, technology-savvy reformer who would get India back on track and deliver prodigious economic growth.

Welcoming Modi's victory, business leaders and investors who had been sulking for the last three years, brimmed with hope again. But no company was more ebullient than Flipkart. Why couldn't two Indians create a great Indian internet firm – this was the ambition that had spurred Sachin and Binny to leave Amazon India and start Flipkart against the advice of almost everyone they knew. Now, here they were, seven years later, with the dream within their grasp. Even their colleagues, people who had worked closely with them for many years, were in awe. The Bansals were keenly aware of their new supreme status.

In the halls of Flipkart's headquarters, Binny referred to the funding round in mysteriously dramatic fashion. He said to a colleague, '*Funding ho rahi hai* – we're raising another round of funds.'

'*Kitni?*' How much?

'*Bahut badi.*' Massive.

'*Kitni badi?*' How massive?

Without saying a word, Binny simply raised one finger.[3]

On the night of the billion-dollar funding announcement, a group of Flipkart leaders, including Sachin and Binny, had gone to a nearby bar in Koramangala to celebrate. In the middle of revelries, the bar's television played one of the many interviews the Bansals had given that day. Everyone stopped to watch the interview and the attendant reels of adulatory headlines in silence, as it sunk in that Flipkart – and the Bansals – had just levelled up to an entirely new league.

Sachin savoured the billion dollars more than anyone else. For the second time in a few months, his favourite number had been realized. When Sachin spoke after the fund raise, it was clear that he believed he was a man of destiny. 'This is a big milestone not just for Flipkart, but for internet firms in India in general. We believe India can produce a $100 billion company [in sales] in the next five years, and we want to be that. Whether it takes five or ten years, we are here for the longer term.'[4]

He was saying that he wanted to build The Great Indian Internet Company.

WOULD FLIPKART BECOME India's greatest internet company? Could it achieve revenues of $100 billion? In five years? Or ten? Was Sachin Bansal India's answer to Jeff Bezos and Jack Ma?

At least one thing was certain: Bezos was going to have a part in framing the answers to all these questions. The legendary CEO and founder of Amazon was pained by his company's collapse in China. This made his desire to succeed in India even more intense.

The day after Flipkart revealed the $1 billion fund raise, Bezos announced that Amazon would invest as much as $2 billion in India. Emphasizing the 'huge potential' of India's economy and its e-commerce market, he predicted that India could become the fastest country in Amazon's history to deliver a billion dollars in gross sales. He finished with a flourish: 'A big "thank you" to our customers in India – we've never seen anything like this.'[5]

Two months later, Bezos visited India on a publicity tour. He met with the new prime minister and spent time with the Amazon India team. On a Sunday morning, outside the Amazon office in the World Trade Centre building in northern Bangalore, Bezos put his flamboyance on full display. Decked in a white *bandhgala* and maroon *dupatta*, he stood on top of a truck of local make, and handed Amit Agarwal, the head of the India business, a mock blown-up cheque of $2 billion, as the media clicked photographs. As if this wasn't enough, later in the day, amid many guffaws, Bezos proclaimed to journalists that the India business was 'extremely important'[6] to him, and that Amazon had 'blown past the initial set of goals'[7] here. The message was clear: Amazon would do whatever it took to win in India.

At Flipkart, Sachin Bansal woudn't bite. He called Bezos' visit to the country a 'panic reaction to the fact that Amazon is not able to make any inroads in India.' He boasted that Flipkart's market share had only increased that year.[8]

A month after the Bezos publicity blitz, another firm joined the party. In October 2014, Snapdeal, which was still

India's second-largest e-commerce firm, announced that it had received more than $600 million from the Japanese investor SoftBank Group. Kunal Bahl had successfully positioned the company as an anti-Flipkart. He had persuaded his investors that e-commerce was a battle of business models in which his vision of a bazaar would prevail over the inventory-led operations of both Flipkart and Amazon. His confidence, charisma and showmanship had won SoftBank over, and diverted them from the fundamental weaknesses of the company, poor logistical and warehousing infrastructure being some of them. Even startup investors outside Snapdeal began to believe that Kunal, in fact, was the real visionary entrepreneur who would build a bigger business than Flipkart and Amazon while spending far lesser. While announcing the SoftBank funding, Kunal couldn't resist taking a dig at his rivals. He said in an interview that Snapdeal didn't hold inventory, and that 'we don't do private label because we don't want to compete with our sellers'. Everything he denounced in this part of the interview were essential features of the business models of Flipkart and Amazon.[9] It was now officially a three-way war.

Along with showering Snapdeal with cash, SoftBank invested in two other startups: Ola, an online cab company, and Housing, a real-estate portal. That wasn't all. SoftBank's founder Masayoshi Son announced that he would plough $10 billion into Indian companies over the next decade. In any other year, that estimate, so apparently wanton, may have been met with scepticism. But not in 2014. And not when Son was involved. Son invested in tech businesses with an unmatched zeal. Despite being driven to the edge of ruin during the dotcom bust, he continued to strike big deals in the telecoms business and pour cash into unproven tech ventures. His faith had borne fruit: SoftBank's stake in Alibaba, the largest e-commerce company in China, was worth a fortune. He was keen to invest in India, a nascent, but evidently promising market.

By now, a serious funding boom for startups was underway.[10] Yet again, the herd mentality of investors was on display. Like the e-commerce funding boom of early 2010 triggered by Tiger Global's outsized injection of $10 million in Flipkart, the whopping $1 billion investment in the same company organized by the same fund had set in motion an investment frenzy in 2014. This cycle would be far more intense than that of 2010–11 when it was restricted to just e-commerce startups. This time, not only e-commerce companies but even startups delivering food and groceries, providing electrical repairs and plumbing services, brand hotels, websites selling crafts, sporting goods and women's clothing, found takers.

Many of these companies were launched by engineers who were barely out of college. Suddenly, internet entrepreneurship – long considered an unserious, feeble initiative, had become fashionable. Thousands of young men – they were almost always men – in engineering colleges ventured into entrepreneurship, certain that the surest, easiest way to become rich, acquire fame, get laid, was to become a startup founder. Engineering degrees obtained, they were going to transform India by harnessing the power of technology. Chastened grey-haired venture capital investors who had lorded it over entrepreneurs reversed course, now chasing these young nerds, begging them to take their money.

What had prompted this startling turn, this outpouring of love and capital on Indian startups, was the coming together of a few disparate events. Perhaps the most important factor was the astonishing wealth creation in the internet ecosystem of China. In May 2014, China's second-largest online retailer, JD.com, had gone public at a valuation of more than $25 billion.[11] A few months later, in September, JD's bigger rival, Alibaba, listed its shares in the US. It was a record offering, valuing the company at more than $225 billion.[12] This made Alibaba the world's most valuable e-commerce company, its market capitalization easily exceeding that of Amazon and eBay. Alibaba's rise had been many years in the making. Founded in 1999 by an English teacher named Jack Ma, Alibaba had vanquished Amazon and eBay by dint of its agility and superior local knowledge, as some accounts suggested.[13] Over the years, it had mushroomed into an internet conglomerate with interests in retail, payments, logistics, gaming and various other areas. The public listings of JD.com and Alibaba had resulted in a tremendous windfall for its backers. Tiger Global, the largest investor in Flipkart, was also an early investor in JD.com, while SoftBank owned as much as a third of Alibaba. The Alibaba listing valued SoftBank's stake at more than $75 billion and made Masayoshi Son the richest man in Japan.[14] Many other Alibaba investors profited as well.

Enriched by their bets on Chinese internet companies, these venture capitalists as well as investment firms in the US, Europe and Asia that had missed out on the Chinese boom, flocked to India in search of their next loot. In October 2014, Son came to India after nearly a decade. To his eye, India was the China of a few years ago. In New Delhi, he told a newspaper reporter, 'Ten years ago, China was the best opportunity, and now India has the best opportunity.'[15]

Twenty-five years earlier, another corporate VIP had expressed a similar view. Jack Welch, chairman of the American conglomerate General Electric, had predicted that India and China were the new big markets of the future.[16] Even at the turn of the century, hopeful analysts and consultants had posited that the two countries would become 'superpowers', more or less simultaneously. It didn't matter that by then China's economy was already about three times the size of India's. It was the same belief that had prompted investors to bet on offline retailers in the 2000s. They were convinced that India would go China's way and rapidly modernize its retail sector. However, this never happened. Even after nearly two decades of continuous investment, modern retail had a paltry reach in India.[17] In fact, Kishore Biyani, India's would-be Sam Walton, had been forced to sell off key businesses in order to repay debts.[18]

By 2014, China's economy was five times as large as India's. Despite this, investors reverted to their old conviction, certain that India's internet space would turn out to be a goldmine. On the surface, it did have a few similarities with China's internet sector of the noughties. Every month, millions of new Indians were using the internet for the first time on cheap but powerful smartphones. The bulging internet population was poised to expand even faster as prices of mobile internet connections fell. The introduction of 4G services would result in lightning internet speeds.

And then there was Flipkart, the indigenous e-commerce champion standing tall, proving that Indian entrepreneurs could indeed make it big in the internet business.

17

THE COMEBACK

By the time of the billion-dollar fund raise, Sachin Bansal was fighting his own battles within Flipkart.

In the eighteen months that Sachin had been on the margins of the company, it had turned into a retailing juggernaut. After taking the reins in late 2012, Binny had strengthened Flipkart's spine. Kalyan Krishnamurthy, on secondment from Tiger Global, had vastly improved the finance function and empowered the sales team. Under Amod Malviya, Flipkart's technological edge over rivals had widened. The logistics fleet, technically owned by WS Retail, was expanding at a dizzying pace under Sujeet Kumar, who had returned from exile to lead the company's relaunch of its large electronics category and then its supply chain. Vaibhav Gupta, a former McKinsey consultant, had emerged from anonymity to lead the business finance function which, along with the sales division, had become the driving force of the company. Ankit Nagori had been promoted to lead the company's marketplace business.

Flipkart had started this initiative of adding third-party sellers on its platform in 2013, to address regulatory concerns about its structure as well as expand its assortment of goods. These executives, along with other senior leaders at Flipkart, made a formidable team. But it was a team that had little room for Sachin. In fact, many of these executives had an uneasy equation with the Bansals, and especially with Sachin. Every once in a while Sachin would call his colleagues, mostly to complain about something. The recipient of the call, not pleased at having to hear what had upset or excited their boss, would roll their eyes before answering and say to their nearby coworkers: '*Aa gaya phone* – here comes the call.'

Until the end of 2012, when Sachin was at the peak of his powers, he had undoubtedly been the pivotal figure at Flipkart. His ability to conjure a grand vision for the company, his knack for coming up with the big ideas that unlocked the promise of e-commerce, combined with his audacity in pursuing these ideas, made him a peerless entrepreneur. He had run Flipkart through instinct as well as careful thought.

But it wasn't just Flipkart's anatomy that had changed considerably in the time he had been away from the action; even the e-commerce market had grown by magnitudes. Flipkart, which was at the frontier of this change, had expanded considerably along with it. There were new dynamics; power equations between senior executives had altered. Teams coordinated with each other in new ways. This process had been organic, as it often is at a fast-growing startup. Employees would joke that one year at the company seemed like the equivalent of five at any other. All the senior leaders had strong personalities and had built fiefdoms of their own. They wielded enormous power, primarily because their performance was beyond reproach. Since the end of 2013, Sachin had been trying to recover his former authority, but it hadn't been easy. Indeed, for months, he had been consumed by a strange, almost schizophrenic feeling – finally, when after years of being dismissed, Flipkart was finally being feted by the world outside, when Sachin himself was being lionized, he actually had little influence at his own company, and not much to do with its recent successes. He now had the fame and the glory, but not the entrepreneur's satisfaction of directing his company's affairs. And he felt its lack keenly. Especially since the billion-dollar funding had been finalized in July 2014, Sachin had been burning to get back onto the battlefield of daily operations.

Sachin's criticism about the 'lack of innovation' in the company's product function had become more forceful in 2014, and in the latter part of the year, he grew strident. He had been particularly unhappy with the development of the mobile website and app. He strongly believed that the mobile would soon replace the desktop as the primary medium of shopping. He vented to some of his colleagues, 'Our technology and product teams have become slaves to the sales team.' If things continued in this way, Flipkart would be destroyed, he complained. He also pulled up Flipkart's engineers for continuing to spend their energies on tinkering with the website for soon-to-be-irrelevant desktop computers. 'Desktop is the past; the present and future is on the mobile – that's where the company needs to channel its resources,' he insisted.

Much of this criticism was aimed, either directly or by implication, at Kalyan Krishnamurthy, who had by now become the most powerful figure at Flipkart. Under him, business was booming. Yet, Sachin believed that Kalyan's empowering of the sales and finance functions over technology would harm Flipkart over time. Both Sachin and Binny thought that the discount-heavy approach favoured by Kalyan wasn't sustainable either. For Sachin, Flipkart wasn't simply a buy-and-sell trading business. He had always seen Flipkart as a 'technology company, not a retailer'.[1] His relationship with Kalyan, never great to begin with, was deteriorating.

A few months after Kalyan was promoted to Senior Vice President, Sachin and Binny had offered him a permanent role at Flipkart. Kalyan's influence and popularity with the management team was plainly visible. It seemed like an obvious move, a just reward for his stellar performance. Besides, formalizing Kalyan's position would sever his links with Tiger Global and give the Bansals direct, unquestionable supervision over him. They offered him a prestigious position, one that would elevate Kalyan as the seniormost leader at Flipkart after the Bansals. They also offered Kalyan a large amount of stock options in the company.

To their shock, Kalyan declined. He informed the Bansals he wasn't ready to move to Flipkart permanently, that he wanted to return to Tiger Global at some point. Later, Kalyan told colleagues that he had refused the offer mainly because he believed that he and Sachin couldn't work together. Their colleagues already knew that the two would always be at odds. Sachin considered himself a 'product' champion, a technologist who cut through the complexities of intractable problems with software and delivered outstanding service to his customers. Kalyan was a man of finance, driven by numbers, margins and the idea of saleability. Their visions for Flipkart couldn't have been more different.

For much of 2014, Sachin and Kalyan coexisted awkwardly. In fact, Sachin clashed often with many senior executives that year. He had even fallen out with Sujeet Kumar. They had now known each other for nearly fifteen years. After Sujeet was sidelined at the end of 2012, the two had only exchanged words at team meetings. The cause of their rift was unclear to their colleagues, but it was evident that they were no longer close, not even cordial.

The environment at the upper management level grew increasingly toxic through the year. Powerful senior executives like Sujeet and Kalyan, who had little regard for Sachin, made their opinions clear to colleagues. They believed that he had little understanding of the day-to-day workings of e-commerce, and they had grown weary of his fault-finding, which they found to be unreasonable. They openly bad-mouthed Sachin and made fun of him within their inner circle.

On the other side of the tensions, Sachin was growing more zealous. Like many strong-headed entrepreneurs, he had always been unusually passionate about his ideas – it was a passion bordering on vehemence. Now in 2014, as he saw that he wasn't being taken seriously by the likes of Kalyan and Sujeet, his manner during meetings became more imperious with each passing month, with each milestone Flipkart achieved. When asked for supporting data or evidence during arguments, Sachin would often counter by saying that his opinions were informed by his 'gut feeling'. But when his colleagues proffered instinctive views and ideas, Sachin would dismiss them with ridicule. Once, in a heated discussion, Sujeet fired back, 'Sachin, the same rules should apply to everyone. Your gut is gut, but with others, it's gutter?' Sachin had looked offended. But Sujeet wouldn't back down.

To impose his directives on advancing the technology function, Sachin had made some changes. In late 2013, he asked Mekin Maheshwari, the company's first engineering head, to take over human resources. For the past year, Mekin had been heading Flipkart's digital content and payments businesses (which were shut down at separate times). Sachin believed that with Mekin's background in engineering, the HR division, and the company as a whole, could be infused with a technological ethos. Sachin also gave Sameer Nigam a senior position in the engineering team.

Sameer had joined the company in 2011 when Flipkart had bought his startup Mime360. That business, which eventually morphed into the digital music platform Flyte, was shut down after it failed to grow in good time. But Sameer had developed a close relationship with the Flipkart CEO. An engineer with a business degree from The Wharton School, Sameer was a talented tech leader. Like Sachin, he, too, saw himself as an innovative technology entrepreneur. After Flyte was shut down, Sameer had been given charge of digital marketing. In that role, he sometimes clashed with Kalyan. Sameer was focused on attracting new users to Flipkart, while Kalyan wanted the digital marketing team to spend more on promoting sales events. Sachin had been impressed by Sameer's belief that technology should drive marketing; he had also seen Sameer holding his own with Kalyan and other leaders. He decided that Sameer would add heft to the engineering team.

Finally, in July 2014, a week before Flipkart announced its

billion-dollar capital infusion, Sachin found his window of opportunity.

Over the past few months, Sachin and Binny had spent a considerable amount of time in China. The internet boom that would make China the largest e-commerce market in the world, had taken their breath away. They observed that the business models of Chinese companies bore little resemblance to those of the more familiar American firms. These visits left a deep impression on the Bansals; Sachin, in particular, was dazzled by the success of Alibaba and the emergence of Xiaomi, the startup that made smartphones, accessories and other electronic devices.

The Bansals had, in fact, been to China primarily to put the seal on a partnership with Xiaomi. Flipkart's sales team had been courting Xiaomi executives, urging them to sign an exclusive partnership. The hugely successful Moto G phone launch had changed the way brands looked at Flipkart; smartphone-makers that had earlier rejected its exclusivity request were now eager to pursue such an arrangement. But for Flipkart, securing a deal with Xiaomi was paramount, as its executives believed that these Chinese phones would enthral Indian shoppers.

Along with Michael Adnani – Flipkart's electronics chief – Sachin and Binny met the Xiaomi founder Lei Jun several times, in both Bangalore and Beijing. Over Chinese food, they talked about their businesses, exchanging insights and lessons that could inspire each other. It was, in all fairness, the Flipkart executives who did most of the listening. In his mid-forties, Lei Jun was already an accomplished entrepreneur. His previous venture, an online book retailer, had been bought by Amazon in 2004. His present startup, Xiaomi, was a spectacular success.

Within five years of starting out, it would fetch a valuation of more than $40 billion, becoming one of the world's most valuable startups. Its low-priced, powerful phones had become so popular that Xiaomi was outselling in China the world's mightiest phone-makers, Apple and Samsung.[2] Naturally, Flipkart was eager to bring Xiaomi's phones to India.

In July 2014, Xiaomi agreed to grant Flipkart's request – its phones would be available only on Flipkart. The first sale was planned for 22 July. Xiaomi had a distinct method of selling their phones: flash sales. It eschewed spending on advertising. Xiaomi believed that its phones were so good, their prices so compelling, that advertising was unnecessary. Like new members of a cult, users of Xiaomi phones raved about their devices, urging family, friends, colleagues and acquaintances to try them out. The company further stoked its cultish aura by rationing the availability of phones, creating artificial scarcity, which made consumers even more impatient for the products.

Knowing how sought-after its phones were, Xiaomi had bargained hard to extract the most favourable terms from Flipkart. Not only did the company obtain financial concessions, they also got the Bansals to promise that Flipkart would do all it could to ensure Xiaomi's launch was a success. Sachin and Binny didn't care if they had overcommitted; they were thrilled to have achieved exclusivity with Xiaomi. Flipkart hastily strengthened its tech infrastructure to handle the flash sale. Expectations from both camps were high as the sale opened in the last week of July.

The demand from customers blew all these expectations away. Flipkart's website crashed, such was the flood of traffic.[3] The sale was literally over in a flash; Flipkart had sold thousands of phones in a matter of minutes. Only a fraction of users who came to the site were able to buy the phones. Every Xiaomi sale for the next few months played out along similar lines. Only the sale duration reduced each time, phones selling out in seconds rather than minutes. For Flipkart, the Xiaomi business turned out to be even bigger than Motorola's, which had so far been the largest contributor to its sales.

It was these two phone deals that kickstarted India's e-commerce boom in earnest, considerably enhancing Flipkart's popularity and that of online retail. Over the next few years, smartphones would become the predominant category for online retailers and, in turn, e-commerce would become the most important channel for smartphone brands. Apart from Motorola and Xiaomi, brands such as Apple, Samsung, OnePlus and several others, would generate a significant portion of their Indian business from e-commerce. By the end of 2015, smartphones would constitute anywhere between forty to fifty per cent of online retail. This was an oddity, not only when compared to e-commerce in other countries but even within India. In the country's overall market, groceries were the single-largest product category, followed by fashion;[4] smartphones made the top ten but was certainly not at the top. Yet, in the online space, smartphones dwarfed all other categories. In 2014–2015, much of this burgeoning smartphone business naturally sought out Flipkart, which had successfully led phone-makers to e-commerce.

Sachin revelled in the success of the Xiaomi partnership. Even though it was his colleagues in the sales team who had actually worked out the details of the deal, he took great pride in having established a rapport with Lei Jun, who was regarded as one of the foremost technology entrepreneurs in China. By association, Sachin implied to his colleagues that he belonged in the same league. Now at the end of July, a week after the first blockbuster Xiaomi sale, his confidence soaring, Sachin declared his ambition to grow Flipkart into a $100 billion company. His plans of realizing this vision were, in fact, already in motion.

In August, Sachin called a small group of colleagues to his house in Koramangala. The agenda was to discuss what Flipkart needed to do so it could become a $100 billion company. He called the mission Flipkart 3.0. Sachin and Binny had led the company's first phase, from its birth until the end of 2012. The second phase, dominated by Binny and Kalyan, had lasted eighteen months. It had been a great spell, one that had made the company into an efficient machine. But its time was up, Sachin believed. He also complained that this phase had introduced structural weaknesses that had to be undone. Flipkart had moved away from its technology mission. To become a $100 billion company, Flipkart needed a new vision, a new path. Now, he told his colleagues, the time had come for the company to undergo its biggest-ever transformation.

Three other individuals, apart from Sachin and Binny, would be present at the Flipkart 3.0 meetings. They were Mukesh Bansal, Amod Malviya and Vaibhav Gupta.

After the Myntra deal, Mukesh had grown close to the Bansals. Amod and Sachin shared a close professional relationship as well; despite their occasional conflicts, each held the other in high regard.

Vaibhav Gupta, simply called VG, had been at Flipkart since 2011. He was Sachin's senior from IIT Delhi, but the two hadn't known each other well at college. In his first year at Flipkart, VG had struggled to establish himself as a product executive in the supply chain division. But he had helped implement Sachin's supply chain software, Flo. Over the past eighteen months, VG had also led the business finance function that had played a key part in the company's revival and in its fundraising spree. He was one of the few Flipkart executives who was rated highly by both Sachin and Kalyan.

Later, Sachin created another group he called the Flipkart Think Tank which included a few other senior leaders who were responsible for directing the company's daily operations. This group was to oversee the implementation of Sachin's new vision.

As conspicuous as those present was the absentee: Kalyan Krishnamurthy, the man who was running much of the company – but this would have to change. In his mind, Sachin was clear about who would or wouldn't have a place at Flipkart 3.0.

It was clear to Kalyan, too. By the middle of 2014, Kalyan had decided to return to Tiger Global sometime later in the year. His strained relationship with Sachin wasn't getting any better.

SACHIN HAD BEGUN to reimagine the company in the midst of preparations for a special shopping event.

In early 2014, Binny and Kalyan had attended a gathering of the portfolio companies of Naspers, one of Flipkart's investors. At the meeting, a Polish e-commerce firm had made a presentation about its shopping festival. It had set Binny thinking about hosting one on Flipkart's site, and he charged Kalyan with organizing it. Online shopping festivals are common in the big internet markets of the US and China. In the US, Cyber Monday takes place at the start of the shopping season, a few days after the Thanksgiving holiday. Chinese companies have their own – the biggest, hosted by Alibaba, is called Singles Day.

Kalyan was confident that Flipkart could pull off such an event in India. In October 2013, a few days before Diwali – the biggest shopping season of the year – the company had held a hastily arranged sale event. Despite the lack of planning, customers came in droves, taking Flipkart by surprise. That month, the company raked in sales three times higher than the monthly average.

Now, in 2014, Flipkart set a far bigger target for the one-day event: ₹600 crore in gross sales. It was Sachin who came up with the name for the sale: Big Billion Day. It was to be held on 6 October, a few weeks before Diwali. The date of the sale, 6–10–2014, contained the numbers in the address of the NGV apartment – 6–10 – where the Bansals had founded Flipkart.[5]

Kalyan set about preparing for the event. The finance and sales teams under Kalyan busied themselves with preparations for months. Large orders for products were placed with vendors. Existing warehouses were expanded. Temporary warehouses were rented. Thousands of temporary delivery workers were hired. Courier companies were told to be ready for a spike in deliveries. Third-party sellers were persuaded to offer big discounts, which would be made up for with increased sales and higher visibility to customers. Everyone at Flipkart worked overtime. Amod Malviya and Sameer Nigam, the highest-ranking engineers at the company, made their team work fourteen to sixteen hours daily in the weeks leading up to the sale. New software tools for promotions and marketing were readied. Large tracts of additional server space were reserved to absorb the higher influx of users. The sturdiness of the systems was tested for the anticipated spike in traffic.

But just before the sale, Kalyan became worried that the company might not be able to achieve its ambitious target. The number was exceptionally high – on a regular day, gross sales would amount to about ₹30 crore. Sales would have to multiply by twenty times for the company to attain its goal. Kalyan feared that they had overreached. In a panic, he decided to spend a lot more money on discounts and promotions. The Flipkart sale event was splashed all over newspapers, billboards and TV channels in the first week of October. In the big cities in particular, Flipkart was omnipresent. It was a classic advertising blitz. The company promised to sell some of its products, including gadgets and various accessories, for as low a price as ₹1. The weekend before the sale, Sachin and Binny wrote a joint email to customers, inviting them to shop on the site. 'To celebrate Flipkart's journey, we are going to have a sale to end all sales,' they said.[6]

Soon, Flipkart's rivals responded. On 4 October, two days before the sale, Amazon launched a three-day sale event of its own. They were calling it the Mission to Mars. Cleverer still was its move to buy the domain name BigBillionDay.com – anyone who typed 'Big Billion Day' on their browser landed on the Amazon site. Snapdeal, too, engaged in guerrilla warfare of its own. On 6 October, the final Big Billion Day ad on the front pages of newspapers urged customers, 'Today, don't look anywhere else. India's greatest sale is here.' Snapdeal ran an ad right next to it, with the cheeky tagline, 'For others it's a big day. For us, today is no different.' It was the 2014 version of the Cola wars.

That day, the Flipkart leaders were tense. At daybreak, they assembled at the company's new offices in Bangalore's Outer Ring Road area, a few kilometres from the central office in Koramangala. Here, the Bansals, Kalyan and a few others sat in a 'war room', from where they would watch the sale unfold. Outside the room were the rank-and-file employees, many of whom hadn't gone home for days. The density of people was such that the Wi-Fi crashed. Employees were asked to spread out. It wasn't an encouraging omen.

The sale began at 6 a.m. The first two hours had been reserved for Flipkart employees. At 8 a.m., the sale was finally opened up to customers.

By 8.10 a.m., Flipkart's website and mobile app stopped working. Despite the extensive preparations, the sites were overwhelmed by the deluge of customers. In India, the government railway booking website, irctc.co.in, attracted the highest volume of users among e-commerce businesses. On 6 October, Flipkart's website received in an hour the volume of traffic that IRCTC drew across several days. Initially, Kalyan and his associates were thrilled. By 10 a.m., Flipkart had already achieved almost half of its ₹600 crore sales target. Though the website was still down for most customers, the Flipkart team believed it would be fixed soon. But at 11 a.m., the site was still not working.

Outside, everyone was celebrating. Every time a team achieved its target, horns were blown, loud cheers went up, employees danced on their desks. Inside the war room, the atmosphere was quiet, dark. The only light was from the projector screens. One screen showed the sales numbers. Another showed the metrics: the number of users and the 'hits' on the website. A third screen displayed tweets and Facebook posts from customers. By noon, the atmosphere had soured considerably. The graphs and patterns on the first two screens kept rising, but on the third screen, customer complaints had multiplied, too, like a drizzle turning into a torrent. Shoppers were very, very angry. They complained that they couldn't access the website, that products had sold out before they could hit 'buy,' that Flipkart intentionally marked up prices just before the sale to make its discounts seem bigger, that every product was 'out of stock', and orders had been abruptly cancelled. It was a barrage. Less than ten per cent of the people who came to Flipkart were able to make a purchase. After the extensive marketing campaign promoting the sale, this was a major embarrassment. The pattern continued through the afternoon. Flipkart's payment system broke, its tech systems crashed, as did the warehousing software.

By 6 p.m., it was done. The target had been achieved in ten hours. Flipkart had miscalculated, grossly underestimating Indians' thirst for discounts. Worrying about a shortage of demand in the run-up to the sale, it had panicked, hurling large amounts of cash on marketing and discounts. The resulting flood of customers had turned out to be a disaster for its systems. The Bansals sent out a joint statement at the end of the sale: 'The Big Billion Day is an unprecedented day for us as this is the biggest sale ever in India. We are delighted by the overwhelming response from our customers since 8 a.m. today.' They mentioned that Flipkart had recorded a 'billion hits' and achieved its twenty-four-hour sales target of $100 million in just ten hours.[7]

Behind the curtain, the reckoning had begun. Around 6.30 p.m., Sachin and Binny began summoning those in charge of the sale, one by one, to one of the conference rooms in the office. Emphatically, Sachin pressed his point: 'This is what happens when technology becomes a slave to business.' One couldn't become too tactical and rely only on discounts to grow the business, he pointed out grimly. Their tech systems had failed. 'This is a huge embarrassment. We've let down our customers badly.' One after the other, the people in charge of Big Billion Day walked out, their faces downcast. Sachin especially blamed Kalyan, later complaining to Flipkart investors that the Tiger Global representative had 'damaged' the company's brand. It was true that, after the sale, the very papers and news channels that had carried Flipkart's ads had published stories about its image taking a battering with customers. The Big Billion Day sale had been the initiation to online shopping for millions of people. This time, customers felt disappointed, angry, as if they had been duped. Whether this constituted permanent damage for Flipkart was questionable. Sachin believed that it did.

The next day, Sachin, Binny, Kalyan and a few other senior leaders gathered in a room to draft a response to their customers. A few of those present at the meeting said that Flipkart should apologize unreservedly and own up to all the errors that people had pointed out. Kalyan, however, stood his ground on one point. He defended the company's pricing practices, arguing that Flipkart hadn't displayed artificially high discounts; the prices had simply reflected the full discount amount on the maximum retail price rather than on Flipkart's everyday prices, which were admittedly lower than the MRP. But he found his argument ignored.

Flipkart released a long email to customers from Sachin and Binny. The Bansals wrote, 'Yesterday was a big day for us. And we really wanted it to be a great day for you. But at the end of the day, we know your experience was less than pleasant. We did not live up to the promises we made and for that we are really and truly sorry.' They conceded that Flipkart's preparation had been inadequate. '... Though we saw unprecedented interest in our products and traffic like never before, we also realized that we were not adequately prepared for the sheer scale of the event.' They acknowledged all the issues that had angered customers and ended by apologizing again. 'Everything that we have achieved at Flipkart is purely on the basis of our customers' trust and faith. This is why we come to work each day and continue to remain extremely passionate about building the best possible customer experience for Indian consumers. We failed to live up to this promise yesterday and would like to apologize once again to every single customer for our failure.'[8]

The Big Billion Day sale of 2014 turned out to be a bittersweet experience for Flipkart, and especially for Kalyan Krishnamurthy. Kalyan had overseen the biggest-ever sale for the company, one that had revealed the true potential of e-commerce. In a single day, nearly twenty million people had converged onto Flipkart. It was truly unprecedented. And yet, a majority of the shoppers had left empty-handed. It was Kalyan the Bansals had blamed for the inadequacy in preparations.

Next month, Kalyan was back at Tiger Global, although, he still remained on Flipkart's board of directors.

According to a former Flipkart official, Sachin and Kalyan had two common characteristics that made them incompatible. They were both alphas, they both 'liked to be the one in command. Neither could take a backseat.' Both of them also harboured extreme opinions about people, either holding someone in very high regard or thinking they were useless.

For many months now, what one thought about the other had been no secret within the walls of the Flipkart offices.

18

REINVENTING THE KART

'He had ceased to be a businessman and become a conceptual artist.'
'He had an animal desire to have what he wanted and not to have what he did not want.'
'He wanted to create the company that invented the future.'
'That was the miracle of Jim Clark: by the end of 1995 he had created a money-making machine in which he was the least easily replaced part.'

– Michael Lewis, *The New New Thing*[1]

In his mind, Sachin Bansal was now a true visionary entrepreneur. Even the world outside was treating him as such: his investors, the media whose scepticism had given way to hero worship, acquaintances, nearly everyone he knew. In hindsight, it seemed as if seven years ago, when he had started Flipkart, he had seen the future. He had done so when his IIT acquaintances had refused to join him, when venture capital firms had counselled him to stay away from e-commerce, when book distributors and courier companies had dismissed Flipkart. It was Sachin who had thought up the big ideas to unlock the potential of e-commerce in Flipkart's early years, it was he who had the vision and the audacity to believe that a startup could be converted into a giant company in no time. Now, he would repeat his feat – on a much grander scale.

Sachin's Flipkart 3.0 team had been meeting once a week at his house to discuss how they could turn Flipkart into a $100 billion company. They debated on the following matters: How was internet usage evolving? How would people's shopping habits change over the next few years? What should Flipkart do to stay relevant over the next five years? How would Flipkart make money? Were the business models of Amazon, Facebook, Google and other American companies suited to the Indian market? Or was the modus operandi of the Chinese internet firms more likely to work in India? What would be the best business model for Flipkart?

In some ways, their discussion was a microcosm of India's conundrum post liberalization and in a globalized age. On one hand were the developed economies of the West represented by the US, where post-World War II prosperity seemed to be waning. On the other hand was China, whose economic transformation launched in the early eighties was only becoming stronger. China's economic achievement has made the country seem like a compelling exemplar to many Indians, not least because of the jealousy aroused when watching a neighbourhood rival that was a fellow backward country break out in such extraordinary fashion. In 2014, Flipkart embodied the anxieties of the Indian economy's place in the world, its promise, its keen awareness of its inferiority vis-á-vis both China and the West. Sachin had been closely studying the business models of Chinese internet companies such as Alibaba and Xiaomi, as well as the business philosophies of the giant American technology companies, Apple, Facebook and Google. Over the past seven years the Bansals had come a long way towards validating their founding idea – that two Indians could build a world-class internet firm in India. Now, when they were in the final leg of that journey, where they had to find the next iteration, the next set of big ideas that would finally lift Flipkart onto the league of the world's most elite internet companies, it wasn't surprising that they were swayed by the business models of the Chinese startups. After all, it was these companies that were redefining the standards of a world-class internet firm.

Sachin had been especially fascinated by Xiaomi; in his eyes, Xiaomi was the ultimate product company. It had become the choice of the Chinese masses because of the excellence of its product design and its technological expertise. Drawing on this melange of sources and trying to adapt it to the realities of the Indian market, Sachin drew up a blueprint to realize his $100 billion dream and achieve profitability at the same time.

It was a plan that necessitated capsizing Flipkart, voluntarily introducing chaos, in the hope that the churn, when over, would produce a far stronger creature – a colossus. Until now, Flipkart had essentially followed the Amazonian principle of pleasing customers at any cost by stocking products at low prices and delivering them quickly. But Sachin and his colleagues came to the conclusion that Flipkart's inventory-based model of direct buying and selling of products would limit the company's reach. It had served the company well so far, but to become a behemoth, to take commerce to the masses, the model might prove inadequate. The range of products under such a model would always be narrow, which would circumscribe its expansion. The diversity and size of the Indian retail market called for a more subtle approach. The Flipkart 3.0 team concluded that if the company continued on its current trajectory, it would 'max out' at $20 billion in sales. Instead, if Flipkart made itself into a 'platform' for all kinds of goods and services, it would become an 'internet company' rather than just a retailer. An internet platform is like a bazaar but with a limitless capacity to host vendors and to grow. Alibaba, the Chinese internet giant, was primarily a bazaar. Even Amazon, the world's largest e-commerce company, had a sizeable marketplace business. The Flipkart council decided that their company would have to build one, too. Strikingly, this is what Kunal Bahl, Sachin's nemesis-in-waiting, had been saying for years. The platform that Sachin was imagining was, however, significantly different from Snapdeal's. In Sachin's view, such a marketplace could only be created at that particular point in time, after Flipkart had helped create an e-commerce ecosystem of suppliers, logistics providers and delivery workers. Without Flipkart's early efforts, a marketplace could not have delivered the kind of excellent service that Flipkart had come to be known for. But now that this ecosystem was in place, Sachin believed it was an opportune time to withdraw from retail and become a bazaar.

Sachin also argued that such a bazaar could only be realized by a 'technology' company, not a retail firm. Hence, decision-making at Flipkart would have to be controlled by the product and engineering teams, and not the sales team. In a sense, history was repeating itself. Sachin's initiation to the internet business had been with Amazon India, set up as part of Jeff Bezos' efforts to prove that Amazon was a 'technology company, not a retailer'.[2] Nearly a decade later, Sachin was pursuing the same mission at Flipkart.

Apart from the shift in its business model, Sachin had decided that Flipkart would have to bring upon itself another upheaval. By now, it was clear that unlike in the US, most people in India would browse the internet on their smartphones rather than on desktop computers. Apart from a few million people who primarily lived in cities, most Indians wouldn't have the finances, or the need, to purchase computers or laptops. Sachin had spotted this trend early, but despite his constant grumbling, he believed that the company hadn't done nearly enough to improve its mobile app. By November 2014, Sachin had expanded the Flipkart 3.0 council to include about a dozen members – the people charged with implementing his grand vision. At their meetings, he started promoting the idea that the company should become an app-only platform.

Sachin argued that the way to make Flipkart into a household name was to beautify its main product – the app. The app would have to be made so technologically advanced, so aesthetically pleasing, that new users would be drawn to Flipkart by word of mouth, just like they were to Xiaomi and Apple in their respective countries. This would save Flipkart hundreds of crores in advertising expenses. The app would offer another advantage: customization. As it gathered data on users' shopping habits, Flipkart would use its technology to analyze the information and display products, matching them with each user's taste. This is how Flipkart would stay ahead of Amazon and its ilk. Sachin was convinced that this could only be possible if the Flipkart engineers, who had been used to building features for the desktop website, devoted all their energies to the app. And they could only be brought around to his worldview if the desktop website was closed down. He told his colleagues, 'The world is moving towards the mobile. Customer experience on the app can be made significantly better than the desktop. So, not only do we have to be the leaders, we need to proactively move traffic to mobile. The only way to do that is to remove the crutch of the desktop.'

Another idea that Sachin had devised was the creation of a large advertising platform. By the end of 2014, Flipkart had quietly been earning sizeable advertising revenues. The Indian digital ads market was growing fast, touching nearly $1 billion annually.[3] Most of this revenue went to one place: Google. The rest was scattered among thousands of websites. In the space of one year, Flipkart had become one of the largest advertising platforms after Google. In October 2014, when it had held the Big Billion Day sale, the company had generated more than ₹25 crore in ad revenues. Companies such as Hindustan Unilever, Coke, Nike and Adidas, which spent heavily on advertising, were all hunting for internet platforms that could bring them large numbers of shoppers, especially from a younger age bracket, with the money and desire to buy consumer goods. Flipkart presented them with a custom-made hoard of such users.

Until recently, Sachin hadn't paid much attention to the fledgling ads business. But after the first Big Billion Day sale, he latched on to it. He recalled how during Flipkart's early days, the ads revenue he had earned from Google and Amazon had been critical in propping up the company. Now he believed that it could be the transformational money-making scheme for Flipkart. Even Alibaba earned a majority of its profits through ads. Sachin had also been inspired by Facebook's success in the US. When the social networking platform had started out in the mid-noughties, the desktop was the primary medium of most internet users. But over the past few years, people had increasingly switched to smartphones, a change that had upended many internet platforms. Not Facebook – it thrived more than ever in the smartphone era.[4] It bought startups, introduced exciting new features on its app, copied rivals when it couldn't buy or better them. Facebook now generated a majority of its revenues from ads served up on its mobile app.[5] Sachin believed Flipkart could – *had to* – do the same here in India where most internet users would soon surf the net primarily on their phones.

In late 2014, Sachin was ready with the outline for the new Flipkart. A vision document was prepared. It was decided that Flipkart would be broken up into three parts. At the centre of the company would be the marketplace business that would be run by Mukesh Bansal. It would mark a stunning rise for Mukesh, who had joined Flipkart only a few months ago. In essence, Mukesh was replacing Kalyan Krishnamurthy.

Sachin and Binny, who had admired Mukesh for years, were even more impressed by him as they began to work closely after the Myntra deal. They appreciated not only his entrepreneurial abilities but his overall personality as well. Mukesh had cultivated a taste for couture after Myntra turned into a fashion-selling site a few years ago. He dressed down consciously. His taste was varied – he admired the fashion sense of Hrithik Roshan, George Clooney and Lisa Haydon.[6] Mukesh was serious about health and fitness – he worked out nearly every day, and had a physique to show for it. He played golf, had friends in Bollywood, and at the same time, was well liked by many of his colleagues at Myntra as well as the company's investors. He was well-read, soft-spoken, articulate. He was all this, a father to two kids, and also a hugely successful internet entrepreneur. For Sachin and Binny, Mukesh was the personification of 'cool'. His life hadn't been dissimilar to theirs. He had grown up in Haridwar, studied computer engineering at IIT Kanpur and written code before becoming an entrepreneur. Like the Bansals, Mukesh, too, was an advocate of using technology in retail. He was as introverted as they were, and yet he had evolved into a rounded, mature person, a man of the world, something the Bansals had always wanted for themselves. Mukesh, in turn, was highly ambitious. He harboured a desire to become CEO of Flipkart in the near future. He charmed the Flipkart co-founders with purpose and, unlike Kalyan, got along well with Sachin, who even encouraged Mukesh's ambitions initially. Convinced that they had found their ideal partner, Sachin and Binny charged Mukesh with the daily running of Flipkart.

The logistics service would be headed by Binny. Not only would it deliver orders for Flipkart, it would also be expanded to become a large logistics firm on the lines of Blue Dart and DHL. Sachin would develop the advertising platform that would, over time, become Flipkart's most important lever in moving towards profitability.

On the whole, the vision document of Flipkart 3.0 was a work of impressive conceptual ingenuity, the corporate equivalent of high-level graphic design or architectural planning.

In November 2014, at a meeting in Singapore, Sachin and Mukesh presented the vision document to Lee Fixel and Flipkart's other board members. More than a dozen Flipkart executives had come to the meeting to make presentations. With Sachin's aid, Mukesh articulated Flipkart's new strategy. Although the plan was radical, there were few probing questions from the board members. And even fewer criticisms. The lone dissenting voice was that of Kalyan Krishnamurthy. Looking at Sachin, Kalyan said that there was one major problem with the strategy: Sachin wanted to turn Flipkart into Snapdeal, which had always been a far inferior company.

Sachin's reply was terse. 'Yes.' Without offering an explanation, he moved on to other matters.

The other board members watched the exchange in silence. In more informal forums, Lee, along with other board members, had expressed some of their doubts to Sachin. Lee had pointed out that if Flipkart tried to become a marketplace overnight, its service might suffer and its carefully cultivated brand could get damaged. He was also a bit alarmed by the app-only plan. Many products were still being bought on the desktop website and millions of customers used both the desktop site and the app to shop on Flipkart. *Why would the company want to lose all this business and hand it to Amazon?* Lee had asked Sachin.

But Sachin, who had anticipated these questions, was prepared. He predicted that people were moving to the mobile in such large numbers that within a few years, all online shopping would take place exclusively through that medium. 'If we have a world-class app, we can create a huge advantage. This is not what Amazon is good at. They're not built for the mobile age,' Sachin would say in defence of his vision.

'So why can't we build a world-class app *and* keep the desktop site?'

'Because the desktop site will only be a crutch that won't let us focus on the mobile app.'

These conversations would continue over the next few months. But it was an intoxicating time, with Flipkart's growth consistently high, its valuation rising all the time, so that all reluctance eventually fell away. Lee signed off on Flipkart 3.0.

In December 2014, Flipkart raised another round of funding. Less than six months after the billion-dollar round, it received another $700 million in fresh capital. Along with Flipkart's present investors, five new firms, including Qatar's national fund, contributed to the round. Flipkart was in such great demand that the company was able to handpick investors from a queue. Its valuation quadrupled to $11 billion in a little over a year.[7] This capital infusion was as strong an endorsement of Flipkart's new vision as there could be. To the Flipkart investors, it didn't matter that the company was unprofitable. The fact that its sales were expanding prodigiously eclipsed any concerns. It was a global trend – investors were backing fast-growing startups in the belief that once these firms acquired a large market share, they would figure out how to make profits eventually.

THE NEW FLIPKART 3.0 council of more than a dozen members would now convene at the large conference room in the Myntra office, about half an hour from the Flipkart headquarters in Koramangala. They also continued to meet at Sachin's house. The discussions there would last until late into the night. At one such meeting, towards the end of 2014, Sachin gave his colleagues a surprise.

They had been discussing how fast the company could implement the new plan. What Sachin had envisioned was a wholesale makeover of Flipkart, a company that employed more than 30,000 people and had thousands of vendors and suppliers. It was a complex, chaos-inducing undertaking that was inherently dangerous. Some Flipkart officials suggested that the company spread out the implementation over three years. They were already unsure about Sachin's decision to break up the company. To them, it made little sense to separate the marketplace business from Ekart, which was the most important component in delivering reliable service to customers. They suggested that Flipkart should at least not make these changes in haste. Staggering the plan over three years would give the company sufficient time to practise and learn without disrupting its present business. But Sachin shot down his critics. 'No, we'll have to do this by the end of 2015, within one year,' he said. His colleagues were in shock. At the start of these discussions, they had been told that the plan would be implemented over the next three to five years. Now, suddenly, Sachin wanted to taste immediate success.

Managing people had never been one of Sachin's strengths. He had always been a demanding, volatile boss. Over the years, his colleagues had found ways to deal with him. But by now, Sachin had become an altogether different man. His abrasive tendencies, his zeal, ran unchecked. His respect for others had diminished. He tended to be dismissive of those who dared to differ. When a colleague complained that he was being too critical of others, Sachin said in response, 'People are ultimately resources. Don't get too invested in them.' All of Sachin's ideas now were radical; his conviction in his vision was so strong, his belief in his ingenuity so unshakeable, that he felt no need for conflicting opinions or the benefits of trial and error. Citing Xiaomi's example, he demanded that the company immediately stop spending on marketing – the app would be so attractive that it would naturally pull users. Citing Apple's example, he called for the shutdown of the desktop website. When some colleagues opposed him, pointing out that a large number of users still shopped on the website rather than on the app, Sachin told them, 'When Apple gets rid of old products, their customers also complain. But the replacements they come out with are so much better that users migrate to the new product. Our app, too, will be much, much better than the website.'

At an early 2015 meeting of the Flipkart 3.0 council in the Myntra office, things came to a head. Many of the dozen members gathered there were again arguing for a more gradual shift to the marketplace. Amod Malviya was one of the dissenters. He reminded Sachin that Flipkart didn't have a good history of implementing big changes. 'We should start small, keep learning and move incrementally,' he advised. If they suddenly became a marketplace, they would have to take a revenue hit. It would compromise customer experience.

'It's OK,' Sachin said. 'We'll take the hit.'

Bemused, Amod laughed out loud.

'Why the fuck are you laughing?' Sachin shot back.

'*Matlab kya hai* – what do you mean?'

'You can't smile at my meetings!'

'You can't speak to me that way!'

The exchange was short but it grew so heated so quickly

that, within seconds, both Sachin and Amod had jumped to their feet, furious. Alarmed, their colleagues had to intervene.

Over the next few weeks, the members of the Flipkart 3.0 council kept dwindling. Anyone who opposed the new plan would not be invited to the next meeting, their approach dismissed as small, limited, limiting.

At the end of January 2015, Sachin was ready to carry out his grand new vision. He wanted to announce it to a larger group of employees in order to bring them around – not simply to persuade them to make the requisite changes, but to encourage them to think of their jobs in a new way. What Sachin ultimately wanted was a sweeping change in the company's culture: the employees of an internet company couldn't think in the same way as the members of a retail company would.

Flipkart invited about a thousand of its highest-ranking employees to an auditorium at the Jyoti Niwas College in Koramangala. It was a fitting choice for the corporate theatre that was about to play out. There, the three Bansals – the company's founders, and with them, Mukesh, now the third-most important man at Flipkart – announced the split of the company into three parts. They explained how Flipkart would become one of the world's leading technology companies. Their speeches were generously peppered with words such as 'big data', 'machine learning', 'artificial intelligence', 'product thinking.'

The response from the spectators wasn't encouraging. On hearing about the drastic changes, the employees who ran Flipkart on a day-to-day basis, expressed doubt.

'How will this work?'

'Why are we doing this?'

'Do we need to make all these changes?'

'Do we need to make all these changes all at once?'

But the three Bansals were unfazed. Like a king presiding over his *janta*, Sachin told his employees that all the changes mentioned were necessary for Flipkart to leapfrog into a $100 billion firm.

Over the next two days, Sachin, Binny and Mukesh, along with other Flipkart executives, elaborated upon the upcoming changes to their respective departments. But employees showed little enthusiasm. 'You're talking gibberish,' some said. 'The more I tried to explain it, the more embarrassing it became,' recalls one of the department heads.

Nevertheless, Flipkart pushed forward with the new plan. Within the next six months, the company would, to some degree, remake itself in exactly the way Sachin had envisioned.

THE NEW FLIPKART would have another essential feature: a new management team. This plan had been conceived by Sachin and Mukesh, and Binny had backed it. The three Bansals together believed that for Flipkart to ascend to the greatest heights, the company would need superior leaders. Sachin, in particular, had no doubt that while the old team had served Flipkart well so far, they had reached the limits of their abilities. Their resistance to Sachin's plans was also inconveniencing. In order to elevate Flipkart to a world-class company and transform it into a true bastion of technology, new managers would have to be found.

Flipkart had already appointed a new finance chief: Sanjay Baweja. In his mid-fifties, Sanjay was a well-respected CFO, having worked at companies such as Airtel and the Tata Group. He had been hired with the long-term objective of taking

Flipkart public. But the most important appointment was that of a chief product officer.

Punit Soni had been the lead product manager for Motorola since its buyout by Google. He had led software development for the new Motorola phones that turned out to be among the bestselling smartphones of 2013–14 across the world. Punit had grown up in Anushakti Nagar, an eastern suburb of Bombay, a few kilometres from the Bhabha Atomic Research Centre, where his father worked as a nuclear scientist. Anushakti Nagar, one of the very few well-planned areas of India's financial capital, served as the housing colony for the scientists, engineers and doctors working at the research agency. After finishing school in this elite environment, Punit would spend six years studying engineering at two ultra-conservative places, first in Haryana at the National Institute of Technology, Kurukshetra, and then at the University of Wyoming, in the eponymous mid-sized American state, the population of which is lower than most Bombay suburbs. After obtaining his master's degree, Punit moved to Silicon Valley just as the dotcom bust was beginning at the turn of the new century. Now in his mid-thirties, Punit was looking to move on to a new job after having spent eight years at Google.

Sachin had met Punit in early 2014 after Flipkart and Motorola became exclusive partners. Punit had betrayed a supercilious manner. Once during a routine meeting, when Sachin asked him about Motorola's upcoming products, Punit pulled out a phone from his bag and showcased its features, some of which were futuristic. Sachin was awestruck, his eyes widening as the product was demonstrated to him. Sachin, always a firm believer in Flipkart's technology prowess, had then drawn a parallel between the new Motorola phone and the Flipkart app, which he claimed was ahead of its time, too. Punit waved his hand dismissively, 'Nah, I don't think so, Sachin. The technology we've built is way ahead of anything Flipkart has created. It's incomparable.' This had made Sachin bristle. But it had also made Punit seem more impressive. Sachin would keep telling his colleagues, 'This is the kind of person we need.'

In the second half of 2014, Sachin offered Punit the role of Flipkart's product chief. He wanted a technologist to carry out his vision of turning Flipkart into a cutting-edge internet company. He thought he had found this pioneer in Punit. Not only was Punit looking to change jobs, like Sachin, he also intensely wanted to make history. Like Sachin, he was a believer in the supremacy of technology and possessed by the dream of creating The Great Indian Internet Company. Punit's academic background and extensive career in Silicon Valley had greatly impressed Sachin. As a bonus, Punit, a bespectacled, observing sardar, was of Indian origin, which meant the cultural adaptation wouldn't be as hard as it might have been for a foreigner. Sachin believed that Punit, with his bright turbans and energetic personality, would be a good fit at Flipkart.

Along with Punit, Flipkart hired another senior engineer from Google. Peeyush Ranjan came in as Chief Technology Officer. Saikiran Krishnamurthy, a senior partner at McKinsey, was hired as Chief Operating Officer of Flipkart's core e-commerce business. To lure these and other coveted executives away from their highly lucrative jobs at companies far bigger than Flipkart, the Bansals offered astonishing compensation packages worth millions of dollars (most of it in stock options). These hires were symbolic of the momentous cultural change that Flipkart had ushered into India's corporate world. A few months ago, it would have been inconceivable for a partner at the world's premier consultancy or senior engineers thriving at the world's leading technology firm, to join an Indian company, much less Flipkart, a little-known startup. Now, it was a compelling proposition. Flipkart and a small number of other Indian internet startups had become exciting places to work, companies at the frontiers of the corporate world, led by technological geniuses reshaping the economy of the new India, set to create spectacular wealth for their investors, founders, employees.

Concurrent to the entry of the new leaders at Flipkart was the departure of the old team. By the middle of 2015, within the space of three months, they exited, one after another. Sujeet Kumar, who had built the company's sales and logistics functions; Amod Malviya, the chief technology officer; Sameer Nigam, the engineering head; Saran Chatterjee, the product chief; Vaibhav Gupta, the business finance leader – all of them left, bitter, angry, unwanted. The significant wealth they had earned notwithstanding, what rankled was that their association with the company had been cut short against their wishes. They may not have been fired, but it was made clear to them that they weren't especially welcome – Vaibhav Gupta went on sabbatical, but on his return, he struggled to find a place for himself at Flipkart. There were only two survivors: Ankit Nagori, who had been promoted to Chief Business Officer, and Mekin Maheshwari, the HR head. Despite seeing many of his old teammates and mentors fall out with the Bansals, Ankit was keen to continue. Flipkart was thriving; its future had never seemed brighter. He had recently been rewarded with a lucrative pay hike, attractive stock options and a promotion. And he had formed a friendly working relationship with Mukesh Bansal. For his part, Mekin had always been close to Sachin. He saw no reason to leave at this opportune time. As HR chief, Mekin had even helped the Bansals find replacements for their old colleagues.

Such an exodus of long-time senior leaders would have been alarming for any company. Jettisoning an entire leadership team that had delivered excellent performance for years in favour of a new group of untested leaders who had little knowledge of e-commerce would have drawn scrutiny, prompted anxious questions from board members and investors, and received criticism from the press. It wasn't that all of them were leaving, it was that they were leaving all at once. But such was the aura around Flipkart and the Bansals that they encountered minimal resistance.

In this regard, as with all the other changes at Flipkart, the decisive factor was the close relationship between Lee Fixel, the company's all-powerful investor, and the Flipkart co-founders, Sachin, in particular. Lee was a hyper-rationalist investor who judged a business or an entrepreneur in a cold, dispassionate manner. Considered ruthless by those who fell out of favour with Lee, he had little personal affinity for entrepreneurs. Those who delivered were rewarded with more capital and higher valuations, while those who failed to meet targets were cut out. There was no place for emotion in his decisions. But with Sachin, it had always been a bit different. Before every board meeting in Singapore or Dubai, which took place once every four months, Sachin would meet Lee over dinner or breakfast. They spoke regularly over the phone. Dinner with the Bansals was a fixture of his India trips. Lee, who called him 'Saa-chin',[8] had known the Flipkart CEO for nearly six years by now. When Lee had first decided to invest in Flipkart in late 2009, he was an unknown figure in the startup world. Since then, from being an anonymous fund manager, he had risen to become one of the smartest young startup investors anywhere in the world. By the end of 2014, the not-yet-thirty-five reclusive fund manager, who had not granted the media a single interview, had devised a unique investment strategy that spanned continents. Few in the business could match his global network of investor connections, his deep knowledge of the internet market ranging from eastern Europe to the subcontinent, his ability to spot the brightest entrepreneurs across these very diverse markets.

But Lee's crown jewel was Flipkart. They had risen together, Lee as an investor, Sachin and Binny as entrepreneurs. Their relationship was symbiotic, they fed off each other's successes. Lee's soaring reputation as an investor had much to do with his bet on Flipkart, on the entrepreneurial abilities of Sachin and Binny. However, Lee had harboured doubts about Sachin's radical plan to remake Flipkart. He had challenged Sachin, and the two had fought each other in vigorous debates. Still, Lee's belief in Sachin's entrepreneurial genius did not waver.

Just how strong Lee's faith was in Sachin would become evident soon. In the summer of 2015, Sachin approached Lee with a startling request: remove Kalyan Krishnamurthy from Flipkart's board of directors. Sachin cited a technicality to seek the replacement of Kalyan – who had become a Singaporean citizen – with an Indian national. It was apparent to all that this was just a ruse. Everyone knew there was bad blood between Sachin and Kalyan. The Flipkart CEO had criticized Kalyan for 'damaging' Flipkart's brand with his mishandling of the

Big Billion Day sale. In turn, Kalyan had denounced Sachin's makeover of Flipkart and his recruitment of a new management team. A few weeks after Kalyan left the Flipkart board, Sachin accused him of hiring Flipkart employees at other companies in Tiger Global's portfolio. A Flipkart sales executive had agreed to join a smaller rival, another Tiger-funded company on whose board Kalyan served as a director. Kalyan had facilitated his exit by vouching for him to the new company. Sachin believed that Kalyan had, in fact, persuaded this employee to leave Flipkart. A furious Sachin complained to Lee that Kalyan held a grudge against him. Kalyan denied this categorically.

This episode was a blip in an otherwise heady season for the Bansals, for Lee, and for Flipkart. In April 2015, Flipkart had finalized another funding round of more than $500 million. The company's valuation now soared to $15 billion. Its business was surging forward. Over the past eighteen months, monthly sales had quadrupled. With the grand new valuation, Sachin and Binny, not yet thirty-five, crossed a new threshold: they, too, had become billionaires. Each held about eight per cent in Flipkart, their ownership having reduced through the successive funding rounds. The $15 billion valuation meant that they were now worth more than $1 billion each.[9] Lee was riding high, too. The following month, he would be promoted by Tiger Global to head all of its private investments.[10]

19

CHAOS AND CONFUSION

On 14 May 2015, Myntra held a press conference. Sachin and Mukesh announced that Myntra would shut its website and become an app-only platform. It was no surprise; newspapers had been revealing this over the last several months. A few days ago, Myntra itself had emailed its customers about the shutdown. At the event, Sachin and Mukesh talked about revolutionizing the app by creating an interface like no other.

Myntra had actually been serving as a lab rat for Flipkart. Sachin declared that Flipkart, too, would shut its website over time. It hadn't done so already only because of a lack of 'internal readiness'.[1] Within Flipkart, Sachin's statements caused much consternation. While he had been talking of shutting down the website, a timeline hadn't been agreed upon yet. But Sachin didn't care. He was going to get it done.

Still, Sachin and Mukesh both failed to explain why Myntra and Flipkart couldn't make their mobile apps revolutionary without having to shut down the desktop site. By the company's own admission, Myntra would be forgoing more than thirty per cent of its orders by closing the website. *So, why not keep the website and make the app attractive at the same time?* the media wanted to know. In Mukesh's view, the shopping experience on the app would be so enthralling that people would be compelled to use it over the desktop site in any case. The reporters present were incredulous. Mukesh hadn't specified the changes that would transform the app. Indeed, the app's interface had nearly been the same for months; it wasn't even all that different from the Amazon or Snapdeal apps – or Flipkart's own. But the changes were coming soon, Mukesh promised. 'Every single desktop user will have a smartphone. It may take a few months, but every single person will end up using and liking the mobile shopping experience than what they are used to [on] the desktop.'[2]

The Flipkart engineers had been under pressure for months to deliver this magical interface. They were told that the Flipkart app would have to be so good that 'customers should have an orgasm' from using it. It was certainly an unbeatable way to take commerce to the masses.

Few people, either within or outside the company, were convinced that the app-only move was a smart one. Still, it had become the talk of the startup world. Investors, analysts, entrepreneurs, journalists – everyone put forth their own theories. Some drew on strategy literature to make sense of the decision, some ascribed it to thoughtfulness, others to ulterior motives. No possible explanation was left uncovered. But the simple fact was that Sachin was propelled more by impulse than by hypotheses. It was clear that smartphones would become the primary medium of internet consumption in India. Sachin decided that Flipkart should drop everything else and make its app the best shopping platform in the world – it would then surely become the preferred choice of customers. Of course he drew on influences and cited data; he had also considered the repercussions. But eventually he did give in to an impulse; it was his 'gut feeling' that drove him to take this decision. Sachin had always been a radical entrepreneur. And now, the urge to be a visionary was irresistible.

Sometime around the middle of 2015, Sachin called for a meeting of the seniormost Flipkart leaders. By now, most of the dissenters had resigned from their positions. Sachin asked his newly appointed lieutenants to voice their opinions about the app-only initiative and prepare presentations backing their arguments. Many of these leaders agreed that the company should shut its desktop site. One presentation quoted the Irish intellectual George Bernard Shaw: 'Doing what needs to be done may not make you happy, but it will make you great.'[3] Sachin loved it. By the end of the meeting, he had decided that Flipkart would shut its desktop site before October. The app-only project was named Project Shaw.

In July, Flipkart called an all-hands meeting. Sachin and Flipkart's product chief Punit Soni were to announce the decision to the rank and file. But at the time of the meeting, Sachin was nowhere to be found. Punit addressed the crowd by himself. He had privately been lukewarm about the plan. But as he addressed the gathering, Punit became the champion of the idea, savouring his moment in the spotlight.

He was surprised that Sachin hadn't turned up. After making the announcement, Punit turned to some of the departing senior Flipkart officials, who were standing nearby, and said,

'Sachin and I were supposed to do this together!' They were greatly amused, unable to control their laughter.

IN AUGUST 2015, the *New York Times* published an investigative story about the work culture at Amazon. It showed Amazon to be a ruthless organization engaged in the single-minded pursuit of growth, marked by a 'purposeful Darwinism' that pitted employees against each other. It detailed several instances of ruthless treatment of employees including one where a breast cancer survivor was put on a 'performance improvement plan'. Amazon was 'conducting a little-known experiment in how far it can push white-collar workers, redrawing the boundaries of what is acceptable,' the article suggested.[4] These disturbing aspects aside, the piece also revealed – as have other accounts, including Brad Stone's *The Everything Store* – how even after employing more than a hundred and fifty thousand people,[5] the company was able to impose a uniform corporate culture.

After Flipkart had divided itself into three parts in early 2015, its employees were spread out over three large offices. The company had taken up two opulent spaces in Bangalore's Outer Ring Road area. Its technology team was housed in one building; the other new office, nearly two kilometres away, hosted a large part of the sales department. Binny's supply chain team remained at the Koramangala headquarters. This wasn't by design – finding a large enough office space in that area for a company of Flipkart's size had proved quite difficult. The segregation would have a considerable impact: soon, these three offices started working so independently of one another they may as well have been three different companies.

While Sachin had always believed in the supremacy of technology, he did recognize – especially at the time Flipkart was founded – the importance of having a strong operations function. In a 2010 interview with the news website vccircle.com, he had emphatically stated that e-commerce was a 'very execution-heavy' business.[6] What he meant was that success in e-commerce was determined to a large extent by a firm's ability to instil discipline among its suppliers, run warehouses, operate a logistics fleet and other such labour-intensive tasks that had little to do with writing code. But by 2015, Sachin was so obsessed with making Flipkart a technology company that he displayed a revulsion towards most things real, or physical, that could not be governed by algorithms. To him, the sales team that had run the company for the last two years were now little more than 'relationship managers' with brands rather than executives with much-needed business acumen. Sachin wanted everyday decisions – which products should Flipkart buy, in what quantities and at what prices – that had earlier been taken by sales executives to be made the domain of the technology team. It was like asking literature graduates to become accountants.

The already-weak unity between the technology and sales teams now disintegrated. Punit's role was perhaps decisive here. Sachin and Mukesh had given Punit and his team almost complete control of Flipkart. Punit was only too happy to take up the mission of converting a retailer into a technology firm with Silicon Valley mores. He had become the most important executive at Flipkart after the three Bansals and he ensured everyone knew that. Ever since he had joined Flipkart in March 2015, Punit had been eagerly expanding his turf. He introduced some of the rigorous technology practices and procedures of American technology companies at Flipkart. Borrowing a practice from his former employer, Google, Punit started a weekly beer rendezvous for Flipkart employees. He worked as per a strict regimen, and refused to entertain anyone on its outside. His time was precious, every minute of which had to be utilized productively. Colleagues couldn't just walk into his office. Even senior leaders had to wait their turn to meet him. He rejected the timeless custom of Indian Standard Time. If someone was late for a meeting with him, he would openly admonish them, regardless of their position.

Colleagues who got to know him closely claim that Punit came across as a man with two diametrically opposite personalities. Outside the office, he was a warm, garrulous guy with whom one might enjoy getting a drink. At work, he was almost compulsively disagreeable, too enthusiastic about promoting himself, uncompromising in his dealings with the heads of other divisions. He was especially dismissive of the sales executives, whom he saw as neanderthals.

Taking their cue from Punit, his juniors in the technology team, too, would treat their sales counterparts with contempt. One senior sales executive recalls that product managers, many of whom had barely spent a few months at the company, would openly insult sales officers. 'The tech–product guys had almost stopped holding meetings with our team. And when the meetings would happen, we would come back demotivated,' he claims.

The disunity between the technology and sales teams gradually led to a mess. Decisions about new category launches would be delayed for months. If the sales team wanted to start a new category, they would ask the technology team to prepare the required infrastructure on the Flipkart app. Inevitably, the engineers would respond, 'We're following our own roadmap and we'll only work according to that.' Flipkart had prepared a plan to start selling groceries at the beginning of 2015. For nearly six months, the plan remained on paper, unimplemented.

In such an environment, the company's sales strategy came to be defined by a comical lack of coherence. Sachin had promoted his new vision for Flipkart as one that would set up the company for long-term success. Astonishingly, one of Flipkart's first moves that year had been to voluntarily forgo the books category, a move it knew would allow Amazon to dominate the category. This was actually a decision that Kalyan Krishnamurthy had made before returning to Tiger Global. For nearly two years, Kalyan had been pushing Flipkart to reduce its budget for books. He had been arguing that the category was a financial wasteland, that customers who bought books were too small in number and rarely ever purchased other goods from the company. Finally, at the end of 2014, his wish was granted by the Bansals. By April 2015, the company's books sales, in real terms, had dropped by half. Other weak categories had also been marked as toxic: laptops, electronic storage devices, and so on. Flipkart lost cash on each order in these 'non-strategic' categories. Binny believed that in a few years' time, laptops would become altogether redundant, replaced by large-screen phones and tablets. He didn't care if Amazon came to monopolize laptop sales – soon the category itself would die. Accordingly, laptops and its ilk were wound down along with books.

Another instance of Flipkart's disjointed approach was its

sudden decision to prioritize sales volumes. Flipkart had earlier set out to achieve ₹3,000 crore in monthly sales by the end of 2015, which meant growing by more than two and a half times in one year. But sometime in the middle of 2015, the Bansals suddenly decided to focus on growing the number of orders instead of sales value. They reasoned that volume, not value, was a truer indicator of demand, and this would grow over time in any case if the demand was strong. Sachin told his team, 'Forget about revenues. Focus on units. We're not a commerce company. We're a data–technology company. Data depends on transactions and volumes.'

The technology team implemented this instruction literally, making immediate changes on the app to provide prominent positioning to low-priced, high-volume products. On the app's opening screen, products such as cheap shoes and slippers were promoted. These goods, offered by inexperienced third-party sellers, sold in high volumes initially, but their quality was poor, leading to higher rates of product returns. Still, sales leaders fell over themselves to stock up on cheaper items. Instead of jeans and shirts, socks, underwear and belts were hawked to customers. These abrupt changes confused and disoriented customers. As with any other retailer, Flipkart offered a mix of low-value, mid-value and high-value products. A customer might have wanted to purchase from all three sections. According to a Flipkart sales executive, the product team needed to understand the importance of striking a balance. This balance could only have been attained by a thoughtful approach, which proved to be elusive because of the broken relationship between the tech and sales divisions.

The company's top leaders had a weak grip over day-today matters. Sachin was busy with the advertising business, Binny had restricted his involvement to Ekart. As the head of the marketplace and commerce business, it was eventually up to Mukesh and his seniormost executive, Ankit Nagori, to ensure that the sales function ran smoothly. But Mukesh would rarely be seen at sales meetings and displayed little interest in discerning how Flipkart's business actually functioned on the ground. Mukesh believed that, as the leader of the commerce platform, he wasn't required to immerse himself in implementing decisions; that was his team's responsibility, and he had accordingly given free rein to executives such as Punit. Meanwhile, Ankit stayed absorbed in expanding the marketplace business – in its bid to move away from the inventory model, the company was adding tens of thousands of third-party sellers on its platform.

In 2015, few people at Flipkart seemed to bother with the seemingly mundane matter of running the company. Engineers were busy launching new innovative features on the app to fulfil Sachin's wish of revamping Flipkart into a technology company. It was often a self-indulgent pursuit. Two new features were launched in quick succession to much fanfare: Ping, a messaging service, and Image Search, which let customers search for products based on pictures. Flipkart's leaders believed that the continuous introduction of such features would lead to a superior shopping experience on the company's app, better than walking into a mall or a high-end store, certainly better than shopping on the jaded old desktop site. Such 'moonshots'[7] were prioritized even though Flipkart was yet to fix fundamental flaws on its app. Its basic search feature was far worse than that of Amazon. This was symptomatic of the heady environment at the company – it was 'solving First-World problems when it had Third-World issues,' many of which hadn't been addressed. In its early years, Flipkart had been characterized by a 'let's do it' spirit. Now, success was considered inevitable – it was Flipkart's entitlement. The management said, 'Think big – for the long term.' 'And everyone started thinking big,' says a mid-level sales executive. 'Everyone was building for the future. No one was focusing on the present. It was assumed that the moonshots we were pursuing will automatically translate into growth. But how would sales actually increase – no one was going into [these] details. *Bas hawey mein baat ho rahi thi* – everyone was building castles in the sky.'

The marketplace business wasn't faring too well either. Sachin had been insistent that the company immediately shift to the marketplace model. Accordingly, Flipkart tried to move sales of most products – smartphones, its biggest category, was the exception – to third-party sellers. On Sachin's orders, the marketplace team led by Ankit dedicated most of their time towards bringing thousands of new sellers on to Flipkart. Sure enough, every month, the seller count kept going up. Periodically, Flipkart released press statements, celebrating its ever-increasing seller numbers, as if it was breaking records. But no one, apart from Flipkart, was interested, no one was keeping score. Certainly not Flipkart's customers. The headlong shift to the marketplace model, in fact, caused considerable damage to Flipkart's brand. Inexperienced sellers failed to deliver the high standard of service customers expected from Flipkart. Some sellers would ship black T-shirts when customers had ordered grey, or red shirts instead of maroon. Some of them shipped inferior or second-hand goods; many lacked the rigour to meet delivery timelines; fraudulent activities weren't uncommon. Flipkart had been built to be a retailer; its technology tools, processes and logistics systems were designed to serve a retail business. It didn't have the means to run an efficient online marketplace, which is an altogether different business. The company could only have built it over time, but it wasn't ready to wait.

In one especially egregious case, third-party sellers defrauded Flipkart of several crores of rupees. The company had set up a fund to indemnify sellers for 'bad behaviour' by customers. As per Flipkart's policy, if customers returned products despite the sellers not being at fault, they would be compensated by the company. Exploiting this policy, some sellers set up an army in a small city that would place orders only to cancel them. It was a few months before Flipkart caught on to this fraudulent business. It wasn't just Flipkart that had to deal with such problems; all online marketplaces, including Amazon and Snapdeal, struggled with a variety of seller and customer frauds that year. It is a common feature in a nascent market that has suddenly exploded; e-commerce firms eventually catch on and are known to then devise mechanisms to weed out such activities.

In the advertising business, too, Sachin effected radical changes. After taking over the fledgling business in early 2015, one of Sachin's first acts was to shut it down, giving up revenues of ₹10–15 crore every month. 'That is peanuts for a company of Flipkart's size and ambition,' he told his team. By Sachin's logic, since the website would soon be shut down, it made little sense to continue posting ads there. Instead, he urged the advertising team to create new software for Flipkart's mobile app. This would be used to display ads by the growing number of third-party sellers. The company also bought an advertising startup, AdIquity, to serve ads by popular brands.[8] Even before the new advertising software had been created, Sachin promised the company's board of directors that Flipkart would generate $100 million in advertising revenues within one year. If Flipkart achieved this target, it would surpass Facebook's India business – a miraculous feat, as Flipkart enjoyed less than a tenth of Facebook's users. Yet, Sachin was convinced Flipkart would outsmart Facebook the way the American company had outlived old rivals and bested new startups in the US when it had expanded its business to the mobile app a few years ago. Sachin named Flipkart's ads technology FAN – the Flipkart Ads Network. It was inspired by Facebook's FAN – the Facebook Audience Network.

Flipkart was undoubtedly operating in a make-believe technology utopia. In the advertising business, executives spent many weeks working on complex mathematical equations, not to solve business problems but just to distil the performance of the unit into two or three metrics that could be presented to Sachin, on the basis of which he would determine the health of the business and make decisions. It seemed that the Flipkart CEO considered the traditional ways of running a business too backward and unbecoming of himself.

In 2015, Flipkart was both the zeitgeist and a product of its times. It wasn't just Flipkart, engineers at all internet startups had entered their own, self-contained tech utopias. The eighteen months starting from early 2014 was truly an epoch for Indian startups. More capital went into startups in that period than what all Indian internet startups combined had received in the preceding decade.[9] Earlier, if things went well, an investment would be completed within a few months. But in this period, deals were struck in a matter of days. One venture capitalist, Niren Shah, recalls how he was informed, as he was on his way to a scheduled meeting with an entrepreneur, that he would no longer be needed – the entrepreneur had already signed an investment deal minutes before, and within minutes. At a startup conference in 2015, a budding entrepreneur told a journalist that his startup would launch a product that would 'kill' Uber and Ola. Not satisfied with demolishing these transportation companies, he said, 'in confidence', that he was also working on a new search engine that would vanquish Google within two years.[10]

IN AUGUST 2015, the *Economic Times* published an interview with Snapdeal CEO Kunal Bahl. Snapdeal was on a high at the time. It had just received $500 million in capital from Alibaba, Foxconn and SoftBank, in addition to the $850 million it had raised from SoftBank and other investment firms in the previous year. Kunal made a startling claim in the interview: Snapdeal would overtake Flipkart by March 2016. He added that Myntra's app-only move had helped Snapdeal expand its fashion business. He mocked Sachin, calling his move 'the most consumer-unfriendly idea' he had ever heard.[11]

Flipkart executives were furious. They had always considered Snapdeal a pest, not to be taken too seriously, but an irritant nevertheless. But this was too much. A few days later, Mukesh Bansal responded. Flipkart would sell goods worth $10 billion in 2015–16, and 'nobody will be even half of that'.[12]

The hyperbole was indicative of how intense the rivalry between Flipkart and Snapdeal had become after their mega funding rounds of 2014. The two companies were desperate to be seen as the top dog in e-commerce. But they weren't just battling each other. Amazon had made quiet inroads into the minds that mattered most – of shoppers.

Amazon India had set up shop in June 2013, but its expansion had been slow. When Flipkart decided to cut its books budget, Kalyan Krishnamurthy and Binny had been of the opinion that Amazon would not gain much even if they got monopoly of books sales online. It would not be able to cause Flipkart serious damage. The books market was small, less than half a per cent of the overall retail market. It was of no significance, they had concluded. Soon, it became clear that they had made a strategic blunder.

Until late 2014, Amazon had failed to topple Flipkart in any major category. But after being handed the books market on a platter, Amazon had replaced Flipkart as the largest seller of books in the country by the middle of the year. The triumph in books, along with the concurrent victories in laptops and electronic accessories, strengthened Amazon's belief in its India strategy, energized its executives and spurred the company to move faster. It provided Amazon the ideal launchpad from where it could eventually stake its claim to market leadership. By the end of 2015, Amazon had come a long way towards becoming a full-fledged retailer, offering – apart from books – fashion, smartphones, tablets and other products. While Flipkart had wasted many months splitting hairs about whether it was a technology company or a retailer, Amazon had been consumed with attracting and retaining customers, learning the nuances of the Indian retail market and introducing innovations to adapt to it.

Amazon's India head Amit Agarwal was earning his nickname of Jeff Bot. Every week, Amit and his leadership team would gather in a room at the company's headquarters in Bengaluru to discuss the previous week's performance. The meeting would start off with a customer call. It usually got ugly. People could be seen 'bristling, recoiling in their chairs because the customer [was] going on and on' about how Amazon had disappointed them. The call would set the tone for the meeting. Amit himself received many customer emails directly. The worst were those forwarded by Bezos himself (Amazon encouraged customers to write to its leaders directly whenever they faced problems with its service). Amit had read so many such emails that by now he could, like an algorithm, predict an issue after reading a few lines.[13]

The famous Amazonian pursuit of pleasing customers was working out well, especially in the urban areas, where much of online retail was concentrated. In the metros, Amazon's low prices and fast delivery times were winning over an increasing number of shoppers. It was outspending Flipkart and Snapdeal in every area of e-commerce and assembling a product assortment so vast that customers could spend their lives shopping on the platform. Amazon was also occupying massive warehouses every other month, relentlessly expanding its logistics network.

AS THE MONTHS went by, Sachin's impatience grew. Flipkart had still not moved decisively towards shutting the website, and its marketplace shift wasn't happening fast enough for his liking. In September 2015, Sachin issued instructions to remove discounts and other incentives from the desktop site – these would be offered only on its app. He went a step further in October, when Flipkart held its second Big Billion Days sale. It would be a five-day event this time. Sachin had laid down the law to his colleagues and customers: the sale would be held only on the app. Shoppers who went to the Flipkart website were prodded to turn to their apps or install it if they hadn't already. Sachin wasn't just preparing for the mobile-only era, he was trying to hasten its arrival by making a concerted effort to shift shoppers onto the mobile.

Unlike the first Big Billion Day sale, this time it went off without incident. It was held during the middle of October, a few weeks before Diwali. The preparations had been thorough. The technology infrastructure was overhauled. Demand was rationed by assigning one day each to key product categories such as smartphones, electrical appliances and fashion. As with the inaugural sale, Flipkart employees once again worked through nights in the week leading up to Big Billion Days. During the five-day event, Flipkart even stationed an ambulance[14] outside its office, to ferry exhausted workers to nearby hospitals if required. Flipkart had some of the best-paid engineers in the country, working in luxurious, air-conditioned offices stocked with energy bars, food and Red Bulls. No effort would be spared to ensure their upkeep at this juncture; Flipkart was a company with a conscience.

Despite the extensive preparations, Flipkart fell slightly short of its revenue target. It was clear that restricting the sale to the app had caused the deficiency. Still, the Flipkart team was in a celebratory mood: at least the sale had been carried out without major glitches. The company organized a party for all its employees at the end of October. Ayushmann Khurrana, actor and television host, was the host of the party. The singer Vishal Dadlani performed with his band. The headlining act was by film star Akshay Kumar, who entertained several thousand Flipkart employees with a dance routine. It was an extravagant affair – the company had spent more than $1 million on a party that celebrated a sale event just because it had gone off without blunders. It was a measure of how much Flipkart had changed.

Though the decision to restrict the sale to the app had limited Flipkart's reach, Sachin's conviction about the app-only idea hadn't wavered. For him, such fleeting pain was but a trifle. He had his eyes on the far more important objective of establishing absolute dominance in the next big thing – shopping on the mobile. He pointed out to his colleagues the surge in app usage in the past ten months. The number of app downloads had jumped to nearly fifty million from ten million since the end of 2014. Sachin insisted that Flipkart push ahead with its app-only drive. In the weeks after Big Billion Days, Flipkart continued to hold app-only sale events, posting higher prices on products on its website.

But by the end of October 2015, Flipkart's management team had begun rebelling against Sachin's push to close the desktop site. Even Punit expressed opposition to it. After website discounts were halted in September, Flipkart had been deprived of hundreds of millions of dollars in sales. For the second month running, sales targets had been missed – the shortfall roughly amounted to the drop in demand on the desktop website. It wasn't making sense. Flipkart leaders also told Sachin that the company should maintain its retail business and suspend the expansion of the marketplace until it had improved its technology tools and learnt how to run a marketplace platform efficiently. There was enough evidence that the company was suffering badly from the radical shifts it had effected.

Towards the end of the year, Sachin's obsession with going app-only met with its first real backlash from the outside world. Flipkart's largest smartphone supplier, Xiaomi, informed the company that it would no longer work exclusively with Flipkart. It was keen on expanding its retail presence. In private, Xiaomi executives told their Flipkart associates that the exclusivity arrangement was no longer satisfactory. Flipkart had lost its status as the preponderant e-commerce brand. Its service had become unreliable and inconsistent, and its app-only rhetoric made little sense to brands or to shoppers. On the other hand, Amazon, the legendary international e-commerce champion, was the rising power in India. Its user numbers and sales were expanding much faster than Flipkart's. It was clear to Xiaomi, the most sought-after brand in e-commerce, whose future was brighter. And to sweeten the deal, Amazon was offering more lucrative terms than Flipkart. It was a no-brainer: Xiaomi decided it would now supply its latest phone models to Amazon instead of Flipkart.

In December 2015, the worrying pattern – a slowdown in Flipkart's sales growth – that had developed over the past three months, endured. In fact, nearly all the important business metrics showed an alarming decline. New users weren't coming in droves any more, customer loyalty was down, customer satisfaction scores were at an all-time low. Losses had gone up, not frighteningly, but every metric was tainted by the diminishing sales figures. The advertising business that Sachin was overseeing had also failed to take off. Contrary to his promise of delivering ad revenues of $100 million by the middle of 2016, less than five per cent of this figure had been achieved by the end of 2015. It was evident that his target was ludicrously out of reach.

Meanwhile, Amazon expanded at terrifying speed. Flipkart wasn't in crisis yet, but the crisis wasn't far.

Sensing that his management team had lost confidence in his vision, Sachin was becoming anxious. Lee Fixel and the other board members had been questioning him for nearly three months, demanding to know why Flipkart had missed its targets and how it was planning to get back on track. In the internet space, one poor quarter was bad, two catastrophic. Sachin would have to make some big adjustments.

20

AFTER BANSAL, BANSAL

It was a few days before Christmas. Sachin Bansal told Lee Fixel over a call that it was best for the company if he stepped down. He added that Binny, who was also part of the call, should be made CEO instead. 'Binny is better at operations and execution and that is what we need right now.'[1]

Lee was taken aback, but he was also relieved.

Over the past few weeks, he had received damning feedback about the Flipkart management team from Kalyan Krishnamurthy and others. While Kalyan had left the company and resigned from its board of directors, he had kept in touch with many Flipkart managers. When in Bangalore, Kalyan often worked out of a Novotel just across the road from the Flipkart headquarters. He ensured that he received regular updates on all matters Flipkart from his former underlings. These employees had painted for him a picture of a company in turmoil, one that had lost it bearings. They called the new senior leaders hired from Google and McKinsey 'clueless'. They also decried the leadership of Sachin and Mukesh, both of whom, they said, were operating in a make-believe world. Kalyan had relayed these reports to Lee. In addition, citing data and insights provided by a local market research firm that Tiger Global had engaged, Kalyan warned Lee that Flipkart was on the verge of being overtaken by Amazon.

At Kalyan's prompting, Lee had also spoken with a small group of former Flipkart executives whom he held in high regard. These executives, including two of Kalyan's closest associates, had left the company earlier in the year after falling out with Sachin. And just like Kalyan, they were also in touch with their friends at Flipkart. Lee found out that they had heard Sachin and Mukesh were out of their depth. 'Flipkart is being ruined,' one of them said to Lee. Like Kalyan, they had been seething after being cast aside by Sachin. Now they seized their chance to retaliate. Railing against Sachin's radical plan to remake Flipkart, they told Lee that it was fundamentally flawed and 'badly executed'. They presented Lee with a remedy: bring back Kalyan. They stressed that it was no coincidence that Flipkart's best years – 2013 and 2014 – had come to pass under Kalyan's stewardship. He was the only one who could rescue Flipkart, they claimed.

After noting the forcefulness with which so many of Sachin's former colleagues and friends were attacking him, Lee was concerned, especially as the decline in Flipkart's business was evident. The company had missed its sales targets for several months. The much-touted advertising business looked hopeless.

Before he had chosen to step down as CEO, Sachin had considered another option: to take over the daily running of the company himself. With his colleagues opposed to the app-only move and the total conversion to a marketplace, the only way Sachin could enforce the changes was by directly taking charge of the commerce platform – Mukesh's role – himself.

When Sachin discussed this with Binny, he was surprised at his co-founder's response. For much of 2015, Binny had been withdrawn. He had restricted himself to overseeing Ekart, the logistics service. Throughout the year, Binny hadn't openly articulated his views about Sachin's attempted overhaul of Flipkart, including the app-only move. Employees weren't entirely sure if Binny was for or against it. He didn't oppose Sachin, at least not in front of others, nor was he a proponent of Sachin's ideas. Finally, in private, Binny rejected the option that Sachin put forward. Instead, he staked his claim, 'You've been CEO for eight years. It's my turn now.'[2]

Sachin knew he would have to give in. Binny was a co-founder, he knew the company as well as anyone, and he commanded respect. Sachin and Binny had always had a tacit understanding about handing over the reins of the company to each other if needed. This had happened roughly every fifteen to eighteen months in the recent past. Sachin had been in command for the first five years of Flipkart's existence. Binny had taken over at the end of 2012, only to make way for Sachin in the second half of 2014. It was now Binny's turn at the wheel. Although this time there was one big difference: Binny had insisted on the CEO tag, ensuring that his ascendance would be irreversibly formalized.

After the Bansals spoke with Lee, the other board members, including Subrata Mitra of Accel Partners and Oliver Rippel of Naspers, were informed. By Christmas, it was done. Binny would be promoted to CEO while Sachin would step aside and take up the role of Executive Chairman.

A few days after the first call, Sachin spoke with members of the Flipkart board again. He pitched the idea of making Mukesh Bansal CEO of Flipkart. He proposed a structure in which Binny would be the Group CEO, with the heads of Flipkart and Myntra reporting to him. But Lee immediately rebuffed Sachin. Not only did he hold Sachin and Mukesh responsible for the poor implementation of their big ideas, he now believed the ideas themselves had been calamitous. To overcome the debacle, Flipkart needed someone who excelled in operations, who knew the company in and out. Flipkart's poor performance in the past year and his exchanges with the former Flipkart executives had convinced Lee that while Mukesh had been an excellent entrepreneur at Myntra, he wasn't equipped to manage a company of Flipkart's size.

In January 2016, on the second Monday of the new year, the company went public with the news. The three Bansals went on overdrive to insist that these changes would strengthen Flipkart. Sachin tweeted: 'Welcome @binnybansal as the CEO of @Flipkart. Together we'll create magic.'[3]

In an email to employees, Sachin's tone was unequivocally upbeat: 'We want to prove that India can produce a world class internet company that can outshine and outclass any global behemoth. We also want to play a pivotal role in shaping the internet and the commerce ecosystem of India.' Binny, too, proclaimed that Flipkart had all the 'necessary ingredients of brilliant talent and great technology' to continue being successful.[4]

Reassuring emails notwithstanding, the employees at all

levels were in shock. This wasn't something anyone had seen coming; even Flipkart's senior leaders were caught unawares.

Flipkart had recently expanded its leadership team. It had hired yet another senior engineer from Google, Surojit Chatterjee, into the product division. Samardeep Subandh, who had worked for more than fifteen years at the large consumer goods companies, Hindustan Unilever and Marico, was recruited to head marketing.

After taking over as CEO, Binny called for a discussion with his management team. At the meeting, his words were blunt, urgent. 'This is a crisis. I'm declaring emergency.' He warned that the next few months would be 'very tough'. But, he promised: 'We'll turn it around.'

Towards the end of January 2016, Binny repeated this message at the quarterly meeting of Flipkart's board of directors in Dubai. The environment there was very different from the triumphant vibe of many past meetings. The board members were sombre; Lee was especially concerned. The months-long decline in Flipkart's business was showing no sign of improvement. At the same time, Amazon India was thriving. They would soon announce that in the last three months of 2015, the company had generated higher sales than in the entirety of 2014.[5]

Lee and the other board members reminded Sachin about all the targets that Flipkart had missed and everything that had gone awry.

Jumping to his own defence, Sachin urged everyone to have patience. 'These things take some time.' They have made a decision and now they needed to see it through.

Lee was too anxious to let the matter rest. Flipkart was his biggest holding. In fact, it was more than just an important investment – Lee's career depended on it. The success of his massive bet hinged on a continuous, enormous expansion in Flipkart's sales for years to come. And yet, for the past five months, sales had barely advanced. To see Flipkart's growth stall already was unpalatable. Lee would have to take action, even if it meant upsetting one of his favourite entrepreneurs.

He proposed to the Bansals that Flipkart should bring back Kalyan Krishnamurthy, whom he regarded as a turnaround specialist. But Sachin, expectedly, wouldn't have it. He had arranged for Kalyan's exit from Flipkart barely a year ago. He had then ensured that Kalyan wouldn't have any role on the company's board. There was no way he would allow Kalyan to return.

Lee persisted, now appealing to Binny. But Binny, too, wasn't convinced. It wouldn't be the right move, he said, and asked for some time to consider it. He assured the board members that Flipkart would soon reverse the slowdown in sales growth. Not only that, he also promised to reduce the company's costs and resurrect its excellence in customer service.

At the meeting, no one had anything to say to Mukesh. Over the past year, he had played a leading role at board meetings, making presentations, elaborating on Flipkart's transformation and discussing quarterly performance. This time, he was on the periphery, a worried spectator.

IT WAS NOW unanimous that Flipkart had faltered the previous year. The company needed to work out who were accountable. At Flipkart, this meant one thing: senior executives would have to go.

The first obvious candidate was Punit Soni. As Chief Product Officer, Punit had wielded immense power. His imperious manner and love of the limelight had earned him many enemies. The big features he had introduced, such as Ping and Image Search, hadn't taken off. Sales had suffered. Even the app hadn't improved noticeably; customers were certainly not raving about it, much less having an orgasm. Although he had been at Flipkart for less than a year, it was decided that he had to be removed immediately – hiring him had turned out to be a blunder. It was Mukesh who took the decision. Binny, now Mukesh's boss, couldn't care less. Sachin, who had recruited Punit, had also grown weary of him. Less than a year after he had moved back to India, Punit was cut loose – by the end of his term, he had little to show for it and no one willing to defend him.

A few days after Mukesh fired Punit, he was called into a meeting by Binny. It was now his turn at the guillotine. Binny told him summarily that he was no longer needed. As the head of the company's commerce platform, Mukesh had been responsible for the overall business performance. He would have to pay for the sales slowdown with his job. After building up Myntra into a successful e-commerce firm, Mukesh had become one of the best-known internet entrepreneurs in India. He had considered Sachin and Binny his equals, and was seemingly treated as one by the Flipkart co-founders. When he had been given charge of the daily running of the company in early 2015, Mukesh had believed it was just a matter of time before he would be made CEO. But he had been found wanting. He had failed to impose order, to bring unity between the various teams of which he was in charge. He had let the technology division indulge in excesses to disastrous effect on the company's business and culture. Mukesh believed that he had been hamstrung by Sachin's constant interference. But he would still have to go. That's how it had always been at Flipkart: a chosen one would be built up as a star, the Next Big Thing, until suddenly they were not, at which point they were coldly discarded. Mukesh still had an excellent reputation as an entrepreneur and was highly regarded by venture capitalists. He decided to return to entrepreneurship.

Around the same time, Ankit Nagori, the chief business officer, resigned. After joining Flipkart in 2010 at the juniormost level, Ankit had risen to the top echelon of the company. All that was left was for him to occupy the hot seat. But it wasn't to be. His stature had taken a hit after it became clear that the headlong shift to the marketplace model had damaged the company. While Ankit hadn't conceived the project, he was responsible for its implementation, which had been poor. All of thirty, Ankit decided to leave on his terms while he still could. Before he came to Flipkart, he had started a company of his own; now he felt ready to become an entrepreneur again.

Even though Ankit and Mukesh left on a bitter note, their exits were graceful, especially by Flipkart's dreadful standards. Sachin and Binny praised their contributions, and both were given warm farewells.

But there was another person, apart from Mukesh and Punit, for whom Binny had no room in his team. It was his friend and business partner, Sachin Bansal. For years Binny had admitted to colleagues that he wished Sachin would develop better interpersonal skills to mitigate his harsh personality. But he had always maintained that Sachin's technology acumen, his relationships with investors, and above all, his audacity for coming up with transformative ideas, overshadowed all negatives. After the debacle of last year, however, Binny had changed his mind. He made himself clear: Sachin would have no say in Flipkart's daily operations. It was one of his boldest acts ever, surprising colleagues who had seen him willingly play second fiddle to Sachin for so many years.

WITHIN A FEW weeks of taking over, Binny prepared a plan to reinvigorate the company. As COO, Binny had been the prototype of a behind-the-scenes operator. He wasn't known to be especially decisive or imaginative – that was Sachin's forte. Binny's inclination and expertise lay in managing the more mundane matters, the internal organs that made the company tick.

As CEO, Binny was suddenly a man transformed. It was the first time he had been formally recognized as the top boss at Flipkart, and he revelled in the limelight. Just like Sachin, he was thrilled to be in charge, eager to outline a new path for Flipkart. He shared Sachin's dream of building Flipkart into a giant internet company. But his methods were different, and he discarded many of his co-founder's ways. Sachin's two big ideas – the app-only focus and the marketplace conversion – were immediately reversed.

In fact, around this time, even Myntra had decided to reopen its website, in yet another indictment of Sachin's failed vision. The previous year, Myntra had appointed Ananth Narayanan, a former director at McKinsey, as CEO. Within a few months of taking the reins, Ananth had informed Sachin and Flipkart's board that he wanted to re-launch the website. Myntra was losing out on a large chunk of sales and some of its loyal customers had been alienated by the app-only move. When he was hired, Ananth had been promised complete independence in directing Myntra. Now, even though Sachin was disappointed, he kept his word and let Ananth have his way. The board, on the other hand, was thrilled. After a few months of preparation, Myntra restarted its website in June 2016, a year after it had been shut down.[6]

Back at Flipkart, Binny was of the opinion that the company had forgotten how to do the simple things well. There had been too much talk about technology, but little action. Despite Sachin's sincere intent to introduce technology in every aspect of the business, he and his chosen leaders had failed to come up with a meticulous or practical approach to make it happen. In the process, the fundamentals had been ignored. Binny strived to take the company back to its roots and throw all its resources towards delivering the best shopping service to customers – what Flipkart had once been known for. He repeatedly told his team: 'Let's get our mojo back.'

As a start, Binny immediately ordered a reduction in costs. He called for frugality and set a goal of breaking even at the gross margin level before the end of the year. He had taken this upon himself; the company's board of directors were primarily concerned about the slowdown in sales. But of all the leaders in Flipkart's eight-year history, Binny had been one of the few who had constantly emphasized the need for building a self-sustaining business. He was clear that the time had come to create a strong, lasting foundation. To do that, it was essential to fix the cost structure. He was determined to break Flipkart's dependence on fresh capital – the company couldn't be at the mercy of investors forever.

Binny was convinced that he could accomplish both tasks together: cut costs *and* revive sales growth. He blamed the sales stagnation on issues such as the decline in the quality of goods and the lack of depth in product assortment, especially when compared with Amazon. 'If Amazon has five products, we have one,' he complained. He concluded that Flipkart should identify high-quality, high-volume products in each category and stock up on these items rather than try to compete with Amazon on offering the broadest range of goods. They needed to take a depth-over-width approach. He also pointed out that the search function on Flipkart's website was terrible – even if Flipkart had a product on offer, customers would all too often fail to find it.

Binny was certain that if Flipkart fixed these issues, growth would return on its own. He deciphered that the growing cost bill and sales slowdown were in some ways linked. Since Flipkart now relied on third-party sellers, the quality of products had understandably deteriorated, which led to higher product returns. This, in turn, pushed up logistics costs. Additionally, with Flipkart's sales function having lost its rigour, its product assortment was a mess. In effect, Flipkart's service was neither cost-efficient nor particularly appealing to customers: a most wasteful combination. If the quality of goods improved and its assortment could be enhanced, the company would see an increase in sales as well as a drop in costs. Such was Binny's confidence in this assessment that he instructed his team to reduce discounting. He wasn't interested in 'buying revenues' by offering mindless discounts or entering a price war with

Amazon in the smartphones business, which comprised about half of all e-commerce in India. Though these moves were evidently risky, he was willing to give up a few millions in sales to make the business truly healthier.

In March 2016, Binny elaborated on his strategy in an email to all employees: 'Going forward, we will follow a clear set of priorities – first and always deliver product quality and service quality to our customers as a non-negotiable starting point – we cannot scale without this. Only after we deliver this should we pursue growth – this is what made Flipkart different when we started and we have to go back to these fundamentals.'[7]

When Flipkart was still new, Binny had spent considerable time conceiving the structures and processes according to which the company should function. Where Sachin saw himself as a technologist and attempted to mould Flipkart in that image, Binny was a corporate literature geek. He, too, was convinced about the supremacy of technology but he was equally fascinated by management theories. Despite his demanding schedule, he had been a voracious reader for many years, often getting through a book a week. He favoured non-fiction, especially books on management. He read a large range of business books. His favourites included *Playing to Win*, a book about Procter & Gamble, co-authored by A. G. Lafley, the company's former CEO, and *Zero to One*, the startup bible co-written by Peter Thiel, an American entrepreneur and venture capitalist. He also loved reading the *Harvard Business Review*, the management magazine published by Harvard University. Binny would sometimes adopt the exact language of the books he had just read. After finishing *Playing to Win*, instead of asking colleagues, 'What's the strategy?', he would say, 'What's your playground? What are you trying to win?' His colleagues found it amusing. 'It's almost like he regretted not going to management school,' reflects a colleague who worked closely with Binny in 2016.

Binny quickly identified the executives who would implement his directives. He handed the key sales function to Samardeep Subandh, or Samar, as everyone called him. With his vast experience in sales and marketing, Samar was an authority on the consumer goods market. For Ekart, he chose Saikiran Krishnamurthy (Saiki), who had held a senior position in the marketplace business the previous year. A graduate of IIM Ahmedabad, Saiki had joined Flipkart after spending more than fifteen years at McKinsey, where he had risen to become senior partner. Though the commerce platform had fared miserably the previous year, Saiki, as one of its seniormost executives, had escaped censure. Like many good consultants, he was a charming, smooth-talking salesman. Hair combed neatly, dressed in an understated manner, Saiki exuded good vibes. Binny was instantly impressed with him. Saiki was given a broad mandate: improve Ekart's delivery speed, introduce more automation at Flipkart warehouses and prepare Ekart to serve other companies as a courier service. Given its substantial infrastructure, Binny believed that Ekart could become a large courier company, a rival to DHL and Blue Dart.

Another leader who quickly became an integral part of Binny's team was Nitin Seth. After graduating from IIT Delhi and then IIM Lucknow, Nitin had worked as a consultant and run an internet startup during the dotcom boom of the early 2000s. But his healthcare startup failed miserably, after which Nitin went on to head the offshore operations of McKinsey and Fidelity International in India. Like many others who had seen the dramatic rise of Flipkart from the outside, Nitin had been enthralled by the prospect of building The Great Indian Internet Company and its immense wealth-creating potential. When he joined Flipkart as Chief People Officer in March 2016, Nitin admitted that it was 'very inspiring to see Binny and Sachin's vision of creating a world-class company out of India.'[8] A devout Hindu, one of his favourite books was the Bhagavad Gita, which he had read many times over. Nitin's hiring had been finalized by Sachin and Mukesh before Binny became CEO. But after Nitin joined, Binny was impressed by his energy and willingness to act boldly. Nitin sported a handlebar moustache and would regularly wear T-shirts with the Flipkart logo. In his mid-forties, he was nearly a decade older than Binny, who addressed Nitin as 'sir'.

In early April, Binny made two more additions to his team, persuading Sameer Nigam and Rahul Chari to return to the company. In 2011, Flipkart had bought Sameer and Rahul's music software startup Mime360. Sameer had left the company in July 2015 after falling out with Sachin. Rahul, who had been Sameer's close friend for nearly two decades, followed him a few months later. By early 2016, they had decided to launch a mobile payments startup together. Unified Payments Interface (UPI), the new national digital payments infrastructure, was to be introduced later in the year. PhonePe, Sameer and Rahul's startup, would build a UPI payments app. PhonePe had, in fact, attracted a good deal of interest from venture capital firms that believed UPI would become the primary mode of digital payments in the country.

Amidst all of this, Sameer had kept in touch with Binny.

Flipkart had always wanted to establish a payments business but had failed to come up with an attractive product. The advent of UPI and the technological expertise of Sameer and Rahul seemed a compelling proposition to Binny, who offered to buy out PhonePe even before its app had even been designed. The negotiations continued for many weeks, as Sameer sought assurances that the constant volatility at Flipkart wouldn't derail PhonePe's advance. Finally, at the end of March, a deal was agreed. While PhonePe would become a subsidiary of Flipkart, it would function independently. The transaction was structured in a mutually beneficial way – as PhonePe expanded, it would trigger increasing amounts of stock payouts to Sameer, Rahul and their colleagues. The bigger PhonePe got, the more wealth its executives would accumulate, making it an overall win for Flipkart.

Sameer extracted one critical concession: if Flipkart replaced its current CEO, the stock payouts due to Sameer and his PhonePe colleagues would be accelerated.

BY EARLY 2016, the euphoria around Indian startups had all but vanished. Venture capitalists found that they had vastly overestimated the size of the internet market as well as the speed at which startups could be built here. They had seen many companies devour capital and still produce only meagre revenues. After realizing that many of their portfolio companies had no future, investors turned tail. Instead of finalizing a deal in days, they dwelt over decisions for months. The balance of power that had fleetingly moved in favour of entrepreneurs was now restored to the side of the venture capitalists. An engineering degree from an IIT plus a bright idea were no longer enough to attract millions in capital. Startups that had already raised capital were ordered by their patrons to cut losses. This proved to be fatal for many firms, whose business models had not been set up for self-sustenance. As soon as the supply of capital was severed, small and mid-size internet startups immediately diminished in size. Several startups wound down like pricked balloons. Some were sold at cut-price deals. Thousands of startup employees lost their jobs.[9]

For now, the biggest startups had enough capital to avoid such an outcome. Far too much money had already been invested in these companies. The fate of their investors hinged on their survival. And so, these companies, too, faced a reckoning. The most prominent among them was Snapdeal. In August 2015, Kunal Bahl had claimed that Snapdeal would overtake Flipkart by the end of the year. A few months later, it had come nowhere close. Snapdeal had relied on incessant discounting to win market share. By the end of 2015, it had become clear to SoftBank as well as Snapdeal's other shareholders that persisting with this approach would lead to destruction. Amazon wasn't going to lose a price war. Flipkart, too, had far more capital. Never mind toppling Flipkart, Snapdeal would now have to fight for its life. The only means of survival was to reduce costs, discounts, salaries, marketing, everything.

Discounted phones had comprised a large part of Snapdeal's sales. As soon as the discounts were lowered, customers deserted the platform. To nobody's surprise, a big chunk of Snapdeal's business vanished. While Flipkart and even Amazon had dangled low prices to lure customers, Snapdeal's dependence on this tactic was the highest. And unlike its rivals, Snapdeal lacked a substantial infrastructure of warehousing and logistics; in effect, it was simply a website showcasing goods.

In normal circumstances, Snapdeal's loss should have been Flipkart's gain. But Flipkart was slow to react, too busy sorting itself out to accept the gift. The business that Snapdeal lost forever in early 2016 went instead to Amazon. As Snapdeal's smartphone sales collapsed, it was overtaken by Amazon almost overnight. It marked a stunning turn for the American retailer in India. Even though it had launched many years after Flipkart and Snapdeal, Amazon had already accumulated the widest range of products. It offered about fifty-five million products as opposed to Flipkart's forty million and Snapdeal's thirty-five million offerings. Among the three, its sales composition was the most diverse and well-balanced. It had built up a massive network of e-commerce infrastructure. It now operated twenty-one warehouses and supported fifty others owned by its sellers. Flipkart had just seventeen.[10] Now that it had overtaken Snapdeal, Amazon had Flipkart within its sight.

Amazon had already persuaded Xiaomi to break its exclusivity pact with Flipkart in late 2015. A few months later, it even lured away Motorola from its rival. And apart from spending on infrastructure, Amazon splurged tens of millions of dollars every month on discounts, marketing and subsidized order deliveries. The company believed it had, in all likelihood, lost out in China because it hadn't invested enough in expanding its operations there. It wouldn't make that mistake in India. Amazon's ascent to the top of the Indian e-commerce market seemed unstoppable.

At Flipkart, Binny wasn't overly bothered by Amazon's rise. Flipkart was nimbler than its greatest rival, which, after all, was just an outpost of a large multinational company with its attendant bureaucracy. Flipkart, on the other hand, was an agile startup, a local company, created by Indians, for Indian customers. Binny believed that Flipkart's understanding of the market was far more nuanced. He took great pride in Flipkart's record of coming up with market-changing innovations. Though the company had lost its way for a few months, its business was largely intact, unlike the case with Snapdeal. It had held on to its position as market leader, if only by a thread. Binny was convinced that if Flipkart resolved its problems, the company would easily prevail over Amazon.

Unfortunately for him, the first five months of 2016 happened to be an especially vexatious period in e-commerce, even worse than the second half of 2012 when Flipkart's business had suffered a sudden slump. Not only did he have to contend with a global technology champion with limitless capital, he was operating in an altogether new, frightening reality: a slowdown in the e-commerce market. This came as a terrible blow to the entire startup ecosystem. Investors, entrepreneurs, bankers and analysts who had predicted unabated expansion for many years to come, couldn't believe that the market had already reached a standstill. They were shocked that the retail market had proved to be far trickier than the one they had seen in Powerpoint presentations and on Excel sheets. It made mockery – yet again – of the belief that the retail business in India could be as smoothly organized and rewarding as China's. The slowdown had been caused primarily by the reduction in discounts by local e-commerce firms. When prices on shopping sites inched closer to the MRP, many shoppers deserted these platforms. It also came to light that some of the sales at these companies had, in fact, come from wholesalers, who had exploited the low prices by buying in bulk! As policies were introduced to plug this loophole, sales fell further. Flipkart's internal problems, of course, didn't help either. It was Flipkart and its innovations that had propelled the e-commerce market for years. But in 2016, Flipkart had lost the capacity to steer the market, preoccupied as it was in recovering from last year's blunders.

In February 2016, Flipkart had been hit by another shocker. Morgan Stanley, a Flipkart investor, depreciated the value of its holdings in the firm by as much as twenty-seven per cent. A few months later, two other mutual fund investors in Flipkart also reduced the value of their holdings. These were only estimates: no transaction had been carried out at the marked-down prices. Nevertheless, the markdowns made for juicy news stories, especially as the firms behind them were Flipkart's own investors.[11] For a startup, valuation is seen as the ultimate measure of success. Startups aren't like public companies. Movement, upwards or downwards, in the shares of a listed firm is a matter of course, but if a startup suffers a fall in valuation, it's a major embarrassment for its founders and investors. Flipkart's markdowns solidified the impression that it was in deep trouble. The negative headlines just wouldn't stop. In May 2016, the company deferred the joining date of its IIM hires by six months, citing an 'organization redesign'.[12] It was an unavoidable outcome of Binny's plan to reduce costs. This was hardly a tragedy, but it did tarnish Flipkart's image. It seemed like the company was in free fall.

By the end of May, Binny had, in fact, started bringing about some big improvements in Flipkart's business. In just five months, costs had reduced dramatically – by more than thirty per cent. Flipkart's customer satisfaction scores were gradually inching upwards. Delivery times were improving. In an interview, Binny emphasized that Flipkart's biggest priority was to be 'very, very consumer-focused'.[13] The most important metric at the company now was net promoter score, a key measure of customer satisfaction. If Flipkart kept customers happy, it was a matter of time before sales would start expanding, he assured.

But Binny's investors weren't placated. So far, in his five months as CEO, Binny had failed to recapture sales growth. Entrepreneurs are expected to find the balance between the pursuit of long-term objectives and the achievement of everyday goals. Flipkart's investors believed that Binny was so consumed by long-term objectives that the current, more pressing matters – especially growing sales and holding off Amazon – weren't getting the required attention. They believed it was high-minded of Binny to build a self-sustaining company, but it could not be done at the cost of growth. For investors, it was ultimately the only thing that really mattered: growth – how much, how fast. They had no inclination to pour any more money into Flipkart. Other investors would have to be found. Moreover, showing consistently high sales expansion was the only way to attract capital. It was also the sole means for its present investors to get at least some returns on an investment that was unravelling.

Flipkart was battling for its survival, and yet, its approach, under Binny's leadership, didn't seem to reflect this urgency. Increasingly, investors found it hard to shake off the feeling that Binny wasn't moving fast enough. Their patience was running out.

In April 2016, *Time* magazine named Binny and Sachin in its annual list of the '100 Most Influential People' in the world, calling them 'nimble tacticians and hardheaded realists'.[14] It was the latest recognition of their status as entrepreneurial icons. For a long time, it would also be the high point of their professional lives.

21

THE TIGER CUB RETURNS

After Nitin Seth joined Flipkart as Chief People Officer, to look after the Human Resources division, he rapidly became one of the most influential leaders at the company. The much-mocked HR division is often seen as a necessary but annoying function filled with lazy paper-pushers. But Nitin wasn't a typical HR chief. Having run large companies, he was very ambitious – for him, HR was just a point of entry into Flipkart. Within a few months he had not only formed a close relationship with Binny and Sachin, Nitin had also won the trust of some key board members at Flipkart. Nitin had prepared a blueprint to fix Flipkart that Binny encouraged him to present to the board. Thereafter, he would sometimes speak directly with Lee Fixel and Subrata Mitra of Accel Partners.

Lee had assigned two major goals to Nitin. The first was to reduce costs. This was something he had started working on even before meeting Lee. On his arrival at Flipkart, Nitin had been shocked by the state of the company. It was losing millions of dollars every week at an unacceptable rate. The company had become bloated, overstaffed, directionless. He saw that it would be foolish to add more employees. Within a few weeks of joining, he halted recruitment, after which he moved to implement the company's biggest-ever job cuts. He also deferred the hiring of the IIM graduates that Flipkart had agreed to employ before he joined.[1] These decisions made him a villainous figure at the company. Though Nitin conducted nearly two dozen town-hall meetings to explain his decisions, many employees refused to be mollified. At these meetings, he was viewed with resentment and suspicion. But he didn't mind. Flipkart was in crisis. Difficult measures would have to be taken.

While Nitin was seen as a ruthless leader greedy for power, his boldness and decisiveness won over Binny and Sachin as well as the board members. Few others had shown the willingness to take up the unpopular but essential assignment of shedding jobs. But after it was done, Flipkart was able to shrink its wage bill and conserve cash. Binny rewarded Nitin by expanding his role, trusting strategy, analytics and other divisions in his care.

The second task Lee had assigned Nitin was more perilous: convince Binny to bring back Kalyan Krishnamurthy. Although the Bansals had resisted Lee's proposal to reinstate Kalyan in January 2016, he had later brought it up several times with Binny. Lee had also enlisted the services of a few Flipkart executives to persuade Binny, among whom Nitin was the most influential. It wasn't just Lee who was agitating for Kalyan's return. Some juniors of Nitin from IIT Delhi who were senior managers at Flipkart also spoke highly of Kalyan, urging Nitin to bring him back. An introductory meeting was arranged between Kalyan and Nitin. They had a few things in common.

Both were strong-willed, high-octane, all-action men, burning with ambition. Both were in their mid-forties and had no doubt that the best part of their careers was yet to come. The meeting went well and they stayed in touch regularly thereafter.

Until early June, Binny kept vetoing Kalyan's return. Whenever Nitin or Lee or anyone else raised the topic, he would insist that they didn't need Kalyan. Binny had many misgivings about him. Kalyan might be able to improve sales but the company's culture would suffer, he said. 'It's always my way or the highway for Kalyan.'[2] Binny also did not approve of Kalyan's reliance on discounts to raise sales in many categories. 'It's too short-term,' he pointed out. What would they do when money ran out?

Eventually, Binny's resistance proved futile. One of the reasons was that Binny's relationship with the Flipkart investors had altered. Until the end of 2015, Lee had had tremendous faith in Sachin and Binny. But the failure of Sachin's attempted transformation of Flipkart had shaken him up. He mainly held Sachin responsible for the disaster. But it was true that Binny, too, had been an integral part of that project. Though not as weakened as Sachin's, Binny's standing with Lee had diminished as well.

Finally, in early June, Lee prevailed over him. Flipkart's sales were still stagnant. There was a strong likelihood that Amazon could overtake the company at any moment. Binny reluctantly agreed to bring back Kalyan on one condition: Kalyan would be kept on a leash, his role limited and temporary. Around mid-June, Flipkart reappointed Kalyan in a strangely titled role, Head – Category Design Management.

In truth, Kalyan's title was a subterfuge. It was inevitable that he would have complete control of Flipkart's sales and marketing functions. His immediate mandate was unambiguous: revive sales growth and prevent Amazon from dislodging Flipkart.

It was a tough ask. Amazon had built up serious momentum and was within touching distance of Flipkart. The gap between the two companies was less than $100 million in monthly gross sales. With each passing month, Amazon was closing in. This was a staggering achievement given that it had started out in India just three years ago. Of course, unlike Flipkart, Amazon wasn't constrained by the task of having to raise capital. Still, its ascent had been remarkably swift. In April 2016, Jeff Bezos had promoted Amit Agarwal, the Amazon India head, to his 'S-Team'. This team comprised the seniormost leaders at Amazon globally under Bezos. Amit, who had a love of mountaineering, savoured the moment – at the age of forty-one, he had risen to Amazon's summit. In an email to employees, Bezos said, 'Amit and our India team are doing remarkable things. Amit and his experience in India will be a key resource for all of us on S-team as we work to figure out what it is to be a true global company.'[3] By promoting Amit, Bezos had displayed his great satisfaction with the performance of the India business.

A few weeks later, he went for the kill.

In early June, around the same time that Kalyan was preparing to return to Flipkart, Bezos announced that Amazon would invest an additional $3 billion in India, having nearly exhausted its earlier investment pledge of $2 billion. He made the announcement in Washington, D.C. at the US India Business Council's global leadership awards ceremony, where he was feted by Indian Prime Minister Narendra Modi. He spent nearly half an hour in conversation with Modi. Bezos gushed about the 'huge potential' of the Indian economy and mentioned that the Amazon India team was 'surpassing even our most ambitious milestones'.[4]

One year later, Bezos again met Modi at an industry event in the US state capital. At this conference, he found another well-known CEO courting the Indian PM: Doug McMillon, head of Walmart, the world's largest retailer.

IN HIS FIRST stint at Flipkart, Kalyan, as Lee Fixel's man on the ground, had initially been feared. Very soon, however, his straight talk and deep knowledge of e-commerce had won over colleagues. Unusually for a Tamil Brahmin, Kalyan preferred to speak in Hindi, in which he was fluent. He was blunt, unrelenting, like a robot, with little time for anything apart from work.

This time round, Kalyan was in no mood for niceties.

As he was walking into the office on his first day back at Flipkart, Kalyan was greeted by a division manager who was sipping chai outside. Warmly, this executive asked, 'How are you, Kalyan? It's been a long time.'

'Good. And you?' said Kalyan.

'Very good.'

'Very good? Look at what you guys have done to the company. You find it good? I find it irresponsible!'[5]

Leaving the employee speechless, Kalyan strode into work.

At the office, he immediately called for a meeting of key Flipkart executives. He asked them pointed questions about their roles and the performance of their functions. 'I'm happy to have come back and am looking forward to working with everyone – there's obviously a lot of work to be done,' Kalyan told them.[6] When a colleague asked about his role, the title being vague, Kalyan made sure there was no room for doubt about his authority. 'I'll run the show now,' he said. 'I will decide how things are to be done here.'[7]

In his very first week back at Flipkart, Kalyan showed just how serious he was about that statement. Based on the intelligence that his acolytes had supplied to him beforehand, Kalyan had singled out executives in the sales function who would have to go. As soon as his return was finalized, he demanded their removal. It had the legitimacy of an edict. These executives weren't even allowed a chance to defend themselves. What made it all the more shocking was that two of them had been Kalyan's protégés during his first tenure; they were people he had eagerly promoted. Now, Kalyan betrayed no qualms about discarding them. Nitin Seth, who had pledged to work closely with Kalyan, facilitated these exits. Kalyan had convinced Nitin that he needed freedom to operate and couldn't be hindered by bureaucracy. He would need to form his own team; senior leaders would have to be sidelined. Kalyan made it clear who he would work with and for whom he had no time. Given the trouble that Flipkart had found itself in, there was no time to play nice, Kalyan told Nitin. And just as Kalyan wanted, changes were instantly executed. The people Kalyan had chosen were immediately given new roles to support him; those who didn't have his blessings were made irrelevant, regardless of their title.

The message to the rest of the organization was clear: Flipkart was now going to be merciless. If you didn't deliver, you would be cast away without a second thought. There was too much money involved, too many important careers that hinged on Flipkart's turnaround. No one could be allowed to come in Kalyan's way, collateral damage be damned. A group of Binny's closest associates found this out at close quarters within a few days of Kalyan's entry. In a meeting, these executives were debating whether Flipkart should hold the Big Billion Days sale that year. While it would boost Flipkart's sales, the company would also end up losing large amounts of cash. Did it really bring any lasting benefits to Flipkart, they asked one another. Kalyan was infuriated by the discussion – that such a debate was being held in this most critical of periods told him that these people were amateurs. 'You guys can discuss whatever you feel like but I've already started placing orders for BBD,' Kalyan said to them, before storming out.

Kalyan's acerbic manner and his decision to summarily remove important sales executives had the desired effect. It shocked the sales division – which had become moribund – into action, as they kick-started a frantic turnaround effort. Kalyan's most urgent priority was to prepare Flipkart for the festival season sales face-off with Amazon that had now turned into a knockout contest for his company. Kalyan had no doubt that the Big Billion Days sale was the most important event of the year in the Indian retail business. A good performance would set the tone for the coming year. Brands, suppliers, employees would all be reassured; surely, investors would follow. A poor showing would be unacceptable in any year; this time, it could spell the end for Flipkart as an independent company.

To avoid such an outcome, Kalyan went back to the formula that had worked in his first stint: procure smartphones on an exclusive basis, cut prices in other categories and carry out speedy order deliveries. Over the past few months, Flipkart had struggled to rekindle sales partly because it no longer had exclusivity with the key smartphone brands. The loss of Motorola and Xiaomi had been particularly damaging. For Kalyan, repairing relationships with these brands was paramount. Motorola and Xiaomi phones, by themselves, could contribute more than fifteen per cent of Flipkart's sales in some months. If Flipkart could win back exclusivity with these brands, sales growth would be assured.

Kalyan's chosen team went to work. It was a group filled with relatively junior managers, many of whom had worked with Kalyan in his previous stint. They were all overachievers, aggressive, earnest and completely willing to work themselves to exhaustion in order to carry out Kalyan's will. Among the familiar faces who returned from other functions into sales roles were three of Kalyan's favourites – Amitesh Jha, Sandeep Karwa and Smrithi Ravichandran. He put another person, Ayyappan R., in charge of the day-to-day running of the smartphone business. One man stood out in this crowd: Ajay Veer Yadav. Ajay had joined Flipkart as head of smartphones in May after a spell as COO of The Mobile Store, a chain of smartphone stores. In his mid-forties, Ajay was a decade older than most of his colleagues. He had cut his teeth at United Spirits, Vijay Mallya's liquor company. Working for the liquor baron and his associates in the heyday of United Spirits, Ajay had picked up colonial mannerisms. Tall, broad-shouldered, he would turn up at work in a suit and tie, shoes spotlessly polished. He spoke correct English and addressed people formally. His appearance and manner amused his colleagues who, like other startup professionals, dressed in casual attire as a principle and spoke in colloquial Hindi or a pidgin of Hindi, Telugu, Kannada and English.

Along with Ajay and Ayyappan, Kalyan spent much of June and July on the road, trying to rebuild relationships with smartphone-makers. Working eighteen hours every day of each week, Kalyan met executives at all the important smartphone companies. Initially, they were sceptical. Flipkart had been hit by a barrage of negative headlines for nearly six months. The company had changed its CEO at the start of the year, only to appoint Kalyan in a vaguely titled position a few months later, on the orders of his boss, Flipkart's largest investor. It seemed to these companies that a power struggle was ongoing between Tiger Global and the Flipkart founders. This was hardly reassuring. Senior leaders also kept leaving the company. Flipkart's valuation had been marked down by its own investors. There were even rumours about how long its cash reserves would last. From the outside, Flipkart looked like a mess, its image at an all-time low. Against this, Amazon projected an aura of stability, power and competence.

At the offices of Xiaomi and other smartphone companies, Kalyan, Ajay and Ayyappan were pounded by questions and doubts.

'Are you in for the long term?'

'Can you guarantee Flipkart won't lose focus again?'

'Amazon is going to outspend you. How do you plan to take them on?'

'There's a lot of churn. You guys keep changing leaders.'

And on it went.[8]

Kalyan was honest. He admitted that Flipkart had lost its way but pleaded with the smartphone chiefs to trust him. 'Give me a chance. We will do whatever it takes to make you successful.'

Flipkart had also devised a new smartphone strategy that

Ajay and Ayyappan presented in detail at these meetings. It was fuelled by a novel insight, which caught the attention of the phone-makers. Customer shopping patterns on Flipkart seemed to indicate that people who already had smartphones were hunting for better phones. Worryingly, Flipkart didn't register searches from new users. For some reason, people who owned feature phones didn't seem to want to upgrade to smartphones for the time being. Essentially, the demand would come from people replacing their old smartphones, not from people buying smartphones for the first time. This was surprising – smartphone sales had been fuelled by the multitudes who were swapping their simple handsets. With the entry of cheap Chinese smartphones, it had been assumed that this shift would continue for many years to come.

Looking at its customer shopping data and the general slowdown in online retail, Flipkart had come to the conclusion that industry sales volumes would hardly grow this year, contrary to the general consensus. This new market reality necessitated a change in strategy by both Flipkart and smartphone-makers. Flipkart divided the market into layers based on prices. In every niche, the company set out to accumulate a small but deep assortment of powerful Android phones. It had also decided to buy sizeable quantities of iPhones, the most premium brand, to attract the small number of customers who would want to indulge themselves during Diwali. But it would avoid buying too many phone models: depth over width. This strategy was risky – Amazon, with its goal of offering the widest range of products in any category including phones, would have everything for everyone. If Flipkart had misread the smartphone market, it would spell disaster.

The company also prepared what it called the 'affordability construct' for customers. It was to nudge people into making purchases by offering to buy their old phones at decent prices. Customers were given the option to purchase phones on interest-free credit. The company had primed its supply chain for fast deliveries of phones at the expense of other products.

On the whole, the comprehensive package and the depth of Flipkart's research impressed phone brands. Finally, the company outbid Amazon and promised sales volumes that far exceeded what the brands had expected. This sealed it.

The first to return to Flipkart was Xiaomi, in late July, less than two months after Kalyan's comeback. Soon after Xiaomi, Motorola and Lenovo followed suit. Kalyan's presence helped in a significant way to reassure these brands about Flipkart. His courtship of brand executives – CEOs don't usually travel to attend meetings with brand partners – flattered them and reaffirmed Flipkart's seriousness in competing in the category again.

As with the smartphone operation, Kalyan imposed similar rigour in other categories. He centralized power, but his ruthlessness which was jarring to those outside his team, also brought decisiveness and agility. In August 2016, his efforts started yielding improvement in the sales numbers, which finally inched up after many months of decline.

Simultaneously, Flipkart's customer service scores were advancing. Binny's imposition of structure and processes at the company had brought much-needed discipline, especially in the supply chain function. Under the leadership of Binny's chosen lieutenant, Saikiran Krishnamurthy, the logistics service was recovering the speed and consistency in order deliveries that had once made Flipkart the favoured shopping destination of online shoppers.

Slowly, the company was regaining its mojo.

Flipkart made another big move to preserve its leadership position. In late July 2016, the company swooped in to buy Jabong, the struggling fashion e-commerce firm, for $70 million. For months, Snapdeal had been locked in talks to buy Jabong. The discussions had reached the final phase, with the two companies converging on an agreeable price. This is when the Jabong investors reached out to the Myntra CEO Ananth Narayanan, encouraging him to make an offer. Ananth took the deal to the Bansals and Lee Fixel. After moving from McKinsey, Ananth had brought about a rapid improvement at Myntra, increasing its margins and accelerating sales growth. He was held in high regard by Flipkart's board. They gave him the nod to make an offer. While Jabong's business had collapsed because of corporate governance problems, its brand still resonated with fashion shoppers. Besides, it was too risky to let Jabong be bought by a rival. Fashion was the one category in which Flipkart's dominance was unchallenged; it would be foolish to enter into an expensive fight over this in case Jabong was snapped up by Amazon or Snapdeal. In four days, the deal was done.[9]

If Flipkart was going to lose to Amazon, it wouldn't be for lack of agility.

AS SOON AS Kalyan returned to Flipkart, Sachin Bansal's internal alarms went into overdrive. After he had relinquished the CEO position, Sachin, as Executive Chairman, had been kept on the margins of Flipkart, like a pariah. He had spent his time conducting management reviews, which had turned into rather meaningless obligations for Flipkart executives who knew that Sachin had no say in the running of Flipkart. But the moment Kalyan came back, Sachin jumped into action, trying to reassert his authority. He tracked Kalyan's moves obsessively, worried about the growing influence of his former subordinate.

A new power dynamic had developed at the company. It wasn't just Binny and Kalyan wrangling for power, or even Sachin, who was the keenest to contain the Tiger cub. In a matter of months, Nitin Seth had become the most powerful leader at Flipkart, after Binny. In fact, all three top leaders – Binny, Kalyan, Sachin – leaned heavily on Nitin to make their way. Kalyan, because he needed Nitin to get around the bureaucracy and escape interference by the Bansals; Binny, who banked on Nitin to keep Kalyan in check; and Sachin, who not only wanted to contain Kalyan but also make himself relevant again. Initially, Nitin tried to make the best of his role as the go-between. He even attempted to bring the three of them together. He believed that all three had major strengths which, if harnessed, would yield miraculous results for Flipkart. Sachin possessed technological prowess and an instinctive ability to think big, Binny was skilled in implementing sound processes and was determined to build a self-sustaining firm, and Kalyan was a dynamic leader with an instinctive grasp of sales and finance – all powers combined, these leaders would make a formidable team.

But it was a forlorn initiative, destined to fail, as Kalyan and Sachin's visceral dislike of each other was insurmountable. They rarely exchanged words and when they did, the cracks in their relationship instantly became clear. At one senior-level meeting, Sachin excitedly described a small-town store visit and listed some of the missing pieces in Flipkart's offering to customers.

In a scathing tone, Kalyan responded, '*Achha, toh ab aap ko samajh aa gaya consumer ko kya chahiye, e-commerce kaise chalta hai?*' So now you've understood what consumers want and how e-commerce works?[10]

There could only be one winner in this battle. And the improving sales numbers had only bolstered Kalyan's position. Nitin's relationship with Kalyan was also becoming stronger. The two would meet many times every day over chai. They would speak over the phone first thing in the morning and before turning in at night. Nitin was highly impressed with Kalyan's purposefulness and passion. He saw him as a propulsive force that could repel Amazon's onslaught – to him, Kalyan was very much the man of the hour.

Nitin persuaded Binny to expand Kalyan's role in August 2016. The ludicrous title, Head – Category Design Management, was rendered completely meaningless. Kalyan was given charge of the company's marketplace, retail and advertising businesses. The functions of marketing, private label, customer experience and product would all be formally overseen by him. On paper, the Tiger Global representative reported to Binny; in truth, his boss was Lee.

Binny, keenly aware of this dynamic, still sought to restrain Kalyan. Around the time Kalyan was promoted, Binny complained to the Flipkart board that Kalyan's overly aggressive manner was putting off too many employees and eroding the management's team spirit. In a concession to Binny, the Flipkart board chastened Kalyan, but he continued to operate without any real fetters.

WHILE FLIPKART'S SALES numbers had begun rising again, Amazon's advance hadn't halted. Indeed, in July 2016, it overtook Flipkart in monthly sales for the first time ever.[11] At the end of the month, Amazon launched the famed Prime membership service in more than 100 cities, offering one-day and two-day delivery on lakhs of products for a fixed annual price of ₹499. Prime had made the company indispensable to millions of customers in its home market of North America. Amazon executives had no doubt that it would do the same here. In August, Amazon once again outsold Flipkart.[12] Amit Agarwal was riding high. A decisive victory over Flipkart, which could be sealed by winning the upcoming Diwali sale, would be the highlight of his career. After being wallopped in China by Alibaba and others, to become the largest e-commerce firm in India in just three years would be no small feat. There was little doubt that Amazon had achieved the momentum to do so.

It was up to Flipkart to prove that it had the strength and the will to turn the tide. This was a crucial period for the company and for the startup ecosystem in India. Flipkart was too big, too symbolically important, it had consumed too much capital – a lot depended on its success. If it failed, investor confidence in Indian startups would be destroyed – if Flipkart couldn't make it, what hope did the others have? Its failure would be the Indian equivalent of the Lehman Brothers bankruptcy, or as if India's Goldman Sachs had collapsed.

The stage was set for the most important battle in the short history of India's startup ecosystem.

IN SEPTEMBER 2016, Flipkart released the Big Billion Days dates: the sale would go live in the first week of October. Like last year, it would be held across five days, with the big categories such as smartphones, electronic appliances and fashion all being assigned different dates to accommodate the expected surge in traffic. Amazon's rival sale event, The Great Indian Festival, was also scheduled for the same week. It would be a direct, head-to-head contest.

In 2014, when Kalyan had overseen the first Big Billion Day, he had come up short despite extensive preparations. Flipkart's systems had collapsed under the weight of the traffic. This time, its arrangements would be far more thorough. The company had given its everything; it had prepared for the sale as if its survival depended on the success of Big Billion Days.

The sale started off well. In the smartphone category in particular, Flipkart had easily beaten Amazon. On smartphones day, Flipkart claimed that its gross sales had touched ₹1,400 crore, the highest single-day figure ever for an Indian e-commerce firm. Binny called it a 'historic moment'.[13] This feat was a validation of Kalyan's high-risk tactics.

The pattern continued through the sale, and by the end of the week, Flipkart had emerged as the clear winner. It had sold 15.5 million units compared to Amazon's 15 million; the gap in value was even more widely in Flipkart's favour.[14] Binny taunted his rival in media interviews, saying that Flipkart had sold products that people loved to buy during festival season – smartphones and TVs, as opposed to the 'churan, hing, detergent' and other grocery items Amazon claimed to be selling in high volumes. Amit Agarwal shot back with the counter that in a little over three years, Amazon had accomplished what Flipkart, despite launching much earlier, hadn't 'come close to doing.'[15]

But there was no denying that Flipkart had won this round. Confidence restored, morale raised, it would live to carry on the war with Amazon. Flipkart milked the moment. In another interview, Binny pointed out how important the win had been for the company. 'One thing that is heartening in the wide lead established by Flipkart is that a homegrown company can successfully fend off a twenty-two-year-old global behemoth pouring in money to buy market share. This is very important as it's a question on everyone's mind today, especially on the minds of entrepreneurs: how will we take on global giants if they come into India? The answer is that you can. You need to do it with the right customer focus, local innovation and local knowledge. And that would always win against just pure capital.'[16]

Those were rousing words. Evidently, Flipkart's mojo was back; Binny's certainly was. But behind the curtains, as far as Flipkart's investors were concerned, there was only one man who would get the credit for the turnaround.

22

KALYAN RAJ

After the Diwali battle, it was Kalyan Krishnamurthy who became the main man at Flipkart. He had taken charge of the Big Billion Days sale and delivered a stupendous performance under the circumstances. His standing with the company's investors, already strong on account of his status as a Tiger Global representative and his successful first stint at Flipkart, was elevated further. It was an opportune time for Kalyan to show his hand. A few weeks after Diwali, in December 2016, Kalyan made his move. He declared that he wanted to be the CEO of Flipkart.[1] Kalyan, still nominally a Tiger Global employee, made it clear to the Flipkart board that if they wanted him to stay on, his role would have to be formalized and expanded. He contended that it was only fair, and even logical: to create maximum impact, he would need to have control over the whole company, not just parts of it.

In fact, Kalyan's proposed ascension had been months in the making. When he had re-joined Flipkart in June, Kalyan had made a promise to himself: this time he wasn't leaving, this time, he would stay for good. It wasn't just his ambition, Lee Fixel had also foreordained it.

In early 2016, Lee had come to believe that the Bansals were no longer suited to run Flipkart. In the short history of software and internet businesses, very few entrepreneurs – the same figures that the Bansals idolized – had displayed the endurance and capacity to keep improving by magnitudes every few years as their startups burgeoned into huge companies. Jeff Bezos, Bill Gates, Mark Zuckerberg, Jack Ma – they were the exceptions, the rarest of the rare entrepreneurs. Even Steve Jobs had failed to cope the first time at Apple, which led to his ouster from the company. It was Lee's assessment that the Bansals belonged in that group which didn't measure up, not where the running of a gargantuan company was concerned. There was hardly any shame in it. Binny and Sachin had already proved to be outstanding entrepreneurs. But it was now time for them to give way to a 'professional CEO'. This view was, of course, not shared by either of the Bansals, each of whom had no doubt that only he – individually – could run Flipkart.

This undercurrent of dissonance necessitated a somewhat gradual approach by Lee. It was this compulsion that had prompted him to enlist the services of some influential Flipkart executives close to Binny in his endeavour to bring Kalyan back. Though Lee had assented to Binny's elevation as CEO, it soon turned out to be of secondary importance in his scheme. It mostly served to lay the groundwork – through the removal of Sachin from the CEO position – for the essential feature of his plan: the re-entry of Kalyan. Now that Kalyan had repaid his faith by reviving Flipkart's flailing business, Lee's belief turned into conviction. Kalyan would have to continue at Flipkart – as far as Lee was concerned, the turnaround was in its infancy. Kalyan's agility and sales acumen had won the day. But the struggle to take Flipkart to a position where it could go public or attract a buyer had just started; Lee's struggle to extricate himself from Flipkart was only just beginning.

There was strong evidence that the mistakes Flipkart had made in 2015 had caused serious damage, had derailed it for years perhaps. Alibaba, which had become the world's most valuable e-commerce firm since its stock market listing in 2014, had shown interest in buying a minority stake in Flipkart in early 2016.[2] Joseph Tsai, the Alibaba co-founder and executive vice chairman, had flown to Bangalore to meet the Bansals. The discussions were pleasant but they went nowhere. Tsai had indicated that a deal could happen only at a significantly lower valuation than the $15 billion Flipkart had fetched in its previous funding round. This was unacceptable to the Bansals. Then came the barrage of markdowns, like hammer blows. One after another, nearly half a dozen shareholders in Flipkart hacked its valuation. After this, whenever Flipkart engaged with investors, the company was told it would have to accept a lower valuation. Several firms passed up Flipkart because it refused to lower its asking price.[3]

A few weeks before the Big Billion Days sale in October 2016, Walmart, the world's largest retailer and a bitter rival of Amazon, had approached Flipkart. In recent years, Walmart had considered the Indian market warily, unable to decide whether its promise was real or illusory. The company had already been burnt once when its joint venture with Bharti Enterprises had collapsed in 2013 because of corporate governance issues and poor performance.[4] Besides, the biggest obstacle still seemed impregnable: the Indian laws preventing a foreign 'multi-brand' retailer like Walmart from entering on its own. But gradually, Walmart executives resumed their pursuit of opening shop here, encouraged by Narendra Modi's eagerness to attract foreign investment.

At the same time, Walmart, in its home market, had assumed a new, aggressive approach to adapt to the force that threatened to upend its business: the internet. For many years Walmart had been criticized for lacking a sound e-commerce strategy even as Amazon was rapidly increasing its share of the retail market in America. While Walmart was still the far bigger company, every year the once-laughable idea that it could one day be overtaken by Amazon seemed less ridiculous. In 2016, Walmart significantly increased its online investments in the US and began an acquisition spree of internet startups. Its biggest deal came in August 2016 when it purchased Jet.com, an e-commerce firm started by Marc Lore, who was reputed to be one of the very few entrepreneurs with the will and ability to take on Jeff Bezos.[5]

In India, the combination of Flipkart's remarkable rise and the seemingly everlasting promise of the market seemed attractive to Walmart. For now, the American firm was interested only in a minority investment in Flipkart. Senior executives from the two companies met at their respective headquarters in Bangalore and Bentonville, a small city in the southern American state of Arkansas. But the talks left Walmart unimpressed by Flipkart's sales growth, margins and other metrics. The meeting ended in disappointment.[6]

The rejection by Walmart, Alibaba and other investors was

humbling for Flipkart, for Lee, and most of all, for the Bansals. Until the end of 2015, Flipkart had seemed destined to become a massive company. It had handpicked investors and set the terms of engagement. Now, while it wasn't out begging for money, its aura had considerably diminished. As had the exhilarating pull of building the $100 billion enterprise.

At this juncture, it was all about survival. For Flipkart's investors, especially Lee, it was about coming out unscathed. Since he first invested in Flipkart in early 2010, Lee had poured roughly $1 billion into the company, including some $600 million in the span of just one year starting in July 2014. This was an unconventional bet by any measure.[7] Any venture capital firm typically invests large amounts of cash only in specific stages of a startup's life to reduce its risk. But with Flipkart, Tiger Global had led a majority of all the funding rounds. Lee's breaking with the norms of venture capital investing had been influenced by his conviction in the entrepreneurial genius of the Bansals, especially Sachin, and the evident promise of the e-commerce market in India. By the end of 2016, both these convictions were shaken. Not only had Sachin faltered, Lee had grossly underestimated the time and capital it would take to create a successful e-commerce business.

The $100 billion dream had primarily been Sachin's; Lee had backed Sachin unequivocally because the former stood to be one of its biggest beneficiaries. But barely eighteen months after Sachin had first imagined a $100 billion company, his dream had died even though he didn't know it at the time. In early 2016, after Lee had received alarming feedback about Sachin and the Flipkart management being out of their depth, and after those views had been corroborated by a shocking decline in Flipkart's business, Lee had made up his mind: he had to secure an honourable exit.[8] As soon as possible. His career, his reputation, his wealth, his dreams, rested on it.

In this environment, there was just one man who could deliver him from ruin: Kalyan. Unlike Sachin or Binny, Kalyan had no grand ideas about Flipkart. He simply wanted to turn it into an efficient, fast-growing retailer that consistently expanded its business and delivered higher valuations. It was this approach that was best suited to Lee's plan of securing the fastest possible way out of Flipkart.

It was a happy coming together of two minds: Lee's need to secure an exit and Kalyan's burning desire to become the top man at Flipkart. It would be a stunning rise for Kalyan, from a little-known finance manager at eBay to the highest position at India's premier startup. It would also be the harshest rebuke for Sachin, who detested Kalyan and had opposed his re-entry into Flipkart.

In early 2016, at a panel discussion, Sachin had passionately spoken about how important it was for entrepreneurs and their investors to be 'aligned'. 'If investors are not aligned with what you want to do, you will have a hard time … You need to be very, very clear to them at the start itself that this is exactly what I'm going to do, this is my playbook, this is what I believe in, I don't believe in this. If you like this, come in as an investor. [Or] you can find somebody else, I can find somebody else.'[9]

To use his own word, Sachin and Lee were no longer 'aligned'. And Sachin was indeed having a hard time.

As he watched his company slip away from him, Sachin cut a desolate, sullen figure. He was helpless, on the margins, unable to influence the direction of Flipkart. He had been kept out of daily affairs by Binny. Sachin's opposition to Kalyan's return and subsequent promotion had been ignored. When he complained about the lack of innovation at the company, nobody paid heed beyond making token gestures.

Though his attempted transformation of Flipkart had nearly brought disaster, Sachin was still convinced that his ideas had been sound, his vision exemplary. He blamed 'bad execution' for their failure. He blamed the senior leaders he had trusted. And he blamed Amazon's 'capital dumping' at a December 2016 technology conference arranged by Carnegie India. When Flipkart was at its peak, Sachin had taunted Jeff Bezos. A little more than two years later, Sachin was now asking for sanctuary from Amazon. Denouncing American companies such as Amazon and Uber at the Carnegie conference, he called for India to adopt China's model of banning foreign internet companies in the country: 'What we need to do is what at some level China did. They told the world that we need your capital but we don't need your companies.'[10]

The idealism of Flipkart's early years long gone, the bravado of the subsequent years exhausted, Sachin had been reduced to calling for government protection against his former employer. Strictly speaking, Flipkart itself wasn't an Indian company – its holding company was registered in Singapore – but this was a technicality. Flipkart may not have even been founded had it not been for Amazon, which had once employed Sachin and Binny. This kind of hypocrisy is hardly uncommon in business. Indeed, Sachin's willingness to ignore all these truths may have been a manifestation of the street smartness of a young entrepreneur with the ability to play dirty, if need be, against one of the most powerful companies in the world.

But what his statement clearly betrayed was the real agenda of his mission to create The Great Indian Internet Company: it was simply another capitalist's pursuit of wealth and power packaged in noble rhetoric, the Indian equivalent of the deceptive 'we will change the world'[11] messaging of American internet companies.

The Chinese model that Sachin was advocating would no doubt enrich entrepreneurs and their startups, but it would come at a cost, which for any democracy would be unacceptable. China is known to use its homegrown companies and their technologies to enforce authoritarian measures through Orwellian schemes of surveillance, propaganda and restrictions on free speech.

In November 2016, about a month before Sachin spoke at the Carnegie conference, the BJP government had announced that it would, with almost immediate effect, demonetize ₹500 and ₹1000 banknotes. The justification given by the prime minister was that this move would destroy 'black money' and exact revenge upon traitors who had for years cheated the country by hiding income.[12] A high and forceful wave of nationalism was sweeping through India. One can't be sure if Sachin was intending to ride on it – he had been thinking of creating a lobby group for Indian startups even before demonetization. But it was a disturbing conflation – the idea of technology companies that store massive quantities of information about citizens receiving patronage by a government whose authoritarian tendencies have been widely criticized.

In the 1950s, Nehru had labelled dams, factories, power plants and other large technological industrial projects by public sector companies as the new 'temples' of India.[13] More than sixty years later, twenty-five years after India liberalized its economy, public sector companies were irrelevant in the technological arena. In the internet age, globally, a country's technological prowess was increasingly being measured by the success of its private technology companies. For the US, it was Amazon, Apple, Google, Facebook and Microsoft. In China, it was Alibaba, Tencent and Baidu. In 2014, Sachin had been determined to put Flipkart in that league. Two and a half years later, when his dream was in tatters, his technological vision rejected by customers, colleagues and investors, it was expedient to call for protection. The seed for the Flipkart project – the idea that Indian engineers can create a world-class internet company – had thus germinated into a nation-building exercise that India was neglecting to nurture at its own cost. This evocation of the Chinese model was an instance of the formulation that, years later, one of India's best-known intellectuals would describe as the 'RSS meets Jio' ideological world."[14]

In any case, the viability of Sachin's mission rested primarily on his ability to deliver massive amounts of wealth to its shareholders, a basic principle of capitalism. And Sachin, a fervent capitalist, had lost the confidence of his shareholders, the people higher up in the capitalist chain who no longer believed in his mission.

At the end of 2016, the Flipkart investors had, in fact, begun persuading Sachin's co-founder, Binny, to hand over the daily running of the company to Kalyan. Lee, Kalyan and a couple of other key Flipkart shareholders were relentless in this pursuit. It took just a few weeks. In early January 2017, exactly one year after he had taken over from Sachin, Binny succumbed. Sachin's opinion on the matter hardly counted. Starting in 2012, Flipkart had made drastic management changes at the end of every year. The tradition would continue.

Just like the previous year, on the second Monday of 2017, Flipkart announced its management changes. The company elevated Kalyan Krishnamurthy as its new CEO. Kalyan, who would turn forty-five later that week, couldn't have asked for a better birthday present. Binny was given the Group CEO position, in light of the fact that Flipkart was shaping up as an internet conglomerate. Apart from its eponymous business, it owned two fashion-selling sites, Myntra and Jabong, as well as the mobile payment app PhonePe, which was picking up nicely, having received an unexpected boost from demonetization. Kalyan as well as the CEOs of Myntra, Jabong and PhonePe, would report to Binny. As was the case even earlier, Kalyan was really answerable to only one man: Lee Fixel. Still, Binny's position wasn't ceremonial. He would have a say in Flipkart's strategy and management appointments. Sachin's role remained unchanged: he would continue as Executive Chairman.[15]

There were other sweeping changes. About half a dozen Flipkart leaders who had worked closely with Binny, were moved to meaningless positions. It was Kalyan's show now, and he had no use for them.

Before Flipkart had gone public with the news, Binny had informed his team in private. They were stunned. They were established corporate bosses who had held senior roles at companies far bigger than Flipkart. They had come to Flipkart, attracted by hefty compensation packages and to fulfil their dream of taking part in building India's biggest internet company. But even before they could truly get a grasp of its workings, they were devoured by the vortex of its politics.

'I'm sorry, but this is how it has to be,' Binny told one of them.[16] Within weeks, as many as five of Flipkart's seniormost leaders would leave.

The only major player at Flipkart who came out unscathed was Nitin Seth. He had been promoted to Chief Operating Officer. He would now supervise Flipkart's massive logistics business, apart from fulfilling his present charges of HR, strategy and other divisions. Though Nitin and Kalyan had struck a close friendship, Kalyan's campaign for the CEO title had taken even Nitin by surprise. When Kalyan had re-joined the company, he was nominally at a lower level than Nitin. Nitin had played a crucial role not just in Kalyan's return but also in his promotion a few months later. After realizing that it was futile to coax the Bansals and Kalyan to work together, Nitin had felt compelled to take sides in order to get things done.

He had chosen Kalyan, convinced that the Tiger Global representative would be the ideal sales head for Flipkart. Nitin had no idea that Kalyan would make a claim for the CEO post just a few months later. He had hoped that if Binny made way for anyone over time, the Flipkart co-founder would choose him. Instead, five months after helping secure Kalyan's position at the company, Nitin found himself reporting to Kalyan. Nitin was a veteran of corporate politics, but even he had been blindsided by this twist in a coup he had helped carry out. In the process, he had alienated the Bansals who believed that Nitin had betrayed their trust. Some of the other senior managers at Flipkart also disliked Nitin, certain that he was greedy for power and had trodden over several capable leaders to get his way. As a COO, Nitin found himself in a strange place.

If he didn't know it already, he would soon realize that titles held little meaning at Flipkart.

AMID THIS EVIDENT volatility, it would have surprised no one if Flipkart's business began to suffer. Somehow, this wasn't the case. The company hadn't been run this efficiently in a long time. Costs were being brought under control, customer service was improving, Flipkart was continuously introducing smart business innovations such as a no-cost EMI scheme and a phone exchange programme, and most importantly, its sales were growing every month.

Flipkart had even kept Amazon subdued. After winning the crucial festival season sale battle, Flipkart continued to pull in higher sales than Amazon over the next few months. Kalyan's ruthless quest for power had been carried out over months, but it hadn't distracted him from the task of rejuvenating Flipkart. As CEO, his grip on the business had strengthened. With no one standing in his way, he made swift decisions.

Apart from Nitin Seth, Kalyan did away with most of Flipkart's senior leaders, and instead worked directly with executives in the mid-management layer. Rather than hire experienced executives – as the Bansals had done – Kalyan preferred to groom junior managers whom he could mould as per his vision. He directly took charge of day-to-day affairs as opposed to CEOs who mostly concern themselves with strategy and high-level matters. He had dozens of people reporting directly and indirectly to him, far more than Binny or Sachin had when they were the chiefs. Most of the important sales roles were filled by his capable underlings, who were untiring in their efforts to implement his will. In a matter of months, he had shaped the entire company in his image. This was an unorthodox approach but one that was working well for the moment, as the improving sales numbers showed.

It was an opportune time for Flipkart to hit the market for capital. Though it had more than $1 billion in the bank, its coffers had to be replenished.[17] New categories such as groceries were planned, existing categories like furniture would have to be relaunched, new infrastructure built, all of which would require lots of money. Besides, it had been nearly two years since Flipkart had last raised funds. A fresh dose of capital would remove any doubt about its decline, reassure all stakeholders, send a forceful message of counter-intimidation to Amazon. And it would allow the Flipkart team breathing room to run the business without apprehension.

Flipkart began to approach new investors in January 2017. Even after the valuation markdowns, the e-commerce slowdown, the harrowing experience of nearly being steamrolled by Amazon, and all the negative headlines, Flipkart executives still harboured some hope of raising funds at their preferred valuation of $15 billion. It didn't take long for the illusion to be shattered. After meeting more than half a dozen investors, they found that no one was interested in doing a deal at that price. The company would have to acquiesce to a down round.[18] A down round is seen as a humiliation by any fast-growing startup, and it was the same at Flipkart. But no one at the company pondered over this for long. Flipkart's priority right now was survival, and endurance.

While Flipkart's standing had diminished, it was still, by far, India's most outstanding internet startup. To investors, the company pitched itself as a nimble startup that had held off the formidable Amazon. It also dangled the untapped potential of e-commerce. Though e-commerce was well-established in Indian cities, a majority of the country's people lived in semi-urban and rural areas. It was this market that Flipkart would now pursue, the company promised investors. Hundreds of millions of Indians in semi-urban areas still weren't shopping online – they were all Flipkart customers of the future.

Once the company was willing to lower its asking price, discussions moved quickly. By the end of February 2017, Flipkart was confident that a deal was within its grasp. Talks with nearly half a dozen investors – all marquee firms like Google, Microsoft, Tencent and Paypal – had reached an advanced stage. By early April, the fund raise was finalized. Microsoft, Tencent as well as eBay had together agreed to invest $1.4 billion, valuing Flipkart at $11.6 billion.

Apart from Flipkart's core business, the new investors had put a high value on the fashion platform Myntra, which was pulling off the rare feat of reducing losses while growing faster. They were also excited by the potential of PhonePe, which looked set to become a major player in the booming payments space. As part of the deal, Flipkart acquired the India business of eBay. It brought to an end a long struggle for the American company. Years before Amazon launched in India, eBay had kicked off in 2004, buying up a local startup called Bazee. Since then, however, eBay India had been tracking its parent company's declining fortunes. Once considered superior even to Amazon, eBay was now – and had been for several years – seen as a second-rate company. In India, it had failed to get its act together despite the early start. EBay had considered buying Snapdeal twice but couldn't summon the courage to move decisively. It now had to settle for a meagre price of $250 million for its India business.

But the funding round was primarily a vindication of Kalyan's impact at Flipkart as well as a win for Nitin Seth, who had played a key role in formulating the pitch that the company made to investors. It was also a victory for the company's founders. Sachin and Binny declared the round a 'landmark deal' for 'Flipkart and for India', and a 'resounding acknowledgement that the homegrown tech ecosystem is indeed thriving'.[19]

Sachin, in particular, seemed energized by the deal. As soon as Kalyan had been promoted to CEO, Sachin had begun to assert himself again with force. He would demand specific data and business metrics from the sales, marketing and technology teams and comb through them for any signs of weakness. At a board meeting in early 2017, he found fault with Kalyan. 'Sales from this set of customers has gone down. What's the reason for it?' he said to the CEO. The customer set Sachin referred to was small and its significance wasn't apparent. Perplexed, Kalyan could give no answer.

Sachin would accuse Kalyan of not sharing data with him on a regular basis. He would also ask pointed questions to Nitin – whom he considered Kalyan's proxy – about the rising attrition rate in the engineering team. It was an extension of his favourite theme: promoting technology. He admonished both Kalyan and Nitin, warning that Flipkart would lose its 'innovation culture' if it kept losing engineers.

But Nitin was confident that he was on safe ground. He had got off to a good start at Ekart, his primary responsibility at that point. When he had been given charge of the logistics service in January 2017, his mandate had been to reduce costs. He had accomplished this by abandoning wasteful automation efforts and cutting the share of orders that Flipkart outsourced to third-party couriers. He was looking forward to the board meeting at the end of April. Ever since he had joined the company, Nitin had been lauded by board members for his boldness and competence.

This time, though, instead of praise, what awaited him was censure. Lee started the inquisition, which turned into a barrage of criticism, knocking Nitin off his feet. 'Our delivery times have gone down. Our service quality has deteriorated. What have you been doing?' Lee demanded.

Others joined in. 'Engineering attrition is high because of the rot in the culture.' And it was Nitin who was responsible, they said.

Unprepared for this turn of events, Nitin had no comeback.

By the end of the meeting, Nitin had been informed that his role was being cut. He was asked to hand over Human Resources to his boss, Kalyan. This was yet another shock. Only last year the Bansals had resisted Kalyan's return partly because they were worried about the influence it would have on the company's 'culture'. Now, they were fine with Kalyan taking charge of HR!

Nitin had no option but to agree. Still, the backlash against him continued. Even his equation with Kalyan seemed to change overnight. A few days after the board meeting, Kalyan advised him to resign. 'The board has lost faith in you. You should leave,' said Kalyan.

'Have you gone mad!' Nitin replied. He couldn't understand what was happening. Only four months ago he had been promoted to COO, the second-most powerful position at the company. He had helped prepare the strategy for the critical fund raise and cut Ekart's costs. He was in the process of moving his family – his wife and three children – to Bangalore from Gurgaon. He had enrolled his daughters in a new school. He had spent lakhs buying expensive furniture for the new house. Everything had been going so well. Then came this sudden thunderbolt.

Nitin refused to resign. He was a veteran corporate leader, well respected in the software business in India, had led organizations that employed thousands of people. And he was COO of Flipkart, where he had thrived. Even if somehow someone at Flipkart had decided that his performance hadn't been satisfactory, no company would be insane enough to lose faith in its second-most powerful executive after just four months. He would fight for his job.

Over the next few days, Nitin tried speaking to all the major players at the company to understand what had gone wrong. He received vague, non-committal responses. One month after the board meeting in April, Kalyan called him into a meeting room at the headquarters. Alongside the Flipkart CEO was the company's public relations head. Kalyan had brought him along in case things got 'ugly'.

Kalyan came straight to the point. Handing Nitin a piece of paper, he said, 'Here's your termination letter. We will have to do this unless you agree to resign.' He added that if Nitin chose to quit on his own, Flipkart would arrange a nice farewell and issue a glowing press statement about his contributions. He also promised to give Nitin the stock options that were to vest soon, along with a bonus payment due to him.

Nitin stormed out.

That night, he got an email saying he had been removed from the company.

23

THE SON

The unending tensions, power struggles and shocking turns had compelled many of its employees to liken Flipkart to the popular television series, *Game of Thrones*. Over the years, many executives had staked their claim to power, ruthlessly casting aside rivals, peers, friends, only to meet the same fate themselves. But it was a flawed analogy, as there was no question about who was both king and kingmaker at Flipkart: Lee Fixel.

Not only was Lee's firm the largest shareholder in Flipkart, owning about a third of the company, Lee also had excellent relationships with every major player at Flipkart. His influence over other shareholders and board members, his standing with Sachin and Binny who had tremendous respect for him, his network of investor contacts and ability to arrange fund raises, and his overall credibility in the startup world, were unrivalled at the company.

The funding round in April 2017 had secured Flipkart's future for the next few years. But it had been an unpleasant experience, eroding the company's valuation. Lee believed that it would be ideal to accumulate so much cash that Flipkart wouldn't have to worry about raising capital until it was ready for a stock market listing. It would forever liberate Flipkart executives from the troublesome process of fundraising and allow them to direct all their energies towards running the business.

Most importantly, Lee really needed to show some returns on his investment. It had now been seven years since he had first put money into the company. That was a very long time in the venture capital business. He had also bet a huge amount: $1 billion. Parking that kind of sum in any company is risky, and when the company turned out to be as volatile as Flipkart, it was nerve-shredding, not only for Lee but also for his partners at Tiger Global and his fund's investors to whom he was answerable. Lee needed to take some cash out.

Even before the $1.4 billion funding round had been completed in April 2017, he rang up SoftBank founder Masayoshi Son. Lee and Son had known each other for many years. They were co-investors in many startups. In 2012, Son's conversation with Flipkart about an investment had ended abruptly as he had taken off on a long-pending vacation. By the time he returned, Flipkart's engagement with Naspers had already moved to an advanced stage. Son later ended up investing a large sum in Flipkart's rival, Snapdeal. Now, he had become one of the most influential figures in the technology business. He had shocked the world by drawing up plans for a $100 billion fund to invest in startups globally, including in India. SoftBank had become the preferred supplier by default for any startup needing large amounts of capital.

When Lee approached Son in early 2017, SoftBank had a mess on its hands with Snapdeal. After vying with Flipkart and Amazon for dominance of the e-commerce market for years, Snapdeal had become a much smaller company in 2016. It couldn't raise the capital required to continue competing with its rivals. Still, Snapdeal's new reality didn't affect the bravado of its CEO Kunal Bahl, or his ability to spin headlines. As he said in an interview in 2016, for Snapdeal, 'GMV was so 2015.' GMV, or gross merchandise value, reflects gross sales, an unreliable measure of a startup's financial health. What Snapdeal wanted to do now was 'to build a real business'.[1]

But by early 2017, Son had given up on the company and Kunal. He had always known that Snapdeal's infrastructure and e-commerce operations were inferior to those of Flipkart and Amazon. He had hoped that the e-commerce market would become so large that Snapdeal's leaner business model would emerge victorious. He also had tremendous faith in Kunal's ingenuity. Then, after the e-commerce slowdown of 2016, he realized that the market wouldn't sustain more than two large retailers and that Snapdeal wasn't going to be one of them – Kunal had failed him. It made little sense for SoftBank, which had already invested $1 billion in Snapdeal, to continue pouring money into the struggling company.[2]

So, when Son received the call from Lee, he was receptive to the idea of investing in Flipkart. He had one condition: Lee had to help him out with his Snapdeal problem. Son proposed that Flipkart buy Snapdeal, after which SoftBank would invest in the merged company. He would also buy shares from Tiger Global, giving Lee the much-needed part exit from Flipkart.

The merger made little business sense. Snapdeal was a

marketplace platform with completely different technology and logistics systems from Flipkart's. It was seen as a downmarket brand whose service was unreliable. Managing Snapdeal was going to be a nightmare for Flipkart executives. One newspaper pointed out that the proposed merger was a rather 'desperate attempt at financial engineering by the country's two most influential startup investors'.[3] Still, for the Flipkart team, SoftBank's allure overshadowed all their misgivings about absorbing a struggling rival. SoftBank's cash and its disposition as a freewheeling investor would be of great help to Flipkart against Amazon. Besides, they could always just shut down Snapdeal after buying it. And of course, the price would have to very low – a fitting end for a company that had prided itself on offering the best deal.

An outline of the sale was agreed upon in April 2017. SoftBank would invest about $1–1.5 billion in Flipkart directly, and buy Flipkart shares worth $500 million to $1 billion, chiefly from Tiger Global. Flipkart would take over Snapdeal for about $1 billion or lesser in stock. It was a hugely disappointing outcome for the Snapdeal investors, of whom there were more than two dozen. Just as Lee had spotted Flipkart's potential, they had seen Snapdeal as a once-in-a-lifetime investment that would shape their fortunes. A sale at $1 billion was a terrible comedown for a company that had been valued at $6.5 billion just one year ago. And the compensation wouldn't even be in cash.

This time, even Kunal seemed to have lost his swagger. His colleagues muttered to one another that the man who had seemed indomitable had all of a sudden aged visibly in months. The sale process, chronicled almost daily in the media, was a humiliating experience for Kunal. He had thought of himself as a first-rate entrepreneur, superior even to the Bansals of Flipkart. It was a view that had been reinforced for years by the Snapdeal investors. To be forced to sell out for a pittance to his rivals – people he had criticized and ridiculed for many years – was deflating. No one was calling him a genius any more. He had become irrelevant. Even some of his own investors had turned against him. In April 2017, Kunal indicated that the fate of the company was out of his hands. In an email to employees, he wrote that Snapdeal investors were 'driving the discussions around the way forward'.[4]

It was true that the Snapdeal investors had taken matters into their hands, but the real picture was more complex. Not only had some of them lost faith in Kunal, they had also turned against each other as they scrambled to salvage their own interests. For many months, the board had become dysfunctional, with individual members locked in a civil war.[5] A former Snapdeal executive aptly called it the tragedy of the commons.[6]

Snapdeal had, in fact, been forced to pass up two funding offers because of the rift between the board members. At the heart of the matter were greed and egos. SoftBank had offered to invest more in Snapdeal but its conditions would have led to a slide in the ownership of other shareholders and given SoftBank almost complete control over the company. This was unacceptable to the other shareholders, who promptly exercised their veto to bury the deal. The impasse continued for months even as Snapdeal's cash reserves fell to alarmingly low levels.

After months of parleying, SoftBank finally brought around some of the key players by offering settlements in July 2017. The Snapdeal founders, too, reluctantly agreed to explore the sale offer, provided that their terms – lucrative cash payouts for them, no job losses for employees, and a few other conditions – were met. The Snapdeal and Flipkart teams leading the negotiations were set to meet in Bangalore on the last day of the month to seal the merger. Just one day before the meeting, however, it was cancelled. Tragedy had struck again. Pouncing on the indecisiveness among Snapdeal shareholders, the company's founders called off the sale.[7] SoftBank's hope of salvaging its investment was buried. The other warring investors were left with a holding that had lost most of its value. Snapdeal would continue as an independent company, but only in a much-shrunken form, selling assets, cutting jobs, vacating many product categories. But at least the company's founders and their investors had their pride intact.

Back at Flipkart, its executives and investors were overjoyed. They were saved the distraction of managing a complicated asset, and they would still enjoy the benefits of the engagement. This was because SoftBank had decided that it would invest in Flipkart regardless of the failed merger. On 10 August 2017, less than two weeks after the sale fell apart, both SoftBank and Flipkart announced the investment. SoftBank would pour more than $2.5 billion into the online retailer, the biggest deal ever at an Indian startup. About $1.4 billion would go directly into Flipkart and shares worth more than $1 billion would be purchased from Tiger Global and a few other Flipkart shareholders. Flipkart's cash reserves now swelled up to more than $4 billion, providing the company enough ammunition for many years to come.[8]

As an observer put it, Flipkart had got 'the milk without buying the cow'.[9]

IT HAD NOW been more than eighteen months since Sachin Bansal had last been CEO of Flipkart. In this time, he had been a remote presence at the company, kept at a distance first by Binny, then by Kalyan. He could do little about it other than feel agitated. He was raring to come back to an operating role. He had started preparing the ground for a return. In May 2017, he had taken the government relations function back from Nitin Seth. He had begun to spend time with Flipkart's engineers, discussing innovative ideas and the new technologies in which the company needed to invest. He had been urging Kalyan to appoint a chief product officer in order to further the technology agenda, which he believed was being neglected.

His clashes with Kalyan had continued unabated, even after Nitin Seth's exit. Their relationship was so evidently broken that it prompted an intervention from the alarmed Flipkart board members, who suggested that the two, along with Binny, see a leadership coach to resolve their differences. This was a popular practice at Silicon Valley startups where many entrepreneurs, including Steve Jobs, Jeff Bezos and Larry Page, had engaged leadership coaches.[10]

Lee Fixel arranged for Jim Kochalka, an experienced coach that Tiger Global had employed previously, to work with Sachin, Kalyan and Binny. Kochalka, an American in his sixties, met the three Flipkart leaders and conducted sessions where they were asked to air their views – even the unpleasant ones – about one another. Kochalka recommended that Sachin and Kalyan spend time with each other, just the two of them. By speaking with each other regularly, they would be forced to sustain a working relationship at the very least. Around the middle of 2017, Sachin and Kalyan began to meet regularly and, over the following months, their relationship showed signs of improvement.[11]

In July 2017, Sachin introduced a new brand he had personally conceptualized. It was, unsurprisingly, called Billion. Unlike a traditional brand that restricts itself to a specific category or group of categories, Billion would serve all categories from home appliances and fashion to phones and other electronic goods. It was Sachin's first major initiative after he had stepped down as CEO in January 2016. The purpose of the brand was to offer products designed specifically for Indians, who Sachin believed weren't satisfactorily served by most international or domestic brands. He explained that the name Billion represented 'a billion aspirations for a billion people'. Billion would create products that met these aspirations in 'the best possible manner'.[12]

As the year progressed, Sachin's vibrancy grew. He was in a particularly ebullient mood after the SoftBank funding round. While his colleagues were locked in negotiations with their counterparts at SoftBank, Sachin had built a rapport with Masa Son. Son loved big-thinking, daring entrepreneurs like Sachin and they had hit it off. Sachin knew that it was no small thing to have the backing of the world's most powerful tech investor.

A few months after the SoftBank funding round in August 2017, certain that he would have Son's support, Sachin expressed his desire to Lee: he wanted to become CEO of the Flipkart Group. Sachin believed that he had spent enough time on the margins. Now that Flipkart had stabilized, he was ready to take back the reins. Now, with more than $4 billion at Flipkart's disposal, he was eager to resume the pursuit of his $100 billion dream.

Lee was alarmed. Having lost faith in Sachin's ability to run Flipkart, he wasn't sure what to do. Sachin had proved to be an abrasive, polarizing manager. Lee also knew that Kalyan would never agree to work for Sachin. The two were almost irreconcilable. Though their relationship had improved, the rift had not been closed. For the purpose of recruiting senior leaders, Flipkart had formed a committee that included Sachin, Kalyan and Binny. But in the whole of 2017, the company failed to finalize a single hire primarily because Sachin and Kalyan could never come to an agreement. Both had veto powers which were exercised generously. It was indeed inconceivable that the two of them would work together. Not to mention, Flipkart was doing well under Kalyan, meeting its targets every month, operating like a well-oiled machine. Lee had no inclination to cause any disruption in this most essential of tasks that he had himself set for the CEO.

Eventually, to placate Sachin, Lee told him that he would first have to improve his leadership and interpersonal skills, rebuild his relationships with his colleagues and continue with the leadership coaching. Sachin agreed. He believed that the sessions with Jim Kochalka were going well. Just as he had in 2014, Sachin was convinced that he would, after his long hiatus, return to the driver's seat.

24

A JOURNEY TO BENTONVILLE

> 'Nobody is a permanent friend, nobody is a permanent enemy. Everybody has his own self-interest. Once you recognize that, everybody would be better off.'
>
> – Dhirubhai Ambani in *Ambani & Sons*, Hamish McDonald[1]

The large infusion from SoftBank had satiated Flipkart's capital needs. Now the company could think of preparing for an IPO. It was going to take many years, and by any measure, it was a long shot. In the financial year 2016–17, Flipkart's losses had shot up, by nearly seventy per cent, to ₹8,771 crore. Its revenues had increased, by twenty-nine per cent, to ₹19,854 crore.[2] These weren't pleasing numbers – neither the revenue growth that was paltry in a vast, promising market, nor the loss figure that was outright shocking. It was true that the results had been distorted by one-time charges, but it was also evident that Flipkart was nowhere near attaining profitability, a must for any company looking to list its shares publicly. There was a lot of work to be done. For all of Sachin Bansal's obsession with the one billion figure and with taking e-commerce to the masses, less than ten million people shopped on Flipkart every month.[3] This number would have to multiply many times over for the company to have any chance of pulling off a successful listing. Its dream of going public looked all the more improbable because, for their part, Amazon wasn't letting up. It was pushing Flipkart to the hilt every month, expanding its range of products, entering new businesses such as payments and food retail. There was no doubt that for many years to come, Amazon would continue to throw billions of dollars just to achieve its goal of toppling Flipkart.

Still, the fresh capital from SoftBank had reassured everyone at Flipkart. SoftBank's financial might and global network in the technology world would undoubtedly be a robust prop as Flipkart pursued its IPO dream. Certainly, after a long period of ceaseless volatility, the Flipkart team could look forward to working in a relatively stable, productive environment.

It thus came as a surprise when, around the time Flipkart finalized the SoftBank deal, the company was approached by a now-familiar figure: Walmart. The world's largest retailer had walked away from a deal with Flipkart exactly a year ago. The Walmart executives were so underwhelmed by what they had learnt about the company that they hadn't even bothered mentioning to Walmart CEO Doug McMillon that he should look into the Indian e-commerce company. Flipkart liked to think of itself as a large company, but for Walmart, 'big' had a different meaning altogether. In the financial year 2016–2017, Walmart recorded sales of $486 billion.[4] This was nearly a quarter of India's entire economy. But it wasn't that Walmart sought only large deals. In e-commerce especially, it was open to smaller, innovative businesses. But the firm had to be growing very fast; for Walmart, that was the only draw where an internet business was concerned. In 2016, when Walmart had considered investing in Flipkart, the Indian startup was in the early stages of its turnaround, and all its key metrics were askew. But the fact that Walmart had indicated serious interest in buying a stake was encouraging. Some Flipkart investors were convinced that the American retail giant would return to the negotiating table in the future. India's restrictive foreign investment rules meant that, for Walmart, Flipkart would remain an attractive point of entry into the local market.

Their conjecture turned out to be right. However, Walmart had also approached other local e-commerce firms including Snapdeal. Over the last year, Walmart's seriousness about making a minority investment in an Indian retailer had grown considerably. Its executives wanted to avoid making a late entry here, their anxieties intensified by the sight of Amazon charging ahead. Walmart had also become more confident about the market. It had been running a wholesale unit in India since 2013 which was advancing nicely.

In September 2017, a meeting was set up between Binny Bansal and Dirk Van den Berghe. An imposing Belgian in his fifties, Dirk had been promoted to CEO of Walmart Canada and Asia a few months ago. Binny and Dirk met over breakfast in a private suite at a five-star hotel in central Bangalore. Binny expressed his admiration for Walmart and expressed his hope that the two companies could work together. Flipkart had a lot to learn from Walmart, especially in the groceries business which was Walmart's forte.

After this amicable first meeting, things moved quickly. Walmart had also met Snapdeal executives, but the company was in a shambles, shrinking in size every month, barely getting by. There was no comparing it with Flipkart, which by now was thriving again.

The following month, in October 2017, the Flipkart team flew to the Walmart headquarters in Bentonville, Arkansas, to carry on the discussions. The weather there was cold, with temperatures dropping to the single digits at night. Bentonville, a city with a population of less than 50,000, is an unlikely base for a retailing behemoth. In such a small southern American city, it is startling to spot a number of Indians, who have moved there to fill up the satellite offices of IT firms. Expectedly, Walmart's presence is inescapable. The company is the city's biggest employer, its stores and offices are landmarks. Walmart also maintains a museum that records the company's history since its founding in 1962. Some of the older residents in the city personally knew Sam Walton, the company's founder who died in 1992.

At the Walmart offices, the Flipkart executives met with Doug McMillon and other senior leaders of the company. Doug was only the fifth CEO in Walmart's history. He was a Walmart lifer, having joined the company as a teenager. At fifty-one, he had already been CEO for four years. Doug had steadied Walmart after its image had been tainted by a bribery scandal in Mexico. He had made some bold moves, buying several online retailers and increasing the use of technology in Walmart's operations. He was known as an 'intensely friendly' CEO.[5]

Doug was taken with the Flipkart team, particularly by Sachin, who came across as a sincere, innovative entrepreneur.

The Flipkart executives returned to Bangalore at the end of the month, confident that a sale of five to ten per cent of the company's shares would soon be finalized. A strategic partnership with the American retailer would surpass all previous deals, including the gigantic SoftBank funding. Walmart was the most feared name in retail and its determination to prevail over Amazon was even stronger than Flipkart's own. With the might of Walmart, SoftBank and Tencent backing Flipkart's, Amazon would face an uphill task in overtaking its local opponent.

By now, Flipkart had already posed a direct question to Amazon: did it want to continue battling Flipkart? At an elite financial services conference in the US – around the time Walmart had approached Flipkart – Sachin had come across a known but unfamiliar rival: Jeff Bezos. He had wondered if he could tempt the Amazon founder – whose eagerness to succeed in India was well-established – into making a bid for Flipkart. Sachin had known that Bezos would be attending and had prepared extensively for the meeting. He had assembled data on the latest sales, losses and other business metrics at both Flipkart and Amazon India. He presented to Bezos these numbers which showed that Flipkart was still comfortably ahead of its rival in sales despite spending far lesser. This was because of the superior local knowledge and innovative abilities of Flipkart, claimed Sachin. Flipkart now had more cash than ever and it was only going to get stronger, he insisted. Did it then make sense for both companies to keep burning cash by fighting each other? Wouldn't it be better to join forces, combine each other's strengths and dominate the market profitably, asked Sachin of the Amazon founder.

Sachin had his own reasons for courting Bezos. He saw a deal with Amazon as his shot at redemption. The entry of a powerful new investor would considerably diminish the influence of Tiger Global, and by extension, of Kalyan Krishnamurthy. With a new partner, Sachin could start afresh and resume his $100 billion mission. To Sachin's surprise, Bezos expressed interest. He had respect for how Flipkart had fought off Amazon so far. He also found Sachin to be very impressive, and his arguments persuasive.

Bezos tasked a senior acquisitions specialist at Amazon to look into the possibility of buying Flipkart. But as this Amazon official spoke with Sachin and the Flipkart team, it became clear that the engagement would be fruitless. Just like in 2011, when Amazon had first considered buying Flipkart, its estimation of the company's worth came out to be unacceptably low. The talks fizzled out.

Soon, however, Amazon would be forced to reconsider its appraisal. A few weeks after they returned from Bentonville, the Flipkart officials were in for a surprise.

TOWARDS THE END of 2017, Doug McMillon and the other Walmart board members convened for a routine board meeting. The most influential member of the board was Greg Penner. In his late forties, Greg wasn't just the Walmart chairman, he was one of the heirs to the Walton family fortune. The Waltons are one of the richest families in America who own fifty per cent of Walmart. Greg had met Carrie Walton, granddaughter to Walmart founder Sam Walton, at university in Washington. They married a few years later, after which Greg joined Walmart at the end of the nineties. Greg also started a private equity firm and worked as a venture capitalist. In 2015, he became the chairman of the Walmart board, replacing his father-in-law, Rob Walton. Greg's parents, Clifford and Joyce Penner, were famous in their own right, having authored many sex-advice books.[6]

Now, Greg turned out to be a strong advocate for a deal with Flipkart,[7] so much so, that he put forth a new proposal: if Flipkart was an innovative, fast-growing retail company with an excellent brand, why not buy it out altogether, or certainly acquire a majority ownership? For years, Greg had been especially keen on expanding in Asia. Even though Walmart had been burnt earlier in India, the environment in the country had become more favourable for a fresh attempt. Now that the Indian market was up for grabs, Greg insisted that Walmart had to seize this chance. Like Greg, even the Walmart CEO Doug McMillon pushed for a majority ownership of Flipkart. This would give Walmart control of Flipkart's management and enable it to bring about major improvements at the company by introducing its enduring retailing practices. By the end of 2017, a decision had been taken: Walmart would offer to buy more than fifty-one per cent of Flipkart.

The stunned mergers and acquisitions team at Walmart began making preparations for negotiating an entirely new deal. It was certainly an audacious idea. Flipkart had been valued at $10.2 billion in its recent funding round. Any buyout offer would have to be significantly higher. If realized, the deal would be Walmart's biggest ever, exceeding its $10.8 billion purchase of British retail chain Asda in 1999.[8]

AT FLIPKART, SACHIN was getting increasingly restless about his proposal to become CEO again. He had been hankering for a return to power for months now. In anticipation of a comeback, Sachin had already increased his involvement at the company. Apart from the Billion brand, he had announced a new project in the area of artificial intelligence called AIforIndia. He had promised to invest hundreds of millions of dollars to apply AI across Flipkart. He had also started work on another initiative: designing a new smartphone. For years he had been inspired by Xiaomi. He now wanted to beat Xiaomi at its own game by creating an even cheaper phone that could compete with the Chinese company's enduringly popular models. It was a wild idea, and it was right up Sachin's alley. He hadn't felt this confident, this alive, in a very long time.

Towards the end of 2017, Sachin pressed the board to act. After lingering over Sachin's request for months, Lee was obligated to respond definitively. A '360-degree feedback' was commissioned by Flipkart's board to evaluate Sachin's candidature. It was to be overseen by Jim Kochalka, the leadership coach who had been working with Sachin, Binny and Kalyan for months now. This process involved soliciting feedback about Sachin from his peers, subordinates, bosses and anyone else who may have worked with him. The objective was to determine his behavioural patterns and gauge his managerial abilities.

As soon as the process started, it became clear that Sachin's mission was being blocked by two of Flipkart's seniormost officials: Kalyan Krishnamurthy and Sameer Nigam, the head of PhonePe. They were steadfastly opposed to his return. Kalyan's antipathy was well-known. He had been fine as long as Sachin was tucked away in the distant position of Executive Chairman. He had even cooperated with the board's efforts to repair his relationship with Sachin. He had been meeting Sachin regularly, as Kochalka had recommended. But if Sachin became Group CEO, Kalyan would have to answer to him formally. That would be unacceptable.

Kalyan warned the Flipkart board that if Sachin returned, he would move on; he wasn't going to work for Sachin again. Sameer Nigam's opposition was more surprising given that he had once been close to Sachin. But in July 2015, he had quit Flipkart on a sour note, furious at the way Sachin had displaced him by hiring managers from Google. When Flipkart bought PhonePe in April 2016, Sameer had secured a guarantee that if the company changed its CEO, the stock payouts due to him would be accelerated. This was now about to come true. Like Kalyan, Sameer also stated that he had no desire to report to Sachin again. It took several weeks for Sachin's evaluation to be completed.

Apart from Sachin's colleagues, Kochalka played a decisive role in the evaluation process. Through his sessions, he had formed an opinion about Sachin's interpersonal skills and managerial abilities, and it wasn't a favourable one. The verdict was unambiguous: Sachin was found 'unfit' to be CEO of Flipkart. It was inevitable, and in the end, it was an easy decision for Lee and the other board members. Having lost confidence in Sachin's leadership skills long ago, they felt ill-disposed to grant his request. The evaluation conducted by the leadership coach simply supplied the evidence to back up their stance.

Around the end of the year, Sachin was told that his candidature had been rejected. He was crushed. All his energy and enthusiasm of the past several months vanished. He began to think that he had been set up. The leadership coach who had conducted the process was well known to Tiger Global – Sachin now doubted that such a person could make an impartial assessment of his abilities. In any case, the Flipkart chairman recovered quickly – he would fulfil his wish in other ways.

IN FEBRUARY 2018, Doug McMillon and other top Walmart officials flew to Bangalore to discuss their new proposal to buy a majority ownership of Flipkart. Doug visited the Flipkart office on Bangalore's Outer Ring Road, where detailed presentations were made to the Walmart team about Flipkart's business. Later, senior officials of the two companies also met at the Hilton located within a software park near central Bangalore, a forty-five-minute drive from the Flipkart headquarters. Over dinner, Flipkart paraded its team to the Walmart officials.

This is where Sachin sprung a surprise on his colleagues. Standing next to the Walmart Asia CEO Dirk Van den Berghe, Sachin tapped his glass to get the audience's attention. He expressed enthusiasm about leading Flipkart in this next phase of its evolution. He said that he and Dirk had held encouraging discussions about the path forward. 'I want to raise a toast to our partnership. For the next ten, twenty, thirty years, we will rule the Indian market together.' It was clear to Sachin's colleagues that he was as resolute as ever to return to the hot seat. His speech was intended to send a message to both the Walmart officials and his Flipkart colleagues; he was making his status as the main man at Flipkart clear to the new owners, and to his colleagues he seemed to be saying that he had the backing of the Walmart leaders. As they listened to Sachin speak, the dozen or so Flipkart executives who were present, exchanged glances, pondering the import of his speech.

Nevertheless, the meetings were productive, a huge step forward.

The Flipkart investors were thrilled by this development. For Lee Fixel, this would be a satisfying conclusion to his long, exacting association with the company. It had seen many highs, but the lows had been the most nerve-wracking experiences of his career. Less than eighteen months ago, Flipkart had been in serious trouble; its survival had been in question. To have come out of this predicament so soon could only be seen as one of the great escape acts in the startup world. Lee became the champion of the deal at Flipkart. His partner in advocating Flipkart's sale was none other than Sachin, for a very different, but very predictable reason: he was determined to reclaim the title of CEO.

As the Flipkart team was negotiating the minutiae of the transaction with Walmart officials, Sachin spoke directly with Doug McMillon. They had several agreeable conversations about the direction of Flipkart after the sale. As they understood it, Sachin's involvement was going to be essential.

WHEN A COMPANY is up for sale, it is a norm to conduct an auction in order to extract the highest possible price. And so it was with Flipkart.

In early 2018, Flipkart representatives invited other potential suitors to make an offer. One of these was Alibaba, which was a large investor in Paytm, a rival of Flipkart. Paytm is a mobile payments provider that had also expanded into e-commerce. Stirred by Amazon and Walmart's pursuit of Flipkart, Alibaba, too, indicated its interest in discussing an investment. However, it soon became clear that Alibaba was keen only on a minority stake. Another complication was the valuation of PhonePe, Flipkart's payments business that was threatening to overtake Paytm. In deference to Paytm, Alibaba was offering a scanty price for PhonePe, which had become a prized asset for Flipkart. Within weeks, the talks with Alibaba broke down.

Flipkart also relayed Walmart's offer to Amazon officials. Bezos and his team were shocked. When they had evaluated the possibility of buying Flipkart last year, they had not for a moment believed that any other company would have the audacity and the means to make a rival bid. Flipkart was a hugely unprofitable retail business in a notoriously tricky market. It would require years of patient nurturing before the company could start showing profits. Surely, only Amazon, with its well-established reputation of making risky, long-term bets, could pull off such a deal. Secure in this belief, Amazon's opening offer had been wilfully inadequate, convinced as it was that the Indian company had no choice but to accept its terms. After learning of Walmart's interest, the Amazon officials restarted negotiations with Flipkart in earnest.

The two biggest international names in retail were now competing to buy Flipkart.

Still, the Flipkart team was aware of Amazon's notorious reputation for engaging in discussions just to play spoiler. This time, though, Amazon was quite serious. Jeff Bezos himself hosted Sachin at his house in Seattle. As proof of Amazon's sincerity, Flipkart extracted a provision that would make Amazon liable to pay a breakup fee of more than $4 billion. This sum would be due to Flipkart in case the two companies signed a merger agreement that later had to be terminated, no matter what the reason.

Sachin had been very excited about the merger with Amazon India. When he had met Bezos, Sachin had pitched the idea that Flipkart should remain independent and continue to be overseen by him and the company's present management team. The Flipkart team was clearly superior, Sachin had told Bezos. Sachin proposed that Amazon India should continue to exist, but occupy a supplementary, subordinate position. He believed that such a transaction would be a historic achievement for Flipkart, in real and symbolic terms. Not only would the merger yield an extraordinary bonanza, it would be a thumping validation of the local startup ecosystem: an Indian company taking over a promising unit of a global internet conglomerate was considered a fanciful idea.

Despite Sachin's enthusiasm for a deal with Amazon, the talks had moved slowly. Even as late as March 2018, Amazon hadn't made much progress in evaluating Flipkart. The Indian firm was wary of sharing details about its business. If a deal didn't materialize – and at the moment there was no guarantee that it would – Amazon would have secured a massive advantage by getting an inside look at its rival. Naturally, Flipkart only yielded minimal intelligence, resisting most of Amazon's requests for information. Nevertheless, representatives of the two companies kept in touch. Apart from Sachin, even SoftBank founder Masa Son was keen on a deal between the two companies. Son belived that Amazon's technology expertise would make the company an ideal owner of Flipkart. He was also attracted by the proposition of establishing a long-term alliance for SoftBank with Amazon, which could be kick-started with this deal. He spoke directly with Bezos and the two kept open the possibility of a merger even though the talks had gone cold for the time being.

The favoured suitor of Lee Fixel and most of the other Flipkart investors had always been Walmart. Apart from their reluctance to share information with Amazon, they were also concerned that India's anti-trust regulator wouldn't approve a deal between Flipkart and Amazon, given that the two companies enjoyed a virtual duopoly in e-commerce. On the other hand, the engagement with Walmart was deepening rapidly. Flipkart executives had visited Bentonville several times to make presentations and the two companies had come to an agreement on important matters, including Flipkart's valuation. Both Walmart and Amazon had offered to value the company at more than $20 billion, nearly double the valuation that Flipkart had fetched less than a year ago in its last funding round.

While Sachin had played an energetic role in the discussions with Walmart, it was Lee who had been pulling the strings and had provided the confidence to the Walmart officials to push on. Lee was no fly-by-night operator. He had a stellar reputation in the startup world and his presence and assurances about Flipkart went a long way towards smoothing the bumps in negotiations.

AS THE SALE discussions were ongoing, another obstacle in Sachin's path back to the CEO seat had been cleared towards the end of winter 2018. To everyone's surprise, Binny had made up his mind to leave the company. He had indicated to Flipkart's board that his work at the company was done. After an exhausting ten-year run, he wanted to do something less taxing, something that would leave him with a lot more time for his wife and their eighteen-month-old twins. Binny was willing to facilitate a smooth transition, but he was determined to move on.

This was acceptable to Sachin, who had taken charge of the deal discussions. Working closely with Goldman Sachs, the investment bank that Flipkart had hired to represent itself, Sachin came up with an outline for the deal. Flipkart would sell fifty to fifty-five per cent of the company to Walmart, giving it ownership control. But it would retain SoftBank and Tencent as shareholders and persuade Microsoft to increase its stake in the company. After his experience with Tiger Global, Sachin didn't want Walmart to be the sole authority on the Flipkart board. It was best to distribute power. Flipkart also solicited Google and Paypal for minority investments. Essentially, what Sachin had in mind was an overarching anti-Amazon alliance. Sachin had personally spoken with Google CEO Sundar Pichai, who seemed open to the proposal. Another Indian-origin CEO, Microsoft's Satya Nadella, had expressed willingness to raise his company's holding in Flipkart.

Additionally, to prove his commitment to the cause, Sachin had sought to increase his ownership in Flipkart. He had begun discussions with financial institutions about taking a personal loan of anywhere between $450 million to $1 billion in order to purchase Flipkart shares and lift his stake to more than ten per cent, nearly double of what he presently held. He had even discussed the possibility of borrowing from Walmart to fund part of this purchase.

Sometime in March 2018, after Binny had expressed his wish to leave Flipkart, Sachin moved again to assert his claim to the throne.

Lee had presented the Flipkart team to Walmart as an ideal, complementary mix of skills. There was Sachin, the technologist who had the ability to imagine the improbable;

Binny whose forte lay in operations; Ananth Narayanan, the former McKinsey senior partner who had turned Myntra into an efficient, fast-growing retailer while nurturing the company's innovation impulses; Sameer Nigam, a nimble entrepreneur who was building a digital payments app that could become a massive business in the future. But it was Kalyan Krishnamurthy who had been marked out as indispensable, the man who had turned Flipkart around, who made it tick every day.

Sachin, however, had a different picture in his mind. The Flipkart co-founder made it clear to his company's board that he wanted to become Group CEO. Though his candidature had been rejected by the board earlier, Sachin believed he had solidified his claim by proposing to double his ownership in the company. This constituted a huge personal risk, as Sachin would have to borrow hundreds of millions of dollars to fund the purchase. But he didn't care; it was a statement of his conviction about Flipkart's future, about his willingness to risk everything in order to return to the driver's seat at his beloved company. Sachin believed that he had atoned for his mistakes by spending time away and giving Kalyan and Binny the freedom to run Flipkart as they saw fit. He had even agreed to leadership coaching and to improve his interpersonal skills. It was now time for him to get his due, especially in light of Binny's desire to leave the company. He had no doubt that an innovative startup such as Flipkart had to be run by its founder. Though Kalyan had his uses, he was ultimately just an employee. It was Sachin who had the entrepreneurial drive and vision. Kalyan would have to learn to work with him.

Binny's impending exit compelled the Flipkart board to act on Sachin's claim. This time, Lee took it upon himself to survey the Flipkart team so he could judge Sachin's suitability for the role he wanted. Sachin was informed that he could only become CEO if his colleagues supported his candidature. They were the ones in charge of the daily administration of the company and it was essential for the stability of the firm that any CEO have their support.

Yet again, when they were asked, Kalyan and Sameer Nigam reaffirmed their opposition to Sachin's nomination. It was a strange scenario. Sachin had co-founded Flipkart and had led the company as CEO for most of its existence. He had also ostensibly played the leading role in the negotiations with Walmart and Amazon. To any outsider, it would seem obvious that Kalyan and Sameer were lower than Sachin in the pecking order. It would even seem obvious that Sachin wielded more authority than them. But this wasn't the case at all. This was Flipkart, a company that had always invented its rules. Paradoxically, it was Kalyan and Sameer who, in effect, had the power to choose their boss. They exercised that power without inhibition, and for the second time in months, Sachin's candidature was rejected. Over the years, hundreds of people had found to their shock that titles were of little significance at Flipkart. It was now Sachin's turn to learn this difficult truth.

IN APRIL 2018, Flipkart's discussions with Walmart moved to the penultimate stage. Walmart's audit of Flipkart's financial records was nearly complete. Now Sachin made another attempt to revive the engagement with Amazon, at the prompting of Masa Son. The two companies restarted their parley in haste. Sachin was confident that his chances of becoming CEO were high if Amazon bought Flipkart. He believed that he had established a cordial rapport with Bezos, who saw Sachin as a visionary entrepreneur in his own image. Even publicly, Amazon's previous antagonism towards Flipkart seemed to have ebbed. In a newspaper interview published that month, Amit Agarwal called the Bansals 'missionary entrepreneurs'.[9]

But the biggest obstacle remained: Lee's concerns about antitrust action against the proposed merger. By the middle of April, Flipkart had made its decision, bringing an end to the protracted auction. Lee had persuaded the other Flipkart investors to reject the Amazon proposal in favour of Walmart. A fellow Flipkart shareholder who was ambivalent about the choice, expressed his admiration at Lee's ability to 'win friends and influence people'. There was a hint of resentment. By now, Lee had also decided to retain a small holding in Flipkart. If Walmart ever took Flipkart public, the thought of being in the audience was too painful – this was his career's most significant work.

In the third week of April, Lee and the Flipkart team were scheduled to visit Bentonville for one last round of talks to finalize the sale. Until now, there had been no major hiccups. There was no reason to believe that this meeting wouldn't go well.

A few hours before the Flipkart team was to arrive, Sachin landed in Bentonville by himself. It was his final chance to make his case. He had decided to meet with Doug McMillon and Greg Penner to convince them that it was in Walmart's best interests to allow him considerable leeway in running Flipkart. Though the Flipkart board had rejected his candidature, Sachin believed they had no authority to decide his future. Flipkart's takeover was imminent; surely Walmart, in its capacity as the new owner, would want to have the final word on crucial matters such as this. After Sachin's meeting with Doug and Greg, the respective teams were left to put together a final transaction agreement.

Sachin told the Walmart officials that he wanted contractual guarantees about his role at Flipkart. He insisted on one particular right: the privilege to appoint the CEOs of Flipkart, Myntra and PhonePe. It wasn't that Sachin wanted to make any changes right now. But he believed he should certainly have the right to do so in the future. He had no doubt his demands were righteous. Not only had he founded and nurtured Flipkart, by doubling his ownership in the company he was proving his commitment to stay the course. There was no other individual who had more at stake. He was also the company's executive chairman – if the position had any real meaning, he certainly deserved this right. Though Sachin had accepted that he lacked the support of the Flipkart team to become CEO at the moment, he believed that it was natural for him, as co-founder and chairman, to inherit this right from Binny, who was on his way out. In addition, Sachin asked for superior voting rights to be given to minority shareholders in the matters of strategy and related-party transactions. These rights would ensure that Walmart held lesser voting power than its numerical ownership represented. Given that Doug McMillon had seemed willing to let Sachin have the freedom to run Flipkart, Sachin was sure he could obtain these rights.

When Sachin expressed his demands, the Walmart officials were startled. These details hadn't been part of the negotiations so far. They now referred the matter to Lee, Binny and the rest of the Flipkart team.

The Flipkart officials were furious that Sachin had inserted new demands at this juncture when all that was left to do was for the two companies to sign the agreement. They had even planned a celebratory dinner that night in anticipation of consummating the prolonged affair. Lee believed that Sachin's demands could wreck the sale that had been so painstakingly put together over the past seven months. He was convinced that neither Walmart nor the Flipkart team was going to yield so much ground to Sachin. With victory so close, the great escape within his grasp, Lee sprang into action. He wouldn't let anything ruin this buyout, even if it meant having to throw Sachin out of Flipkart. It would eventually have to be done in any case, as it was crucial that Kalyan continued to run the company. Lee was certain that only Kalyan could oversee Flipkart in a satisfactory manner. Sachin would have to be sacrificed. He had become too unreasonable.

But removing Sachin wouldn't look good either, as he had been an active participant in the talks with Walmart. Walmart executives would surely be unsettled by the exit of both the Flipkart founders. To ease their doubts, Binny would have to abandon his desire to quit Flipkart, if need be. Binny had kept himself on the periphery of the merger negotiations for the past few months. Now, he was thrust back onto the battlefield. Like Sachin, Binny stood to make more than $1 billion from the Walmart sale. Just a few weeks more and this astounding wealth would be his, at least on paper. As he weighed his options, this became the most important consideration for Binny. Unlike Sachin, he had little inclination to toil for another decade or longer at Flipkart. He also truly believed that Sachin wasn't equipped to run Flipkart as CEO. The debacle of 2015 had convinced Binny that Sachin lacked the discipline and rigour to run a company of Flipkart's size. Binny had so far remained silent about Sachin's demands; now he would have to reveal his stance. It was unavoidable, as Sachin was counting on the backing of his co-founder in his endeavour to extract the desired concessions from Walmart. When he had taken over as CEO in January 2016, Binny had surprised everyone who knew him by keeping Sachin out of the company's affairs. Two and a half years later, he would reprise this act, even if it was with some reluctance.

Back at the Walmart offices, Lee, Sachin, Binny and the rest of the Flipkart team had assembled with the Walmart officials for one last discussion. It had become clear to everyone in the room that Sachin's terms weren't going to be met. It made no sense for Walmart to buy a majority stake and not secure equivalent voting rights. For Flipkart's part, it was equally inconceivable that Kalyan would agree to Sachin being given the right to fire him. In exasperation, Lee urged Sachin to drop his demands, and accused him of putting the transaction at risk.

In the nine or so years that they had known each other, it was the first time that Lee had lost his temper with Sachin. After a moment's shock, Sachin recovered and turned to Binny. He had been sure that Binny would support his claim. But Binny made it clear that he wasn't on Sachin's side either. Nevertheless, Sachin stood his ground and raged that Lee had been plotting to turn both Walmart and Flipkart teams against him.

Disturbed by this civil war between the seniormost officials of the company that was to be its biggest-ever acquisition, the Walmart team suspended the discussions. They told the Flipkart executives to get their act together and present one final list of terms agreed upon beforehand.

Towards the end of April 2018, the Flipkart team returned to Bangalore from Bentonville, unsure about the status of the sale.

Leaving Sachin out, the Flipkart board conferred over a brief call. Everyone agreed on what had to be done. It was left to three members of Flipkart's board – one of whom was Binny Bansal – to inform Sachin that his demands weren't being met and that he was being cut out of the deal altogether.

Sachin couldn't believe that, in a matter of days, the transaction he had supposedly fronted for Flipkart was being summarily snatched away from him. It was hard to comprehend that Lee Fixel could banish him so coldly. He was in disbelief that his co-founder had deserted him. Most of all, he couldn't come to terms with the reality of having to leave the company that he had thought of as his own.

In the last week of April, Flipkart officials informed their Walmart counterparts about Sachin's departure. The news was jarring for the Walmart team. They asked for some time to consider this development.

While Walmart was weighing its next move, the Flipkart officials began to draw up a plan to announce Sachin's exit. It would have to be handled delicately. Binny took Flipkart's PR chief in confidence and began preparing a communication strategy. As they discussed the strategy in a small conference room at the Flipkart headquarters, Binny found that he couldn't stop trembling.

On 26 April, less than two days after Sachin's exit had been finalized, a reputed technology news website published an article which claimed that Binny may leave Flipkart after its sale to Walmart.[10] For months, the media had been giving a blow-by-blow account of the Flipkart–Walmart–Amazon saga. Rumours about Binny's supposed exit had been circulating amongst reporters, but the website factordaily.com was the first to publish a story on the subject. The irony, of course, was that the piece had come out just as Binny's stay had been prolonged, perhaps indefinitely.

Binny woke up to the article the next morning. He had no appetite for appreciating the irony. He was already on edge, aware that the Flipkart PR chief was perceived to be Sachin's man. Before the end of the day, Binny fired him.

A few days later, Walmart officials informed the Flipkart management that they would proceed with the deal on two conditions: one, Lee would have to continue on the company's board for a few more years; and second, Binny would have to remain Group CEO as well as take on the role of Chairman.

THE PICTURE SAID IT ALL.

On 10 May 2018, Flipkart released an ostensibly warm blog post in which Binny bid farewell to Sachin. At the end of the post was a picture of Sachin, Binny and Kalyan.[11]

They were standing close together. But it was the position of the three that caught the eye, revelatory, like a Freudian slip. Sachin was on the left, Kalyan in the middle and Binny to his right with an arm around him. The supposed camaraderie brought to one's mind how Kalyan had been installed by investors to replace Binny as CEO only last year. The photograph had actually been taken several months ago – it was inconceivable that Sachin would agree to such a photo after recent events – but it was an apt representation of how things had turned out between the Flipkart founders.

The day before the blog post was published, Walmart and Flipkart had announced the long-awaited deal. Walmart would pay $16 billion for a seventy-seven per cent stake in Flipkart, valuing the online retailer at $21 billion.[12] It set all kinds of records: the largest-ever acquisition in India, the greatest sale in e-commerce worldwide, and Walmart's biggest purchase. This transaction dwarfed the previous record acquisition in the Indian startup sector – Snapdeal's $400 million buyout of a mobile recharge firm. The press statement announcing the Flipkart–Walmart deal was accompanied by a picture of Binny shaking hands with Doug McMillon. Completely missing from the statement was any mention of Sachin's name.

It was true that, for the last two weeks, Sachin had been locked in negotiations with Flipkart as they finalized his exit agreement. The discussions had expectedly turned bitter. By the end, Sachin had extracted a very short non-compete clause. He was restricted from starting any business that directly or indirectly competed with Flipkart, but only for eighteen months.[13]

Sachin would earn more than $1 billion in cash after selling his approximately six per cent stake in Flipkart.[14] But this didn't help his acute sense of loss. He was distraught. Flipkart had been his life. He had few interests outside work. He couldn't imagine life without the company.

There was just one man Sachin could turn to for solace, his old friend and Flipkart's second employee: Tapas Rudrapatna. Tapas was perhaps the only Flipkart associate, former or present, with whom Sachin could still speak freely. Of all the people at Flipkart he had ever been close to, Tapas was perhaps the only one with whom his relationship with still intact. Since 2012, Tapas had maintained some distance from the company's internal workings. Flipkart had grown too big, too noxious for his liking. Still, he had remained a friend to Sachin, maintaining an unwavering, selfless allegiance to him. Tapas would often work on his laptop under a tree outside Flipkart's Koramangala office, across the road from a large park. His routine hadn't changed much. He still loved his chai–sutta, he still ate little, and showed up at Sathya's next to his small bungalow every other evening.

Sathya's is one of those cheap, cosy bars frequented by both the rich and the middle class, men and women alike. It stands on one end of a long, tree-lined street in Koramangala with bungalows on each side interspersed with the odd office building. The blackboard at the entrance states that the bar opened in 1983. Since then, it has enjoyed great loyalty from its patrons.

On several days during the summer of 2018, Tapas could be seen at Sathya's, drinking with his friend and former boss who had just become astonishingly wealthy, a real billionaire, and had freshly been named India's pioneering internet entrepreneur. Estranged from almost everyone he had known closely at his startup, Sachin Bansal had now returned to Sathya's, the cheerful bar he used to frequent in Flipkart's early years. In the fluorescent light of the bar, amid the buzz of conversation, Sachin sat quietly with his one real friend, as his former employees, associates and investors, in the Flipkart office just a few kilometres away, basked in the glory of a historic achievement.

EPILOGUE

Even under a new owner, Flipkart hasn't lost its taste for volatility.

In August 2018, Walmart completed its acquisition of Flipkart after receiving approval from the Competition Commission of India.[1] On 13 November 2018, Flipkart made a shocking announcement: Binny Bansal was resigning from the company as Group CEO and Chairman of the board. His resignation came in the aftermath of an internal investigation into an allegation of 'serious personal misconduct'.[2] While Flipkart didn't specify the details of the allegation, various publications reported that it was a complaint of sexual harassment against Binny.[3] It emerged that the complaint was lodged by a woman with whom Binny had had a consensual extramarital affair. This woman of unknown identity had once worked in Flipkart's customer support team. The affair allegedly started sometime in 2016, long after she had left the company, and ended the same year. It is unclear why the woman filed her complaint with Walmart executives about two years later, in July 2018. Walmart is known to have hired a law firm to investigate the matter.

The months-long probe could not gather any evidence to support the allegation. But it did show 'lapses in judgement' on Binny's part, Flipkart revealed in a press statement in November. The episode also revealed 'a lack of transparency' in how Binny had responded to the situation.[4] In a goodbye email to Flipkart's employees, Binny wrote, 'The allegations left me stunned and I strongly deny them.' But he admitted that the investigation did 'bring to light lapses in judgement'.[5] The company didn't share the details of these lapses, but media reports indicated that they were linked to how Binny had handled the termination of the affair.[6] Binny had been made aware of the matter only days before the announcement of his resignation. He had, in fact, made several public appearances in the months leading to his exit.

It was a tragic departure for the Flipkart co-founder. Walmart had asked him to stay back at the company as Sachin would no longer be a part of it. Binny leaving would also put Walmart in a tricky situation. Walmart had decided to go public after concluding it was too risky to hold back the details of a vexatious issue, especially in light of Binny's 'lapses'.

Binny continues to be a board member at Flipkart and holds more than three per cent stake in the company. In early 2019, he moved to Singapore with his family. He now serves as Executive Chairman at xto10x Technologies, a consultancy firm co-launched by him and former Flipkart executive Saikiran Krishnamurthy. Since 2015, Binny has also been a prolific investor in startups.

After Binny resigned from the company, Flipkart abolished the post of Group CEO. It consolidated all its e-commerce businesses under Kalyan, who was made the head of Myntra and Jabong, in addition to Flipkart. Kalyan's ascension was followed by the exit of Myntra CEO Ananth Narayanan. For months, Kalyan had been making the case for running Flipkart and Myntra–Jabong in a more complementary manner. His wish was finally granted by Walmart in November 2018. Putting Myntra and Jabong under Kalyan's charge immediately yielded cost savings for Flipkart. Whether the move will continue to benefit the company in the future is unclear. In the past, Flipkart had considered a separate listing of Myntra's shares. That possibility is all but dead now.

Kalyan is no longer seen as an associate of Lee Fixel or a Tiger Global representative; he is a powerful CEO in his own right with the full backing of Walmart. The American retail giant has appointed several executives to important posts in Flipkart's finance and legal functions, but Kalyan has been given considerable leeway to run the company as he sees fit.

So far, Kalyan has delivered fine results. In the one year or so after its takeover, Flipkart has increased its lead over Amazon. Surprisingly, after Walmart's entry, Amazon's competitive intensity seems to have reduced. The company is close to exhausting the $5 billion in capital it had pledged for expanding its India operations. How much more capital the company will commit towards India remains to be seen. It is becoming increasingly clear that Amazon will take longer to realize its stated objective of making India its second-biggest market after the US by 2025.[7]

Lee Fixel left Tiger Global in June 2019 after a spell of thirteen years,[8] during which time he established himself as one of the most promising young investors in the startup world globally and accumulated a personal fortune that will soon approach $1 billion. Much of his wealth is on account of the Flipkart wager. Lee plans to start an investment firm of his own. He continues to serve on the Flipkart board.

While Kalyan's record in delivering market share gains has been almost exemplary, he is yet to prove that Flipkart can attain profitability. After agreeing to buy Flipkart in May 2018, Walmart had stated that it would seek a public listing of Flipkart shares within a few years.[9] To date, this remains only a distant possibility, as Flipkart presently burns through approximately $1 billion in cash every year. Kalyan now has to reduce costs without sacrificing too much sales growth. It won't be easy: e-commerce in India is an inherently expensive business.

One surprising windfall for Walmart could come from PhonePe. When Flipkart bought PhonePe in April 2016, it was optimistic that the latter would become a serious player in the digital payments space. PhonePe has surpassed Flipkart's expectations. In early 2019, PhonePe entered discussions to become independent of Flipkart and raise capital from outside investors. The company could be valued anywhere between $5 billion to $10 billion.[10] It would come as a huge win for Walmart if PhonePe is able to pull off a funding round at the higher end of the spectrum. Whatever the price, the PhonePe founders, Sameer Nigam and Rahul Chari, are sure to be worth hundreds of millions of dollars.

Apart from PhonePe, Flipkart has spawned several other successful startups. Not only did the company help turn internet entrepreneurship into a desirable occupation, dozens of its employees have left to start their own companies over the years. The most prominent among these curiously reside next to each other in HSR Layout, a few kilometres away from where Flipkart was started: CureFit, a fitness and food platform that was launched by Mukesh Bansal and Ankit Nagori; and Udaan, a marketplace that facilitates business-to-business commerce that was birthed by Sujeet Kumar, Amod Malviya and Vaibhav Gupta.

In a sense, the founders of Phonepe, CureFit, Udaan and the other Flipkart-spawned startups are all indebted to Sachin. Many of them played important supporting roles to Sachin, but in the final reckoning, without his imagination and audacity, Flipkart would probably have been just another internet startup. Thinking big is now a mantra for startup founders; its prevalence can be traced directly to Sachin and to Flipkart's success.

Meanwhile, Sachin has started a new venture. In late 2018, he incorporated a holding company by the name of BAC Acquisitions Private Limited. He has already invested a large part of his wealth into startups and financial services firms. At BAC Acquisitions, he has teamed up with Ankit Agarwal, his former hostelmate at IIT Delhi and NGV flatmate. Sachin's LinkedIn profile states that he is 'pursuing opportunities in the BFSI (Banking, Financial Services and Insurance) space.'[11]

It may seem like a plain statement, but Sachin's zeal for pursuing the improbable remains undiminished. Sachin now wants to create a new corporate behemoth: a $100 billion enterprise in financial services. One could assume that this company, too, will have all the characteristics of a Big Billion Startup.

AFTERWORD

At a meeting with Flipkart employees in April 2019, Walmart CEO Doug McMillon was asked an awkward question. A year ago, Walmart had bought a seventy-seven per cent stake in India's largest online retailing group for $16 billion. A Flipkart staffer asked Doug why Walmart hadn't shared its famed knowhow in operating supply chains, an especially vexatious problem in India, with the Flipkart team. Doug responded that they had deliberately adopted a cautious approach. 'We're a giant and even our hugs can feel claustrophobic,' he said.[1]

Since the acquisition, Walmart has largely given free rein to Flipkart, thanks in no small part to Kalyan Krishnamurthy. After the exits of Flipkart co-founders, Sachin Bansal and Binny Bansal, Kalyan has established an unshakeable grip over the company. Resisting Walmart's advice to hire more accomplished executives, he has retained his preference for promoting from within talented young leaders who are more impressionable and therefore amenable to his ways. He has also remained immersed in daily operations instead of restricting himself to high-level matters.

When he became CEO, Kalyan had a point to prove even to

his own colleagues. His understanding of technology had been questioned by the Flipkart founders in the past, and the sales team he used to oversee before his ascendance to CEO often clashed with engineers. Kalyan has since made special efforts to show that he's tech-savvy. He spends a considerable amount of time with engineers and product managers, pampering them with special treatment in the form of fat bonuses and creative leeway, and has backed several tech acquisitions proposed by them. He keenly talks up Flipkart's tech innovations such as its Indian-language interfaces and voice assistant that have attracted millions of new users in smaller cities and towns who struggle to navigate English-language apps.

But his technology focus has come at a cost. He was so eager to prove that he 'gets tech' that he went to the 'other extreme', according to a former product manager. Kalyan overly defers to Flipkart's tech leaders because he doesn't have an engineering background, refraining from drilling down on them the way he does with those on the business side, as confirmed by several former employees.

Even though Flipkart has suffered some setbacks, such as a so-so performance in the 2019 Big Billion Days event, on the whole Walmart seems pleased with Kalyan. In June, the international CEO Judith McKenna said at a conference in New York that Walmart had been 'happy at every step of the way' with Flipkart's performance.[2] It's not hard to see why.

For more than two decades, Amazon has posed an existential threat to Walmart. Its $870 billion market cap dwarfs Walmart's $390 billion. Bezos is closing in on the wealth levels of the Walton family that controls Walmart; his stature overshadows theirs. In 2021, consumers in countries outside China spent more on Amazon than Walmart for the first time ever, according to a report in the *New York Times*.[3] Amazon is no.1 in online retail in almost all its major markets, including the US, Japan, UK, France and Germany.

India remains a notable exception, due to Flipkart's efforts. According to estimates by the Wall Street firm Bernstein, Flipkart Group's GMV touched $23 billion in 2021, higher than Amazon's $18–20 billion.[4] Flipkart's supremacy largely rests on Myntra, with the help of which it dominates fashion sales. While Flipkart's lead is hardly insurmountable, in recent years, Amazon hasn't done enough to indicate that it can overtake its rival.

Before the Walmart takeover, Flipkart had operated like a typical startup. The focus was on breakneck expansion rather than doing things by the book. Shockingly, for a company of its size, it didn't have a specialist legal head at the time of its takeover. Unsurprisingly, Walmart secured the rights to oversee Flipkart's finance, legal and accounting matters and made substantial changes in these functions.

Walmart leaders had also expected to work with Flipkart on aspects like supply chain improvement, but Kalyan has ensured that Walmart is barely involved in business matters. Walmart has ceded some ground to him even in the functions it controls. In 2018, Walmart appointed one of its senior executives, Emily McNeal, as Flipkart's finance chief. After McNeal left in 2020, Walmart named Sriram Venkataraman, a senior Flipkart leader nominated by Kalyan, as her replacement.

In July 2021, Flipkart raised $3.6 billion in capital from a group of investors at $37.5 billion, roughly a tenth of Walmart's current market cap.[5] It was a mark of Flipkart's appeal that the group included SoftBank, GIC and Qatar Investment Authority, who returned as investors after selling out to Walmart in 2018. Walmart, also a participant in the round, now owns about seventy-two per cent of the company.

Flipkart's payments unit PhonePe has fared even better than its parent. It is now India's biggest UPI app, comfortably ahead of Google Pay and other competitors. PhonePe's valuation touched $5.5 billion in December 2020, and it is reportedly raising another round of capital at a valuation of about $13 billion.[6]

There is, however, some tension between PhonePe and its parent firm. PhonePe is tentatively venturing into e-commerce, a move that could pit it against Flipkart. It has joined a government-backed e-commerce initiative that aims to break Flipkart's and Amazon's dominance. Flipkart too is expanding its financial services business and competes with PhonePe in a few areas.

Even though Flipkart and PhonePe are yet to turn profitable, Walmart has rewarded Kalyan and PhonePe CEO Sameer Nigam with cash bonuses worth several millions of dollars each, apart from far larger amounts in stock options. Their leadership teams too own lucrative stock options. This incentivizes the managers of the two companies to seek IPOs even more eagerly than Walmart, which intends to retain a majority holding after a Flipkart listing.

Since late 2020, Reuters and Indian newspapers have carried reports that a Flipkart IPO is due anytime.[7] Flipkart has begun to adopt measures mandated by the Sarbanes-Oxley Act – a law governing public companies in the US – such as improving reporting processes for making regulatory disclosures. But insiders say that the company has a long way to go in meeting all the requirements; an IPO is therefore unlikely for a few years to come.[8]

An IPO will expose Flipkart to scrutiny it is not prepared to handle. Zomato, Paytm, Nykaa and the few other Indian unicorns that have listed their shares have lost billions of dollars in market value. Though they are still growing quickly, most of them are not profitable. The message is clear: public market investors value profitless growth far less than venture capitalists. Globally too tech stocks have been routed; the biggest tech companies have cut thousands of jobs. Flipkart's latest numbers – in the financial year ending on 31 March 2022 its two main India entities reported a combined net loss of roughly $1 billion[9] – indicate its valuation is inflated by public market standards.

Flipkart's arch-rival Amazon has been one of the biggest losers in the ongoing tech downturn. In India, Amazon is chugging along. Even though it is running close to Flipkart, it hasn't achieved the dominance it craved. Amazon has also been the target of open hostility from India's politicians and regulators.

In January 2020, Jeff Bezos, then the world's richest person, returned to India to smooth over relations with the government and boost the morale of the India team. Ready with another big-bang investment commitment, Bezos was eager to get a sign-off from the BJP government, months into its second term.

Bezos' publicity campaign was more extensive than the one in 2014, when he had posed on a local truck wearing a bandhgala and given several media interviews. During the three-day trip in January 2020, Bezos, sporting different Nehru jackets, went on a (real) kite-flying expedition in New Delhi, visited the Gandhi memorial in the capital, drove around in an Amazon-branded e-rickshaw and hung out with Bollywood stars in Mumbai. He announced that Amazon would invest another $1 billion in India, on top of the $5.5 billion it had previously committed and nearly exhausted.

But instead of a pat on the back, the BJP government responded with a public snub. At a conference in the capital, trade minister Piyush Goyal snorted at Bezos' announcement and said that Amazon was hardly doing a 'great favour to India'.[10] Goyal described a recent antitrust investigation into Amazon and Flipkart as 'an area of concern for every Indian', as if it was a national security matter, without explaining why.

That Flipkart has avoided such gratuitous hostility must surely have brought some comfort to executives at Walmart, which not too long ago was seen as a paradigm of the predatory foreign company.

But while Flipkart has surpassed Walmart's initial expectations, it faces many questions and threats. For starters, its deep loses are an embarrassment for a firm that has been the market leader in e-commerce for most of its fifteen-year existence. While its valuation has risen impressively, the true measure of its worth can only be known when it goes public. Most worryingly for Flipkart, the expansion of the $64 billion online shopping market may be tapering just as competition from the likes of Reliance and the Tata Group is intensifying.[11]

In addition, there is the issue of leadership. Kalyan's management style has made the company dependent on him to an unusual degree. His inclination for avoiding big-name hires means there are few, if any, leaders at the firm who can succeed him. Nominally a professional CEO, Kalyan runs Flipkart like a founder – with all the attendant benefits and dangers for the firm.

ONE OF FLIPKART'S actual co-founders has struggled with personal and professional setbacks since his exit from the firm.

In February 2020, Sachin Bansal was accused of very serious crimes by his estranged wife, Priya Bansal.

Priya filed an FIR at the Koramangala police station in Bangalore against Sachin, his parents and brother, listing several complaints against them. She alleged that the four had demanded dowry from her family around the time of their wedding in April 2008, a few months after Flipkart was founded. In her complaint, Priya alleged that her father had given Sachin ₹11 lakh 'in lieu of buying a car' and that Sachin and his family 'were pressuring her for more dowry and harassing her physically and mentally'. She also alleged that Sachin had physically assaulted her in October 2019, 'after demanding that the properties they owned jointly must be signed over to him'. She further claimed that Sachin had sexually harassed her sister.[12]

In response, Sachin moved the Karnataka High Court to quash the complaint and obtained relief from the court in the matter. Priya, however, challenged the order in the Supreme Court, which is yet to declare its decision.[13]

The allegations against Sachin have cast a shadow over his status as an iconic pioneer of India's startup ecosystem. They may also have affected his new financial services venture.

Sachin has invested a majority of his Flipkart fortune into this venture, Navi Technologies (previously BACQ). It is an astonishingly bold statement of intent – few entrepreneurs are inclined to gamble all their wealth on a new venture, especially when external capital is available. As he said in a recent interview, 'The only way I know to do things is to go all in.'[14]

Through Navi, Sachin had applied for a universal banking licence that will allow him to pursue his goal of building a Flipkart-like behemoth in financial services. Obtaining a banking licence, however, requires a squeaky-clean record. In May 2022, the RBI rejected Navi's application. News reports suggested that the court case involving his wife and others against him from his Flipkart days may have influenced the RBI's decision.

Sachin is nevertheless charging ahead, to the extent regulations allow him. Navi has made several acquisitions, picking up ventures in micro-finance, asset management and insurance at fire-sale prices. His vision for Navi has drawn two large investors, IFC and Gaja Capital, but he has continued to hold on to about ninety-seven per cent of the company. Scarred by his experience at Flipkart, maintaining management control now seems paramount to him: 'I never wanted to sell, I never imagined I would not be in Flipkart.'[15]

Navi is already preparing to go public. Its listing application was approved by India's stock market regulator in September. The company seeks to raise ₹3,350 crore and invest in its lending and insurance units.[16] Improbably, Sachin's second startup will list its shares faster than his first.

His second $100 billion mission is well underway.

AUTHOR'S NOTE AND ACKNOWLEDGEMENTS

This book is based on more than two hundred and fifty interviews, emails, regulatory documents, news reports, and video interviews of Flipkart executives available online. In most cases, the dialogues and quotes that appear in the narrative have been used verbatim from news reports or from interviews that I conducted. In the odd case, they are reconstructed from statements made to me in interviews.

While I have interviewed them several times in the past, the Flipkart co-founders Sachin Bansal and Binny Bansal declined to speak to me for the purposes of the book. Flipkart did not participate either. I reached out individually to all the major characters at Flipkart who appear in the book. Some of them declined to talk or did not respond to my requests. However, I had deep access to many of the people who played a crucial role in the making of Flipkart since its founding in 2007.

I first wrote about Flipkart in 2013. In the four years before its sale to Walmart, Flipkart had been the main subject of my coverage for *Mint*. The book is the culmination of this experience.

Apart from Flipkart, the book traces the development of the wider startup ecosystem in India, by which I refer mostly to the internet companies that serve shoppers. A smaller part of this ecosystem comprises startups that provide software for companies, as opposed to shoppers. Their development, while somewhat related to the internet companies, has not been covered.

Many people deserve thanks for contributing directly and indirectly to this book: Sukumar Ranganathan, my former editor, for giving me the opportunity to write on startups and for backing me fully on controversial and sensitive stories. I learned a great deal from him. My friend and former colleague Shrutika Verma, together with whom I learned about startups, and news reporting. Vinay Kamat, my current editor at *Mint*, who generously allowed me the time and space to work on this book. It was truly gracious of him. Pankaj Mishra, my former boss at *Mint*, who compelled me to track startups before he left. Somak Ghoshal, who introduced me to my agent and provided helpful advice on various matters. My agent Anish Chandy for believing in this book and working diligently to bring it out. His feedback on the book and advice on related matters were critical. A special thank you to Teesta Guha Sarkar, my editor at Pan Macmillan India. She was the arbiter of the book's tone and quality, and if the book is readable, it is thanks to her. And, of course, thank you to my family – my grandmother, parents, brother, and in remembrance, my late grandfather – for their unwavering support. I'm indebted to my partner Chandni. She offered unfailing encouragement, patience and generosity during the year I spent working on the book. Her support kept me going when I had doubts and her suggestions helped me make important changes to the manuscript.

Most of all, I thank all the Flipkart officials and everyone else who participated in the development of this book. Thanks especially to those who spoke without inhibition. I am unable to name them for obvious reasons. But without their help, it is unlikely that this book could have been completed. These people spoke with me several times, spending many hours detailing their experiences and perspectives. It helped me immensely in piecing this story together.

NOTES

1 BREEDING GROUND

1. *New York Times*. 2004. 'Google Goes Public', 20 August, available at https://www.nytimes.com/2004/08/20/opinion/google-goes-public.html
2. Sabarinath M. 2005. 'Meet Kishore Biyani, the Sam Walton of India', *Economic Times*, 15 October, available at economictimes.indiatimes.com/articleshow/1263228.cms?utm_source=contentofinterest&utm_medium=text&utm_campaign=cppst
3. *Business Standard*. 2004. 'eBay buys Baazee for $50 million', 24 June, available at https://www.business-standard.com/article/management/ebay-buys-baazee-for-50-million-104062401142_1.html
4. BBC. 2004. 'BJP admits "India Shining" error', 28 May, available at http://news.bbc.co.uk/2/hi/south_asia/3756387.stm
5. BBC. 2009. 'India billionaires double in 2009', 11 March, available at http://news.bbc.co.uk/2/hi/south_asia/8562957.stm
   James Crabtree. 2018. *The Billionaire Raj: A Journey Through India's New Gilded Age*. Tim Duggan Books.
6. While Shockley was a brilliant physicist, he was a terrible manager whose mismanagement pushed his colleagues to leave his firm

and start Fairchild Semiconductor, a pioneering hardware startup. For more, see: Scott Rosenberg. 2017. 'Silicon's Valley first founder was its worst', 19 July, available at https://www.wired.com/story/silicon-valleys-first-founder-was-its-worst/

7. Raj Chengappa. 2013. 'Bangalore clocked to be the fastest growing metropolis in India', *India Today*, 22 July, available at https://www.indiatoday.in/magazine/cover-story/story/19830415-bangalore-clocked-to-be-the-fastest-growing-metropolis-in-india-770617-2013-07-22
8. *Hindu*. 2005. 'The Bean City' available at https://www.thehindu.com/mp/2005/02/22/stories/2005022201010300.htm

   Divya Shekhar. 2017. 'Krishnaraja Wadiyar IV: The philosopher-king who laid foundation for modern Bengaluru', *Economic Times*, 14 September, available at economictimes.indiatimes.com/articleshow/60510235.cms?utm_source=contentofinterest&utm_medium=text&utm_campaign=cppst

   Divya Shekhar. 2017. 'Date with history: The 107-year-old home in Bengaluru that is a tribute to Mysore's first Dewan', *Economic Times*, 12 January, available at economictimes.indiatimes.com/articleshow/56499881.cms?utm_source=contentofinterest&utm_medium=text&utm_campaign=cppst

   T. J. S. George. 2016. *Askew: A Short Biography of Bangalore*. Aleph Book Company.

   Janaki Nair. 2005. *The Promise of the Metropolis*. Oxford University Press
9. Chidanand Rajghatta. 2004. 'Bangalored: function – transitiveverb!', *Times of India*, 23 July, available at http://timesofindia.indiatimes.com/articleshow/787599.cms?utm_source=contentofinterest&utm_medium=text&utm_campaign=cppst
10. Thomas Friedman. 2005. *The World Is Flat: A Brief History of the Twenty-first Century*. Farrar, Straus and Giroux.

Friedman's theory of the modern world being flat has been discredited by many intellectuals as an overly simplistic idea that distorts the understanding of globalization and its workings.

11. Amazon. 2004. Available at https://press.aboutamazon.com/news-releases/news-release-details/amazoncom-acquire-joyocom-limited
12. Amazon. Available at https://www.amazon.jobs/en/principles
13. Divya Shekhar. 2016. 'Aga Ali Asker, the Persian horse trader whose legacy lingers on in Bengaluru', *Economic Times*, 21 January, available at https://economictimes.indiatimes.com/magazines/panache/aga-ali-asker-the-persian-horse-trader-whose-legacy-lingers-on-in-bengaluru/articleshow/50667052.cms
14. LinkedIn. Sachin Bansal, available at https://www.linkedin.com/in/sachinbansal/

2 THE BANSALS GO TO IIT

1. Mihir Dalal. 2018. 'Why startups are exiting Bengaluru's Koramangala', *Livemint*, 3 September, available at https://www.livemint.com/Companies/LnV18zLsDCfIGcckMb9tsI/Why-startups-are-exiting-Bengalurus-Koramangala.html
2. Chandigarh official website, available at http://chandigarh.gov.in/knowchd_gen_historical.htm

   Sunil Khilnani. 1997. *The Idea of India*. Farrar, Straus and Giroux.
3. Shraddha Sharma. 2013. 'Binny Bansal with YourStory in TechSparks2013', available at https://www.youtube.com/watch?v=zPFptdATk_s
4. Aditi Tandon, 2000, 'Record number of city students make it to IIT', *Chandigarh Tribune*, available at https://www.tribuneindia.com/2000/20000530/cth1.htm
5. Chetan Bhagat. 2004. *Five Point Someone*. Rupa & Co.

6. Anand Daniel. 2019. 'Insights #22: Binny Bansal', Soundcloud, available at https://soundcloud.com/insights-podcast-accel/binny-bansal-final-podcast
7. Term used by Nicholas Carr in his book *The Glass Cage*. It refers to the philosophy of Frederic Winslow Taylor, a pioneer of the scientific management theory. Taylor was obsessed with improving the efficiency of labour and machines in factories and in industry overall.
8. Shekhar Gupta. 2015. 'Walk the Talk with the founders of Flipkart', available at https://www.youtube.com/watch?v= ye2LLhZdHLM

3 EXODUS FROM AMAZON

1. Walter Isaacson. 2011. *Steve Jobs*. Simon & Schuster.
2. Nick Bilton. 2013. *Hatching Twitter: A True Story of Money, Power, Friendship, and Betrayal*. Penguin.
3. Ibid.
4. Shekhar Gupta. 2015. 'Walk the Talk with the founders of Flipkart', available at https://www.youtube.com/watch?v=ye2LLhZdHLM
5. Based on statements made in interviews to the author.
   Rachel Chitra, 2018. 'Binny Bansal: Flipkart happened as Google rejected me twice', *The Times of India*, 10 August, available at https://timesofindia.indiatimes.com/business/india-business/flipkart-happened-as-google-rejected-me-binny-bansal/articleshow/65346358.cms
6. NextBigWhat. 2010. 'Sachin Bansal: When Flipkart Was A Startup', available at https://www.youtube.com/watch?v=sLvW_8xNXq8
7. Based on statements made in interviews to the author.
   Binny Bansal. LinkedIn profile, available at https://www.linkedin.com/in/binnybansal/
   Neha Jain. 2018. 'Working at Amazon was riskier than starting Flipkart – Binny Bansal', YourStory, 10 August, available at https://

yourstory.com/2018/08/working-amazon-riskier-starting-flipkart-binny-bansal

8. Seattlepi.com. 2006. 'Google hires Amazon's search chief', available at https://www.seattlepi.com/business/article/Google-hires-Amazon-s-search-chief-1195185.php
9. Brennon Slattery. 2010. 'Google Buys Jambool: Social Networking Battle Begins', PCWorld, 16 August, available at https://www.pcworld.com/article/203335/google_buys_jambool_social_networking_battle_begins.html
10. Krishna Motukuri. LinkedIn, available at https://www.linkedin.com/in/krishnamotukuri/
11. Shraddha Sharma. 2013. 'Binny Bansal with YourStory in TechSparks2013', YourStory, available at https://www.youtube.com/watch?v=zPFptdATk_s
12. *Economic Times*. 2018. 'When Amazon got big fat bonus back from Flipkart's Sachin Bansal', 10 August, available at https://economictimes.indiatimes.com/news/company/corporate-trends/when-amazon-got-big-fat-bonus-back-from-flipkarts-sachin-bansal/articleshow/65352858.cms

4 THE DESERTION

1. NextBigWhat. 2010. 'Sachin Bansal: When Flipkart Was A Startup', available at https://www.youtube.com/watch?v=sLvW_8xNXq8
2. Mihir Dalal and Shrutika Verma. 2016. 'Flipkart's Godfather in New York', *Livemint*, 29 July, available at https://www.livemint.com/Companies/QD9B2wsY5WMMfYuLYi6jEM/Flipkarts-godfather-in-New-York.html
3. Amazon annual report 2007.
4. NextBigWhat. 2010. 'Sachin Bansal: When Flipkart Was A Startup', available at https://www.youtube.com/watch?v=sLvW_8xNXq8
5. Based on statements made in interviews to the author.

6. Neha Jain. 2018. 'Working at Amazon was riskier than starting Flipkart - Binny Bansal', YourStory, 10 August, available at https://yourstory.com/2018/08/working-amazon-riskier-starting-flipkart-binny-bansal

5 UP, DOWN, HELLO, GOODBYE

1. Bijoy Venugopal. 2015. 'Flipping back pages with the first Flipkart customer', Flipkart, 15 October, available at https://stories.flipkart.com/first-flipkart-customer/
2. Aakar Patel. 2009. 'When will the Brahmin-Bania hegemony end?', *Livemint*, 28 August, available at https://www.livemint.com/Leisure/ 3u2QUPuXBEFPaBQXU2R8mJ/When-will-the-BrahminBania-hegemony-end.html

   Harsimran Julka and Radhika Nair. 2013. ' Why young Aggarwals dominate India's e-commerce start-ups', *Economic Times*, 13 February, available at https://economictimes.indiatimes.com/tech/internet/why-young-aggarwals-dominate-indias-e-commerce-start-ups/articleshow/18454259.cms
3. Archana Rai. 2010. 'Flipkart: Country's largest online bookstore', *Economic Times*, 30 June, available at https://economictimes.indiatimes.com/flipkart-countrys-largest-online-bookstore/articleshow/6108317.cms
4. Bijoy Venugopal. 2015. 'Flipping back pages with the first Flipkart customer', Flipkart, 15 October, available at https://stories.flipkart.com/first-flipkart-customer/

   Based on statements made in interviews to the author.
5. Anand Daniel. 2019. 'Insights #22: Binny Bansal', Soundcloud, available at https://soundcloud.com/insights-podcast-accel/binny-bansal-final-podcast
6. LetsVenture. 2018. 'Story of Flipkart | Binny Bansal and Subrata Mitra at LI Bangalore', available at https://www.youtube.com/watch?v=2LyLyV46vEo

7. Based on statements made in interviews to the author.
8. Binoy Venugopal. 2016. 'Ambur Iyyappa – The Man Who Saw Tomorrow', Flipkart, 11 January, available at https://stories.flipkart.com/ambur-iyyappa-human-erp/
   Based on statements made in interviews to the author.
9. VCCircle. 2013. 'Sachin Bansal on how Flipkart built a Rs 2,000 Cr business in 5 years', 7 March, available at https://www.youtube.com/watch?v=Y70OZ6D4UPg&app=desktop

6 THE KART GETS ROLLING

1. Ministry of Corporate Affairs

7 THE EYE OF THE TIGER

1. Mihir Dalal and Anirban Sen. 2018. 'Ashish Gupta, the angel who struck gold in Flipkart sale to Walmart', *Livemint*, 11 May, https://www.livemint.com/Companies/J25VyjJIhvYZ8o7a5EMr0J/Ashish-Gupta-the-angel-who-struck-gold-in-Flipkart-sale-to.html
2. Rohin Dharmakumar. 2012. 'Can Flipkart Deliver?', *Forbes*, available at http://www.forbesindia.com/article/boardroom/can-flipkart-deliver/33240/4
3. Brian O'Keefe. 2008. 'Tiger's Julian Robertson roars again', CNN, 29 January, available at https://money.cnn.com/2008/01/28/news/newsmakers/okeefe_tiger.fortune/index.htm
4. Mihir Dalal and Shrutika Verma. 2016. 'Flipkart's Godfather in New York', *Livemint*, 29 July, available at https://www.livemint.com/Companies/QD9B2wsY5WMMfYuLYi6jEM/Flipkarts-godfather-in-New-York.html

8 'BINNY KE BATCH SE HO?'

1. Harini Subramani, 2012. 'Fund infusion values Flipkart at $850 million', *Livemint*, 30 January, available at https://www.livemint.com/Companies/df5k5Pqn1h3UlB2PGhjyTM/Fund-infusion-values-Flipkart-at-850-million.html
2. Amazon leadership principles which inspired the Bansals to institute similar 'values' at Flipkart.
3. Henry Blodget. 2009. 'Mark Zuckerberg On Innovation' Business Insider, 1 October, available at https://www.businessinsider.com/mark-zuckerberg-innovation-2009-10?IR=T
4. Network effect refers to a process in which the more people use a service, the more valuable and improved the service becomes.

9 BOOM

1. Deepti Chaudhary. 2011. 'E-commerce firms get an edge over others on valuations', *Livemint*, 22 July, available at https://www.livemint.com/Companies/BddlAITwuM3uJ3wRiFyf1N/Ecommerce-firms-get-an-edge-over-others-on-valuations.html
2. Rohin Dharmakumar. 2011. 'E-commerce in India – The Second Coming', *Forbes*, 25 July, available at http://www.forbesindia.com/article/boardroom/ecommerce-in-india-the-second-coming/27042/1
3. Telecom Authority of India. Available at https://web.archive.org/web/20130927084149/http://trai.gov.in/WriteReadData/Recommendation/Documents/Rcommendation81210.pdf
4. The Boston Consulting Group. 2010. 'The Internet's New Billion', available at https://www.bcg.com/documents/file58645.pdf
5. Deepti Chaudhary. 2011. 'Flipkart raises $20 million from Tiger Global for supply chain expansion', *Livemint*, 16 June, available at https://www.livemint.com/Companies/

BTIzPAoIV7HHHsTKYO4YbL/Flipkart-raises-20-mn-from-Tiger-Global-for-supply-chain-ex.html

6. Registrar of Companies.
7. John Cassidy. 2002. *Dot.Con*. HarperCollins.
8. Ministry of Corporate Affairs
9. Based on statements made in interviews to the author. Shrutika Verma. 2012. 'FDI Escapades' BusinessWorld, available at http://www.businessworld.in/article/FDI-Escapades/08-11-2014-67048/
10. Ministry of Corporate Affairs

10 THE KING OF SHAKTIPEETH

1. IIT Bombay. 2016. 'Fireside Chat – Sachin Bansal & Rahul Yadav @ E-Summit 2016', available at https://www.youtube.com/watch?v=ZZR_mSOP5Mg
2. Hugh MacLeod. 2009. Ignore Everybody: and 39 Other Keys to Creativity Hardcover. Penguin.
3. '*Lala*' is a derogatory term used to describe the promoters or owners of certain kinds of Indian companies. Such companies are usually associated with retrograde business practices and poor corporate governance.
4. Ministry of Corporate Affiars
5. Happy mcgarrybowen. 2011. 'Flipkart.com - The Granny & The Mouse', available at https://www.youtube.com/watch?v=U2yh9pjnuTQ
6. TiE. 2016. 'Keynote Conversation', available at https://www.youtube.com/watch?v=u97hLvCO3Kw
7. Flipkart. 2011. 'Flipkart: No Kidding. No Worries. (Cafe)', available at https://www.youtube.com/watch?v=rLnJJ0CNBok

11 SETBACK

1. Satish John. 2008. 'Biyani moves on with 4 new stores in 5 days', *Livemint*, 29 September, available at https://www.livemint.com/Home-Page/ZlzTlEGr521WcHPbrqsoXJ/Biyani-moves-on-with-4-new-stores-in-5-days.html
2. TiE. 2016. 'Keynote Conversation', available at https://www.youtube.com/watch?v=u97hLvCO3Kw
3. Brad Stone. 2013. *The Everything Store: Jeff Bezos and the Age of Amazon*. Little, Brown and Company.
4. Deepti Chaudhary. 2012. 'Flipkart acquires Letsbuy.com', *Livemint*, 10 February, available at https://www.livemint.com/Companies/HSkOJC5yIpsOTsy8ZKr4bP/Flipkart-acquires-Letsbuycom.html
5. Anupam Saxena. 2012. 'Flipkart Shutters LetsBuy; Why Not Keep Two Storefronts?', Medianama, 29 May, available at https://www.medianama.com/2012/05/223-letsbuy-shuts-down/
6. Mihir Dalal and Deepti Chaudhary. 2013. 'Flipkart raises $200 million amid e-commerce fund drought', *Livemint*, 11 July, available at https://www.livemint.com/Companies/Dkaigg2rge8dNbXGO6DxJJ/Flipkart-raises-200-million-from-existing-investors.html
7. Biswarup Gooptu. 2014. 'Snapdeal co-founder Kunal Bahl: A rising star of India's e-commerce space', *Economic Times*, 28 February, available at https://economictimes.indiatimes.com/tech/internet/snapdeal-co-founder-kunal-bahl-a-rising-star-of-indias-e-commerce-space/articleshow/31125419.cms
   Based on statements made in interviews to the author.
8. Shayon Pal. 2012. 'Amazon launches Junglee.com in India', *Hindustan Times*, 2 February, available at https://www.hindustantimes.com/tech-reviews/amazon-launches-junglee-com-in-india/story-yY35tJFsT0gPVh9K1qzQ4H.html

12 NO RESPITE

1. Rohin Dharmakumar. Linkedin. Available at https://www.linkedin.com/in/rohin/
2. Rohin Dharmakumar. 2012. 'Can Flipkart Deliver?', *Forbes*, available at http://www.forbesindia.com/article/boardroom/can-flipkart-deliver/33240/4
3. Indrajit Gupta. 2012. 'Flipkart CEO responds to our cover story', Forbes, 25 June, available at http://www.forbesindia.com/blog/editors-blog/flipkart-ceo-responds-to-our-cover-story/
4. *Economist*. 2003. 'Finding Nemesis', 21 October, available at https://www.economist.com/news/2003/10/21/finding-nemesis
5. Deepti Chaudhary. 2012. 'Flipkart raises $150 mn from investors', *Livemint*, 24 August, available at https://www.livemint.com/Industry/fGAYKfohxjwyHNK7JjTtlN/Flipkart-raises-funding-from-Naspers-ICONIQ-Capital-and-oth.html
6. 'Too big to fail' is a phrase used to describe companies that are so large and so important to an industry that their collapse would threaten the survival of that entire industry. In this case, Flipkart's failure would cast doubt about the survival of the entire e-commerce business in the country.
7. Shrutika Verma and Mihir Dalal. 2014. 'Inside Flipkart's complex structure', *Livemint*, 25 November, available at https://www.livemint.com/Companies/VXr8oJzNJ4daOYSO5wNETN/Inside-Flipkarts-complex-structure.html
8. Ministry of Corporate Affiars.
   Shrutika Verma. 2012. 'FDI Escapades' *BusinessWorld*, available at http://www.businessworld.in/article/FDI-Escapades/08-11-2014-67048/
9. Ministry of Corporate Affairs.
   Shrutika Verma and Mihir Dalal, 2015. 'Sujeet Kumar, head of Flipkart's largest seller WS Retail, quits', *Livemint*, 18 May,

available at https://www.livemint.com/Companies/5Z9dMYCZA2GjZsdhRhO9lI/Sujeet-Kumar-head-of-Flipkart-seller-WS-Retail-quits.html

10. Shrutika Verma. 2012. 'FDI Escapades' BusinessWorld, available at http://www.businessworld.in/article/FDI-Escapades/ 08-11-2014-67048/
11. Anupam Saxena. 2012. 'Enforcement Directorate To Probe Flipkart For Alleged FDI Norms Violation', Medianama, 11 December, https://www.medianama.com/2012/12/223-enforcement-directorate-to-probe-flipkart-for-alleged-fdi-norms-violation/
12. Based on statements made in interviews to the author.

TiE. 2016. 'Keynote Conversation', available at https://www.youtube.com/watch?v=u97hLvCO3Kw

13 THE TIGER CUB

1. Kalyan Krishnamurthy. LinkedIn. Available at https://www.linkedin.com/in/kalyankrishnamurthy/
2. Paul De Bendern and Henry Foy. 2011. 'Manmohan Singh fails to dispel policy paralysis fears', *Reuters*, 29 June, available at https://www.livemint.com/Politics/DwkoGovkYHoDxZzX28SwWO/Manmohan-Singh-fails-to-dispel-policy-paralysis-fears.html
3. Anirban Sen. 2014. 'Infosys not satisfied with recent performance: Narayana Murthy', *Livemint*, 27 February, available at https://www.livemint.com/Companies/r0q9bVUle15fLbngVSgHtK/Infosys-not-satisfied-with-its-recent-performance-Murthy.html
4. Mihir Dalal and Deepti Chaudhary. 2013. 'Flipkart raises $200 million amid e-commerce fund drought', *Livemint*, 11 July, available at https://www.livemint.com/Companies/Dkaigg2rge8dNbXGO6DxJJ/Flipkart-raises-200-million-from-existing-investors.html

5. Mihir Dalal and Deepti Chaudhary. 2013. 'Flipkart raises $200 million amid e-commerce fund drought', *Livemint*, 11 July, available at https://www.livemint.com/Companies/Dkaigg2rge8dNbXGO6DxJJ/Flipkart-raises-200-million-from-existing-investors.html
6. Mihir Dalal and Deepti Chaudhary. 2013. 'Flipkart boosts war chest, gets $160 mn more from investors', *Livemint*, 10 October, available at https://www.livemint.com/Companies/pbOfYVBQigpqm1D2FguQDO/Flipkart-raises-160-million-in-another-round-of-funding.html
7. Shrutika Verma and Mihir Dalal. 2014. 'Inside Flipkart's complex structure', Livmeint, 25 November, available at https://www.livemint.com/Companies/VXr8oJzNJ4daOYSO5wNETN/Inside-Flipkarts-complex-structure.html
8. Deepti Chaudhary, Mihir Dalal and P. R. Sanjai. 2013. 'Ibibo buys online bus ticket agent redBus', *Livemint*, 22 June, available at https://www.livemint.com/Companies/NBINnTouWd7lGrixgF2xZK/Ibibo-buys-online-bus-ticket-agent-redBus.html

14 HELLO, MOTO

1. Based on statements made in interviews to the author.
   Shrutika Verma. 2012. 'FDI Escapades', *BusinessWorld*, available at http://www.businessworld.in/article/FDI-Escapades/08-11-2014-67048/
2. *Economic Times*. 2013. Available at https://economictimes.indiatimes.com/et-now/daily/et-awards-2013-entrepreneur-of-the-year-sachin-bansal/videoshow/27036411.cms
3. Mihir Dalal. 2013. 'Snapdeal CEO says inventory model is 'dead', looking for deals', *Livemint*, 13 April, available at https://www.livemint.com/Industry/D2Xufph6zu7w9ZYg8Ze0dM/Snapdeal-CEO-defends-marketplace-model-looking-for-acquisit.html

4. Ashish K. Sinha. 2013. 'Exclusive: Snapdeal raises $50 million from eBay and existing investors', NextBigWhat, 1 April, available at https://nextbigwhat.com/ebay-invests-in-snapdeal/
5. PTI. 2013. 'eBay invests an undisclosed amount in Snapdeal', 4 June, available at https://economictimes.indiatimes.com/tech/internet/ebay-invests-an-undisclosed-amount-in-snapdeal/articleshow/20428923.cms
6. Mihir Dalal. 2017. 'How smartphone sales revived Flipkart's fortunes', *Livemint*, 22 September, available at https://www.livemint.com/Companies/AgpQ0QQSCWBW3v3oTnFcLL/How-smartphones-changed-Flipkarts-fortunes.html
7. Mihir Dalal. 2017. 'How smartphone sales revived Flipkart's fortunes', *Livemint*, 22 September, available at https://www.livemint.com/Companies/AgpQ0QQSCWBW3v3oTnFcLL/How-smartphones-changed-Flipkarts-fortunes.html
8. Mihir Dalal. 2014. 'Flipkart on course to touch $1 bn in annual sales', *Livemint*, 7 March, available at https://www.livemint.com/Industry/BzamePoHG135hdYwUwz31K/Flipkart-on-course-to-touch-1-bn-in-annual-sales.html

15 ANOTHER BANSAL JOINS THE FAMILY

1. Mihir Dalal and Shrutika Verma, 2014. 'How Flipkart Sealed The Deal With Myntra', *Livemint*, 23 May, available at https://www.livemint.com/Companies/p5nkYHmjFR5jNqn1Q9ZZLO/How-Flipkart-sealed-the-deal-with-Myntra.html
2. Mihir Dalal and Shrutika Verma, 2014. 'How Flipkart Sealed The Deal With Myntra', *Livemint*, 23 May, available at https://www.livemint.com/Companies/p5nkYHmjFR5jNqn1Q9ZZLO/How-Flipkart-sealed-the-deal-with-Myntra.html
3. PTI. 2014. 'Flipkart acquires Myntra', 22 May, available at https://timesofindia.indiatimes.com/tech-news/Flipkart-acquires-Myntra/articleshow/35472797.cms

4. Mihir Dalal and Shrutika Verma. 2014. 'E-commerce firms continue to attract investments', *Livemint*, 27 May, available at https://www.livemint.com/Companies/lbfXg1DXl0Etm13uEedIpJ/Flipkart-raises-210-million-from-DST-Global-others.html

16 A BILLION DREAMS

1. Mihir Dalal and Shrutika Verma. 2014. 'Flipkart bags $7 billion valuation after mammoth fund raise', *Livemint*, 29 July, available at https://www.livemint.com/Companies/X49vLQnJNq1QHnx8GwPjzL/Flipkart-raises-1-billion-in-latest-round-of-funding.html
2. *Economic Times*. 2014. 'Flipkart raises $1 billion in funds, company may be valued at $7 billion', 30 July, available at https://economictimes.indiatimes.com/industry/services/retail/flipkart-raises-1-billion-in-funds-company-may-be-valued-at-7-billion/articleshow/39233188.cms?from=mdr
3. Based on statements made in interviews to the author.
4. Mihir Dalal and Shrutika Verma. 2014. 'Flipkart bags $7 billion valuation after mammoth fund raise', *Livemint*, 29 July, available at https://www.livemint.com/Companies/X49vLQnJNq1QHnx8GwPjzL/Flipkart-raises-1-billion-in-latest-round-of-funding.html
5. Amazon. 2014. 'Amazon Announces Additional US $2 Billion Investment in India', 30 July, available at https://www.amazon.in/gp/feature.html?docId=1000818573
6. Mihir Dalal, Leslie D'Monte and Shrutika Verma. 2014. 'Amazon's Jeff Bezos loves India business, ready to invest more', *Livemint*, 29 September, available at https://www.livemint.com/Companies/RBZ8yTWUu1MsNRbZ9CIEiN/I-love-this-business-in-India-Amazons-Jeff-Bezos.html
7. Samidha Sharma and Boby Kurian. 2014. 'Amazing India

energizes me: Amazon CEO Jeff Bezos', *Times of India*, 29 September, available at https://timesofindia.indiatimes.com/business/india-business/Amazing-India-energizes-me-Amazon-CEO-Jeff-Bezos/articleshow/43757725.cms

8. Samidha Sharma. 2014. 'Flipkart taunts Bezos with welcome ad', *Times of India*, 27 September, available at https://timesofindia.indiatimes.com/tech-news/Flipkart-taunts-Bezos-with-welcome-ad/articleshow/43563597.cms
9. Shrutika Verma and Mihir Dalal. 2014. 'India e-commerce gets latest push from SoftBank', *Livemint*, 29 October, available at https://www.livemint.com/Companies/TelpPwsX51qyj8ZkFduKyK/Snapdeal-raises-627-million-from-Japans-SoftBank.html
10. Samidha Sharma. 2014. 'Online startup boom: What made the year 2014 special', *Economic Times*, available at https://cio.economictimes.indiatimes.com/news/corporate-news/online-startup-boom-what-made-the-year-2014-special/45689585
11. Amrutha Gayathri and Denny Thomas. 2014. 'China's JD.com IPO raises $1.78 billion, augurs well for Alibaba', *Reuters*, 22 May, available at https://www.reuters.com/article/us-jddotcom-ipo-idUSBREA4K19H20140522
12. William Alden. 2014. 'Alibaba's Shares Close Up 38% on First Day of Trading', *New York Times*, 19 September, available at https://dealbook.nytimes.com/2014/09/19/live-blog-tracking-the-giant-alibaba-i-p-o/
13. Duncan Clark. 2016. *Alibaba: The House That Jack Ma Built*. Ecco.
14. Laura Lorenzetti. 2014. 'Alibaba's IPO has made Masayoshi Son Japan's richest man', *Fortune*, 17 September, available at http://fortune.com/2014/09/17/alibabas-ipo-has-made-masayoshi-son-japans-richest-man/
15. Shrutika Verma and Mihir Dalal. 2014. 'India e-commerce gets latest push from SoftBank', *Livemint*, 29 October, available at https://www.livemint.com/Companies/TelpPwsX51qyj8ZkFduKyK/Snapdeal-raises-627-million-from-Japans-SoftBank.html

16. T. N. Ninan. 2015. *Turn of the Tortoise: The Challenge and Promise of India's Future*. Penguin.
17. Nandita Bose. 2012. 'Retailers retrench as reform hopes dashed', Reuters, 11 June, available at https://www.livemint.com/Companies/7idDw8Li2bfjwuWRuZOK6O/Retailers-retrench-as-reform-hopes-dashed.html
18. Sapna Agarwal. 2012. 'Aditya Birla to buy Pantaloons retail chain', *Livemint*, 1 May, available at https://www.livemint.com/Companies/7gYxcYC8xH8OjggQWmIfAJ/Aditya-Birla-to-buy-Pantaloons-retail-chain.html

17 THE COMEBACK

1. Phrase used in *The Everything Store* by Brad Stone, Little, Brown and Company.

   Priyanka Pani and Rajesh Kurup. 2013. 'I will never sell Flipkart', *Hindu BusinessLine*, 19 December, available at https://www.thehindubusinessline.com/info-tech/i-will-never-sell-flipkart/article20701868.ece
2. Eva Dou. 2015. 'Xiaomi Overtakes Samsung in China Smartphone Market', *Wall Street Journal*, 4 August, available at https://blogs.wsj.com/digits/2014/08/04/xiaomi-overtakes-samsung-in-china-smartphone-market/
3. Danish Khan. 2014. 'Xiaomi Mi3 sold out in a few seconds; Flipkart website crashes again', *Economic Times*, 5 August, available at https://telecom.economictimes.indiatimes.com/news/devices/xiaomi-mi3-sold-out-in-a-few-seconds-flipkart-website-crashes-again/39681826
4. Technopak Advisors.
5. Mihir Dalal, Shrutika Verma and Sapna Agarwal. 2014. 'Flipkart hits $100 million Big Billion Day Sale target in 10 hours', *Livemint*, 7 October, available at https://www.livemint.com/Industry/

TM8tDvrv3OfeYjeXkEPXZI/Flipkart-hits-100-million-sales-target-in-10-hours.html

6. Mihir Dalal, Shrutika Verma and Sapna Agarwal. 2014. 'Flipkart hits $100 million Big Billion Day Sale target in 10 hours', *Livemint*, 7 October, available at https://www.livemint.com/Industry/TM8tDvrv3OfeYjeXkEPXZI/Flipkart-hits-100-million-sales-target-in-10-hours.html
7. Mihir Dalal, Shrutika Verma and Sapna Agarwal. 2014. 'Flipkart hits $100 million Big Billion Day Sale target in 10 hours', *Livemint*, 7 October, available at https://www.livemint.com/Industry/TM8tDvrv3OfeYjeXkEPXZI/Flipkart-hits-100-million-sales-target-in-10-hours.html
8. Mihir Dalal, Shrutika Verma and Sapna Agarwal. 2014. 'Flipkart hits $100 million Big Billion Day Sale target in 10 hours', *Livemint*, 7 October, available at https://www.livemint.com/Industry/TM8tDvrv3OfeYjeXkEPXZI/Flipkart-hits-100-million-sales-target-in-10-hours.html

18 REINVENTING THE KART

1. Michael Lewis. 1996. *The New New Thing: A Silicon Valley Story*. W. W. Norton & Company.
2. Phrase used by Brad Stone in *The Everything Store*.
3. *Economic Times*. 2015. 'Digital ad spend to rise significantly in India', 14 April, available at https://economictimes.indiatimes.com/industry/services/advertising/digital-ad-spend-to-rise-significantly-in-india/articleshow/46913789.cms
4. Mike Isaac. 2015. 'Facebook Revenue Surges 41%, as Mobile Advertising and Users Keep Growing', *New York Times*, 4 November, available at https://www.nytimes.com/2015/11/05/technology/facebook-q3-earnings.html
5. Seth Fiegerman. 2015. 'Facebook's annual revenue topped $10

billion for the first time in 2014', Mashable, 29 January, available at https://mashable.com/2015/01/28/facebook-q4-earnings-2014/

6. Masoom Gupta. 2015. *Economic Times*. 'Fashion is 'highly personal' for Myntra's Mukesh Bansal', *Economic Times*, 1 January, available at https://economictimes.indiatimes.com/magazines/panache/fashion-is-highly-personal-for-myntras-mukesh-bansal/articleshow/45713210.cms
7. Mihir Dalal. 2014. 'Flipkart raises $700 million in fresh funds', *Livemint*, 20 December, available at https://www.livemint.com/Companies/jsYNvJSmfB6tbWKqRL9vhK/Flipkart-raises-700-million-in-fresh-funds.html
8. Mihir Dalal and Shrutika Verma. 2018. 'How Lee Fixel, Flipkart's godfather in New York, changed India's start-up ecosystem', *Livemint*, 18 May, available at https://www.livemint.com/Companies/5Cds0A5aOSil178CM4J9vM/How-Lee-Fixel-Flipkarts-godfather-in-New-York-changed-Ind.html
9. Saritha Rai. 2015. 'India's E-Commerce Poised To Mint First Two Billionaires: Flipkart's Sachin And Binny Bansal', *Forbes*, 30 March, available at https://www.forbes.com/sites/saritharai/2015/03/30/indias-ecommerce-poised-to-mint-first-two-billionaires-flipkarts-sachin-bansal-binny-bansal/#2d69e69f42e2
10. Mihir Dalal and Shrutika Verma. 2016. 'Flipkart's Godfather in New York', *Livemint*, 29 July, available at https://www.livemint.com/Companies/QD9B2wsY5WMMfYuLYi6jEM/Flipkarts-godfather-in-New-York.html

19 CHAOS AND CONFUSION

1. Sayan Chakraborty. 2015. 'Myntra expects gross sales of $1 billion by March 2016', *Livemint*, 14 May, available at https://www.livemint.com/Companies/tFSlv1vhpYpv9PGQAQzX0O/Myntra-eyes-gross-sales-of-1-billion-by-March-2016.html

2. Ibid.
3. Based on statements made in interviews to the author.
4. Jodi Kantor and David Streitfeld. 2015. 'Inside Amazon: Wrestling Big Ideas in a Bruising Workplace', *New York Times*, 15 August, available at https://www.nytimes.com/2015/08/16/technology/inside-amazon-wrestling-big-ideas-in-a-bruising-workplace.html
5. Amazon. Available at https://ir.aboutamazon.com/static-files/d6263104-b6fa-401a-aa29-3b66ec713f76
6. Brad Stone. 2013. *The Everything Store*. Little, Brown and Company
7. Tech jargon for wild experimentation that sometimes leads to highly profitable discoveries, but more often doesn't yield a viable business idea.
8. Vikas S. N. 2015. 'Flipkart acquires mobile advertising firm AdIQuity amid major advertising push', *Economic Times*, 6 March, available at https://tech.economictimes.indiatimes.com/news/internet/flipkart-adiquity-advertising/46474074?redirect=1
9. Data supplied by Tracxn
10. Based on statements made in an interview to the author.
11. Biswarup Gooptu. 2015. 'Snapdeal on course to topple Flipkart from top, says CEO Kunal Bahl', *Economic Times*, 31 August, available at https://tech.economictimes.indiatimes.com/news/internet/snapdeal-on-course-to-topple-flipkart-from-top-says-ceo-kunal-bahl/48738224
12. Jayadevan P. K. and Pankaj Mishra. 2015. 'Flipkart's Mukesh Bansal knocks Snapdeal with $10 billion quip', *Economic Times*, 2 September, available at https://brandequity.economictimes.indiatimes.com/news/business-of-brands/flipkart-s-mukesh-bansal-knocks-snapdeal-with-10-billion-quip/48767875
13. Mihir Dalal. 2016. 'The Rise and Rise of Amazon', *Livemint*, 20 May, available at https://www.livemint.com/Companies/zs1JqXLNTv7ML2xeE9joRL/The-rise-and-rise-of-Amazon.html

14. Radhika P. Nair. 2015. 'Flipkart to pamper employees for smooth 'Big Billion' sales', YourStory, 13 October, available at https://yourstory.com/2015/10/flipkart-pampering-employees-for-big-billion-sales

20 AFTER BANSAL, BANSAL

1. Reconstructed from statements made in interviews to the author.
2. Ibid.
3. Manu P. Toms. 2016. 'Flipkart names Sachin Bansal executive chairman, Binny Bansal CEO', VCCircle, 11 January, available at https://www.techcircle.in/2016/01/11/flipkart-names-sachin-bansal-executive-chairman-binny-bansal-ceo
4. Shrutika Verma and Mihir Dalal. 2016. 'Flipkart flips CEO post, Binny Bansal replaces Sachin Bansal', *Livemint*, 12 January, available at https://www.livemint.com/Companies/j8ebSI6fTpKEO4wp2nrfCJ/Flipkarts-Binny-Bansal-replaces-Sachin-Bansal-as-new-CEO.html
5. Vikas S. N. and Aditi Shrivastava, 2016. 'Amazon CFO Brian Olsavsky reiterate that India is one of Amazon's biggest investment areas', *Economic Times*, 29 January, available at https://economictimes.indiatimes.com/industry/services/retail/amazon-cfo-brian-olsavsky-reiterate-that-india-is-one-of-amazons-biggest-investment-areas/articleshow/50772697.cms
6. Mihir Dalal. 2016. 'Myntra blinks, will relaunch desktop site on 1 June', *Livemint*, 4 May, available at https://www.livemint.com/Companies/gGCm6sa8fCHRUGwVQC67SL/Myntra-blinks-to-relaunch-desktop-site-on-1-June.html
7. Shrutika Verma and Mihir Dalal. 2016. 'Flipkart CEO Binny Bansal brings back old hands in turnaround efforts', *Livemint*, 20 June, available at https://www.livemint.com/Companies/C0XdvsTAu6R6fZ5krS3bZK/Flipkart-CEO-Binny-Bansal-brings-back-old-hands-in-turnaroun.html

8. Flipkart. 2016. 'Nitin Seth To Join Flipkart As Chief People Officer', 17 February, available at https://stories.flipkart.com/nitin-seth-flipkart-cpo/
9. Saritha Rai. 2016. 'Dotcom deadpool returns as India's start-up boom turns to bust', Bloomberg, 25 August, available at https://www.livemint.com/Companies/iJbrRvXUzF6lpyTxMyrJXO/Dotcom-deadpool-is-back-as-Indias-startup-boom-turns-to-bu.html
10. Mihir Dalal. 2016. 'The Rise and Rise of Amazon', *Livemint*, 20 May, available at https://www.livemint.com/Companies/zs1JqXLNTv7ML2xeE9joRL/The-rise-and-rise-of-Amazon.html
11. Sayan Chakraborty and Mihir Dalal. 2016. 'Flipkart valuation marked down by Morgan Stanley fund to $9.39 billion', *Livemint*, 28 May, available at https://www.livemint.com/Companies/3ZRMwOZqipkZyYUOeBeL4N/Morgan-Stanley-fund-cuts-Flipkart-valuation-again-to-939-b.html
12. Shrutika Verma and Mihir Dalal. 2016. 'Flipkart defers joining dates of IIM graduates by 6 months', *Livemint*, 25 May, available at https://www.livemint.com/Companies/lCEhM8TUrbBUpUyhxIm01L/Flipkart-defers-joining-dates-of-IIM-grads-by-6-months.html
13. Mihir Dalal. 2016. 'Binny Bansal charts a fresh course for Flipkart', *Livemint*, 24 May, available at https://www.livemint.com/Companies/GrYplHVrP5hlOqZdSqNVzH/Binny-Bansal-charts-a-fresh-course-for-Flipkart.html
14. *Time*. 2016. 'Binny Bansal and Sachin Bansal', available at https://time.com/4300001/binny-bansal-and-sachin-bansal-2016-time-100/

21 THE TIGER CUB RETURNS

1. Shrutika Verma and Mihir Dalal. 2016. 'Flipkart defers joining dates of IIM graduates by 6 months', *Livemint*, 25

May, available at https://www.livemint.com/Companies/lCEhM8TUrbBUpUyhxIm01L/Flipkart-defers-joining-dates-of-IIM-grads-by-6-months.html

2. Based on statements made in interviews to the author.
3. Shilpa Phadnis. 2016. 'Amazon CEO Jeff Bezos inducts India MD into core team', *Times of India*, 26 April, available at https://timesofindia.indiatimes.com/tech-news/Amazon-CEO-Jeff-Bezos-inducts-India-MD-Amit-Agarwal-into-core-team/articleshow/51985963.cms
4. Uttara Choudhury. 2016. 'Amazon to invest $3 bn more in India, Jeff Bezos tells PM Modi', Firstpost, 8 June, available at https://www.firstpost.com/business/amazon-to-invest-3-bn-more-in-india-jeff-bezos-tells-pm-modi-2822524.html
5. Based on statements made in interviews to the author.
6. Mihir Dalal and Anirban Sen. 2017. 'Why Flipkart Has Turned To Kalyan Krishnamurthy', *Livemint*, 10 January, available at https://www.livemint.com/Companies/7i4dqvxfz16nfBfboE9f1K/Why-Flipkart-has-turned-to-Kalyan-Krishnamurthy.html
7. Based on statements made in interviews to the author.
8. Mihir Dalal. 2017. 'How smartphone sales revived Flipkart's fortunes', *Livemint*, 22 September, available at https://www.livemint.com/Companies/AgpQ0QQSCWBW3v3oTnFcLL/How-smartphones-changed-Flipkarts-fortunes.html
9. Shrutika Verma. 2016. 'How Flipkart plucked Jabong from under Snapdeal's nose', *Livemint*, 27 July, available at https://www.livemint.com/Companies/iicvIYFijqp9VRAx0ON46I/Flipkarts-Myntra-acquires-Jabong.html
10. Based on statements made in interviews to the author.
11. Mihir Dalal and Shrutika Verma. 2016. 'Has Flipkart lost No 1 slot to Amazon?', *Livemint*, 23 August, available at https://www.livemint.com/Companies/c6vY9ta120G7cwewrCg6bI/Has-Flipkart-lost-No-1-slot-to-Amazon.html

12. Mihir Dalal and Shrutika Verma. 2016. 'Amazon outsells Flipkart for second straight month', *Livemint*, 12 Septmeber, available at https://www.livemint.com/Companies/BoAqx1908xWAXWRhKU0FwL/Amazon-outsells-Flipkart-for-second-straight-month.html
13. Aditi Shrivastava, Mugdha Variyar and Payal Ganguly. 'Flipkart claims to have made one-day record of Rs 1,400 Cr in sales', The Economic Times, 5 October, available at https://tech.economictimes.indiatimes.com/news/internet/flipkart-claims-to-have-made-one-day-record-of-rs-1400-cr-in-sales/54687693
14. Anirban Sen and Mihir Dalal. 2016. 'Flipkart outsells Amazon during festive sale', *Livemint*, 8 October, available at https://www.livemint.com/Companies/fWmdwrhLeDBcDQcw50aUbO/Flipkart-outsells-Amazon-during-festive-sale.html
15. Anirban Sen and Mihir Dalal. 2016. 'Amazon has done in 3 years what rivals didn't in 10: Amit Agarwal', *Livemint*, 10 October, available at https://www.livemint.com/Companies/I4wWqFZjVofti2rRRa4sKK/Amazon-has-done-in-3-years-what-rivals-didnt-in-10-Amit-Ag.html
16. Mihir Dalal and Anirban Sen. 2016. 'Diwali sales prove Flipkart can hold its own against Amazon: Binny Bansal', *Livemint*, 2 November, available at https://www.livemint.com/Companies/sRln64YFWz9J3L4t6xeZnI/Diwali-sales-prove-Flipkart-can-hold-its-against-Amazon-Bin.html

22 KALYAN RAJ

1. Based on statements made in interviews to the author.
2. Shrutika Verma and Mihir Dalal. 2016. 'Alibaba in talks to buy Flipkart stake', *Livemint*, 4 February, available at https://www.livemint.com/Home-Page/qcQWDTZFoir7LpaGZZbnGP/Alibaba-looks-to-buy-stake-in-Flipkart.html

3. Mihir Dalal and Shrutika Verma. 2016. 'Have Flipkart, Snapdeal hit a valuation wall?', *Livemint*, 14 April, available at https://www.livemint.com/Companies/TmJdiG503Lhn7AfzEJI8YM/Have-Flipkart-Snapdeal-hit-a-valuation-wall.html
4. Walter Loeb. 2013. 'Walmart: What Happened in India?' *Forbes*, 16 October, available at https://www.forbes.com/sites/walterloeb/2013/10/16/walmart-what-happened-in-india/#350ae09c7d1c
5. Leslie Picker and Rachel Abrams. 2016. 'Walmart Rewrites Its E-Commerce Strategy With $3.3 Billion Deal for Jet.com', *New York Times*, 8 August, available at https://www.nytimes.com/2016/08/09/business/dealbook/walmart-jet-com.html?searchResultPosition=5
6. Based on statements made in interviews to the author.
   Reuters. 2016. 'Wal-Mart in talks to buy stake in Indian online retailer Flipkart: sources', 28 September, available at https://www.reuters.com/article/us-flipkart-walmart-stake-idUSKCN11Y1JO
7. Mihir Dalal and Shrutika Verma. 2016. 'Flipkart's Godfather in New York', *Livemint*, 29 July, available at https://www.livemint.com/Companies/QD9B2wsY5WMMfYuLYi6jEM/Flipkarts-godfather-in-New-York.html
8. Based on statements made in interviews to the author.
9. IIT Bombay. 2016. 'Fireside Chat – Sachin Bansal & Rahul Yadav @ E-Summit 2016', Youtube, available at https://www.youtube.com/watch?v=ZZR_mSOP5Mg
10. Sadhana Chathurvedula. 2016. 'Indian start-ups call for a level playing field against global peers', *Livemint*, 8 December, available at https://www.livemint.com/Companies/q05WS9DW8pxTpHBnIJ5o7N/Indian-startups-call-for-a-level-playing-field-against-glob.html
11. George Packer. 2013. 'Change The World', *New Yorker*, 20 May, available at https://www.newyorker.com/magazine/2013/05/27/change-the-world

12. Madhura Karnik. 2016. 'Narendra Modi just banned Rs500 and Rs1000 notes to fight corruption and terrorism', Quartz, 8 November, available at https://qz.com/india/830774/rupee-notes-in-india-narendra-modi-just-banned-rs500-and-rs1000-notes-to-fight-corruption-and-terrorism/
13. *Hindu*. 2003. 'Jawaharlal Nehru (1889 - 1964): Architect of India's modern temples', available at https://www.thehindu.com/thehindu/mp/2003/07/07/stories/2003070700880200.htm
14. Pratap Bhanu Mehta. 2019. 'We might enter an "RSS meets Jio" ideological world', *Indian Express*, 1 May, available at https://indianexpress.com/article/opinion/columns/the-new-techno-nationalism-technology-elections-5703564/
15. Anirban Sen and Shrutika Verma. 2017. 'Flipkart replaces Binny Bansal with Kalyan Krishnamurthy as CEO', *Livemint*, 10 January, available at https://www.livemint.com/Companies/DyAMlbXXJ08b3m6zVYvEON/Flipkart-replaces-Binny-Bansal-with-Kalyan-Krishnamurthy-as.html
16. Mihir Dalal and Anirban Sen. 2017. 'How Flipkart got back in the game', *Livemint*, 23 February, available at https://www.livemint.com/Companies/UYyYvB3UCV73lP26Uh10CP/How-Flipkart-got-back-in-the-game.html
17. Based on statements made in interviews to the author.
18. A down round is a capital infusion into a private company in which it sells its shares at a lower price than any of its previous financing rounds.
19. Mihir Dalal and Anirban Sen. 2017. 'Flipkart raises $1.4 billion from eBay, Microsoft, Tencent, acquires eBay India', *Livemint*, 11 April, available at https://www.livemint.com/Companies/RjjyJUShEtiZ2DjgzUBczM/Flipkart-to-buy-eBay-India-as-part-of-14-billion-fundrais.html

23 THE SON

1. Shrutika Verma. 2016. 'GMV is so 2015: Snapdeal CEO Kunal Bahl', *Livemint*, 8 July, available at https://www.livemint.com/Companies/Is7DaiQTryifFa8OPNpVeJ/GMV-is-so-2015-says-Snapdeal-CEO-Kunal-Bahl.html
2. Tracxn data
3. Shrutika Verma and Mihir Dalal. 2017. 'Snapdeal acquisition to benefit Tiger Global more than Flipkart', *Livemint*, 21 April, available at https://www.livemint.com/Companies/j90l1s80uF5WjxpOtQBahP/Snapdeal-acquisition-to-benefit-Tiger-Global-more-than-Flipk.html
4. Shrutika Verma and Mihir Dalal. 2017. 'Snapdeal's co-founders hint firm's fate not in their hands ', *Livemint*, 10 April, available at https://www.livemint.com/Companies/thfpvAkDTUPb5oSmquLYRN/Snapdeal-founders-move-to-calm-employees-amid-rumours-of-Fli.html
5. Mihir Dalal and Shrutika Verma. 2017. 'Snapdeal misses out on funding as SoftBank feuds with Kalaari, Nexus' *Livemint*, 31 March, available at https://www.livemint.com/Companies/o5auXKZnB9updwQk45sqTI/Snapdeal-misses-out-on-funding-as-SoftBank-feuds-with-Kalaar.html
6. Based on statements made in interviews to the author.
7. Mihir Dalal and Anirban Sen. 2017. 'Snapdeal-Flipkart deal falls apart in win for founders Kunal Bahl, Rohit Bansal', *Livemint*, 1 August, available at https://www.livemint.com/Companies/CAQ1JvAmT7uNDCpOLLKXfM/Snapdeal-wont-sell-to-Flipkart-to-run-on-its-own.html
8. Mihir Dalal and Anirban Sen. 'Flipkart's big billion day, courtesy SoftBank', *Livemint*, 11 August, available at https://www.livemint.com/Companies/7Ws4blkEFk1RVg7m8Y6q6J/SoftBank-fund-invests-in-Flipkart-after-Snapdeal-takeover-co.html

9. Anirban Sen and Mihir Dalal. 2017. 'Snapdeal calling off sale may benefit Flipkart the most', *Livemint*, 2 August, available at https://www.livemint.com/Companies/6aRyQLUTwhlEjOsrpbZ5PM/Snapdeals-decision-to-go-solo-may-benefit-Flipkart-the-most.html
10. Robert Hof. 2011. 'Tech Startup Secrets of Bill Campbell, Coach of Silicon Valley', *Forbes*, 27 July, available at https://www.forbes.com/sites/roberthof/2011/07/27/startups-secrets-of-bill-campbell-the-coach-of-silicon-valley/#5184295b6931
11. Based on statements made in interviews to the author.
12. Mihir Dalal and Anirban Sen. 2017. 'Flipkart launches "made for India" budget brand Billion', *Livemint*, 31 July, available at https://www.livemint.com/Companies/qpeSAKzWaGvBmVbAEF5zAP/Flipkart-launches-made-for-India-budget-brand-Billion.html

24 A JOURNEY TO BENTONVILLE

1. Hamish McDonald. 2010. *Ambani & Sons*. Lotus.
2. Yuvraj Malik. 2018. 'Flipkart FY17 loss widens 68% to Rs8,771 crore, revenue up 29%', *Livemint*, 3 February, available at https://www.livemint.com/Companies/GlgtSXUpAdTYw3wsnGBZFP/Flipkart-FY17-loss-widens-68-to-Rs8771-crore-revenue-up-2.html
3. Anirban Sen. 2018. 'Amazon, Flipkart power new user base growth in e-commerce in India', *Livemint*, 20 December, available at https://www.livemint.com/Companies/lurjUhGPebAdExiucyJeAN/Amazon-Prime-Flipkart-Plus-lead-ecommerce-user-base-growth.html
4. Walmart. 2017. Annual Report. Available at https://s2.q4cdn.com/056532643/files/doc_financials/2017/Annual/WMT_2017_AR-(1).pdf
5. Brian O'Keefe. 2015. 'The Man Who's Reinventing Walmart',

Fortune, 4 June, available at https://fortune.com/2015/06/04/walmart-ceo-doug-mcmillon/

6. Bloomberg. 2014. 'Greg Penner Emerges as Heir to Wal-Mart's Chairmanship', 9 June, available at https://www.esmmagazine.com/retail/greg-penner-emerges-as-heir-to-wal-mart-s-chairmanship-5133
7. Rasul Bailay. 2018. 'How Greg Penner went all guns blazing for Flipkart', *Economic Times*, 10 May, available at economictimes.indiatimes.com/articleshow/64104098.cms?utm_source=contentofinterest&utm_medium=text&utm_campaign=cppst
8. Shrutika Verma and Mihir Dalal. 2018. 'Flipkart dialled Amazon after Walmart revived deal talks', *Livemint*, 6 April, available at https://www.livemint.com/Companies/76rtJCuWWfZvyUmcCcoPhL/Flipkart-dialled-Amazon-after-Walmart-revived-deal-talks.html
9. Anirban Sen and Mihir Dalal. 2018. 'Flipkart Walmart deal would be good for e-commerce: Amazon India head', *Livemint*, 23 April, available at https://www.livemint.com/Companies/Y2dY7W35z2MRMA4UEgCvWP/Flipkart-Walmart-deal-would-be-good-for-ecommerce-Amazon-I.html
10. Sunny Sen. 2018. 'Is Binny Bansal saying bye to Flipkart in the Walmart sellout?', FactorDaily, 26 April, available at https://factordaily.com/walmart-flipkart-deal-binny-bansal-exit/
11. Mihir Dalal and Shrutika Verma. 2018. 'The behind-the-scenes story of Sachin Bansal's exit from Flipkart', *Livemint*, 18 May, available at https://www.livemint.com/Companies/9743fblAncsi4dbfOxCxRM/The-story-of-Sachin-Bansals-exit-from-Flipkart.html
12. Shrutika Verma, Mihir Dalal and Anirban Sen. 2018. 'Walmart buys Flipkart for $16 billion, shifts battle with Amazon to India', *Livemint*, 9 May, available at https://www.livemint.com/

Companies/PltclXOj0whPWMGUFWqs9O/Walmart-buys-controlling-stake-in-Flipkart-for-16-billion.html

13. Mihir Dalal and Shrutika Verma. 2018. 'Sachin Bansal: From outsized Flipkart presence to outcast', *Livemint*, 12 May, available at https://www.livemint.com/Companies/7TpoCOdT6RSoRlVVeZyptJ/Sachin-Bansals-changing-fortunes-From-outsized-Flipkart-pr.html
14. Mihir Dalal and Shrutika Verma. 2018. 'Sachin Bansal: From outsized Flipkart presence to outcast', *Livemint*, 12 May, available at https://www.livemint.com/Companies/7TpoCOdT6RSoRlVVeZyptJ/Sachin-Bansals-changing-fortunes-From-outsized-Flipkart-pr.html

EPILOGUE

1. Anirban Sen and Mihir Dalal. 2018. 'Flipkart-Walmart deal crosses key CCI hurdle', *Livemint*, 8 August, available at https://www.livemint.com/Companies/h63fBTnFc7HE8WBaufifAN/FlipkartWalmart-deal-gets-CCI-approval.html
2. Anirban Sen and Mihir Dalal. 2018. 'Binny Bansal resigns from Flipkart over charges of personal misconduct', *Livemint*, 14 November, available at https://www.livemint.com/Companies/FaAYjt9xkHNObVOiNAWfkN/Binny-Bansal-resigns-as-CEO-of-Flipkart-group.html
3. Samidha Sharma and Madhav Chanchani. 2018. 'Binny Bansal was informed of probe by Walmart lawyers on Monday', *Economic Times*, 15 November, available at https://tech.economictimes.indiatimes.com/news/internet/binny-bansal-was-informed-of-probe-by-walmart-lawyers-on-monday/66628361
4. Anirban Sen and Mihir Dalal. 2018. 'Binny Bansal resigns from Flipkart over charges of personal misconduct', *Livemint*, 14 November, available at https://www.livemint.com/Companies/

FaAYjt9xkHNObVOiNAWfkN/Binny-Bansal-resigns-as-CEO-of-Flipkart-group.html

5. *Reuters*. 2018. 'Flipkart's Binny Bansal denies allegations of personal misconduct', 13 November, available at https://www.livemint.com/Companies/j1YnAeiKqUdIEgZ68M0jRM/Flipkarts-Binny-Bansal-denies-allegations-of-personal-misco.html
6. Saritha Rai and Matthew Boyle. 2018. 'How Walmart decided to oust Binny Bansal, an icon of the tech industry', Bloomberg, 15 November, available at https://www.hindustantimes.com/business-news/how-walmart-decided-to-oust-an-icon-of-india-s-tech-industry/story-oC6UlvCt9WxknrGgGE3tjJ.html
7. Vivienne Walt. 2015. 'Amazon Invades India', *Fortune*, 28 December, available at https://fortune.com/longform/amazon-india-jeff-bezos/
8. LinkedIn. Lee Fixel. Available at https://www.linkedin.com/in/leefixel/
9. Sankalp Phartiyal. 2018. 'Walmart may launch Flipkart IPO in as early as 4 years', *Reuters*, 12 May, available at https://www.livemint.com/Companies/LPNtdifRIolqoeKu6WWc3N/Walmart-may-launch-Flipkart-IPO-in-as-early-as-4-years.html
10. Saritha Rai. 2018. 'Walmart got a $10 billion PhonePe surprise after buying Flipkart', Bloomberg, 10 July, available at https://www.livemint.com/companies/news/walmart-got-a-10-billion-phonepe-surprise-after-buying-flipkart-1562726957843.html
11. LinkedIn. Sachin Bansal, available at https://www.linkedin.com/in/sachinbansal/

AFTERWORD

1. Based on a yet-to-be-published story written by the author for restofworld.org.

2. Pranav Balakrishnan. 2022. 'Flipkart has shown clear proof of value, will hit profitability: Walmart's Judith McKenna,' *Economic Times*, 16 June, available at https://economictimes.indiatimes.com/tech/technology/flipkart-has-shown-clear-proof-of-value-will-hit-profitability-walmarts-judith-mckenna/articleshow/92089947.cms?from=mdr
3. Karen Weise and Michael Corkery. 2021. 'People Now Spend More at Amazon Than at Walmart,' *The New York Times*, 17 August, available at https://www.nytimes.com/2021/08/17/technology/amazon-walmart.html
4. Tushar Goenka. 2022. 'Flipkart's seller base now at par with Amazon,' *Financial Express*, 16 September, available at https://www.financialexpress.com/industry/flipkarts-seller-base-now-at-par-with-amazon/2668692/
5. Manish Singh. 2021. 'Flipkart valued at $37.6 billion in new $3.6 billion fundraise,' *TechCrunch*, 12 July, available at https://techcrunch.com/2021/07/11/flipkart-valued-at-37-6-billion-in-new-3-6-billion-fundraise/
6. Saritha Rai. 2022. 'Walmart's Payments Startup PhonePe Seeks to Raise $1 Billion,' *Bloomberg*, 8 December, available at https://www.bloomberg.com/news/articles/2022-12-08/walmart-s-payments-startup-phonepe-seeks-to-raise-1-billion?leadSource=uverify%20wall
7. Sankalp Phartiyal and Nivedita Bhattacharjee. 2020. 'Exclusive: Walmart's Flipkart eyes overseas listing as early as 2021: sources,' *Reuters*, 16 September, available at https://www.reuters.com/article/us-walmart-india-ipo-exclusive-idINKBN26725W
8. Based on a yet-to-be-published story written by the author for restofworld.org.
9. PTI. 2022. 'Flipkart losses widened to over Rs 7,800 crore in FY22,' *Times of India*, 7 November, available at https://timesofindia.

indiatimes.com/business/india-business/flipkart-losses-widened-to-over-rs-7800-crore-in-fy22/articleshow/95361766.cms

10. Asit Ranjan Mishra. 2020. 'Jeff Bezos $1 billion investment in India not a favour, says Piyush Goyal,' *Livemint*, 16 January, available at https://www.livemint.com/politics/news/piyush-goyal-s-not-buying-says-investment-not-a-favour-11579197599398.html
11. This paragraph is based on a yet-to-be-published story the author has written for restofworld.org.
12. *Economic Times*. 2020. 'Sachin Bansal's wife files dowry harassment case against him,' 6 March, available at https://economictimes.indiatimes.com/small-biz/startups/newsbuzz/dowry-case-against-sachin-bansal/articleshow/74503368.cms
13. Priyanka Iyer. 2022. 'Navi Technologies IPO: List of ongoing litigations against founder Sachin Bansal,' *Moneycontrol*, 14 March, available at https://www.moneycontrol.com/news/business/navi-technologies-ipo-list-of-ongoing-litigations-against-founder-sachin-bansal-8231361.html
14. Chandra Srikanth. 2021. 'I'm all in, I want to build Navi for the next 20 years, never wanted to sell Flipkart: Sachin Bansal,' *Moneycontrol*, 2 September, available at https://www.moneycontrol.com/news/business/exclusive-im-all-in-i-want-to-build-navi-for-the-next-20-years-never-wanted-to-sell-flipkart-sachin-bansal-7409291.html
15. ibid.
16. Priyanka Gawande. 2022. 'Navi Technologies gets Sebi's approval for IPO,' *Livemint*, 13 September, available at https://www.livemint.com/market/ipo/navi-technologies-gets-sebi-s-approval-for-ipo-11663003491568.html

INDEX

A9 3, 11–3, 17, 45-7; project as Google Killer 17, 47

Accel 88-1, 92, 93, 94, 97, 98, 103, 104, 113, 170; funding from 94, 103, 163

Accel Partners 8, 18, 73, 88-9, 92, 113, 157, 158, 160, 163, 170, 171, 191, 204, 208, 275, 294,

accounting process, new 176

AdIquity 265

Adnani, Michael 197, 222

advertising business 262, 264-5, 272; shutting down of 268

advertising: campaigns 147, 150, 201; expenses 238; first campaign 150; revenues 99-100, 155, 239, 265; team for mobile apps 264-5

'affordability construct' 304

Agarwal, Amit, as 'Jeff Bot' 13, 46, 128-9, 197, 211, 268, 297, 308, 310, 355, 402

Agarwal, Anil 61

Agarwal, Ankit 23-4, 35, 60-1, 83, 367; exit of 357

Agarwals 61-2

Age of Empires 35, 99

Aggarwal, Bhavish 62

Agrawal, Ashish 20

Ali, Sujayath 13, 20-1

Alibaba 156, 206, 209, 213-4, 222, 227, 236-7, 240, 266, 308, 313-4, 319, 348-9; valuation of 214

Alkeon Capital 100-01

Amarnath, N. S. (Amar) 18-9

Amazon 2-5, 8-20, 28, 45-55, 60-2, 71, 76-7, 90-2, 97-8, 100-3, 107-9, 118, 123, 127-30, 144, 148-55, 159-60, 163-4, 185, 189-90, 197-9, 204-14, 222, 228, 235-42, 255-7, 260-4, 267-8, 271-4, 277, 283-4, 288-92, 296-310, 314, 317-9, 322-4,

331-2, 339-43, 348-55, 360, 365, 369-73; advancing 308; in Bangalore 11, 15; for buying Flipkart 342-3; 'capital-dumping' 317; and China venture 47, 198, 211; corporate culture in 16; customer happiness in 18; 'The Emperor Has No Clothes' award 17; Great Indian Festival 309; investigative story on work culture 257; launch in India 47, 187–8, 190; launching Junglee 163; 'leadership principles' in 17; Mission to Mars sale 228; motto: Get Big Fast 98; overtaking Snapdeal 289; playbook 60, 109; Prime membership service 308; recompense to O2 16; replacing Flipkart on books 267; warehouses of 268; work culture in 16-17

Amazon.com 100–1, 130

Amazon India 15-6, 18, 28, 46-7, 52, 62, 71, 76, 97, 155, 197, 209, 211, 238, 267, 277, 297-8, 342, 350

Amazon Web Services (AWS) 13

Ambani, Dhirubhai 154, 338

American internet companies 9, 121, 318

annual shopping event 143, *see also* Big Billion Day sale

Apple 6, 41, 199, 202, 223-4, 236, 238, 245, 312, 319

app-only platform 238, 242, 254-6, 266, 270-1, 275, 281-2

176, 179, 188–9, 197, 199–200, 203, 208, *see also* smartphones

Aramex 119

artificial intelligence 246, 345

Asda 344

auction 348, 355

Ayyappan, R. 301-3

BAC Acquisitions Private Limited 367

Bahl, Kunal 162-3, 198, 212, 237, 266, 288, 331-3

Baidu 209, 319

Bain 124

Bajaj, Amanpreet 160

Bajaj, Avnish 8

Balachandran, Mahendran 71

Balakrishnan, M. 39-40, 62

Bangalore 2-4, 6-15, 19, 23-5, 37, 43-4, 48-50, 62, 64, 66-9, 80, 84, 86-7, 93, 95-7, 101-3, 113, 118, 121-6, 132-3, 136-

7, 144, 148, 168, 205, 211, 222, 229, 257, 273, 313-4, 327, 334, 340-2, 347, 359, 374; Electronic City 23; Koramangala 23-4, 53, 64, 67-8, 72, 75, 92, 121, 142-4, 172, 210, 225, 229, 243, 246, 257, 362, 374; Nehru on 6, 24-5; NGV (National Games Village) 23-4, 44, 51, 55-6, 60, 64, 67, 69,123, 227, 367; office at Outer Ring Road 347; as tech centre 7

'Bangalored' 7

Banias 61–2

Bansal, B. K. 173

Bansal, Binny 5, 24-7, 30, 33, 37-45, 47, 50-9, 62-74, 77-8, 80, 82, 84-5, 93, 95-9, 102-6, 115, 119-24, 128-9, 131, 133-4, 142-3, 147, 149, 155-6, 163-5, 167, 171-3, 177-80, 183-7, 194-6, 203, 205, 209-10, 216, 219, 222-6, 228, 231-2, 240-1, 247, 252-3, 257, 260-2, 267, 273-96, 300, 304-12, 316-22, 325, 329, 335, 337, 340, 354, 351-3, 356-64, 368, 376; at Amazon 45; approach of 184; as CEO 276; as Chief Operating Officer 73; complaint of sexual harassment 363; computers and 26; as Group CEO 320; for leaving Flipkart 351; marrying Trisha 105; oversee operations 187; resignation of 363; and Sachin 357; taking over as COO 281; at xto10x Technologies 364

Bansal, Mukesh 62, 90, 163, 203-5, 225, 240-2, 246-7, 251, 254-5, 258, 262, 266, 274-76, 278-80, 286, 367; exit of 280

Bansal, Rohit 37, 62, 162-3

Bansal, Sachin 5, 19-21, 23-46, 50-67, 69, 71-4, 77-86, 94-100, 102-9, 111-4, 119, 122-3, 128-38, 141-51, 153-4, 156, 159, 163-5, 167-73, 176-80, 183-6, 191-200, 202-5, 208-11, 216-28, 231-86, 293-6, 305-7, 312, 315-20, 322, 325, 329, 335-62, 367-8, 374-76; in Amazon 19, 62; billion-dollar fund raise of 216; Business sense and 21; candidature of 345-6, 353-5; as Chief Executive Officer 73, 351; clearing IIT-JEE 27-8; for contractual guarantees 356; courting Bezos 342; for deal with Amazon 350; departure of 359; as Entrepreneur of Year 2013 194; as Executive Chairman 276, 305, 320, 345; file-sharing software by 34; at Flipkart 28; on Flipkart shutdown 254; for as Group CEO 346, 353; and Kalyan 219, 226, 231, 241, 252-53, 335-7; LinkedIn profile of 361; for making $100 billion company 225; manipulation of Google and 66; marriage with Priya 67, 105, 374; missions of 319, 345; and Mukesh 242, 247, 254, 258, 274, 276, 286; research internship and 35; speech by 347; stepping down as CEO 274, 336; for superior voting rights 356; tech skills of 34; tweet by 276; and video games 36

Bansals (Binny Bansal and Sachin Bansal) 19, 24-7, 29, 40, 44, 47, 49, 5152, 54-86, 89-94, 97-108, 113, 120, 123, 128-38, 147, 154-8, 161-3, 168-74, 178-9, 181, 186-7, 197-8, 207-10, 217, 219, 222-3, 225, 227, 229-32, 236, 241, 246-53, 258-61, 275-8, 295, 305-6, 312-3, 315, 321-2, 326, 333, 355; common among 25-6; and selling out Flipkart 79; sharing personal phone numbers 66

Barlow, John Perry 144

Bazee 4, 89, 324

Bentonville 341, 343, 351, 355, 359

Bernard Shaw, George 256

Bezos, Jeff 2-3, 11, 13, 18, 127-8, 162, 210-1, 238, 268, 297-8, 312, 314, 317, 335, 342-3, 349-50, 355, 369, 372-3

Bhagat, Chetan 37, 117

Bhagavad Gita 286

Bharti Enterprises 313

Bhartiya Janata Party (BJP) 4, 209, 318, 372-3

Bhutani, Ajay 1, 5, 17, 20, 30, 55, 62

Big Bazaar 4, 114

Big Billion Day sale 143, 227-8, 230-2, 239, 253, 269-70, 300, 309, 311, 313, 369; 'billion hits' 230; email to customers 232

BigBasket 126, 161

BigBillionDay.com 228

Bikhchandani, Sanjeev 9
Biyani, Kishore 4-5, 126, 152, 215
Blossoms bookstore 65
Bombay 80-1, 95-6, 118, 122, 126, 132, 136-7, 148, 154, 159, 248
book: buyers 87, 95; distributors 65, 85-7, 95-6, 115, 133, 235
book-by-book delivery system 95
BookExpo America 115
books business 60, 73, 87, 114-5, 117, 182, 260; low margins of 76; online selling 67; shelf-based process 95
Boston Consulting Group 127, 185
Brand advertising 181
Brand, Stewart 144
buyout 78, 344, 357; Lee, Sachin and 358

Café Coffee Day 86
'Can Flipkart Deliver?' 167,
Canaan 50
capital 74-5, 87-8, 158-9, 163, 170, 173, 265-6, 287-8, 292, 308, 310, 315-6, 321, 326, 330-1, 365, 370-1; infusion 172, 174, 208, 222, 243, 338; investment 99
capitalism 5, 144, 146, 208-9, 319
career choices 62
Carnegie conference 317-8
cash on delivery 118,120, 122, 151, 153
cash payments 119-23, 194
cash-flow issues 120
categories, new 106, 123, 169, 259-60, 323
Chakpak 14-5, 50, 53, 66, 70-1, 89, 90, 155; business model of 50
Chandigarh 24-9, 32, 44, 194
Chandigarh Chutiya Association (CCA) 32
Chandra, Ajay 76-7
Chandra, Alok 20
Chandra, V. V. K. 64
Chari, Rahul 155, 286, 366
Chatterjee, Surojit 277
Chaupaati Bazaar 126
Chidambaram, P. 194
chief product officer 248, 279, 335
China 6, 11, 47, 101, 120, 127, 197-8, 208, 211, 213-5, 222-3, 225, 227, 235-6, 289-90, 308, 317-9; internet sector 215
Chinese model 209, 318-9
Chitkara, Ashok 27-8

Chowdhary, Anuj 93, 109, 122, 135
coders 84-5, 97, 110
Competition Commission of India 363
contribution margins 182
'Core Team' 107, 134, 177
corporate: culture 11, 16, 19, 138-9, 146, 167-9, 176, 257; values 147
costs reduction 282
creation myth-making 41-3, 61-2
crisis 68, 82, 84, 88, 176, 272, 277, 295
Crossword 116, 186
cs@flipkart.com 72
CureFit 367
customer obsession 17-9, 94, 98, 107, 145; principle of 17; Thinking Big and Bias for Action 107
customer service 65, 81, 102, 145, 184, 278, 304, 322, *see also* customer obsession
customers 2, 18-9, 50, 53, 56, 60, 61, 65-9, 72, 76, 94, 97-9, 103, 111-12, 115-16, 119-23, 130-33, 136-7, 142-50, 153, 160, 169, 174, 185, 189, 191, 195-6, 200-2, 211, 219, 223, 227-32, 236, 242, 244-5, 254-6, 260-4, 267-9, 279, 282-4, 288, 290, 292, 303-4, 307-8, 319, 324-5; commitment to 68; complaints 72, 94, 175, 230; email to 145, 228, 232; service 65; shopping data 303; on social media 137, 143-4
customization 238
cut costs 283
Cyber Monday 227

Dadlani, Vishal 270
Dalal, Sachin 20, 45, 51-2
Dalzell, Rick 11
Daruwalla, Keki N. 39
Daryaganj 87
Delhi 1, 9, 25, 27, 83, 86-7, 93-6, 108-9, 117-8, 122, 126, 128, 132-3, 136-7, 162, 193, 200-1, 214; office at 87, 93-5, 136
delivery workers 61, 69, 120-1, 136-8, 227, 237
demands 95, 104-5, 110, 117, 122, 129-31, 133, 137, 139, 142, 156, 172, 184, 201, 223, 230, 243, 261, 269, 270, 303; drop in 270; and supply 95, 104, 110, 184
demonetization 318-20

depth-over-width approach 283
desktop site 242-3, 254-6, 262, 269-70, 391; removal of discounts and incentives 267-68; website 239, 242, 245, 270
Dev, Kapil 25
Dham, Vinod 8
Dhand, Harsh 30, 33-5
Dharmakumar, Rohin 166, 385-86, 389
Dhingra, Hitesh 160
discounts 60, 65, 81, 117, 147, 160-1, 181, 185-8, 198, 219, 227-31, 269-70, 283, 288-90, 296
Dorsey, Jack 42
dotcoms 2
Dragoneer Investment 191
DST Global 206-07
Dutta, Indranil 96, 114-5, 118, 148
Dwivedi, Santosh 111

e4e Labs 11
eBay 2-4, 89-90, 126, 161, 180, 188, 198, 214, 316, 324, 384, 396
e-commerce 72, 88-90, 96-105, 115-20, 143, 148-53, 160-4, 168-71, 182, 199, 203-5, 213-5, 220-6, 232, 235-7, 258, 264, 267-71, 284, 298, 323-4, 339, 348, 351, 361, 376, 389, 395, 398-9; businesses 77, 164, 168, 170, 185, 229, 249, 315, 364, 381; ecosystem 163, 237; firms 55, 60-1, 73, 76, 112, 127, 131, 157, 173-75, 191, 197, 207, 212, 226, 264, 279, 290, 305, 308-09, 313-4, 340, , 366, 371, 373, 384, 388-91, 393-4, 397, 403, 406-7; market 125, 129, 211, 217, 222, 289-91, 315, 331; platforms 111, 131; shoppers of 338; slowdown 323, 331; startup 63, 76, 89-90, 96, 103, 126, 129, 160-3, 213; success in 258; as 'very execution-heavy' business 258; website 57, 75
Ekart 135-6, 244, 262, 275, 285, 325-7
electronics category 160, 185-6
emergency funds 158-60, 170
employee stock ownership plans (ESOPs) 138-9, 171
employee, appointment of first official 69
employees: Flipkart 81-2, 105, 142-6, 159, 165, 174, 178, 188, 229, 253, 259, 269-70, 368-9; loss of senior 176

Enforcement Directorate inquiry 175, 193, 382
entrepreneurship 6-10, 15, 28, 40, 48-9, 51, 55-7, 60-3, 67, 71, 77, 110, 130, 141, 159, 172, 194, 213, 280, 366
Equated Monthly Instalment (EMI) scheme 186
Erasmic Venture 50, 71-2, 74, 88; to invest in Flipkart 72
Everything Store, The 257, 380, 387, 388, 390
executives 113-4, 117, 120, 132, 137, 147-9, 152, 155, 167-9, 172, 186, 189-90, 199-200, 204, 222, 226, 242, 247, 266, 274-6, 295, 298, 306, 312, 323, 330-2, 341-2, 347, 351, 368, 370, 373, 376
expansion 98, 106, 123, 128, 136, 182-85, 190, 237, 271, 278, 290-2, 370, 373
78, 94, 108–9, 132, 134–6, 138–9, 191, 193, 197–8, 200, 213–5, 218, 251, 254, 281

FabMart 126
Facebook 50, 56, 90, 110, 146, 155-6, 202, 206, 230, 235-36, 240, 265, 319, 396-97
Facebook's FAN – the Facebook Audience Network 265
Fairchild Semiconductor 6
fashion business 163, 169, 177, 182, 185-6, 203-5, 224, 240, 266-9, 305, 309, 320, 324, 336, 370, 397; sales 181, 204
FDI Escapades 174, 387, 389-91
festival season sales 300, *see also* Big Billion Day sale; flash sale; Moto G sale
Filo, David 12
first employee 70
First Flight Couriers 69-70
first office 11, 69; outside Bangalore 87
first orders 60, 113
Fixel, Lee 100-02, 106, 120, 125, 128, 156-60, 170, 180-1, 192, 196, 206-7, 242, 251, 272-3, 294, 298, 305, 312, 320, 329, 335, 348, 351, 359, 365, 397, 409; leaving of Tiger Global 365
flash sales 223
fledgling entrepreneurs 102
Flexible Payment Service (FPS) 13, 45-7
Flipkart 3.0 225-6, 235, 237-8, 241, 243, 245-6
Flipkart 84-5, 108-9, 132-3, 139-40, 154-8, 176-82, 185-9, 194-6, 216-8, 227-8, 249-51, 278-80, 294-5, 298, 321-

5, 369-77; $1 billion in sale as record 207; as ATM for books 71; divisions in 256-7; dominance 266-7, 305; launch of 99; losses 191, 338; as name 103; revenue of 97; shutting desktop site 255; to start with books 60; website 59, 102, 173, 268
Flipkart app 117, 249, 255, 260
Flipkart Online Services Private Limited 88
Flipkart Think Tank 226
Flipkart.com 59, 131
Flo 142, 176, 226
Flyte 155, 221
Forbes story 167, 177-78
foreign investment 3, 174, 314, 340
founders/co-founders, Flipkart 74, 135, 170, 185-6, 199-200, 250, 278-9, 302, 320-1, 345, 357, 360, 366-9, 373-4, 376
Foxconn 266
fraudulent activities 119-20, 149, 264
Friedman, Thomas 10, 372
funding 68, 70-1, 88, 90, 92-4, 103, 126, 129, 161, 163, 171, 192, 206-10, 212-3, 218, 243, 253, 267, 313, 315, 325, 329-30, 333, 336, 342, 344, 351, 366; as $1 billion 211
funding boom 161, 213
fund-raising 156, 159, 193-4, 323
Future Group 126, 152, 154

games 34-6, 141, 153, 161, 345, 396; *Age of Empires* and *Quake* 35
Ganesan, Shivakumar 97, 109
Gangaram bookstore 65
Garg, Pankaj 35
Gates, Bill 43, 170, 312
General Atlantic 156-60, 169, 176, 183; invest in Flipkart 155; pullout of 157
Genesis Burson-Marsteller 166
Get Big Fast 98, 106
GIC 208, 371
globalization 9-10, 381
Goldman Sachs 308, 352
Google 2-3, 45-7, 50, 53, 66, 90, 99-101, 235-36, 239-40, 248-49, 259, 266, 274, 277, 319, 324, 346, 352, 371, 379, 382-3
Google Killer 17, 47
Gowda, Kempe 6-7
Goyal, Abhishek 18, 70, 88, 97
Great Indian Internet Company 209-10, 249, 286, 318

groceries, selling 260
gross merchandise value (GMV) 331
guerrilla warfare 228, *see* war with Amazon; head-to-head contest
Gupta, Ashish 8, 92-3, 385
Gupta, Pranay 32, 130
Gupta, Shekhar 40, 42, 382
Gupta, Vaibhav (VG) 204, 216, 225, 250, 367
Gupta, Varun 32
Gupta, Vikas 12-3, 46, 48
Gurgaon 9, 138, 327

head-to-head contest 309
Healthkart 130
Helion Venture Partners 92
hierarchy 109, 134-5, 138, 164, 177, 187
Hirachand, Walchand 7
hiring people 2, 14, 19, 20, 48, 80, 84, 96, 108-09, 138, 157, 168, 184, 207, 253, 279, 286, 295, 346
HolidayIQ 89-90
Homeshop 126, 168, 188
HTC 113-14, 186
human ERP 70, 75, 78

Ibibo 170, 383
Iconiq Capital 171, 191
IDG Ventures 74
IIM-Bangalore 121
IIT Bombay 159, 387, 403
IIT Delhi 19, 28-32, 36-7, 39, 42-4, 48, 55, 62, 68, 93, 105, 124, 130, 136, 163, 167-8, 178, 186, 204, 225, 285, 295, 367; graduates 30, 124, 168, 186, 204; Jwalamukhi 31, 136; Shivalik hostel 39, 124, 186
IIT Delhi-mates 167
IIT Guwahati 109
IIT Kanpur 13, 62, 71, 128, 241
IIT Kharagpur 111
IIT-mates 5, 77, 82
IITs 8, 20, 24, 27, 28, 30, 36-7, 42-3, 62, 107, 162; Educated engineers 3
Image Search 262, 279
Indian retail market 237, 268
Indian-American tech executives 8
Indiaplaza 47, 54, 59, 101, 119, 126
Indiatimes 54, 59
Infibeam 14, 20, 47, 76-80, 86, 98, 101, 104, 128, 161; episode 80, 98; launch of 76-7
Infoedge 9
Infosys 7-10, 12, 14, 23, 171, 190-1, 390

innovations 7, 9, 153, 218, 268, 290-1, 310, 317, 322, 325, 353, 369
innovative 152-3, 262, 335, 340, 344, 353
Intel 6
international publishers 115
internet: businesses 8-10, 85, 89, 166, 173, 215, 238, 312, 340; ecosystem of China 214; entrepreneurs 10, 23, 33, 60-2, 241, 278-9; entrepreneurship 6-10, 57, 129, 141, 172, 212-3, 366; startups 8, 14, 29, 47, 50, 68, 71, 73, 76, 88-92, 103, 108, 111, 125-6, 129-30, 138-44, 152, 156-66, 170-2, 192, 206-8, 212-13, 233, 236, 240, 243, 250, 265, 287-91, 308, 312-14, 318, 330, 335, 364, 367
investors 102, 156-161, 170-2, 188, 203-7, 209-212, 241-3, 148-9, 287, 289-91, 313-5, 330-3; Flipkart 156-7, 204-6, 225-6, 231, 240-1, 290-1, 294-5, 310, 314, 317, 339-40, 348, 350, 353
iPhones 126-7, 202, 303
Issacsson, Walter 41, 382
IT boom 29, *see also* internet
IT companies 5, 8
Iyyappa, Ambur 69-70, 75, 81, 385; as human ERP 70, 75

Jabong 185, 305, 320, 365, 401; to buy 305; collapse of 305; investors 305
Jack Ma 210, 214, 312, 394
Jahagirdar, Rohan 145
Jambool 46
JD.com 209, 214; valuation of 214
Jha, Amitesh 186-7, 199-201, 301
Jobs, Steve 41, 312, 335, 382
Junglee 3, 8, 92, 163-64
junior managers 183, 301, 322

Kalra, Deep 9, 103
Karwa, Sandeep 199-201, 301
Khurrana, Ayushmann 270
Kids Campaign 152, 181
Kishore-ji 5
Kochalka, Jim 335-7, 345
Kochhar, Nitin 183
Kola, Vani 8
Krishnamurthy, Kalyan 178, 180-8, 191, 195-6, 201, 204, 216 218-21, 226-32, 240-2, 252-3, 260, 267, 273-4, 278, 295-309, 311-27, 335-7, 343-6, 353-4, 357-60, 364-6,

368-71, 373, 390, 401-2, 404; appointment of 177, 179, 302; approach of 182-83; back at Tiger Global 232; as CEO 319-20, 364; charge of finance and sales 187; as Head of Categories - Retail 196; not for books 182; HR for 326-7; influence of 188; as interim CFO 187; moved to Flipkart 182-3; reappointment of 296-97; rejoining Flipkart 297; removing sales executives 298; as Sr. Vice President 218-9; for as CEO 311-2
Krishnamurthy, Saikiran (Saiki) 249, 285, 304, 364
Kritikal Solutions 62-3
Kumar, Akshay 270
Kumar, Anil 39-40, 67, 123
Kumar, Gagan 71
Kumar, Sujeet 31, 82-7, 93-9, 105, 107-9, 116-17, 119-22, 133-6, 142, 164-5, 171-4, 178-9, 216, 220-1, 250, 367, 389
Kushwaha, Gaurav Singh 15, 20, 48-50, 53, 70-1, 90, 155

Lafley, A. G. 284
Lakkapragada, Raghu 20
Lal, Aditya 20
Landmark 116, 186
laptops 54, 77, 132, 151, 186, 238, 260, 267
Lawania, Ashutosh 205
Le Corbusier 24
leadership coaching 337, 353
Lee Fixel 100, 102, 120, 125, 128, 156-60, 170, 180-1, 192, 196, 206-7, 242, 251, 272-3, 294, 298, 305, 312, 320, 329, 335, 348, 351, 359, 365, 397, 409; and Bansals 181-82, 305; to Binny 277; goals for Nitin 294; investor in e-commerce 119-20; investing Russian firms 206; with Kalyan 180-1, 253, 273-4, 298, 312-3; to Nitin 294-5; with Sachin 252-3, 273, 275, 295-6, 311
legal structures 172-5
Lehman Brothers 84, 88, 308
Lei Jun 222, 224
Lenovo 304
Lenskart 130
Letsbuy 126, 160-1, 164, 380; acquisition of 164
Lewis, Michael 234, 388
liberalization 4-5, 25, 209, 235
logistics 103, 120-23, 133, 135, 138, 142, 149, 173-74, 176,

184-5, 200, 216, 237, 241, 250, 258, 264, 268, 275, 283, 289, 304, 321, 326, 332; of Letsbuy 160
losses 78, 152, 167, 192, 198, 271, 324, 338, 342; of Motorola and Xiaomi 301
Luddite 155

MacLeod, Hugh 146, 147, 387
Mail.ru 170
MakeMyTrip 9, 101, 103
Makhija, Kapil 23
Malviya, Amod 111, 135, 177, 184, 216, 225, 227, 245-6, 250, 367; 'two-pizza' payments team of 17, 111
management team 106, 168, 177, 178, 198, 219, 247, 253, 270-3, 277, 350
Manber, Udi 3, 46
market-changing innovations 290
marketplace conversion 281
marquee funds 74
Matrix Partners 74
McKinsey 36, 101, 216, 249, 274, 281, 285, 305, 353
McMillon, Doug 280, 339, 341, 343-4, 347-8, 355-6, 361, 368
media coverage 166
Mehra, Nipun 185-6, 189
Mehta, Vishal 76-9, 86, 104, 161; for sell Flipkart to Infibeam 76
Micromax 186, 199-200
Microsoft 36, 64, 162, 319, 324, 352, 404
milestones 63, 67, 118, 152, 210, 220, 298
Mime360 154-5, 221, 286
Mitra, Subrata 8, 50, 71, 89-90, 92, 275, 294, 384
Mittal, Alok 8
Mittal, Maneesh 93-4, 135-6
Mittal, Sunil Bharti 61, 154
mobile phones 5, 48, 66, 77, 100, 106, 109, 113, 126-7, 138, 148, 186, 199
Modi, Narendra 209, 297, 314, 404
'moonshots' 262
Morgan Stanley Investment Management 191-92
Moto G phone201-2, 207, 222, *see also* flash sale
Motorola 199-201, 224, 248-9, 289, 301, 304
Motukuri, Krishna 46, 48, 97, 383
Mu Sigma 89
Murthy, Mahesh 152
Murthy, Narayana 154, 190, 390
Myntra 62, 89-90, 126, 161,

163, 174, 185, 203-7, 225, 240-1, 243, 245, 254-5, 266, 276, 279, 281-2, 305, 320, 324, 353, 356, 364-5, 370, 392, 397, 399, 401; become app-only platform 254; buyout of 207; as lab rat for Flipkart 254; shutdown of 254

Naaptol 126
Nadella, Satya 352
Nagori, Ankit 108, 116, 121, 134-5, 155, 164, 176-7, 184-5, 187, 204, 216, 250, 262, 280, 367
Narayanan, Ananth 281, 305, 353, 365
Naspers 170-2, 191-2, 206, 208, 226, 275, 330; engagement with 330; investing in Flipkart 170
National Games Village 23-4, 44, 51, 55-6, 60, 64, 67, 69, 123, 227, 367
NEA-Indo US 74
negative publicity 138
Nehru 3, 6, 24-5, 318, 372, 404
Netscape 6
Nexus Venture Partners 74, 99
Nigam, Sameer 155, 221, 227, 250, 286-87, 345-6, 353-4, 366, 371
Nijhawan, Uma 26
Nilekani, Nandan 10, 23
no-cost EMI scheme 322
Novotel 273

Open Coffee Club 70-1
Open Taps 142
Ordering books online 150
Orkut 50
'Out of Stock' 230
outsourced 326

packaging workers 69, 93, 98, 137
Page, Larry 335
Pandey, Vaibhav 109, 118, 135
Pantaloons 4, 395
partnership, commercial 198; with Xiaomi 222, 224, *see also* Motorola
payment gateways 63, 111-2
Paypal 6, 324, 352
Paytm 348-49
Penner, Clifford 344
Penner, Greg 343, 355, 407
Penner, Joyce 344
'performance improvement plan' 257
performance marketing 181
phone exchange programme 322
PhonePe 286-87, 320, 324, 345-

46, 349, 356, 366-67, 371, 409-10; founders of 367
Pichai, Sundar 352
pigeonhole method 95
Ping 262, 279
Playing to Win 284
Poovalingam, Vinoth 121-2
Prakash, Prashanth 8, 71, 89, 90-1
Premji, Azim 154, 204
Priyedarshi, Satyarth 110
problems 30, 54-5, 107, 113, 120, 137-8, 142-3, 167, 169, 176, 190, 219, 263-65, 268, 290-1, 305, *see also* crisis
Project Shaw 189
promotions 38, 94, 99, 101, 120, 135, 168, 185, 237
public sector companies 318-9
'purposeful Darwinism' 257

Quake 35, 99

Rao, Anand 10, 16, 76
Rathi, Anuj 109
Ravichandran, Smrithi 301
Redbus 192
RedSeer 68, 124
regulatory inquiry 194
restructuring exercise 177
retail market 105, 150, 188, 197-98, 267, 290, 314
returns policy 149-50, 153, 194; fraud and 149
Rippel, Oliver 275
rivals 2, 110, 127, 134, 147, 152, 185, 212, 216, 228, 240, 265, 288, 329, 331, 333; Snapdeal as 162, *see also* Amazon
Robertson, Julian 102
Rocket Internet 161, 174
RSS meets Jio ideological world 319, 396
Rudapatna, as Flipkart's 'Sex Appeal Bringer' 144
Rudrapatna, Tapas 80-2, 87, 93, 107, 144-7, 151, 173, 193, 361-2

salaries 2, 15, 108, 288
sales: and customer service 184; department 187, 257; executive 71, 96, 118, 132-3, 187, 197, 253, 258, 259, 261, 263, 300; Flipkart 253, 261; growth 173, 175, 182, 188, 271, 278 283, 292, 297, 301, 305, 314, 366; missing 274; and operations 110, 132-3, 135, 177, 178-9; stagnation 283; targets 143, 229-30, 270, 274, *see also* Big Billion Day sale; flash sale
Samsung 113, 186, 199-200, 223-4, 395

Sapna bookstore 64
Sarnoff Corporation 44
Satanic Verses by Salman Rushdie 137
Sathya bar 144, 362
sceptics 149, 152 172, 191
search engine optimization (SEO) 53
search engines 2, 12-13, 15, 54, 89-90, 99, *see also* Google
self-sustaining business 292, 306
seller count 263
senior engineers 18, 111, 249-50, 277
senior executives 33, 48, 120, 136, 139, 217, 220, 278, 314
Sequoia Capital 74, 79
service. *See* customer service
Seth, Nitin 285-6, 294-6, 299, 306-7, 321-2, 325-8, 335, 400; as Chief Operating Officer 321; removal of 326-8
Sethi, Sudhir 8
Shah, Niren 266
Shaktipeeth, Headquarter at Bangalore as 136, 141, 191
Shanghvi, Dilip 61
Sharma, Varun 56
Shockley, William 6
Shopclues 126, 161
shoppers 81, 119, 131, 148, 222, 230, 232, 239, 267-71, 290, 305, 377
shopping festival 226, *see also* Big Billion Day sale; festival season sales
shopping on mobile 255; *see also* app-only platform
shortages 77, 98, 147, 230
Silicon Valley 6, 43, 49, 88, 160, 248-9, 258, 335; entrepreneurs 49
Singh, Amarinder 71
Singh, Karandeep 164, 167, 178
Singh, Manmohan 5, 190, 209
Singh, Shailendra 79
Singla, Ram 35, 37
Singles Day 227
Six Sigma 75
slowdown 271, 278-79, 282-3, 290
smartphone business 224, 301; new strategy for 302; price war 283
smartphone-makers 222, 302-3, *see also* Motorola; Xiaomi phones
smartphones 126, 196-200, 215, 222, 224, 238, 240, 248, 255, 263, 267, 269, 284, 300-1, 303, 309, *see also* Moto G phone; Xiaomi phones

Snapdeal 29, 37, 126, 161-3, 188, 198, 211-2, 228, 237, 242, 255, 264, 266-8, 288-90, 305, 325, 330-4, 340-1, 361; apps 255; business loss of 288-9; cash reserves 333; as The Cat With Nine Lives 163; sale offer of 333-4; sales 288; shareholders 334; smartphone sales 289
social media promotions 145
social networks 29, 56, 90
Sofina 192
SoftBank funding 212-4, 266, 288, 330-4, 336, 338-9, 342, 352
SoftBank Group 170, 331, 371
Son, Masayoshi 170, 212, 214, 330
Soni, Punit 248-9, 256, 258-59, 262, 270, 279-80
Soota, Ashok 23
Souq.com 180
special incentives 149
Srinivasan, Karthik 166
startups: ecosystem 112, 125, 137-8, 152-3, 171-2, 190-2, 205-6, 290, 308, 368, 374, 377; Indian 92, 171-2, 207-8, 213-4, 265, 287, 307-8, 318, 334, 339; Indian e-commerce 103, 163-4
S-team 297
stellar founding team 76
Stone, Brad 257, 388, 395-6, 398
Subandh, Samardeep (Samar) 277, 285
Subramanian, Vijay 12, 20, 76-7
Sujan, Suvir 8
supply chain system 82-3, 142, 184, 305, 368, 370
survival 82, 99, 171, 288, 292, 309, 315, 323, 348
Swaroop, Prayank 23

Tata, Jamsetji 7
Tavant Technologies 14, 50, 92
tech systems, crashing of 230-31
tech utopias 265
technology 2, 7, 13, 24-5, 28, 33-4, 44, 55, 62, 77, 82, 86, 105, 107, 110-2, 119, 122, 132-3, 144, 155, 160-1, 166, 170, 178, 184, 189, 204, 209, 213, 218-21, 225, 231, 236-8, 241, 247-50, 267, 271, 276, 280-4, 290, 317, 330, 332, 335, 339, 341, 350, 359, 369; companies 3, 8, 11, 207, 236, 246, 259, 318-9; entrepreneurship 6; infrastructure 269; team 187, 195, 197, 257-61, 325

Techspan 19, 37, 44
television advertising campaign, first 147
Tencent 170, 209, 319, 324, 342, 352, 404
Terry, Marcus 109, 145
Texas Instruments 7
360-degree feedback 345
3i 71
Thiel, Peter 284
third-party sellers 131, 217, 227, 261-5, 283, *see also* distributors *under* book; vendors
Tiger Global 101-05, 115, 120, 125-6, 129, 154, 157-58, 160, 163, 168, 170-1, 178, 180-1, 191, 204, 208, 213-4, 216, 219, 226, 231-2, 253, 260, 274, 302, 307, 311, 315, 321, 330-5, 343, 347, 352, 365
'The Wizard of Wall Street' 102
Tradus 170
Trilogy Software 12, 14, 16
Tsai, Joseph 313

Uber 266, 317
Udaan 367
uGenie (comparison-shopping website) 46, 97
Unified Payments Interface (UPI) 286
uniform corporate culture 176, 257
UnPluggd 43

valuation 2, 128-9, 146, 154, 157, 175, 188, 195, 206-8, 214, 223, 243, 251-3, 291, 313, 316, 323, 330, 346, 349, 371-3, 386, 393, 400, 403; of Flipkart 104, 129, 167, 171-3, 192, 302, 351, 400
Van den Berghe, Dirk 340, 347
Varadarajan, Mohan 20
vendors 54, 142, 176, 227, 237, 244, *see also* book distributors
venture: capital 7-8, 70, 88, 92, 97, 106, 125-6, 147, 152, 160, 166, 173, 191, 213, 235, 286, 315, 330; capitalists 7-8, 75, 88, 97, 103, 125, 153, 206, 214, 266, 280, 284, 287, 344, 372; funds 8, 70, 74; lords 75-7, 88, 98, 102-04
video games 16, 22, 36-7, 51, 55, 196
Vijay, Bharat 3, 10, 16, 46
Visvesvaraya, M. 7
volatility 107-8, 184, 287, 322, 339, 363
Voonik 13

Vora, Ravi 136, 151, 167-8, 181
Vulcan Capital Management 192

Wadiyar IV, Krishna Raja 7
Walmart 298, 313-4, 339-4, 347-9, 351-61, 363-6, 368-71, 373, 376, 385, 403, 406-10; increasing investments in US 314
Walton, Carrie 343
Walton, Sam 4-5, 215, 341, 343, 379
war with Amazon 204, 310, *see also* rivals
warehouses 66, 75, 132, 138, 141-2, 184, 227, 258, 268, 285, 289; renting 227
warehousing systems 135, 160; of Letsbuy 160
website of Flipkart 59, 102, 172-3, 269, 395
Welch, Jack 215
WeRead 154
Wipro 8, 12, 204
Wood, John 64
work culture 16, 46, 169, 257
working capital 117, 182-3, *see also* capital
World Is Flat, The 10, 380
Wozniak, Steve 42
WS Retail Services 131, 147, 172-4, 178, 193, 216, 389

Xiaomi partnership 222, 224
Xiaomi phones 223, 271, 301, 345, 395

Yadav, Ajay Veer 301
Yahoo India 3, 10-2, 16, 97
Yang, Jerry 12

Zero to One 284
Zuckerberg, Mark 43, 312, 386